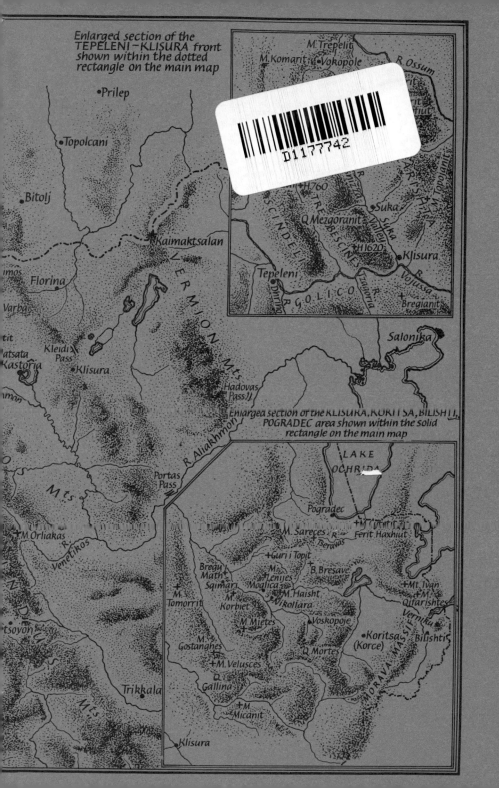

Enlarged section of the
TEPELENI – KLISURA front
shown within the dotted
rectangle on the main map

•Prilep

•Topolcani

•Bitolj

Kaimaktsalan

imos. Florina

Varba

tit

atsata   Kleidi
Kastoria   Pass

•Klisura

Hadovas
Pass

M. Trepelit
M.Komarit •Vokopole
R. Ossum

H.760

Q.Mezgoranit •Suka

Suka
Valley
H.1620   •Klisura

Tepeleni

R.GOLICO   Zagoria   R.Vojussa

+Bregianit

Salonika

Enlarged section of the KLISURA, KORITSA, BILISHTI,
POGRADEC area shown within the solid
rectangle on the main map

LAKE
OCHRIDA

R.Aliakhmon

Portas
Pass

Pogradec

+M.

Ferit Haxhiut

M.Sareces

Tservas

+Guri i Topit

+M.Orliakas

Venetikos

Bregu i
Math
Sqimari

M.
Lenijes
Moglica

B.Bresave

+Mt.Ivan

+M.
Qifarishtes

+M.
Tomorrit

M.
Korbiet

+M.Haisht
Nikollara

Verniku

M.Mietes

Voskopoje

•Koritsa
(Korce)   Bilishti

tsoyon

M.
Gostanghes

Q.Mortes

+M.Velusces

Trikkala

Gallina

+M.
Micanit

•Klisura

THE HOLLOW LEGIONS

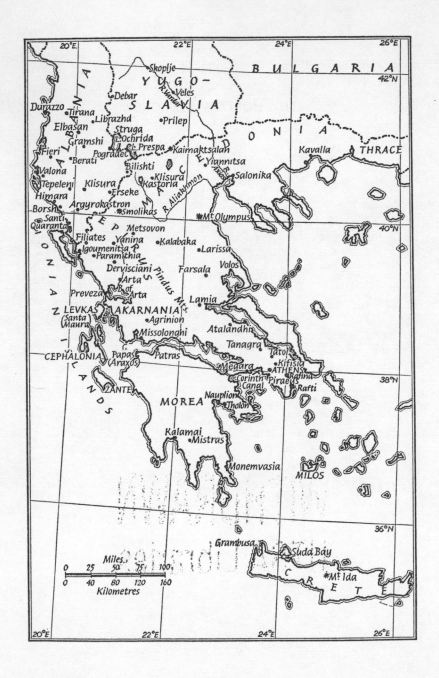

THE
HOLLOW
LEGIONS

Mussolini's Blunder in Greece,
1940–1941

MARIO CERVI

Translated from the Italian by Eric Mosbacher
Introduction by F. W. Deakin

DOUBLEDAY & COMPANY, INC., GARDEN CITY, NEW YORK 1971

Contents

Introduction

This work is a comprehensive study of the military adventure launched by Mussolini against Greece in October 1940.

The author has used, for the first time in a single account, the available memoirs and studies published in Italian, and the latest printed Italian Diplomatic Documents, of which selected extracts are printed in the Appendix.

This study also includes new evidence from Greek sources. The author has already translated the memoirs of General Papagos, the commander-in-chief of the Greek army, and has used the original diary of the Greek Prime Minister General Metaxas. By drawing on other accounts published in Athens, the superficial legend of the persistent attitude of the Greek government as a docile satellite, following without question the perplexed and improvised vagaries of British moves in the Mediterranean during 1940, is modified and corrected with a due sense of proportion.

The book has a dual purpose: to pay tribute to the disillusioned and patient courage of the Italian soldier, untrained and ill equipped for a winter war in the mountains along the Albanian-Greek frontier; and to trace the inept irresponsibility and anarchic direction of the Italian campaign in Greece as a model of Fascist style.

Nearly twenty years of the Mussolinian experience had destroyed the conventional functioning of state administration, particularly in the field of the Armed Forces and the Foreign Office, without creating an alternative system of efficient and organized authority.

On the snap declaration of war on England and France in June
1940, Mussolini had forced the reluctant and rancorous King
Victor Emmanuel to concede to him the supreme command of
the operational Armed Forces of Italy, together with responsibility for their territorial organization—a situation unprecedented
in Italian history. The Duce thus held at the same time the port-
folios of the ministries of War, Navy, and Air, in addition to the
personal direction of hostilities in his capacity of head of the
government.

Marshal Badoglio occupied the undefined post of chief of the
General Staff since 1925, together with the chairmanship of a
nominal and powerless Supreme Commission for Defense. There
was no Committee of Chiefs of Staff to co-ordinate military policy.
The Supreme Command was a building rather than a body. Less
than twenty anonymous staff officers were under the personal
orders of Badoglio. They did not constitute a body of advisers,
and were devoid of any precise functions. The undersecretaries
of the ministries of the Armed Forces and the three vice-chiefs of
staff reported irregularly, directly, and usually separately, to the
Duce, who did not possess or deem it necessary to set up a professional inner body of military advisers.

Overall strategy was the exclusive private concern of the Duce,
conditioned by disconcerting flashes of intuition embodied in contradictory directives. The conduct of war was reduced to homilies
on morale, and the propagation of bombastic slogans on an imperial theme. Operations were ordered and countermanded without
relation to military resources, training, or logistics.

The conduct of Italian diplomacy had been the responsibility
of Ciano since his appointment as Foreign Minister in 1935. Just
as Mussolini had toppled the structure of the Italian Armed
Forces which he had inherited in 1922, so his son-in-law disrupted
and demoralized the apparatus of the Italian Foreign Office, infiltrated his nominees into key diplomatic posts, dispersed the

professional establishment, and created his private sources of intelligence.

Ciano's private office, headed by Filippo Anfuso, became the control center of foreign policy, as confused and contrary in its lack of management and definition of political aims as that of the Duce and his timorous and intriguing military officials, and at the same time exposed to the mercurial domination of the Duce as head of the government.

As in the military sphere, it is misleading for the historian to seek, as the author of this book makes plain, any consistency or rationality in the conduct of Fascist diplomacy. At the most, the stages of facile duplicity can be chronicled; the flashes of cheap optimism and self-deception; the petulant acts of disloyalty towards an indifferent and all-powerful ally, with a total disregard for the political and military realities of Italy's position.

In only one region of Europe did it seem that Fascist Italy might assert her predominant interests with the tacit but watchful acquiescence of Hitler—in the Southeast and the Balkans.

The completion of Italian aims in the Adriatic and Southeast Europe had been frustrated by the Versailles settlement, and it was the "unfinished business" of 1919 that increasingly attracted the attention of Ciano and Mussolini as the rhythm of German expansion mounted, first with the Austrian Anschluss in 1938, and then the entry into Czechoslovakia in April of the following year.

The two immediate Italian objectives were the control, direct or indirect, of Albania, which guarded across the narrow straits of Otranto the vital southern approaches to the Adriatic; and the breaking up of the Yugoslav state, whose original creation Italy had opposed by encouraging internal subversion or by diplomatic cajolery to secure predominance of Italian influence in Belgrade.

The double failure to achieve these latter aims in Yugoslav affairs, and the breakdown of a sophisticated policy of the peaceful penetration of the Albanian administration and economy, slyly countered by King Zog, prompted Ciano to seek to persuade the Duce to take military action. The German entry into Prague and the simultaneous fall of the pro-Axis Yugoslav Prime Minister Stoyadinović, with whom Ciano had been negotiating a secret partition of Albania between Yugoslavia and Italy, created the conditions for Mussolini's benevolent attention to Ciano's plan.

Within less than four weeks of the German action in Czechoslovakia, taken without prior consultation with Rome, Italian troops landed at the Albanian port of Durazzo. King Zog withdrew into exile, and the country was directly annexed under the Italian crown.

The occupation of Albania was the first essential step in Italy's expansion into southeastern Europe. Although Hitler and his advisers had, on several occasions, proclaimed that the whole region should be regarded, in the frame of a new European settlement, as an exclusive Italian sphere of influence, German economic penetration of the Balkan states was a continual source of preoccupation to the Italians. Here lay the minerals, the coal, and the raw materials, whose exploitation would complete the balance and independence of the Italian economy. Control by occupation, or diplomatic pressure, of the area was a prerequisite to the assertion of the paramountcy of Fascist Italy in the eastern Mediterranean.

Italy's attempt to secure a dominant position in Albania in 1919–20 had been thwarted by her wartime allies, and she had been forced to withdraw her expeditionary force stationed there since 1915, and also in the disputed border territories claimed both by Albania and Greece.

In 1923 Mussolini had bombastically flouted the authority of the League of Nations by the naval occupation of the Greek island of Corfu, on the pretext that an Italian general, as a member of an international boundary commission on the Greek-Albanian frontier, had been assassinated by Greek extremists. This challenge was the first test of the League. Mussolini's first display of Fascist bravura ended in an humiliating withdrawal.*

The uncontested invasion of Albania in 1939 not only obliter-

* This episode is the subject of an admirable recent account: James Barros, *The Corfu Incident of 1923* (London, 1965).

ated the failure of 1923, but also revived the boundary contro-
versies entangled in the earlier episode.

By taking over the country, the Italians inherited the traditional
claims of the Albanians to those border territories in Yugoslavia
and Greece—Kossovo and Tsamouria—both inhabited by a majority
of Albanian populations. Italian presence in Tirana implied certain support for "Greater Albania," and a patent threat to the
territorial integrity of her neighbors. Indeed, the assumption by
Fascist Italy of this expansionist role was necessary to secure the
support of the indigenous tribal population of the new Italian
kingdom of Albania.

The origins of the aggression against Greece lay directly in
the unresolved claims to the areas of northern Epirus, populated
by a restless Albanian minority; and a parallel situation posed a
similar threat to the Yugoslav region of Kossovo.

An Italian military force stationed in Albania henceforth represented a standing threat both to Greece and Yugoslavia, and to
peace throughout the Balkans. But no coherent Italian "political
design" emerged in the ensuing months: only an erratic barometer
of appetites charted by the stages of mounting German power,
and accelerated by Hitler's assault on Poland in September 1939.
The outbreak of war with England and France, followed by the
German partition of Poland with the Soviet Union, the occupation
of Holland, Belgium, and Norway, and leading to the capitulation
of France, revolutionized the whole structure of Europe.

Surprised and deceived by Hitler, Mussolini had retreated in
the autumn of 1939 into a grumbling neutrality to meditate on
the implications of German hegemony on the continent for the
future status of Fascist Italy in the new Concert of Europe.

The Duce was aware in detail of the deficiencies of the Italian
military machine, and accepted in private the view of his few responsible experts that Italy could not participate effectively in
general hostilities until 1942 at the earliest.

His declaration of war in June 1940 was a military fraud, and
a diplomatic gamble. Honor required a series of token operations,

unco-ordinated in any general plan, and independent of the German Blitzkrieg, which would end in the imminent capitulation of Great Britain. The early summoning of a peace conference would follow, which was to impose a European settlement representing a long premeditated revenge for Versailles. This must include balancing compensations for Italy for recent German military conquests and occupations and take into account the unachieved Italian war aims of 1915–18—in particular in the Balkans and Southeast Europe.

To Mussolini the heart of the problem lay in relating the territorial claims of Fascist Italy to the imminent revolution in the world balance of power.

When Ciano, as Italian Foreign Minister, made the first soundings to Ribbentrop at Munich, after the French surrender, he received the insulting reply: "One must be moderate, and not have eyes bigger than one's stomach." The measure of Ribbentrop's contempt had to be countered by an insistence on quick profits, even at the expense of clashing with German intentions.

The division of spoils in relation to France and her Empire could only be argued on a diplomatic level: Italian aims in Egypt and Africa, already sketchily represented by the nervous presence of Graziani's army in Libya and Tripolitania, might hopefully and shortly be resolved in a similar manner, when Germany had forced the surrender of England, in all probability by August 1940, by a massive assault on the British Isles. Italy could therefore risk being content with an anticipatory and token military presence and local victory in North Africa. As Mussolini telegraphed to Graziani, in reply to the latter's urgent request for reinforcements, "We must bring home to the peace conference our military conquests."

By the autumn of 1940, however, the failure of the Blitzkrieg against the British Isles was patent. Hitler was now compelled to consider the improvisation of an alternative strategic offensive against England at the center of her imperial position in the

Mediterranean. The destruction of her power in this region would hopefully produce the same results as Operation Sea Lion.

Hitler had been impressed, and fatally, by his talks with Pétain at Montoire. The active and anti-British neutrality of Vichy France, and her secure control of the French Empire in West and Northwest Africa, was essential to future German planning, and seemed to have been achieved. The talks with Franco at Hendaye had failed to bring Spain actively into the Tripartite Pact, but seemed to indicate her readiness to adopt a position of firm neutrality which would not obstruct, if need be, an independent German operation against Gibraltar.

The attention of Hitler and his advisers could therefore be concentrated on the main British positions in the eastern Mediterranean: the fleet at Alexandria, and General Wavell's army in North Africa and Egypt. But any thrust in this direction implied the maintenance of ordered peace in the Balkans, and Southeast Europe. The security of this region was essential to eventual German action, and it was precisely here that a basic conflict of intentions erupted between Hitler and Mussolini, which exposed the artificiality of the paper structure of the Pact of Steel, the decisive flaws inherent in the relations between Germany and Italy, and the absence of a minimal combined military strategy.

Since the Italo-German staff talks at the time of the signature of the Pact of Steel in May 1939, based on the assumption that there would be no general outbreak of hostilities in Europe at least before 1942, there had been no further contacts on a military level. Indeed, Mussolini made it a habit never to bring any military advisers to summit conferences with Hitler: as, for example, at the Brenner meeting in June 1940. Both parties, therefore, operated on a basis of discreet exploration of the immediate intentions of the other through their respective military attachés. Major declarations of policy, and hints at "parallel" operations, were the subject of personal letters exchanged between the two dictators.

Ever since Italy's entry into the war in June, Mussolini and Ciano had watched for an opportunity to exploit any incident which would lead to launching an assault either on Yugoslavia or Greece, or both countries. Drafts of half-conceived military operations piled up in the offices of the Italian General Staff.

Hitler and Ribbentrop continued to emphasize the need to liquidate "the North African problem," still regarded as an exclusive Italian responsibility, before considering any Balkan adventures, which might also alarm the "neutral" Russians and encourage them in similar enterprises in Southeast Europe.

In August 1940 a rare series of open exchanges between the Axis partners took place on a possible Italian operation against Yugoslavia. The German reaction was sharp and negative. Hitler insisted on "order on Germany's southern frontier" and the need to concentrate all efforts for the final destruction of the British position in Africa.

In a letter of August 24 from Mussolini to Hitler, the former argued that "with regard to the Danube-Balkan basin there has been no change in the agreed policy which is to keep that zone out of the conflict. The military measures on the Greek and Yugoslav frontiers are simply precautionary." But both countries were fully mobilized, "and there can be no doubt about the assured complicity of Greece with Great Britain. All the Greek ports are bases against us. Having made this clear, I must say that, unless anything unforeseen occurs, it is not there that I intend to direct the forthcoming Italian military effort, but against Egypt."†

Two days previously, Marshal Badoglio had extracted, to his relief, a directive from the Duce classifying the Greek and Yugoslav sectors as on the level of "observation and vigilance only."

Such declarations by Mussolini did not prevent Ciano from pursuing his own surreptitious plans for a move against Greece, with the active collaboration of certain officers at the Supreme Command. Three further Italian divisions had been moved to

† Quoted in part by the author in the Appendix.

Albania in early September, and a further nine were expected by the end of the month.

According to a Supreme Command memorandum of September 18, it would need only ten to fifteen days to deploy these forces along the Greek and Yugoslav frontiers. Corfu would be occupied to forestall any moves by the British navy. "In the month of October next, therefore, we have the possibility of initiating operations against Greece with a minimum advance notice of twelve days."*

It is vain to seek any rational judgment or motives in regard to the conduct of the war in the minds either of Ciano or Mussolini.

Ciano was bent on pressing Albanian claims to Greek territory in northern Epirus. As General Armellini, a member of the Italian General Staff, wrote in his diary on August 24, "Ciano wants war with Greece to extend the frontiers of his grand duchy (of Albania); Badoglio sees how grave a mistake it would be to set the Balkans alight (and Germany is of this opinion); the Duce agrees at one moment with the one, and at another with the other."

Ciano's activities in preparing for a Greek operation now assumed the attributes of a Renaissance plot, privately contrived by his own agents, and hatched in Tirana. Secret funds were lavishly disposed to promote subversive action among the Albanian population of Tsamouria. The governor-general of Albania, Jacomoni, and the commanding general, Visconti Prasca, displayed sycophantic optimism. Insinuations, unsupported by any evidence, were made that senior Greek officers had received Italian bribes, and that their General Staff was penetrated by treason from within. An operation to seize northern Epirus and Corfu would be a lightning victory.

The question of a further extension of hostilities involving the defeat of the Greek army, and the ultimate occupation of the

---

* Quoted from the Italian Military Archives microfilmed in Washington by G. Warner in a valuable paper "Italian policy towards Jugoslavia and Greece 1939–1940," read at a colloquium in Paris in April 1969 organized by the Comité d'Histoire de la Deuxième Guerre Mondiale.

country could be considered in light of the preliminary and limited invasion. There was no need to plan in detail so far ahead.

Ciano's plot was based exclusively on intelligence from Tirana. The reports of the Italian minister in Athens, Grazzi, and the military attaché, Colonel Mondini, were curtly ignored. The Greek army had in fact been placed on a war footing since August. General Metaxas, the Prime Minister, would fight for the honor of his country if all attempts failed to preserve the neutrality of Greece, for which Metaxas was prepared to strive even to the extent of discouraging British aid under the terms of the guarantee from London of the previous year.

There was no sign of treason within the Greek General Staff; any aggression by Italy could not be confined to northern Epirus; and British "provocation" would be inevitable.

If a general war with Greece was included in the considered aim of Ciano's policy, it would be essential to conduct military operations in alliance with Bulgaria, whose claims on Greek Macedonia and Thrace, and a port on the Aegean, suitably matched those of Italian Albania.

Ciano considered this vital issue of Bulgarian participation in the pending Greek operation with frivolous negligence. Anfuso was sent to Sofia (but not until October 16) on such a mission, and met with a firm snub from King Boris.

Mussolini seems, however, to have accepted Ciano's arguments, and without serious consultation with his military advisers, who themselves were divided into feuding clans. General Soddu, the vice-chief of the General Staff and Ciano's main agent in the game, informed his superior, Marshal Badoglio, on October 13 that orders were to be issued to launch "Contingency G" (the code name for the Greek operation) on October 26. This decision was unknown to General Roatta, the acting chief of the Army Staff (his superior, General Graziani, was in command in Africa), who was not in on the secret. General Visconti Prasca, the leading military "conspirator," and commander in Albania, was summoned to Rome on October 14. In his subsequent apologia, written after the war, he wrote that on that morning he called on Roatta, "who told me that the action against Greece would not take place."

At a meeting on the same day with Mussolini and Badoglio, held to discuss a General Staff plan drawn up in early 1940 for a general attack on Greece, Roatta was told, in an aside by the Duce, that Greece was adopting such a favorable attitude to Britain that she must be occupied by Italy. Roatta estimated that a further twelve divisions were required, and a period of three months' planning would be necessary.

On the following day, October 15, 1940, Mussolini summoned a selected group of advisers to the Palazzo Venezia to reveal his decision to launch the Italian forces in Albania against Greece by October 26. Neither the head of the Italian air force or navy was present, nor were they aware of the impending operation.

The analysis of the minutes of this astonishing meeting, and of the preceding weeks of mutual deception and duplicity in high quarters in Rome are admirably set out by the author of this study.

On October 19, Mussolini wrote to Hitler announcing, without precise details of timing, his intention to move from Albanian bases against Greece. This letter reached Hitler on the Franco-Spanish border at Hendaye, where he was engaged in frustrating talks with Franco.

A hastily arranged meeting between the two Axis leaders was fixed to take place at Florence on October 28, the day on which, unknown to Hitler, the Greek campaign was to be launched as a separate and unheralded Italian enterprise.

The minutes of the Florence meeting conceal Hitler's real reactions to this willful and ill-conceived military parade. He expressed "complete German solidarity with the action begun by Italy against Greece. If it should prove necessary, the Führer would put at the disposal of the Duce parachute divisions which could be used for the occupation of Crete."†

At the meeting Hitler concealed his irritation at the launching

† Italian Diplomatic Documents. Ninth Series, Volume V, pp. 771 ff.

of the Greek operation by Italy and appeared to ignore its inevitable repercussions on the whole Mediterranean position. He indulged instead in a verbose mesmerizing exposition of his latest strategic project: a Napoleonic continental block, which would complete the isolation of Great Britain, to be based on the cooperative neutrality of Vichy France in western Europe and her African empire; which would include Spain; and above all—on a short term—the Soviet Union, "a main element in the European coalition against England."

This self-induced euphoria obscured the fatal implications of Mussolini's adventure on the northern frontiers of Greece, which Hitler professed to regard as a marginal folly.

In private he was more realistic. His military adjutant, Major Engel, recorded, in his hitherto unpublished diary, the Führer's remarks when he learnt for the first time, at Bologna on his way to the Florence meeting, that the Italians had actually invaded Greece.*

"He [Hitler] judged the situation as follows: the Duce feared the economic influence which the Germans had in the Balkans, and Hitler doubted whether Italy was in a position to overthrow Greece, for the Greeks were not bad soldiers. Textually the Führer said, 'This is the revenge for Norway and France.' But he could have only dealt with these operations in secret, because every second Italian was either a traitor or a spy . . . He was greatly disturbed that Italian activity in the whole Balkans would have grave consequences, and give a welcome opportunity to the British to set up an air base in the Balkans."

"Contingency G" was now to be launched as a tragic farce. The Greek army was fully mobilized, and, surprised by the neutrality of Bulgaria (General Papagos had planned for a joint Italian-Bulgar offensive), the bulk of the Greek forces were awaiting the Italians in North Epirus.

* Quoted in Andreas Hillgrüber, *Hitlers Strategie, Politik und Kriegführung 1940–1941* (1965), p. 286 note.

The author quotes from the hitherto unpublished telegram of the Greek minister in Rome, Politis, to his government: "According to information from military sources, the action against Greece will begin in the period between October 25 and 28."

With the exception of General Visconti Prasca, and General Soddu, the senior Italian staff officers, led by Marshal Badoglio and General Roatta, were opposed to the operation, and had hoped, with a puerile and shifty cleverness, to sabotage or at least delay the Epirus operation, by advocating at the meeting of October 15 total war against Greece, which would take months of technical planning.

The chiefs of staff of the Italian air force and navy had no plan, having been omitted from the secret.

At the beginning of the month orders had been issued by General Soddu, Badoglio's immediate subordinate, to carry out the demobilization between October 10 and November 15 of 600,000 out of 1,100,000 men in those units of the Italian army stationed in Italy—in order to help with the harvest. By implication this remarkable order could only give the impression that Mussolini had abandoned any future military adventures. Possibly this move was intended as a deception to distract the attention both of his own military "experts" and his German ally from the pending attack on Greece, but to Badoglio at least it signified that this operation had been privately abandoned.

Instead, Visconti Prasca was to pursue his adventure, confident that his army in Albania of less than 100,000 men would reach their first objectives, without further reinforcements, by November 15. Jacomoni was confident that his subversive plans to provoke a guerrilla rising among the Albanian population of Tsamouria would be a decisive element: in the event, a "commando" of two hundred and fifty men made a lamentable and brief appearance.

The advance into Greece was in general terms to be coordinated, hopefully, in Mussolini's calculation, with a painless offensive in North Africa by Graziani, who would capture Mersa Matruh, and intimidate the British military and naval forces in

Egypt sufficiently to dissuade them from intervening in Greece. The opposite occurred.

It remained to formulate the diplomatic niceties of declaring war upon Greece. This was all Ciano's own work. None of the chiefs of staff nor, of course, the Germans were consulted.

The author describes the scene in Athens with sad and eloquent irony. Neither the Italian minister nor his military attaché had any intimation of the imminence of hostilities. The precise date had, in fact, been changed by the Duce from October 26 to October 28 to coincide with the anniversary of the March on Rome, a subtle touch of Fascist mythology.

On the evening of October 26 a formal reception was held at the Italian Legation in Athens following a special commemorative performance of *Madame Butterfly* in the presence of the son of Giacomo Puccini. Towards midnight a long series of urgent telegrams began to arrive in cipher at the legation. They contained an ultimatum to be delivered by Grazzi, the Italian minister, to General Metaxas at 3 A.M. on October 28 with a time limit to expire within three hours.

The unfortunate and bemused diplomat, who had patiently established relations of mutual confidence over the preceding months with the Greek Prime Minister, gloomily carried out his instructions, and called punctually at Metaxas' villa. Grazzi's postwar account describes the scene. The text of the ultimatum, which was drafted in crude imitation of the German document handed to the Norwegian government in the previous year, stressed that Italy would attack at dawn unless "certain strategic points" were immediately surrendered to Italian forces. Grazzi was not informed by his government as to the identity of these key objectives, and unable to enlighten Metaxas.

On the departure of the Italian minister, Metaxas went to the British Legation, and asked formally for aid from England. He then summoned a Council of Ministers. While this meeting was in session, advance guards of Visconti Prasca's army crossed the frontier of northern Epirus.

The Greek campaign was to expose, as the author unfolds in

this book with restrained and lucid bitterness, the confusion and corruption of the Italian military machine. This is the main historical significance of this disastrous adventure of Mussolini launched in crude and jealous small-scale imitation of the German technique of lightning war.

The drama of this study lies in the contrast between the fatuous military conduct of the campaign and the vain gallantry of the Italian troops doomed to fight a winter war without modern equipment (for example, 107 light tanks out of a paper allocation of 1,750 actually reached the front), and, for the most part, supplied with tropical uniforms.

Part of the air force, unalerted until the last moment, was based on the Italian mainland, and without radio contact with the Tirana headquarters.

The navy was barely able to maintain communications with North Africa. The ancillary operation to occupy the essential Greek naval base of Corfu was abandoned "owing to heavy seas." The transport organization between Italian and Albanian ports collapsed within days. The jagged line of forward positions on the mountain crests, stretching from Macedonia to the western coast of Greece, was thinly held by élite alpine units. Behind them the structure of the divisions making up the Italian expeditionary corps, devoid of supply services and short of field hospitals, were forced to operate in isolated groups with even their command posts seldom in touch with divisional headquarters.

As the initial advance ground rapidly to a chaotic halt, reinforcements were rushed from Italy, moved up to the front in assault companies divorced from any coherent structure on a divisional or even battalion level, and often without artillery support and equipped only with light weapons. Stores and guns piled up in Italian ports. At one point 30,000 mules and horses together with their drivers, vital to the supply columns in mountain warfare, were blocked in Italy.

By the end of the first week of November, the Greeks were on the offensive, and probing in strength northwards on Albanian territory.

The author traces the military vicissitudes of the campaign in stark detail. The "logical and convincing" plan of General Visconti Prasca—in Mussolini's phrase—collapsed within the first weeks, and he was dismissed from his command on November 9. With his customary ironic sense of humor, the Duce replaced him by the arch "planner" of the enterprise, General Soddu, the vice-chief of the General Staff, noted in private for his musical compositions for films. Ciano's contacts with the Italian police had long been employed to tap Soddu's telephone in the offices of the Supreme Command. The intercepts were not encouraging.

With more subtle ingenuity, Mussolini sought to pin responsibility at the military summit. On December 3, Marshal Badoglio was dismissed, to the secret satisfaction of the King and with his formal approval, as Chief of the General Staff, a post to which he had clung with sly persistence since 1925. There was talk in high circles of Caporetto, and Badoglio's unclarified role in 1917. History was mildly perverted to repeat itself for propaganda purposes, and the Greek disaster of the winter of 1940 was glibly named the second Caporetto.

Badoglio's present disgrace simmered in his mind, and contributed to his revenge on the Duce in the coup d'état of 1943.

The appointment of his successor, Marshal Cavallero, the most intellectual and perhaps least experienced in battle command of the Italian generals, followed; but his assumption of direct control of operations in Albania made no dent upon the course of events. He was not, however, short of self-confidence, and announced with a certain premature smugness, "We are back again at Caporetto, and as at that time I have to repair the mistakes of Badoglio."

The slow-moving Greek divisions—Papagos could not grasp the extent of Italian follies and light-headedness—were now in occupation of one third of Albanian territory.

The British had landed Royal Air Force units in southern Greece, and their navy was in occupation of the vital harbors of Crete.

Already on November 12, 1940, Hitler had given orders for Operation Marita, concentrating ten divisions in Rumania and, with the reluctant consent of King Boris, in Bulgaria, to launch a model lightning campaign against the Greek lines on their northeastern frontier, leaving the Italians to sort out the disorder of the Albanian front.†

The unequal clash of the German invading divisions with the British expeditionary force is not a central theme in this book, but is touched on in clear outline to complete the story.

The German command in northern Greece received the surrender of all the Greek armies including those facing the Italians on the Epirus front. In a petulant explosion of temper, Mussolini complained to Hitler at the exclusion of Italian representatives by the local German commander, Field Marshal List, from these armistice negotiations.

On April 23 a special performance was laid on, under direct instructions from Hitler, and General Jodl was sent to Salonika to stage a ceremonious repetition, to include the Italians, of the signature of formal armistice terms with Greece. Metaxas had died in January. The Greek commander of the northeastern front, General Tsolakoglou, accepted the responsibility of the surrender and the fateful role of heading an administration now set up for Axis-occupied Greece. He was fortunate to die a natural death before the victory of the Allies. Field Marshal List refused to take part in the final tragicomedy in Salonika, and the campaign initiated by Mussolini and Ciano in October 1940 ended with an explosion of bitterness between the Axis partners, which was to bedevil their relations for the duration of hostilities.

The Italian assault on Greece, aimed at grabbing territorial, strategic, and economic gains in southeastern Europe as a special monopoly, led to the fatal exposure of every aspect of the Fascist leadership. The extent of the military incompetence of the Italian

---

† A thorough study of the German involvement in Greece has been made in E. Schramm von Thadden, *Griechenland und die Grossmächte im Zweiten Weltkrieg* (1955).

leaders might even have been explained, and such an interpretation on the German side was to gather weight in the future, by deliberate sabotage of the Axis alliance by certain elements within the Fascist High Command and the political leadership itself. German suspicions as to the true role of Ciano certainly date from the Greek adventure; Badoglio was to show his hand in the summer of 1943; Cavallero was driven to mysterious suicide in the ultimate crash of the system.

But the main victims of this tragic episode have been restored to history by this book: the rank and file of the Italian expeditionary force in Albania and Greece. The author has paid a moving tribute to the 14,000 dead, over 50,000 wounded, 25,000 missing, and, grimly added, over 12,000 maimed in the frozen winter months. The gallantry and sacrifice of the alpine units, in particular —to name only one, the Julia Division—are recorded in these pages.*

The tragedy of the Italian divisions in Albania and Greece did not, however, end with the armistice of April 1941. As occupation troops, they were to endure the hidden terror of guerrilla war against partisans in Greece and Albania, and, with the surrender of Badoglio to the Allies in September 1943, these units, for the most part, were to be abandoned to the pitiless ferocity of their former German allies.

The dead of the campaign of 1940–41 were joined by those massacred in treachery by SS commandos in a series of forlorn and isolated gestures of resistance culminating in the mass shooting of 146 officers and 4,000 men of the Acqui Division on the Greek island of Cephalonia.

This book is both a sober and accurate record of criminal incompetence in high places, and a fitting epitaph for the humble victims of the Fascist adventure launched against Greece in 1940.

F. W. DEAKIN

---

* A brief but distinguished essay on the climate of this campaign has been written by Giano Carlo Fusco, "Guerra d'Albania" (1961).

Preface

Thirty years have now passed since the beginning of the Greek campaign. This mistaken war, that cost the Italians and Greeks hundreds of thousands of dead and wounded, and victims of frostbite, can now be looked at more calmly. Not all the wounds have healed; the disabled are still with us, to remind us of the price in suffering that has to be paid for a "mistake" when it is on this fearful scale. But time has removed some of the sting, and hatreds have died down; many psychological and political positions have changed. All the leading figures who bore the responsibility and the burden of events are dead, including Count Francesco Jacomoni, who was the Italian governor-general of Albania—and his testimony is one-sided and self-defensive.

Mussolini is dead, and so are Metaxas, Ciano, and Papagos, the Greek commander-in-chief, and General Visconti Prasca, who led the Italians to the attack, and died nearly an octogenarian. These men left memoirs, official documents, memoranda that take us back to the atmosphere of that distant October night when an agitated Italian envoy handed a declaration of war to a Greek dictator in his dressing gown, and the gray-green columns set out to wind their way through the desolate valleys of the Greek-Albanian border, beginning a Calvary that lasted for months. The generals, poring over maps bristling with red and blue marks, planned operations that were never carried out, and infantry, Alpini, cavalry and Bersaglieri, resignedly grumbling, moved towards an unknown enemy without knowing why or in the name of what mysterious, supreme necessity they were at war with him.

It is a bitter story, and I pondered for a long time before making up my mind to tell it. To the Italians it has neither the glamour of a struggle in a good cause, nor the grim but undeniable kind of fascination that comes from watching the momentum of a superb military machine. The only light in the shadow is the memory of the simple soldiers who fought and did not come back. For their sake, I believe, this unpleasing page of the unpleasing history of the last war should be recalled, so that once more it may be made plain that Italian troops did their duty though they had a thousand excellent reasons for not doing it, while their leaders blundered from the beginning to the end of a campaign outstanding in Italian history as an example of political improvidence, military incompetence, petty ambition, and strategic and tactical shortsightedness.

I am not the only one to say these things, and still less can I claim to have discovered them; they have been stated with varying degrees of explicitness and bluntness by many of the generals and politicians involved in the disastrous enterprise. But all of them have attributed culpability and error to others with a view to saving their own reputations. It is, I believe, unnecessary to emphasize that I have no axe to grind and that this book is not intended to whitewash anyone's reputation. If ever there was a war that was started by chance, out of pure pique, it was this one. In such cases chance, of course, follows the irresistible trend of history, Nemesis if you like. *Quos vult Juppiter perdere dementat prius.* When chance intervenes in the great and terrible framework of a world war, it has its own mysterious and tremendous logic. One day some well-intentioned historian will develop interesting and theoretically sound theories about the conflicts of interests and the strategic imperatives that led to the Greek war. But the fact is that the men who had the power of decision had no coherent plan in mind when they unleashed the slaughter.

This is intended only to be a preface, and I shall not dilate further on this question. But I still find it surprising to read Greek studies and comments—starting with the memoirs of Alexander Papagos[1]—in which a rational and therefore imaginary line of conduct is attributed to their enemy. "The unprovoked and wanton attack," Papagos—a good general but a bad writer—wrote in his Tyrtaean style, "launched on October 28, 1940, by Italy against Greece, who had always been considered an obstacle to the ambitious designs of Italian imperialistic policy of reviving the Roman Empire and extending Italian living space to the Near East, was not devised to further Italian policy alone. Within the framework of the general European conflict, this attack was part of a broader plan previously agreed upon by the two Axis Powers."

That is a myth. It is intelligible that the commander-in-chief of the army that so brilliantly withstood the ordeal should try to give weight to his enemy in order to show himself and his troops in the most favorable light. But all the Greek accounts of the war follow the same line; the picture that they paint is of a great and powerful country, armed to the teeth, attacking their small and almost defenseless homeland after long and meticulous preparation, and yet failing to defeat her because of the superhuman valor of the Greek army. It is a proposition that we should probably support ourselves if we were Greek. It is obviously attractive to the Greeks but it is demonstrably a fantastic distortion of the truth. There was no Axis plan, and there was no serious Italian preparation. The Albanian war was not a battle between David and Goliath, but between two Davids, one of whom had right on his side.

The first and in itself sufficiently convincing evidence of the almost fortuitous origin of the Greek campaign, which is corroborated in every phase of its development, is provided by that very well-known document, Ciano's *Diary*. The extracts that follow are intended to be merely a brief anticipation of the argument that will be more fully developed in subsequent pages. "September 12, 1939. . . . I accompanied Grazzi when he was received by the Duce, who gave instructions for a rapprochement with Greece, a country too poor for us to want." "August 10, 1940. . . . I discussed with Mussolini difficulties which have arisen on the Greek-Albanian border. There is no desire to dramatize the situation, but the Greek attitude is very unreliable. The Duce is considering 'a forceful gesture, because he has had an account to settle since 1923, and the Greeks are deceiving themselves if they imagine he has wiped the slate clean.'" "August 11. Mussolini again mentioned the Greek question and asked for information about Tsamouria. He has prepared a statement for the Stefani agency, which will begin to stir up the question. And he has made me summon to Rome Jacomoni and Visconti Prasca, with whom he intends to confer. He is talking of a surprise attack on Greece towards the end of September. If he has decided on this, I think the timing should be accelerated. It is dangerous to give the Greeks a chance to prepare. . . ." "August 17. [As regards Greece] We put the note that was ready back in the drawer. . . ." "August 22. Mussolini gave me a copy of some military directives he has issued, indefinitely postponing operations against Yugoslavia and Greece. . . ." "October 8. The Duce telephoned, asking for steps to be taken in Rumania leading to a request for Italian troops. He is very angry at only German troops being present in the oil-bearing zones. . . ." "October 12. . . . [The Duce] is above all indignant at the German occupation of Rumania. . . . 'Hitler keeps confronting me with *faits accomplis*. This time I shall pay him back in his own coin; he shall learn from the newspapers that I have occupied Greece. Thus equilibrium will be restored.' I asked him if he had reached agreement with Badoglio. 'Not yet,' he replied. . . ."[2]

In other words, on October 12, two weeks before the attack (the date first fixed by Mussolini was the twenty-sixth, but it was postponed to the twenty-eighth) the chief of the General Staff did not know that his army was about to "break the Greek back." What is more, on the morning of October 14, General Roatta, the army deputy chief of staff, believed that the plan to attack Greece had been dropped. "On October 14 I was summoned to Rome; in the morning I went to see Roatta, who told me that the operation against Greece was off," wrote Visconti Prasca.[3] Such quotations can be multiplied, and in due course we shall cite them in their proper context. Here and now I wish to draw attention to some of the most painful aspects of the prewar situation and the character of a campaign which was morally wrong and was technically bungled and improvised from the outset. It was begun at the worst season of the year against an enemy long since put on his guard by a sequence of arrogant threats, interspersed with unconvincing reassurances. Because of the decision of a Duce motivated by puerile pique, the Italian divisions moved against Greece without conviction, without the advantage of surprise, with obsolete arms and equipment, led by generals divided by careerist jealousies and personal antipathies.

Once in a while it must be admitted that Hitler was partly right, as when he said:

Italy's entry into the war at once gave our enemies their first victories, a fact which enabled Churchill to revive the courage of his countrymen and which gave hope to all the anglophiles all the world over. Even while they proved themselves incapable of maintaining their positions in Abyssinia and Cyrenaica, the Italians had the nerve to throw themselves, without seeking our advice and without giving us even previous warning of their intention, into a pointless campaign in Greece. The shameful defeats which they suffered caused certain of the Balkan states to regard us with scorn and contempt. Here, and nowhere else, are to be found the causes of Yugoslavia's stiffening attitude and her *volte-face* in the spring of 1941. This compelled us, contrary to all our plans, to intervene in the Balkans, and that in its turn led to a catastrophic delay in the launching of our attack on Russia. . . . If the war had remained a war conducted by Germany, and not by the Axis, we should have been in a position to attack Russia by May 15, 1941. Doubly strengthened by the fact that our forces had known nothing but decisive and irrefutable victories, we should have been able to conclude the campaign before winter came.[4]

The Hitler who talked in this way was already psychologically an accused, called on to defend himself in the face of his people and of history. In order to minimize his own mistakes he greatly magnified the consequences of the attack on Greece, i.e., the mistakes of Mussolini. It could be pointed out that the invasion of the Balkans and the sending of a British expeditionary force to Greece deprived the British forces in Africa of precious strength and thus facilitated Rommel's advance. Nevertheless the Greek campaign remains an iniquity and an act of military folly. Hitler's diagnosis, though well founded politically, is thus unacceptable at least on one point. The German dictator attributed to the Italians as a whole failures for which the responsibility belongs solely to Mussolini and those who carried out his contradictory orders. No army could have successfully conducted a campaign in those conditions, with those directives, at that season of the year. Let us leave the shame of defeat where it belongs. Those who fought with courage, loyalty, stoic endurance and deep bitterness can be proud of having done their duty.

THE HOLLOW LEGIONS

1. Dictator *v.* Dictator

It is a paradox that after all his thunderous denunciations of the so-called Judaeo-Masonic plutodemocracies Mussolini should finally have launched his private and personal war against a dictator of the Fascist type. John Metaxas, a general who for many years had been a politician, was a dictator of recent date. His "March on Rome" had taken place on August 3, 1936, and his régime had not adopted the ostentatious choreography of the totalitarian régimes of Italy and Germany. He wore civilian clothes, lived modestly, and his outlook was petty bourgeois; moreover, his plump figure would not have appeared to advantage in uniform. He had an ordinary, fattish face, and a thick moustache. He was not bloodthirsty by nature, but imposed a hard régime on his country, taking advantage of the ruthless efficiency of a Chief of Police named Maniadakis, who unceremoniously banished to the islands all opponents of the dictatorship. The press censorship was severe and the atmosphere oppressive; even certain works of Plato that seemed to conflict with the alleged philosophy of the régime were banned. The Neolia, or youth organization, though it had some undeniable merits in the field of social service, had the demerit of continually obliging boys and girls to march past members of the hierarchy. The régime had adopted the Roman salute, which it nationalistically renamed the Greek salute. There was undoubtedly an ideological affinity between the Greek and Italian régimes: the former could be considered a disciple of the latter. As a good soldier Metaxas admired the Germans—he had been trained in their military academies. His patriotism was deep and sincere. Thus all the conditions existed for a process of political and diplomatic infiltration, for which the path was smoothed by the similarity between the two régimes, and the resounding German successes of the first year of the war would greatly have facilitated the task.

Metaxas was not a man of lively imagination; he might be seen as a less pliable and more provincial Franco. He left a diary[1] which, if it has not been edited and cut—and it does not seem to have been—demonstrates only the limitations of his political horizon and the narrowness of his intellectual horizon. Nevertheless, I repeat, the man was not without a deep sense of national dignity, and he was very much at home on the political backstairs of Athens. In many ways he was Fascism's own man, and he could have been heavily backed and made an ally. There is every sign that this is the course the Germans wanted to follow. The Greek leader had spent four years in political exile at Siena, and felt the Mediterranean "affinity" between Greeks and Italians. "If in all Greece there was a single man who really had a feeling of affection for Italy, that man was John Metaxas," the Italian minister in Athens, Emanuele Grazzi, subsequently wrote.[2] But the time came when Mussolini ceased to be concerned with picking up potentially useful allies cheaply; what he wanted at all costs was enemies, to show Hitler that he too could invade and conquer: in fact, conduct a Blitzkrieg. So he had to declare a war, not issue an invitation to the waltz. The latter he never even attempted.

During the months in which Mussolini vacillated between intervention and non-intervention, between bellicose statements and retreats into moderation, Grazzi, who was a man of good sense and an excellent diplomatist, did all in his power to establish friendly relations with Metaxas, who liked him personally. But it was a strange game of misunderstandings. Grazzi mistakenly believed that he was interpreting Ciano's policy, though in reality the Italian Foreign Minister vacillated too, sometimes in harmony with the Duce but sometimes out of phase with him. Metaxas, however, believed Grazzi to be a faithful executor of Rome's orders, and alternated between phases of optimism and more reasonable phases of extreme suspicion.

The fact of the matter was that no one had a plan worthy of the name. Rome had no plan, and consequently Grazzi, who acted on his own initiative, had none; and Metaxas, who was at the receiving end of these disconcerting changes, had no plan either. Those who desire at all costs to see a line of rational conduct, a historical thread, running through the behavior of the statesmen involved will have to go a long way back to trace the underlying causes of the Greek campaign. I do not believe that in this instance there was any such consistency or deep, non-fortuitous explanation. I believe it unnecessary to look further than the Italian occupation of Albania on April 8, 1939, that almost bloodless operation that set the whole Balkan beehive buzzing, roused Greek and Yugoslav suspicions, and provided the British and French with an excellent opportunity for assuring Metaxas, a dictator who naturally tended to be pro-Mussolinian, that they, the traditional friends of Greece, were ready and willing to come to her aid.

The occupation of Albania took place at the beginning of April. On April 9 the Italian chargé d'affaires—the minister, Raffaele Boscarelli, had been succeeded by Grazzi, but the latter had not yet taken up his post—received a reassuring telegram from Mussolini: "Call personally on Metaxas and tell him from me that I assure him of all my personal satisfaction at the attitude adopted by Greece towards King Zog and that I thank him for all the steps taken for the purpose of preventing actions by Zog that might have cast even the slightest shadow on the friendly relations that unite the two countries, the maintenance of which will be the foundation both of my present and future policy." The Greeks, however, were not reassured; they feared that the seizure of Albania might be the prelude to an attack on Greece (while the Yugoslavs nursed similar suspicions about a possible invasion of their country). For those who wanted evidence of such intentions there was no difficulty in finding it. (". . . the Yugoslavs must be given a dose of chloroform; but later we must adopt a policy of lively interest in Kossovo. That will amount to keeping alive an ir-

redentist problem in the Balkans which will polarize the attention
of the Albanians themselves and represent a dagger planted in
the back of Yugoslavia."—Ciano's diary, April 21, 1939.) Mussolini's and Ciano's political plans were a mixture of everything:
the idea of a "liberation" movement in Kossovo directed against
Yugoslavia, of a similar campaign in Tsamouria (see p. 20)
directed against Greece, the seizure of Corfu, a possible seizure
of Epirus, the invasion of the whole of Greece, peace in the Balkans: a crazy jumble of policies and programs and nothing
properly thought out.

During that first dangerous phase Metaxas took the line that
he was to follow until the day of the Italian ultimatum—apparent
mildness combined with substantial firmness. It was a policy imposed by circumstances and was consistently pursued. At a little
after midnight on April 9 the Greek dictator received the British
ambassador in Athens and informed him that he was determined
to resist any attack, that he would not agree even to a limited and
partial occupation of Greek territory, and that if war broke out it
would therefore be total. Metaxas had not yet received Mussolini's
telegram, but his close contacts with the British diplomatic mission,
and the daily calls on Lord Halifax, the British Foreign Secretary,
by the Greek minister in London, were clearly the prelude to
the Franco-British guarantee subsequently given to Greece.

Greece has always maintained that this guarantee was the result
of an unsolicited Allied initiative. This is formally correct, but
fundamentally it is not so at all. Greece felt herself to be in danger,
and it was natural that she should look for assurances wherever she
could find them. She had no choice in the matter, but was forced
to seek protection from a threat which, seen from Athens, was
far more dangerous and imminent than it was from Rome. On
April 13 Neville Chamberlain announced the British guarantee
in the House of Commons in these words: "In the event of any
action being taken which clearly threatened the independence of
Greece or Rumania, and which the Greek or Rumanian Government respectively considered it vital to resist with their national
forces, his Majesty's Government would feel themselves bound to

lend the Greek or Rumanian Government, as the case may be, all the support in their power." Daladier made an announcement in similar terms in France.

Superficially the flutter of anxiety was of brief duration, but at a deeper level Greek anxiety persisted. King Zog of Albania took refuge in Greece with his wife and family, first at Larissa and then at Volos. To demonstrate Greek neutrality, he was forbidden any kind of political activity, and soon afterwards, to Metaxas' great relief, this somewhat comic opera monarch left the country. While the flurry over Albania was dying away Emanuele Grazzi took over the Athens legation. At a first meeting with Ciano after his appointment he was told to be "polite but cool" in regard to King George II, who justifiably enjoyed the reputation of being an anglophile. Grazzi expected the Foreign Minister to give him exhaustive instructions on the eve of his departure, but these he did not receive. On April 14, 1939, he went to the Palazzo Chigi for an appointment with Ciano. "I waited patiently until about nine o'clock. Filippo Anfuso, the *chef de cabinet,* then appeared in the antechamber and told me that the Minister was dining with Muti, that he had nothing special to tell me, and that he wished me *bon voyage.*"[3] Grazzi believed that his task was to work for a relaxation of tension between the two countries, though Ciano failed to particularize. In reality Ciano cared little about what Grazzi might do or report back. In his policy towards Greece he used other channels and relied on other sources of information.

This was characteristic of the workings of the Italian Foreign Ministry at that time; the small group of officials who constituted the Minister's *cabinet,* or private office, dealt with all important problems behind the backs of the senior officials and many ambassadors, or ministers. The officials of the private office treated their colleagues with the cold, smiling and contemptuous courtesy typical of a *grand seigneur* dealing with worthy citizens not belonging to his caste. Envoys who did not belong to the privileged clique of the Foreign Minister's personal friends were ignored or passed over. (A celebrated instance is that of Bernardo Attolico, whose well-informed reports to Ciano about Hitler's intentions to start a world war were not believed, because one of his subordinates, Magistrati, a relative and intimate of Ciano's, mistakenly insisted on the opposite.) Thus Grazzi, who did not have a direct line to the Palazzo Chigi, was left armed with good will but scanty instructions.

The reports of the Greek diplomatic representatives kept Metaxas[4] in a state of alarm. Skeferis, the envoy at Tirana, had good sources of information. On April 27, 1939, he foresaw the possibility of an attack on Epirus and Preveza; and it was characteristic that plans for such a limited operation indeed turned up from time to time on the General Staff's desks. Meanwhile greater events were pending. Germany and Italy signed the Pact of Steel. Hitler was determined to start a second world war, and in Moscow Ribbentrop and Stalin signed the agreement that gave the Nazis a free hand in the west. Against this vast framework the Balkans—where the situation was still based on the anti-Bulgarian Balkan Entente between Greece, Rumania, Turkey and Yugoslavia—dwindled into insignificance. In fact they turn up from time to time in Ciano's diary rather in the form of picturesque marginal notes. On May 12 he wrote: "Public works [in Albania] are beginning to go well. The whole road-building programe is directed towards the Greek borders. This was ordered by the Duce, who is thinking more and more of an assault on Greece at the first opportunity." The Foreign Minister rather creates the impression of toying with shifting, changeable plans, more or less open intrigues and "irredentisms," for which there were pretexts of varying degrees of substance. When he visited Albania, which was his personal domain, he was received with sovereign honors, and his docile mouthpiece Jacomoni moved the pawns about there in what seemed an easy game of chess. To Mussolini, hypnotized by the dream of *mare nostrum,* Greece was a tempting morsel. But all this was within the framework of a foreign policy that was shifty and irresolute, though it tried to show a strong and determined front to the world.

At the beginning of July 1939, Princess Irene of Greece, King George II's sister, was married in Florence to Duke Aimone di Savoia-Aosta. The King of the Hellenes attended the ceremony, and both the Greeks and the Italians emphasized the private character of the occasion, but to General Papagos, whose wife was one of the ladies in attendance on the princess, the way the event was hushed up by the Italian authorities seemed excessive, and he later complained about it to Luigi Mondini, the military attaché.[5] But this was merely an insignificant frill to events. A crisis developed in the second half of August, only a few days before Germany set out on the conquest of Poland and Europe. The Italians concentrated troops on the Greek frontier for the first time; and Greece, which had always paid most attention to her frontier with Bulgaria, her traditional enemy, prepared for a different and more alarming eventuality, war with Italy. Thus, more than a year before war broke out, Greece was put on her guard, and she made intelligent use of this enormous advantage.

In the second half of August, then, Greek-Italian relations became very tense. Of the five Italian divisions—apart from some independent formations—which were in Albania, four were moved to the frontier with Greece, which Italian aircraft frequently violated. In a heated conversation with Colonel Mondini, General Papagos complained that General Alfredo Guzzoni, then the military commander in Albania—Ciano ridiculed him for being "small, with such a big belly and dyed hair"—was making bellicose speeches, and that the troops were singing songs such as:

> *Andremo nell' Egeo,*
> *Prenderemo pure il Pireo,*
> *E—se tutto va bene—*
> *Prenderemo anche Atene.**

* "We'll go to the Aegean and we'll take the Piraeus, and if all goes well, we'll take Athens too."

Colonel Mondini, who was a sensible man, replied that nothing but normal military exercises could be involved, and added that four divisions, even reinforced, would certainly not be sufficient for an invasion of Greece. Poor Mondini's arguments were based on the futile wisdom of a colonel who was kept systematically in the dark about what was happening at the highest levels of the political and military hierarchy and now found himself in a difficult position; he could not foresee that it was precisely such a force, or a force not significantly superior, that was later considered sufficient to "break the Greek back."

During that August Mussolini was seized several times with anti-Greek anger, certainly inflamed by the Franco-British guarantee and the subsequent Franco-British agreements with Turkey. But it often subsided with the swiftness with which it arose. On August 16 Badoglio, the chief of the General Staff, received orders to prepare a plan for the invasion of Greece. Guzzoni produced it in three days, or rather brought up to date a draft plan he had drawn up in July, after the occupation of Albania. He considered that an invasion with Salonika and Athens as objectives would require eighteen reinforced divisions organized in six army corps. The primary line of attack would be from the Koritsa depression in the direction of Salonika and Athens, and there would be a subsidiary offensive in the direction of Yanina. No strength would be dispersed in occupying the Ionian islands, and no dependence would be placed on Albanian battalions. Four army corps consisting of twelve divisions would be allotted to the Salonika offensive, while an army corps of three divisions would head for Yanina. The remaining army corps, also of three divisions, would be left to guard the Yugoslav frontier. Guzzoni wanted nearly a year of preparation; he insisted that all the divisions must be in Albania and that large-scale road and harbor works must be completed before the beginning of hostilities. This plan was discussed by the military leaders in Rome, but in little more than academic fashion. But General Alberto Pariani, then undersecretary of war, prudently recommended that the eighteen divisions should be increased to twenty.

But this Mussolinian outburst of enthusiasm, like so many others, was of brief duration. On September 11 the Duce informed Grazzi that "Greece does not lie on our path, and we want nothing from her. I have full confidence in Metaxas, who has restored order to his country"; and on September 20, in a conversation with Guzzoni, he said that "war with Greece is off. Greece is a bare bone, and is not worth the loss of a single Sardinian grenadier."[6] Less than a year later, when Visconti Prasca became military commander in Albania, the Guzzoni plan had become a "study" put away in the files, one of the kind that "are normal for every general staff because of obvious necessity and also as a professional exercise."[7]

The Greeks had only very small forces covering the Albanian frontier, and as a countermeasure to the Italian moves in August a partial mobilization was ordered. This was carried out not without muddle and confusion, but it was a valuable experience from which the Greeks profited when general mobilization took place in October 1940. But Mussolini's politico-military planning was mercurial, and the Greek objective disappeared from his horizon. It was now Yugoslavia's turn (these months were characterized by ever changing aggressive plans). The consequence was that Grazzi, who went to Rome for instructions, returned to his post fully satisfied, for he was given official encouragement for his "appeasement" policy. A Greek-Italian treaty of friendship and co-operation which expired on September 30 was not renewed, but a friendly exchange of letters more or less took its place.

Mussolini personally dictated to Grazzi a memorandum that said verbatim:

(1) Italy has already declared under the date September 1 that she does not intend to take any initiative in military operations; (2) this decision of the Council of Ministers, which is general in nature, applies in particular in regard to Greece; (3) thus in the eventuality

of Italy's intervening, by reason of her position as a Great Power, in the conflict (a possibility that she cannot exclude), she will not take the initiative in operations against Greece; (4) in order to demonstrate in the most concrete fashion the feelings towards Greece by which the Italian government and the Duce in particular are animated, the withdrawal of troops to twenty kilometres from the Greek-Albanian frontier will be ordered; (5) the Duce, in spite of existing circumstances, does not exclude the possibility of stabilizing this policy of understanding between Italy and Greece, which might be consecrated in *ad hoc* diplomatic agreements. Rome, September 12, 1939, Mussolini.

The world war had now begun, and Mussolini, having overcome the temptation to intervene during the first few days, was going through a pacifist phase. General Guzzoni, who made inflammatory speeches but wanted eighteen divisions before moving to the attack, was succeeded on December 5 by General Carlo Geloso. When the latter asked for instructions before taking over his command, the Duce told him in lapidary fashion, using the same term that he had used to Grazzi, that Greece "was not on his road." As mentioned, the country that was on his road at that moment was Yugoslavia.

Greece, however, was by no means reassured; evidence of the persistence of her apprehensions is provided, among other things, by her repeated approaches to Germany for some sort of "guarantee" against Italian aims. Metaxas' aspiration for guarantees from all the belligerents was somewhat naïve, but it showed the sincerity of the official Greek policy of neutrality. France, which still seemed militarily a Great Power—it was not till June 1940 that her bluff was called in the most terrible fashion—had ambitions to open a Balkan front. General Weygand, who was in Syria, set in train complex Franco-Turko-Anglo-Greek negotiations. The Greeks were chiefly interested in securing Allied aid in the event of an Italian or Bulgarian attack, while the French wanted to pave the way immediately to military co-operation. Papagos states, credibly enough, that he was opposed to this, and agreed only to a reconnaissance by two French officers in civilian clothes of the airfields that would be put at the disposal of the Allies in the event of war. He says that soundings were made, but no agreements reached. General Gamelin, the French commander-in-chief, noted in his diary on January 4, 1940: "The Greek army chief of staff has let it be known that, if he is assured of effective air support and of anti-aircraft defense, he would be in a position to guarantee the landing of an inter-Allied expeditionary force at Salonika." And on March 10 he noted: "An initiative in the Balkans would be much more satisfactory to us than an enterprise in Scandinavia. Yugoslavia, Rumania, Greece and Turkey would give us the help of about 100 divisions. The forces that the Germans would be compelled to detach from the western front would be of about the same dimensions."[8] The project fell through, according to Daladier, the French Prime Minister, because of the opposition of the British, who wished to avoid provoking Italy. General Gamelin was, however, talking nonsense; his putting 100 ramshackle Balkan divisions on a par with 100 German divisions showed that he had not the faintest idea of the striking power of Hitler's army.

Traces of the Greco-French talks survived in the so-called Charité documents, found by the Germans in a railway carriage at a remote station after the conquest of France. It appeared from these that on December 4, 1939, Papagos made contact with the French military attaché in Athens; that a French officer, Colonel Mariot, was appointed to undertake a mission to Greece; and that reports were prepared on the bases that might have been put at the French disposal if an agreement had been reached. All this was a natural consequence of the political link that had been established between Greece and the Allies as a consequence of the Franco-British guarantee, though an Italian request for an explanation would have been justified if the Italians had wanted to take advantage of such a pretext. Actually no use was made of it except for *a posteriori* argument; and there was not even an official complaint to Greece about her traditional custom of having three

British naval officers as instructors (one at the naval training establishment, one with the submarine service, and one with the fleet air arm).

Ciano used bad pretexts in the service of his bad cause. Put on the alert by the flurry of August 1939, kept under pressure by a constant succession of alarms that were sometimes well founded and sometimes not, the Greeks set in train a clever system of unobtrusive but persistent mobilization. The steps taken are summed up as follows by Papagos in his memoirs:

Development of the scheme of air observation and of active means of air defense; development of the signals network; dispersal of air units for reasons of security, and organization of air defense dispositions on aerodromes; strengthening of the power of the active army by calling up alternately classes of reservists for a month's training and by calling up classes of reserve officers; strengthening of the power of all big units on the frontier through the dispatch of active army forces from the interior; steps for various preliminary mobilization measures [etc., etc.].

The crisis of August 1939 passed. As mentioned, the Greek-Italian treaty of friendship was not renewed, but Grazzi admitted that it was "unlikely that at that moment Greece could conclude a pact of collaboration with us." Such a step would have seemed provocative to the British and the French. The presence in Rome of a recently appointed Greek minister, Politis, who did not understand certain aspects of the Fascist political world, risked dramatizing negligible incidents even during the months of calm. He should have known that arrogance, senselessly provocative language, and a total and ostentatious indifference to international good manners were constant characteristics of Fascist foreign policy. In April 1940, this overzealous diplomatist informed his government that an Italian seizure of Corfu and Salonika was probable, though no one in Rome was thinking seriously of such a thing at the time.

Yet another crisis arose when Italy entered the war. Mussolini gave this assurance to the neutral powers: "I solemnly declare that Italy does not intend to drag into the conflict other nations which are her neighbors by land or sea. Let Switzerland, Yugoslavia, Greece, Turkey, and Egypt take note of these words of mine. It depends on them and them alone whether or not they are rigorously confirmed." This last phrase deprived the statement of a large part of its value. Anyone set on aggression has no difficulty in finding cause for provocation in the behavior of his intended victim. Metaxas, however, made a show of attributing the greatest possible significance to Mussolini's statement, asked to see Grazzi, and hastened to assure him that "Greece is determined to preserve the strictest neutrality," and added that, if Britain tried to violate it, "Greece is determined to defend herself with arms, and Britain has been informed of this decision." He added that "this war will clarify the atmosphere in the Mediterranean and make possible that closer collaboration between Italy and Greece" that had always been both his (Metaxas') and the King's wish, "though Greece has hitherto been compelled to advance cautiously along the road to it in view of her delicate situation."

But in spite of this apparent serenity and confidence Metaxas felt more insecure than ever. "*Sursum corda,*" he confided to his diary on June 17, 1940, after learning of the French capitulation. Twenty-two years earlier, he had made the same bitter comment on the German defeat. In both cases he felt himself spiritually and politically closer to the vanquished than to the victor. During the First World War he had been a monarchist and therefore pro-German—King Constantine I, married to a sister of the Kaiser's, was notoriously on the side of the Central Powers, while Venizelos was pro-Entente—and in the Second World War he was still a monarchist. (George II had returned to Greece after a long exile in England, and his ways and manners were English.) Metaxas did not share the King's anglophilia. He admired the Germans, but felt that the threat came not from London but from Berlin or Rome.

He also had serious worries at home. The resounding German victories naturally strengthened the hand of the pro-Germans in his country, and the Greek dictator, who obviously had nothing to fear from the Allies in the plight they were in, had good reason to doubt the loyalty of certain politicians and military men in the event of a German attack. There is a significant entry in his diary on July 5: "Quiet for the moment. Suspicions about some officials and politicians—a Minister, an admiral, and certainly one general, perhaps more, who want to exploit their well-known German-ophilia."

The British tried to take advantage of the shelter offered by the Greek archipelago to maintain some of their naval supply channels. The suspicion that they did so with the backing of the Greek authorities was inflamed on every possible occasion by that picturesque member of the Fascist quadrumvirate Cesare Maria De Vecchi di Val Cismon, the governor of the Italian islands in the Aegean, who had aspirations to be a strategist.

This crude, arrogant, and heavily moustached individual ruled his "domain" with a heavy hand. He gratuitously and repeatedly offended the susceptibilities of the population, whom he subjected to pointless vexations in matters of language and religion. The Italian legation in Athens was once subjected to a four-page philippic because the island of Patmos had been inadvertently referred to by that name instead of being called Patmo, its Italianized form. De Vecchi listened eagerly to reports made to him by pilots of the Ala Littoria airline who flew over the Greek archipelago; these were worthy young men, generally inspired by ardent Fascist feelings, and they saw British warships and merchant ships everywhere. De Vecchi had a mania for action, and he became very active indeed. There was a widespread saying that attributed to him the ambition to become a reserve king (he was already a reserve general). His agitation infected Rome. On July 3, 1940, Ciano confided to his diary: "I have spoken plainly to the Greek minister. De Vecchi telegraphs that British ships and perhaps also aircraft are being given shelter, supplies, and protection in Greece. The Greek minister feebly tried to deny this, but he went off with his tail between his legs." On July 5 Ciano wrote: "Through her minister Greece has given assurances of her complete neutrality, which the Duce has accepted with reservations, particularly as De Vecchi sticks to his guns."

Ciano's charges were reported as follows by Politis: "On July 13 an Italian submarine was attacked by a British aircraft forty miles off Levkas; on June 28 another submarine was attacked by an aircraft and an anti-submarine craft not far from Zante; on July 29 a submarine was attacked and probably sunk by an aircraft and a submarine chaser coming from Zante; on June 30 and July 1 four British anti-submarine craft were at Milos." The alleged infringements of neutrality of which Ciano complained left the Italian military attachés in Athens skeptical. This is Colonel Mondini on the subject: "Specific details were never supplied by Rome, while all the enquiries made on the spot either by me or by the naval attaché, Captain Morin (who had an excellent observation network) or by his Majesty's consuls invariably had a negative result. We then learnt that the information that gave rise to the sensitiveness in Rome came from the government of the Italian islands in the Aegean, based on news provided by overhasty aerial reconnaissance or by not overscrupulous agents who believed it to be their duty always to be reporting something."

Mondini also remarked, however, that "the behavior of the Greek authorities on the occasion of the engagement that cost us the loss of the cruiser *Colleoni* did not seem very clear, because it seems that the outcome of the battle, in which the *Colleoni* and the *Bande Nere* were at first engaged with a single British cruiser, was decided by a second cruiser, which suddenly appeared from an inlet on the northwest coast of the island of Crete." It was, of course, no easy task for a neutral to carry out the acrobatic exercise of keeping a perfect balance between the belligerent parties. Sometimes the Italians were favored by modest Greek transgressions of neutrality, as when Admiral Sakellariou informed Grazzi

—he was under no obligation to do this—that three British destroyers which took refuge in the port of Malvasia had been ordered to leave it.[9] The Italian navy made no use of this undoubtedly valuable information.

Minor incidents kept taking place. The Italian air force inadvertently bombed a small Greek auxiliary vessel, the *Orion*, which was taking supplies to the lighthouse of Grambusa on the coast of Crete, and the destroyer *Idra* that went to its aid was attacked in its turn. Whenever an excessively long stay by a British naval vessel in a Greek port seemed likely to create difficulties for him, Metaxas, to show his neutral zeal and avoid Italian protests, hastily sent a note of protest to the British. His anxiety not to irritate Mussolini and Ciano appears, sometimes painfully, in his diary. But Ciano, on the model of his father-in-law, remained implacable. On an altogether secondary matter he informed Grazzi, half seriously and half jokingly, that if Metaxas "does not give me satisfaction in regard to the Locris mines, I shall take Corfu from him." In a similar mood of arrogant flippancy he inquired whether it might not be possible to find some Albanian who would "get rid of the King" (i.e., George of Greece, to replace him by his brother Paul, the father of the present King Constantine, who was considered to be more pro-Axis).

These things might have been the sallies, not to be taken too seriously, of a young Minister with an insufficient grip on his tongue, but later events showed that vital decisions were made on no more solid foundations. Italy was never able to provide a shadow of evidence for her accusations, and Grazzi wrote: "I state in the most categorical fashion, and with a full sense of responsibility, what I reiterated to the Italian political leaders in official communications and personal letters, and that is that no British base, either air or naval, existed in Greece before October 28, 1940." But Ciano had no desire to listen to what Grazzi had to say; he even avoided answering the personal letters sent him by his envoy in Greece.

On July 4, 1940, Grazzi assured the anxious Metaxas in perfectly good faith that Italian policy towards Greece was unchanged, and Metaxas replied that he was "determined to defend Greek neutrality against anyone." But Ciano was a long way away, and these statements and assurances did not interest him. On August 3 he insisted on the replacement of the Greek consul at Trieste, Scarpa, on the ground that he was "incurably anti-Italian," and he had his way. Anfuso complained to Politis about Raphael, the Greek ambassador to Turkey, who was guilty of "opposition to totalitarian régimes." Meanwhile the *Giornale d'Italia,* which was the mouthpiece of the Foreign Ministry, published reports pooh-poohing Metaxas' "Fascist" reforms.

On August 4, however, which was the anniversary of the establishment of the Metaxas régime, the Stefani agency, the official news agency of the Fascist government, circulated a statement complimentary to the Greek dictator.

Greece has greeted with great enthusiasm the fourth anniversary of the totalitarian régime. *Te Deums* have been celebrated in all the churches, and Prime Minister Metaxas reviewed 100,000 members of the national youth assembled between Kokkina, near the Piraeus, and Kifisia. At midday members of the Athens-Piraeus Committee offered their congratulations to Metaxas, expressing the gratitude of the Greek people for what he has achieved and for the new rhythm of life imposed on the nation. In the afternoon a great celebration took place in the stadium. In the evening a procession of about 200,-000 persons marched past Metaxas, who took up his position on a balcony at the Agricultural Bank.

This was the last friendly gesture made by Italy to Greece, by Italian Fascism to Greek Fascism. But Grazzi went on nursing his illusions. On July 23 he sent to the Palazzo Chigi a long report on the Platis case, which had caused a stir in the political and military world of Athens. Constantine Platis was one of the three deputy chiefs of the General Staff. He was pro-German by conviction, he had criticized the organization of the armed forces to General Papagos, and had also suggested a change of foreign policy, "associating Greece definitely with the Axis Powers and abandoning the policy of equilibrium hitherto followed, which by being too clever will end in Greece being left with no friends anywhere." He also called for the removal from the government of certain individuals who were "too tied to the pro-British policy." Papagos had put his deputy under arrest, and the latter, strictly following the proper channels, had submitted a memorandum to Metaxas. The government first ordered the general to be imprisoned, but then modified this to house arrest.

It is interesting to note Grazzi's balanced comment on this affair: "Under the present régime the real decisions are made by Metaxas alone, and it is certain that the latter, though personally anything but pro-British, does not yet dare decide on a definite change of Greek policy." In other words, Metaxas was not bowing to Britain, but was afraid of compromising himself. On August 7 Grazzi had one of his innumerable meetings with the Greek dictator, the last before the fatal night of October 28. The two men had established a relationship in which there was as much mutual esteem and trust as was compatible with their respective positions, but now a veil of suspicion had descended between them. Grazzi reiterated that Italy had no intention of threatening Greece, and Metaxas listened with a sad smile. He believed that Grazzi was dissimulating. He could not conceive that the Palazzo Chigi left its representative totally in the dark about what it was plotting (and often also about the plots that it dropped). He could not conceive that the Italian minister had no clue to the intentions of Mussolini, who, according to the passage of Ciano's diary we have already quoted, was now talking about the Greek question again and wanting information on Tsamouria. He had ordered Jacomoni and Visconti Prasca to be summoned to Rome, and was "talking about a surprise attack on Greece towards the end of September." All Italy was shortly to become inflamed over the fate of the Albanian patriot Daut Hoggia, but Grazzi knew nothing of that either.

As Mussolini had decided to settle the "outstanding account" he had had with Greece since 1923 (when the Italian members of a

Franco-British-Italian mixed commission led by General Tellini were massacred while engaged on the delimitation of the northern borders of Albania, and Mussolini landed troops in Corfu, but withdrew them under British pressure), Ciano considered it to be his duty to provide him with some propaganda pretexts. Ciano was a conceited young man; because he controlled the propaganda machine he believed himself to be in possession of men's minds. His ability to turn on and off the flow of journalistic insults and outbursts of indignation just like a tap (the simile is not mine, but Grazzi's, but it strikes me as exceedingly apt) must have given him a sense of omnipotence. The always obliging Jacomoni had already got to work in Tirana, and a brief report he sent to Ciano provided him with a propaganda weapon that would have been useless if the press and public opinion had been free, but was very suitable for exploitation in the conditions existing in Italy at that time. "It is well known to your Excellency," the governor-general wrote more in sorrow than in anger, "that Daut Hoggia, an Albanian from Tsamouria, a man animated by great patriotic spirit, was forced a few years ago to take refuge in Albania because of persecution by the Greek authorities."[10] He went on to explain that this celebrated patriot had been living a quiet life, but as soon as the aspirations of the people of Tsamouria for liberation from the Greeks had been rekindled (after the Italian occupation of Albania), his life had been threatened. His headless corpse had recently been found at Konispoli. In order to claim the price put upon his head by the Greek authorities, his Greek murderers had severed it and displayed it as a trophy to the people of Tsamouria. Before he was murdered Daut Hoggia had been given poisoned food at a meal, "which proves premeditation and plotting," Jacomoni audaciously added.

He went on to say that a note had been found on the body of another murdered Albanian threatening all Tsamourians who tried to reunite their homeland with their mother country with a similar fate, and spoke of "horrible bloodthirsty crimes frequently committed by Greek emissaries." Now, Jacomoni has disclosed that this report was back-dated, as if it had been written before August

11.[11] The truth of the matter was that Ciano asked for it on August 11, when the governor-general and Visconti Prasca were summoned to see the Duce; the object was to provide him with a ready-made plot with a minimum basis in fact. Such were the means by which Ciano, who was anti-German in principle but wanted war in the Balkans, influenced his father-in-law. On August 11 the propaganda tap was turned on by his orders. The *Tomori,* the Fascist newspaper in Tirana, spoke of the "savage aggression" committed on the "great Albanian patriot Hoggia." The Stefani agency took up the theme, and for the benefit of Italian listeners the EIAR, the Fascist broadcasting system, began eulogizing the "veteran fighter for Albanian irredentism in Tsamouria," whose "patriotic life has been sealed in blood." However, his sacrifice "will not be in vain, because the news of this sinister crime has profoundly moved the Albanians of Tsamouria." Farinacci, Polverelli, all the chief Fascist spokesmen, were mobilized to exalt the dead man's virtues, and the newspapers made great play with the plunderings, murders, and deportations from which the unfortunate Tsamouria, "the area between the present frontier, the Ionian littoral extending to the outskirts of Preveza, and the province of Yanina," suffered under the oppressive Greek régime. According to the Fascist propaganda, 80,000 Albanians and only 10,000 Greeks had been living in Tsamouria when the area was incorporated into Greece in 1913.

It is of course easy to appeal to nationalist feeling in border zones where nationalities are mixed and linguistic and ethnic boundaries are much less distinct than political frontiers. (A humorous postscript is worth mentioning here. A few years ago an Italian general, a careless student of documents, roused a hornet's nest by submitting to NATO an ethnic-military study in which Tsamouria, on the basis of these dusty and less than objective documents, was described as ethnically an Albanian area in which irredentist feeling, etc., prevailed.) The man picked on as the hero of the Tsamourian cause did not turn out to have been very happily chosen. The Italian broadcasts and the statement put out by the official Stefani news agency came like a flash of lightning in the sleepy blue sky of Athens sweltering in the August heat. The Greeks issued an official statement in reply. It said that two months before the beginning of the Italian press campaign two Albanians who had entered Greek territory had admitted killing Daut Hoggia during a quarrel. Hoggia was an illiterate cattle-drover and notorious brigand who had been sought by the Greek authorities for twenty years; the "celebrated patriot" had an exceptionally vivid police record. Many years previously he had been sentenced, with three accomplices, by the criminal court of Preveza to penal servitude for the murder of two Muslims, Vehip Tsimo and Zekir Rehip. In November 1919, he had been sentenced in absence by the Yanina criminal court to twenty years' imprisonment for killing two more Muslims. On June 10, 1921, he had been condemned to seventeen years' imprisonment by the Preveza court for cattle stealing and brigandage, and in December 1921, he had been sentenced to another four years for extortion. In 1923 he had been sentenced to eighteen years for attempted murder, in 1925 there had been another sentence for rape, demanding money with threats, and carrying prohibited weapons, and finally in 1925 he had been sentenced to death *in absentia* for acts of brigandage. The statement went on to say that the Greek government had kept the two men who had killed him in prison in the expectation of an Albanian application for their extradition. The Italian legation in Athens was aware of the crime, because in a *note verbale* to the Greek government on July 25 it had informed the latter of the finding of the decapitated body and its identification. This *note verbale,* the Greeks pointed out, had made no mention of any political motivation for the crime, thus making it evident that the whole thing was an unsubstantial and absurd pretext. This statement was, of course, not reported in the Italian press.

Grazzi, taken by surprise at this sensational sequel to an incident which three weeks previously he had hardly noticed, was anything but at ease in the conversation he had on August 13 with the Greek permanent undersecretary of state for foreign affairs, Mavroudis, a senior and astute diplomatist.[12] Mavroudis, who was in a state of unusual agitation, said that Greece had been on the brink of general mobilization, and he could not understand why so much publicity had been given to an episode that could have been amicably resolved. Those were people, he observed with a smile, meaning of course the Albanians, *"qui s'entretuent tout le temps,"* who spent their whole time killing one another. Grazzi, who was in an awkward position, tried to excuse his government by explaining that no one had informed his legation of the arrest of the two Albanians, and so he knew nothing of what the Greek authorities might have done in the matter. "If we decided to make the announcement," he said in embarrassment, "there were no doubt good reasons for it that I was not in a position to discuss."

Meanwhile someone in the Italian Foreign Ministry, taking the Tsamouria affair seriously, drafted a note to be sent by Ciano to Politis.[13] It took the Albanian side in regard to the Tsamourian question and suggested a solution to the problem "on the same lines as the solutions adopted—or being adopted—for similar situations in the Danubian-Balkan region." This was on a level very different from that of the violent press and radio campaign, though the hint of a solution on Danubian-Balkan lines contained an implicit threat. The reference was obviously to the Vienna arbitration by which Ciano and Ribbentrop, the arbitrators, granted Hungary a large slice of Rumanian territory. The note was not presented, however, and in retrospect one can see why. A definitely political step of that kind, as distinct from a propaganda operation, required German consent, and the Germans were totally opposed to creating problems in the Balkans. Ribbentrop took a tough line with the Greek diplomatists, telling them that Greece was in the Italian sphere of influence, but in reality he was anxious to restrain Italian intemperance. There was a noticeably anti-Italian note in the dispatches that Erbach, the German minister in Athens, sent to Berlin. On August 13, after a meeting with Metaxas, reporting the Greek dictator's state of mind, he said that "if Italy believes that this is the right moment to realize its territorial claims in relation to Greece, it is mistaken;" and "Greece will resist all aggression and will refuse to be humiliated by Italy, even if that involves the risk of being destroyed. It is my impression," he added, "that a real determination exists here to resist all Italian intervention, if that should come about, and there is strong backing for this in the general popular feeling against Italy." A few days later, on August 21, while Italian propaganda was still raging, he wrote: "The exploitation of the murder of Hoggia . . . is considered by popular feeling to be a cynical provocation. The resulting indignation against Italy makes it more difficult for the government to accept the Italian demands."

Ribbentrop lost no opportunity of pouring oil on the troubled waters. On August 17, Dino Alfieri, the ambassador in Berlin, wrote to Ciano:

I communicated to Ribbentrop the contents of the telegram relating to the Italian attitude towards Greece and, in accordance with your Excellency's instructions, I enquired what his attitude was in the matter. He replied that he fully appreciated the situation and therefore had nothing to say about the precautionary measures taken. But in this connection he showed that he was concerned about Russia, which might use any action we might take as a pretext for intervening in the Balkans, thus modifying the *status quo* which it is our supreme interest to maintain. In conclusion, Ribbentrop believes that the vital problem with which the Axis is faced is that of defeating Britain. All activity and effort directed to other ends represents a dangerous dispersion of energy which it is essential to avoid. With the fall of Britain, all the other problems will be automatically solved. Thus both the Greek and the Yugoslav questions are seen by Ribbentrop in relation to the final struggle against Britain which has begun.[14]

Ciano assured Ribbentrop in reply that "we are conducting the dispute with Greece on a diplomatic level and are restricting ourselves to reinforcing the six divisions at present in Albania with some additional divisions."[15] Mussolini, adjusting himself to the situation, on August 19 sent a telegram to Graziani, the Italian commander in Libya, saying: "The invasion of England has been decided on, the preparations are being completed, and it will take place. As for the date, it may be in a week or in a month. Well, on the day on which the first platoon of German soldiers lands on British soil you will attack simultaneously. Once more I repeat that I am not giving you territorial limits; it is not a matter of aiming for Alexandria or even for Sollum. I ask you only to attack the British forces facing you." Ribbentrop, still uneasy about Mussolini's frenzied desire for action, followed up his previous comments by pointing out on August 20 that "an Italo-Greek failure to reach diplomatic agreement and possible action by us might provide Britain with an opportunity for making landings and give the Russians a pretext for further intervention in the Balkans." The Axis, he said, should not lend itself to "diversions with unforeseeable consequences."[16]

On August 22, Mussolini, temporarily reasonable and resigned, stated in a secret memorandum that "the Libyan sector becomes the main one on which attention and effort should be concentrated."[17] Hence, he explained, "the other two theaters—the Greek and the Yugoslav—unless the Yugoslavs or Greeks or British take the initiative—become theaters of observation and vigilance, necessary vigilance in view of the equivocal policy followed by those two states and the state of mind of their peoples. The previously arranged rate of deployment in those two theaters may therefore be slowed down, the date for the completion of that on the eastern front to be October 20 instead of September 20 and that on the Greek front to be the end of September instead of the end of August. It is clear, furthermore, that once Great Britain has been defeated the states that have more or less covertly sympathized with London will not make difficulties about falling into line with Axis decisions, whatever these may be." In other words, war on Greece was off. It looked as if the halt called by Hitler would last for a long time. Mussolini believed that Germany was about to engage Britain in the decisive battle and that the Italians were simultaneously about to advance in Africa. But the landing in England never took place, and in Africa the Italians were approaching the disaster of Sidi Barrani.

In his directives Mussolini used pompous language. He fixed dates, postponed them, issued orders, as if he had under his command a highly efficient, smoothly working military machine. From the sentences quoted above it might be concluded that on September 20 the forces in Albania were adequate to meet any contingency, but the reality was less reassuring. Meanwhile there was one man more than any other who contributed to creating and reinforcing Mussolini's and Ciano's illusion that Greece was a negligible quantity, a ripe plum ready to drop at the first military or diplomatic shaking. He did not live in Greece, was ill informed about that country, and subsequently turned out to be exceedingly ill informed even about Albania, which was his special domain. Count Francesco Jacomoni di San Sevino, the governor-general in Tirana, was connected, because of his office, with the Foreign Ministry and, because he was General Cavallero's son-in-law, he had connections with military circles also. As a diplomatist he had intelligence, but of the ambiguous, tortuous kind that puts itself at the service of the powerful rather than of reality and truth, even when the national interest requires that reality and truth should be plainly seen.

He stood out favorably among the many uncouth, ignorant, and presumptuous members of the Fascist hierarchy, and he sincerely defended the Albanian cause. But he attributed to the Albanians and to himself a role which the painful development of the war reduced to far more modest proportions. His cheap Machiavellism deceived no one, either then or later, but his assurances and promises deceived Mussolini and Ciano. He and Visconti Prasca formed a perfect couple for the disastrous campaign; they formed a perfect counterpart to that other couple in Rome, Mussolini and Ciano. On August 17, when Greece as an

immediate objective was receding from Mussolini's mind, he sent
Ciano a memorandum "in preparation for the new event."[18] He
announced that a radio station was being set up at Argyrokastron
which was to broadcast in Albanian and Greek, and that a weekly
newspaper in that town was going to become bilingual, giving
news in Greek as well as in Albanian.

He went on: "Covered by this passionate chorus of popular
voices, I am preparing in the greatest secrecy the politico-military
operation to be begun at a sign from your Excellency." His careful preparations included the following: engagement of men
to undertake guerrilla warfare in Tsamouria and of volunteers to
support the troops who would invade Greece and of others to
cover the Yugoslav frontier. "I have asked his Excellency Visconti
Prasca," Jacomoni said, "for some of the rifles used by the Greek
Army, together with the appropriate ammunition, and for some
foreign bombs for the proposed operations in Greek territory.
Because at a certain stage it may be appropriate to organize an
attack by loyal elements on one of our frontier posts." (As we
shall see, this idea was accepted and approved at the highest level.)
The memorandum also mentioned the training of parachutists
to be dropped in Tsamouria, and improvement of the road system
and harbor works. Jacomoni enclosed a map showing the new
frontier—including Greek territory all the way to Yanina and
Preveza—and added that "the understanding between me and the
military commander Visconti Prasca is constant and complete."

The finishing touch to this exemplary plan was missing, however, and was supplied in another, similarly secret, memorandum,
also dated August 17.[19] This pointed out that, since the people
of Tsamouria were living "in a state of grave poverty," it would be
appropriate that Fascist aid should be provided immediately after
the occupation. "The inspector of the PNF [National Fascist
Party] proposes to make ready five convoys provided with clothing of all sorts, thousands of black shirts, Italian and Albanian
flags, medicines of every kind, canned food, and maize." The
document went into great detail about the composition and organi-

zation of these convoys. But in the midst of his enthusiastic organization of convoys and enlistment of volunteers poor Jacomoni received an unexpected slap in the eye.

On August 22 Ciano informed him that "it has been decided at a higher level to slow down the pace of our operations in the Greek and Yugoslav sectors." Therefore, "while maintaining the potential effectiveness of the arrangements so far made with a view to the objectives in question, their pace should not be increased and, while keeping the question alive, any kind of crisis should be avoided pending further instructions."[20] In other words, as the Venetians say, go ahead so slowly that you are practically moving backwards.* "I am already acting on the lines laid down by you," the compliant Jacomoni replied on August 24.[21] On that day the propaganda tap was turned off. Italy suddenly ceased to be interested in Daut Hoggia and Tsamouria, and after his brief period of renown the great decapitated patriot relapsed into oblivion. Pending further instructions, of course.

Francesco Jacomoni, after keeping quiet for many years, had a book published in 1965: *La politica dell'Italia in Albania nella testimonianza del luogotenente del re.* The book is concerned with many matters that have nothing to do with the Greek campaign, including King Zog's abortive marriage to a woman of the Italian aristocracy. A couple of chapters are devoted to the war with Greece, and these are very interesting. In the course of these Jacomoni emphasizes his "official" (or merely executive) status, and repeats what was already known, that is, that the Foreign Ministry refrained from informing its representatives abroad, even the most distinguished and exalted in rank, about its intentions and the information that it received. That is true enough. It should, however, be added that his personal relations with Ciano were much closer than those of administrative routine. Certainly it can be admitted that Ciano may have hidden some of his secret thoughts even from an intimate (though, since these caused anxiety and alarm in Athens, Berlin, or London, they cannot have

* *Avanti piano, quasi indietro.*

been so very secret or remained so for long). But it is hard to believe that a man as intelligent as Jacomoni undoubtedly was and as versed as he was in the ways of Fascist politics, could have believed what he stated he believed.

He stated that so far as he knew, the Italian politico-military objective was limited to the annexation of Tsamouria to Albania. Political and military pressure was intended to lead to negotiations in which the Athens government would be forced to cede to Albania territory extending to Preveza and Yanina, thus satisfying Albanian claims. Jacomoni states that he neither knew nor imagined that there was any intention of making war on Greece or that the aim was to occupy the whole country. We are faced here with a politico-diplomatic version of the limited operation which on the military plane came to be known as "the large-scale *coup de main*" on Epirus.

All this is unconvincing. However wild and vacillating Mussolini's plans may have been, Italy, engaged in a world war, had no interest in risking vast and unforeseeable complications by taking a step intended merely to annex to Albania a strategically insignificant, poverty-stricken area which was more likely to create economic problems than to confer economic advantages. Tsamouria as a propaganda topic made sense only as a pretext for war on Greece; as an objective in itself it was absurd. Jacomoni maintained that the troops in Albania were really intended only for an "unopposed occupation" of Epirus, which would have been a possibility only in a totally different politico-diplomatic setup. Was it really conceivable that a nation covered by a Franco-British guarantee, with a predominantly pro-British governing class, would consent to the voluntary cession of territory in time of war in the absence of a complete prior reversal of its policy? Grazzi's work in Athens was in a way directed towards bringing about such a reversal. But Jacomoni's maneuvers made sense only in the framework of a wider plan, which was war with Greece, and he could not possibly have been unaware of it.

2. Contingency G

A grave incident took place in Greek waters at 8:30 A.M. on August 15, 1940. A submarine of unknown nationality—the British promptly announced that it must have been Italian, while the Italians declared that it must have been British—sank an aged Greek cruiser, the *Helle,* in the harbor of Tinos. The attack on this venerable warship (2,115 tons, launched in 1912, modernized in 1927) took place on the Feast of the Assumption. The island, on which there is a sanctuary renowned among Orthodox Christians—its fame can be compared to that of Lourdes or Loreto among Catholics—was crowded with pilgrims. The submarine launched three torpedoes, only one of which hit its mark. The others struck the mole of the island's small harbor. The casualties were one dead and twenty-nine wounded. Terrible scenes of panic broke out among the crowd. The place and the occasion were such that the incident seemed a provocation and a sacrilege.

Fragments of the torpedoes which were recovered bore Italian markings, but the Greek authorities, who were most anxious not to offer provocations to an Italy that was looking for them, maintained great reserve about their findings. The Italians behaved as if they had nothing to hide; that is to say, they pointed out that the products of the torpedo works at Fiume were supplied to many foreign countries, including Britain. The affair remained slightly mysterious even to Ciano ("A Greek vessel has been sunk by a submarine of unidentified nationality. The incident threatens to assume graver proportions. It looks to me as if De Vecchi's intemperance lies behind it. I conferred with the Duce, who wants a peaceful settlement of an incident we could have done without."[1]).

Ciano was right. I have already mentioned the frenzy for action with which De Vecchi was seized as soon as war broke out. It was his habit, for instance, to set out in a speedboat, his big moustache quivering in the *Meltemi,* the salt wind of the Aegean, to meet submarines returning from their missions. Ignoring the risk of being fired on by the submarine when he approached it, or of its being the object of enemy attack while taking the impulsive member of the Fascist quadrumvirate on board, he would insist with schoolboy enthusiasm on questioning the commander on how things had gone. At the beginning of 1960 he himself revealed the mystery of the *Helle* in his memoirs, published in a weekly newspaper, thus finally confirming what had seemed highly probable and even certain before, namely that the attack was carried out by an Italian submarine.

"The *Helle* coup, actually an unfortunate one, caused a stink in the international field," De Vecchi wrote. This phrase caused the commander of the vessel that sank her to spring to his own defense. Giuseppe Aicardi, then a lieutenant, was in command of the submarine *Delfino,* and he described in another weekly newspaper how the governor of the Aegean came to Leros from Rhodes on August 14 with Admiral Bianchieri, who showed De Vecchi a letter from Admiral Domenico Cavagnari, the naval chief of staff.

In this document, "Supermarina" stated:

Considering the mercantile traffic emerging from the Dardanelles and the fact that the greater part of it is carried out for the British benefit, and that neutral navies on this route tend to favor only supplies going to the enemy, having taken instructions from the Duce I notify you of the following. You will choose from the submarines under your command the vessel which by reason of the preparedness of its equipment and the ability of its commander seems best fitted for the purpose; and you will impart verbally and personally to the commander of the vessel selected orders inspired by the following principles: (*a*) There will take place, e.g., in the period between August 20 and 25, a brief but intense period of war to the limit on merchant traffic in the waters of the Aegean between the Dardanelles and the Doro canal; (*b*) during the period in question the submarine will torpedo without warning all shipping presumed to be trading on the enemy's behalf, even if covered by a neutral flag; (*c*) the operation will be carried out in such a fashion that the identity and nationality of the submarine cannot be identified; (*d*) at the end of the period laid down the submarine will return to its base, taking precautions to ensure that its berthing is not observed; (*e*) complete radio silence both by and to the submarine will be observed throughout its mission; (*f*) the operation will be surrounded by maximum secrecy. Further decisions will be taken based on the reactions to which the operation leads.

"Supermarina" had taken instructions from the Duce, but it seems evident that the latter did not pay too much attention to them, in as much as the Foreign Minister, who would have to deal with the consequences, was left completely in the dark about them. Moreover, the naval command indicated the period between August 20 and 25 for the operation, and laid down that the objects of attack should be merchant shipping that could at least be assumed to be trading for the benefit of the British. It was difficult to interpret this order as covering the sinking of a neutral warship in the territorial waters of a neutral country.

It is on this that Captain Aicardi bases his charges against De Vecchi. Impulsively and quite unnecessarily, the latter hurried off to Leros, because he was anxious to begin the exciting adventure without losing a moment. He passed on Admiral Cavagnari's orders to Aicardi, but verbally, giving the lieutenant no opportunity to read them—or so indeed the latter insists—gave no date for the beginning of the operation, made no distinction between warships and others, and gave no instructions that passenger ships should be spared. Also he handed Aicardi a sheet of paper on which were the names of two islands, Tinos and Sira, off which the movement of shipping had been observed. Aicardi, to defend himself against the charge of having exceeded his orders or misread their purpose, states that after taking aim at two ships berthed in the harbor of Tinos which were not flying neutral flags (and must therefore, in his view, have been trading on the British behalf), he suddenly saw the *Helle* bearing down on him from behind, and he consequently torpedoed her, having no choice in the matter.

A man who had been given "Supermarina's" vague instructions backed up by wild orders from De Vecchi might easily make mistakes or err by excessive zeal. Whatever Captain Aicardi may say, it is exceedingly unlikely that there were any ships with war material on board at Tinos that morning, which was the day of the Holy Virgin and the occasion of a pilgrimage. It is even more unlikely that the venerable *Helle,* which was sent to the island purely for show purposes, i.e., to add to the formal solemnity of the ceremony at the venerated shrine (a foreigner cannot appreciate what this pilgrimage means to the Greeks), made any sort of hostile maneuver against the submarine. According to the Greeks, she was anchored in the midst of a swarm of ships and boats of all sorts which were dressed overall for the occasion. The torpedoing could not have been more disastrously timed. "Supermarina" in fact changed its mind. "The usual interferences from Rome helped to restrict the submarine's operations," De Vecchi inconsistently remarked, after deploring that its mission had not turned out to be a brilliant success. The Fascist government, whose flair for this sort of thing was unrivaled, had once again managed to commit a futile and iniquitous act, as psychologically damaging as it was militarily useless. The desecration of the Feast of the Assumption gave the Greeks who fought in Albania one of the deepest motives for aggressiveness against their enemy.

De Vecchi remained at his post long enough to provide further demonstrations of his crude arrogance, though the Duce knew that he and Badoglio "were insulting each other by letter" and expressed opinions about De Vecchi "of which he would not have been proud."[2] Let us recall that in the middle of August Italy was determined to make war on Greece, or at any rate to carry out a *coup de main* in "unredeemed" Tsamouria. By August 24 this determination had receded, though it was to regain substance less than two months later.

The prospect of war with Greece of course had brought increasingly into the foreground a personality who has already been mentioned several times. General Count Sebastiano Visconti Prasca, the commander of the Italian troops in Albania, is to some extent the principal character in the story to be related, and it is time to introduce him more fully.

The memoirs that General Visconti Prasca published in 1946 were, in somewhat questionable taste, entitled *Io ho aggredito la Grecia* (I Attacked Greece). Like many of the worst Italian generals, he was an effective writer of memoirs. Papagos wrote a ponderous and pompous book, a kind of unreadable manual of military strategy which I had the misfortune to translate from the Greek; it can, I believe, be read with genuine interest only by those who have an absorbing interest in military affairs. Visconti Prasca's memoirs, on the other hand, make fascinating reading, packed as they are with malicious observations, controversial sallies, petty or scandalous background revelations, accusations and denigrations. No civilian could so effectively have demolished the General Staff and its environment, the men at the top of the Italian military machine. However, certainly without intending to do so and perhaps without even suspecting it, he also demolished himself, perhaps chiefly himself. The book, though written in self-defense, does not succeed in covering up its author's colossal errors and irresponsibility.

Carlo Geloso—who had made some adjustments to the Guzzoni-Pariani plan, among other things reducing the "times" necessary for transferring new units to Albania—was replaced, according to Visconti Prasca, because he got on neither with Jacomoni nor with the Albanians. But by a quirk of fate it was Geloso and not

Visconti Prasca who was one day to be the "occupier" of Greece.
The roots of Geloso's disgrace can perhaps be sought in a conversation he had at Tirana at the beginning of May 1940 with
Galeazzo Ciano. Ciano calmly told him that an all-out operation
against Greece was foreseen within a short time, say two or three
weeks; and Geloso, taken aback, pointed out that this conflicted
with the orders he had received and upset his whole deployment,
which was against Yugoslavia. He added that he would seek instructions from his superiors, and temporized. This prudence on
his part no doubt displeased Ciano. Visconti Prasca may have
been suggested to Mussolini for the Albanian command by
Ubaldo Soddu, the undersecretary for war, who considered him to
be "his" man. The two generals had attended the military school
at Modena together. In the course of his successful career Soddu
may once or twice have tripped up his former comrade, but on the
whole the two had co-operated in covering up for each other in
the General Staff jungle.

Visconti Prasca was the Italian military attaché in Paris up to
1940, and he was given command of the III Army Corps on the
western front on the eve of the Italian entry into the war. He enjoyed the reputation of being pro-French. In January 1940 he
foresaw the eventual defeat of Germany, but that was no sign of
exceptional foresight. In those dead months, while the war stag-
nated in the no-man's-land between the Siegfried and the Maginot
lines and the German war machine had not yet demonstrated its
formidable striking power, almost everyone in Italy, from Mussolini and Ciano downwards, believed in an Allied victory. When
France was knocked out in a few short weeks conversions were
wholesale.

Visconti Prasca was very proud of his physique, which had
helped him in various appointments, and he liked contrasting it
with the mediocre looks of Soddu or Roatta, who were short,
fat, and bespectacled. He described Soddu, though he was a friend
of his, as "having the reputation of a schemer" and being "fierce
in the defense of his own professional interests"[3]—he was on very

cool terms with Roatta, who detested Soddu ("they mutually hated and despised each other, like the leaders of two different cliques, but often, when their joint interests required it, they made common cause like the thieves of Pisa"). When he was on the western front Visconti Prasca noticed that defense works were being constructed which were totally useless since France had no aggressive intentions against Italy, and he explained this by the fact that one of the principal contractors was a close relative of Roatta's. I quote this to illustrate the "cordiality" that existed between these men who should have been working harmoniously together.

Mussolini received the new commander in Albania in audience on May 26, 1940. According to the latter, what the Duce said to him was: "You know Albania and the Balkans well, and you will certainly make use of the tact required with such touchy people. Tact is what is required, tact." There was no mention of war, or of small- or large-scale operations against Greece. Roatta, who was nominally the deputy chief of the Army General Staff but was in fact acting as its chief in the absence in Libya of Graziani, the holder of that office, said good-by to Visconti Prasca in even stranger terms: "You are going to replace a general whom we appreciated and with whom we were satisfied," he said, according to Visconti Prasca, but it must be admitted that his malicious statements generally have the unmistakable ring of truth.

According to Visconti Prasca's memoirs—and their accuracy on this point has withstood all checking—the Italian forces in Albania when he took command in June 1940 were as follows: "The occupation troops consisted of five fine divisions: three reinforced infantry divisions, the Ferrara (General Licurgo Zannini); the Arezzo (General Molinari, later General Ferone); the Venezia (General Pitassi, later General Bonini); the alpine Julia Division (General De Giorgis, then General Mario Girotti); the armored Centauro Division (General Giovanni Magli). Among the independent units were the splendid 3rd Regiment of Sardinian Grenadiers under the command of Colonel Andreini." According to Roatta, the independent units, including some Albanian detachments, amounted in all to the strength of about two divisions.[4] The "fine divisions" to which General Visconti Prasca referred—he displayed a highly enthusiastic and optimistic spirit throughout the Greek adventure—were undoubtedly stronger than others in Italy, but they suffered from the defects common to the whole Italian army—limited mobility, weak armament, little striking power—which were to cost heavy defeats and humiliating encirclements.

Visconti Prasca promptly began playing the part of commander-in-chief, i.e., moving units about with a view to their better deployment. The General Staff in Rome, which had to see and approve of everything though it often knew very little, interfered; and there was also interference by a so-called Army Group South, the headquarters of which were at Frascati under the command of Marshal De Bono. The existence of this command was unknown to most people, and one fine day it simply vanished into thin air without having done anything either good or bad, unless the active service allowance it procured for a number of officers fond of their creature comforts can be counted in its favor. What with delays and orders followed by counterorders that were no more or less of a nuisance to the Albanian than they were to other peripheral commands, things went their way until July, when the Army General Staff, at the instigation of Mussolini—no doubt prodded in his turn by Ciano—entrusted Geloso, now back in Rome but still considered an expert on Albania, with the task of studying "a limited offensive operation against Greece." The objective was the occupation of Epirus, of Akarnania as far as Missolonghi, and the Ionian islands. The plan assumed an intervention by the Bulgarians that would engage the greater part of the Greek forces and the presence of only three Greek divisions in Epirus, or alternatively Greek acquiescence in the occupation.

Geloso drew up a draft plan requiring the use of eleven divisions plus two regiments of cavalry and one of grenadiers; that is, five divisions for the attack on Epirus, one for the occupation of Corfu, two in the Koritsa area, and three on the Yugoslav border. The General Staff used Geloso's draft as the basis of a plan—this was the origin of the so-called Contingency G—that brought the objective of the operation nearer home (the Bay of Arta instead of that of Missolonghi), and economized in the amount of strength to be used, i.e., allotted four divisions instead of five to Epirus and one instead of two to the Yugoslav border. Otherwise the previous plan was adhered to, that is to say, it was proposed to use altogether eight divisions with the addition of some independent formations. This plan, which was based on uncertain or absurd premises, aimed at secondary objectives, and was unambitious militarily and doubtful politically, enjoyed a highly successful career; it did so after all the assumptions on which it was based had one by one collapsed. It enjoyed this success because it did not commit the military to very much and was suitable for production at short notice whenever required.

In the middle of August 1940, it looked as if the die had been cast and as if Mussolini had finally decided what was to be done in the Albanian sector, and when. At that time Italy had a total of 104,000 men in Albania. The divisions, though reinforced, still had shortages of personnel and still graver shortages of arms and equipment.

Visconti Prasca was summoned to Rome on the evening of August 11, and Jacomoni, who was attending a ceremony at Valona, was sent for too. They were promptly received by Ciano, in the presence of Starace, chief of staff of the Fascist militia (who had been secretary-general of the Fascist Party from 1928–39), and Zenone Benini, the undersecretary of state for Albanian affairs. The Foreign Minister announced that the occupation of Tsamouria was imminent. He did not go into details; he merely stated that the troops must be ready to move from August 15 onwards. According to General Francesco Rossi, Visconti Prasca that same evening drafted a memorandum to Roatta asking for reinforcements of two divisions, four groups of mountain artillery, three battalions of Alpini and three of Blackshirts. This, however, seems

to conflict with what he asked for next day. On the morning of
August 12 he and Jacomoni were accompanied by Ciano to the
Palazzo Venezia, where they were received by Mussolini. The
Duce asked the governor-general of Albania for information about
Tsamourian irredentism, and then asked Visconti Prasca whether
the forces available in Albania were sufficient for a swift occupa-
tion of Epirus.

> This point-blank question stated in oversimplified terms seemed
> somewhat strange to me. I replied that in the view of the military
> intelligence service Epirus at that moment was weakly occupied by
> troops on a peacetime footing. An operation of the kind, resembling
> a large-scale *coup de main,* presented possibilities of success, leaving
> out of account, of course, the complications and reactions that such
> a step might provoke either on the part of Greece or her possible
> allies, not excluding Yugoslavia. At all events, since the mass of our
> troops were deployed against Yugoslavia, while only weak forces
> were stationed on the Greek frontier, a certain amount of time
> would be necessary to reverse this situation. . . . The time taken
> by all these steps, which would be difficult to conceal, should not
> exceed a fortnight, or the Greeks would take countermeasures
> which would destroy the advantage of surprise. . . . In any case the
> troops in Albania would have to be reinforced in order to carry out
> the *coup de main.* Since the transport of complete divisions to Al-
> bania would require an amount of time probably greater than that
> which the Greeks would need to send reinforcements to the area,
> it would be appropriate to send a certain number of battalions to
> reinforce the divisions already there. . . . Whether the operation
> against Greece were carried out or not, it would be advisable to send
> the troops in Albania extra batteries of mule-drawn and mountain
> artillery, because the horse-drawn guns that partly constituted the
> artillery at my disposal were useless in that mountainous and road-
> less area.[5]

Thus the Contingency G plan underwent another transforma-
tion and became a "large-scale *coup de main.*" Visconti Prasca
here summarizes his conversation with Mussolini for his own

purposes without, however, succeeding in totally concealing his
own irresponsibility. What is the meaning of the statement "leaving out of account . . . the complications and reactions that such
a step might provoke . . . on the part of Greece"? Had Ciano and
Jacomoni stated that Greece would not fight? In that case five
divisions, with or without reinforcements, would be more than
sufficient. If no war had been in prospect there would have been
no need to trouble General Visconti Prasca; a colonel of the
carabinieri would have been perfectly capable of making arrangements for the garrisoning of "unredeemed" Tsamouria. But the
most obvious complication was that Greece would react, that
there would be war. In that event five divisions, even reinforced,
would obviously not be sufficient, and Visconti Prasca's observation that, while a fortnight would not be enough to bring adequate
reinforcements from Italy, the Greeks would be in a position to
bring up substantial reinforcements in the same period, assumed
an ominous significance.

On the same day, August 12, Ciano wrote in his diary: "I accompanied Jacomoni and Visconti Prasca to the Duce. The Duce
laid down the political and military lines for the operation against
Greece. If Tsamouria and Corfu are yielded without a blow, we
shall not ask for more. But if resistance is put up, we shall carry
through the operation to the limit. Jacomoni and Visconti Prasca
regard the operation as practicable and even easy, provided it is
carried out soon. The Duce, however, remains of the opinion,
for general military reasons, that the operation should be postponed until the end of September." The addition of Corfu to the
Italian objectives gave some strategic sense to the operation,
but made nonsense of its alleged "irredentist" aims, for there were
no Albanians to be emancipated in Corfu. Even in Ciano's mind
the alternative to a peaceable cession of Greek territory—and a
substantial slice of it for a country of the size of Greece—was all-
out war. To explain away the untenability of his position as
champion of Albanian irredentism as soon as the question of seiz-
ing Corfu arose, Jacomoni states: "I do not remember Corfu's

being mentioned in our presence," and adds that "both Ciano and Mussolini spoke only of Tsamouria in our presence."[6]

Visconti Prasca also says that he reported his meeting with Mussolini both to Soddu and to Badoglio. He says that the old marshal's face darkened as he listened to him, and he remarked, referring of course to Mussolini: "He's mad, now he wants Greece too." Visconti Prasca also says that Roatta received him very coolly and told him that for Contingency G he would send him two infantry divisions, four groups of mountain artillery, three battalions of Alpini, four battalions of Blackshirts, and 10,000 rifles to arm Albanian volunteers. He adds that the General Staff wanted to send complete divisions, while he wanted unattached battalions because "the reinforcements mentioned by Roatta were too many and would arrive too slowly to carry out a *coup de main,* while there were too few to engage in a war."

This argument would stand up if it were not obvious that a *coup de main* was war, and that the only difference between the two was in objectives and timing. But the enemy remained the same size. Roatta and Visconti Prasca greeted each other "coolly," the latter says. The fact of the matter was that the General Staff regarded him with great suspicion because of the way he went over the heads of his superiors and his direct relations with Mussolini. (Weeks later Badoglio complained at a meeting of the heads of the three services that "unknown to him an attack on Greece was being organized at the Foreign Ministry through direct contacts with the commander in Albania.")[7]

Badoglio was not a strong chief of staff and put up only a mild and generally futile resistance to Mussolini's decisions and interventions, but he sent Visconti Prasca a covert warning: "Inform General Visconti Prasca that his orders come exclusively from the Army General Staff."[8] This message was dated August 17. When Visconti Prasca returned to Tirana, his first thought was to cover himself by asking the General Staff for the orders he had been promised;[9] and he pointed out—it will be recalled that the troops in Albania were still deployed against the Yugoslavs—that only one division was stationed on the Greek frontier. In reply Roatta informed him that three more divisions were going to be sent.[10] These were the Parma, the Siena, and the Piemonte. The Aosta and Milano cavalry regiments had already been transferred to Albania, and the General Staff arranged to put at Visconti Prasca's disposal by August 25 a motorized machine-gun battalion, a battalion of pioneers, a bridge-construction battalion, a movement control unit, three motorized units, and twelve field hospitals.

All these measures put Albania, hitherto a zone of peripheral calm, on a "tension" footing. For the Italian troops, who in the absence of motor transport had to march wherever they went, a whole series of movements began, from the Albanian frontier to the interior, from there in the direction of the Greek frontier, then again into winter quarters, then towards the Greek frontier again. All these movements followed the shifts and changes of a continually vacillating policy. The troops who had to put up with the comings and goings, the temporary quarters, the orders immediately followed by counterorders, grumbled and swore at the absurdities of a soldier's life and blamed their commanders. They certainly did not imagine that the same uncertainty prevailed at the highest level, not only of the military command, but of the government of their country.

Meanwhile Ciano pressed ahead with his own personal policy. He sent a message to Jacomoni, saying: "Arrange for Albanian press to conduct vigorous campaign against Greece. This will be taken up and echoed by Italian press in the most opportune manner."[11] In short, the Italians barked more and more loudly, but were not ready to bite off either the small morsel of Epirus or the big one of the whole of Greece. Badoglio did not want a war with Greece; Ciano wanted one, but a war of his own kind; Mussolini hesitated, depending on whether the Germans were or were not gaining prestige successes; the General Staff tried to adapt itself to the vacillations of the dictator—who was also the Commander-in-Chief of the Armed Forces and had aspirations to be a strategist—and Visconti Prasca was waiting for the right moment for the *coup de main,* the prospect of which he liked so much but had reason to fear might be vanishing over the horizon. On August 23, the General Staff informed him that deployment on the Greek frontier with a view to Contingency G was to be completed by October 1 instead of September 1. A week later, on August 31,[12] the date was postponed to October 20; and Contingency G became one of three "possible eventualities." These were an offensive against Greece; an offensive against Yugoslavia while remaining on the defensive on the Greek frontier; and remaining in a defensive posture on both fronts.

That was how the General Staff clarified the situation for the commanders in the field. Visconti Prasca was lucky in one respect: his responsibilities were limited to a specific area. Those whose responsibility extended to all sectors, the air force command, for instance, received even more fantastic and contradictory orders at intervals of a few days.[13] Here are some examples. On August 11, for instance, "the Duce orders we must be ready in the east on September 20." On August 30, "recent events in French Equatorial Africa must make us think of possible complications. This General Staff will forthwith begin and rapidly complete studies for the occupation not only of the county of Nice but of all French territory as far as the Rhône." On September 7, "given the situation that may arise in Corsica, I request you as rapidly as possible to study the occupation of the island with troops from Sardinia." And again on September 7, "having to foresee in the future the possibility of action in relation to Tunisia, studies must be initiated with a view to bringing the Fifth Army up to strength."

This jumble of directives was the reflection in the offices of the General Staff of Mussolini's capricious and impetuous zeal for action, which was itself the reflection of the perplexities of a High Command acting—as General Quirino Armellini observes in his diary—on the principle of "first we'll make war and then we'll see." On the same day, September 7, Francesco Pricolo, the air chief of staff, received from Benini, whom Jacomoni regarded as a useless intermediary between the governor-general's office and Ciano and therefore an infernal nuisance, a letter referring to the "operation of which you are aware against the areas of Albania subject to Greece" (Tsamouria and adjoining territories) and drawing attention to the necessity of having parachutists in a state of readiness to drop arms and ammunition in Tsamouria and of training Albanian volunteers to take part in this enterprise. At this point the impression is created that the organizers of the propaganda about Tsamouria had themselves become infected by it, and that they now really believed the area to be in a state of ferment, of which there was not the slightest trace in reality.

It was a strange letter—that is the adjective applied to it by General Santoro, the author of a history of the Italian air force in the Second World War—because it made it evident that Benini, Ciano, and Jacomoni were aware of plans of which the air force officially knew nothing, though they reached Pricolo's ears indirectly, by way of gossip. Pricolo objected to Benini's vague project, based on information from Jacomoni, and explained in reply that before taking action he must have directives from the General Staff stating at least where and in what circumstances the parachutists were to be dropped. But on September 10, General Armellini pricked the bubble of Contingency G with a five-line note. "Dear Pricolo," he said, "I submitted to his Excellency Badoglio the letter from his Excellency Benini and the reply that you sent me yesterday. His Excellency Badoglio mentioned the matter to the Duce and has returned the papers to me with this note: 'Do nothing, Greece is off.' "

The Supreme Command rang down the curtain on the situation on September 10.[14] It explained what was obvious enough to anyone gifted with a minimum of commonsense, namely that "the Duce's orders in regard to possible operations against Yugoslavia, Greece, and France (in the Rhône valley, Corsica, and Tunis)" were not practicable "with the limited forces at our disposal . . . particularly if they were to be simultaneous." These orders therefore were to be regarded as "directives relating to the various contingencies that might arise as a result of the uncertain and changing international political situation." In reality the only fixed point of reference of Mussolini's strategic ideas was not the enemy or neutral states, but Germany. In the dark as he was for most of the time about Hitler's plans and obliged breathlessly to follow in their wake, he was perpetually on the alert for any pickings that might come his way.

The High Command résumé added that Contingency E (for east), i.e., possible operations against Yugoslavia, depended on the political situation in that country being "such as to lead to the expectation of an early revolution" there. "Therefore," the High Command stated, "by the end of October deployment must have been completed so that it may be in a position"—the subject of this clause appears to be "deployment," but the High Command syntax was defective when not revised by the ex-journalist Mussolini—"to take advantage of a possible internal upheaval." As for Contingency G, "the hypothesis must be considered of an armed intervention on our part for the purpose of occupying Tsamouria in Epirus and possibly the island of Corfu, and in a later phase the islands of Santa Maura, Cephalonia, and Zante. The transfer oversea of the reinforcements required by the troops in Albania must be completed by the end of September." As for France, the idea of occupying the Rhône area was off, while in due course orders would be given for the occupation of Corsica ("the operation must be prepared in the strictest secrecy," a phrase that borders on the grotesque), and "it will be possible to carry out" the occupation of Tunisia "by the Fifth Army." At some indeterminate date, of course, because the contingency was merely hypothetical.

The instructions concerning Greece at that moment were merely the result of the grinding of the wheels of the General Staff. On August 24 Mussolini had written to Hitler informing him (perhaps with a touch, or more than a touch, of insincerity) that the measures taken on the Greek and Yugoslav frontiers were purely precautionary; both states were definitely hostile to the Axis and were ready to stab it in the back at the first opportunity. "Greece has shown that her understanding with Great Britain continues. All the Greek ports are being used as bases against us. In spite of this, except in unforeseeable developments, it is not to this sector that I intend to direct my military effort, but towards Egypt."[15] A week later, on August 31, Quirino Armellini noted: "The truth is this. Ciano wants war on Greece to enlarge the boundaries of his grand duchy; Badoglio sees how great a mistake it would be to set the Balkans alight (that is the German position) and wishes to avoid it; and the Duce agrees now with one and now with the other."

Contingency G was shelved. Visconti Prasca, busily allotting theoretical roles for his divisions in the eventuality of a war with Greece, felt on September 16[16] that he was making plans that would never be carried out and were destined to molder in the files. His orders, incidentally reflecting the General Staff directives, anticipated the main lines of the operation begun at the end of October. The Parma Division was to remain on the defensive in western Macedonia, the Julia Division was to undertake a big push towards Metsovon to cut off the Greeks in the Epirus sector from those in the Macedonian sector and "bottle up" the former, the Ferrara and Centauro divisions were to advance along the Dhrino and Vojussa valleys, and the Venezia Division was to clear the Perati–Kalpaki road for the tanks of the Centauro Division and thus open the way to Yanina and Arta for the latter, the Siena Division and the motorized units deployed along the coast were to advance towards the Kalamas and Igoumenitsa, and the Piemonte Division was to remain in reserve. This plan assumed the availability of the Parma, Siena, and Piemonte divisions, which were still being transferred from Italy to Albania. The conception underlying it was still that of the "large-scale *coup de main,*" a limited operation in which Epirus with the Greek forces in it was absurdly assumed to be an independent, self-sufficient entity, almost as if it constituted an independent state and not part of a nation that could not be expected to surrender it without a struggle.

Meanwhile the Greeks were mobilizing. They did not know about all the changes of mind and counterorders (though the Greek envoy in Rome very accurately informed Metaxas of the halt imposed by Ribbentrop on Mussolini's plans for the so-called *coup* in Tsamouria) and believed that behind the big words, the incidents, and the irredentist propaganda in favor of Albania there was a definite will and a consistent plan. A kind of vicious circle arose. Outwardly Greece still strictly observed all the official obligations of neutrality, but Italian aggressiveness forced her into the camp of Italy's enemies, into becoming more and more pro-British; and this dissimulated but undeniable anglophilia, which was very much alive both in the governing class and among the people at large, in its turn inflamed Mussolini's anger and strengthened Ciano's desire to start his favorite "little war"—for that is what he thought it would be. So the Greeks mobilized; and, having learnt their lesson from all the things that had gone wrong during their mobilization of the previous summer, they acted with greater circumspection. The call-up of reservists was carried out according to an ingenious system that avoided creating the impression of large-scale preparations.

"The arms, specialities, corps, and services of every class and group of classes of the call-up," Colonel Mondini, the Italian military attaché, explained, "were given distinctive numbers and initials, and every member of the armed forces on leave knew the number and initial that concerned him, but did not know exactly which classes or specialities the letter and number applied to. Let us assume, for instance, that T47 applied to officers and men of anti-aircraft units belonging to the classes 1931–34 (the Greeks follow the French system of indicating conscription classes not by date of birth but by date of call-up), and that X32 applied to the classes 1935–37 belonging to the same branch of the service, Z36 to radiotelegraphists and telephonists of the classes 1933–34, Y45 to army transport of the classes 1925–27, and V18 to infantrymen of the 1933 class living in definite areas. When the newspapers or the radio or, on some rare occasions, notices on the walls announced the call-up of T47, Z36, and Y45, the great mass of the population and the foreigner had no clue, at any rate at first, to the nature or the size of the call-up."

Greece, with the prospect of an Italian attack hanging over her, was in an extremely difficult position, both militarily and politically. There was the threat from Bulgaria, with her traditional claims to an outlet on the Aegean; Bulgaria, indeed, had always been regarded as the gravest threat. The Greek plan for the contingency of war bore the initials IB, which stood for Italy-Bulgaria. It was generally believed in Greece that if an attack came, it would be a double one, by Italy and Bulgaria simultaneously. Until they knew what the Italian plan of attack was, the Greeks had to provide for a number of contingencies, for possible landings on the islands—as we have seen, the Contingency G plan initially provided for the occupation of the Ionian Islands —and for landings in continental Greece, and hence possible attempts at encirclement. These contingencies made necessary the reinforcement of island garrisons and a consolidation of coastal defenses involving a great dispersion of strength.

Fortunately for the Greeks, the Italians set about resolving these doubts to a large extent. The "political" insistence on Tsamouria pointed to a military operation in Epirus, and the stepping up of troop transfers to Albania further indicated a land attack in that sector. The Greek deployment was adjusted to meet this situation. At the end of August the essential structure of the Greek mobilization (at any rate from the organizational point of view) had been completed, and Papagos' forces on the Albanian border were the following: the 8th Division, of ten infantry battalions, three of which consisted of men recalled to the colors, the 9th Division, of six infantry battalions, one of which consisted of men recalled to the colors, the 1st Division, with four infantry battalions and therefore not up to establishment, and two infantry brigades. These units were supported by artillery and small independent formations.

These forces were still modest. But more troops continued to flow in from the mobilization centers and the interior of the country; and, above all, it was easy to filter troops from the Bulgarian to the Albanian border zone, and between the former and western Macedonia it was especially easy. This was a great contrast to the Italians' situation, handicapped as they were by the bottleneck of the inadequate Albanian ports, and the Greeks made good use of it at the beginning of the campaign. It was not for nothing that Guzzoni had insisted that all the divisions required must be in Albania before any offensive operation was begun. Thus at the end of August the Greek defenses were beginning to have substance, and as the months passed their strength continually increased. There was not the slightest hope of surprise, or chance of success for the *coup de main* to which Visconti Prasca aspired without any military foundation and, as we shall soon see still more plainly, without any political or diplomatic foundation either.

3. Nonexistent Treachery

On November 10, after things had already started going badly wrong, Mussolini stated at a meeting at the Palazzo Venezia at which Badoglio, Cavagnari, Pricolo, Roatta, and Colonel Sorice were present: "Visconti Prasca's plan was based on two factors: one military (a certain number of divisions), the other political (a revolt that was to have broken out in the rear of the Greek troops). Some acts of sabotage that might have been carried out by the fifth column remained doubtful. All this has not happened, instead the exact opposite has happened. While there has been no sign of revolt among the people of Tsamouria in the rear of the Greek troops, very serious phenomena have occurred in some Albanian units." This, as we have already indicated, introduces an element of mystery into the affair. Where did this belief in the prospect of a revolt spring from? To say nothing of the vague but insistent whispers in Foreign Ministry circles about treachery by Greek military leaders.

There is no confirmation of these things from any official source. Ciano makes no concrete reference to them in his diary, and in the postwar period Jacomoni denied having given any assurances in the matter. Metaxas, as we have seen, states in his diary that there were pro-German senior officers in the Greek armed forces (pro-German, not pro-Italian—an important distinction in relation to a war which Mussolini wished to carry out in a sense "against" Hitler). Grazzi, the Italian minister in Athens, knew nothing about them, and neither did Mondini and Morin, the military and naval attachés. General Platis had criticized the policy of the Greek government and General Staff, but openly.[1] To students of the antecedents of the campaign the myth of treachery on the Greek side becomes both a leitmotiv and an obsession. Not only did the information that reached Rome from Athens not hold out the slightest prospect of a revolt in Tsamouria or of Greek treachery, but it gave explicit warning of the methodical and impressive nature of the Greek mobilization.

There could have been no greater contrast between the facts of this mobilization, and a deployment of Greek troops on the frontier that grew more solid day by day, and the wild fantasies about non-resistance or insurrection behind the Greek lines— which incidentally were never seriously evaluated at Mussolini's meetings with his military leaders. The Italian diplomatic documents made public in recent times have not brought to light a single dispatch, a single sentence, coming from Athens to justify the slightest expectation of treachery on the Greek side. At the end of September Grazzi reported in a dispatch that "one cannot talk of an aggressive attitude of Greece towards Italy or even of Greek resistance to our demands, which, as is well known to this ministry, have never been formulated." Grazzi added that the Greek military measures, even if adopted at British instigation, certainly did not portend any "initiatives against us"; and he concluded by emphasizing that the government was making a show of calm, and that Mavroudis, the permanent undersecretary for foreign affairs, had taken ten days' leave for the first time in two years, and had left Athens.[2]

The Greek government showed no sign of yielding, and its pungent comments on the unconstructive bellicosity of the Italian attitude were accompanied by a willingness to negotiate; and— to conclude the picture as painted by the able Italian diplomatic representative in Athens—on October 3 he was still more explicit and outspoken in his warnings. His dispatch of that date remains an example of honest and able diplomacy in the service of arrogant and reckless political masters. He said that Greece was ready for war. "Though making due allowance for informants' exaggerations, it is beyond doubt that Greece has under arms about

250,000 men, most of them already deployed at the frontiers.
. . . It can be deduced from this concentration of armed forces
that the Metaxas government will try to repel any attempt at invasion and that without the use of force it will not be possible
to obtain from it territorial concessions, consent to the occupation
of strategic zones or points, and probably not even concrete acts
of adhesion to the Axis by Greece." Metaxas was as firm as a rock.
"Never has Prime Minister Metaxas had such total unanimity
behind him as in the brief period in which, after brief hesitation,
he adopted the attitude of defending Greek territorial integrity
and neutrality to the limit."[3]

Incidentally it is worth pointing out that Badoglio was informed
of this telegram of Grazzi's. The chief of the General Staff made
no mention of possible Greek treachery, and on October 4 reported the presence of 45,000 Greek troops in western Macedonia and 40,000 in Epirus, with two other big units moving
towards the Albanian frontier. Since the theory of Greek treachery
could not have originated in Athens, it must have originated in
Tirana. Jacomoni throws no light on the question in his book, and
the documents available do not enable one to get to the bottom
of it. But they provide a sufficient explanation of how some trivial,
naïve, and wildly inaccurate information reported from Tirana
to Rome and then growing in Mussolini's and Ciano's minds came
to be taken as foreshadowing a Greek collapse. In his campaign
for Tsamouria Jacomoni set great store by the Dino family, who
were Albanian notables of Tsamourian origin and ardent Fascists.
One of them, Nuri Dino, was federal secretary for Tirana, and the
other, Nebil, was the representative of the party on the Albanian
Higher Council. Nebil Dino used to travel to Tsamouria and
Athens, and when he came back he reported his impressions to
the governor-general, who eagerly swallowed them. According
to Jacomoni, Nebil Dino took the view that the annexation of
Tsamouria was attainable by peaceful means. The reader, who
has been told of the situation as it appeared according to other
sources, can judge for himself the value of Dino's reports.

On August 24 Jacomoni, echoing what the Albanian Fascist leader had told him, wrote to Ciano:

> It is the impression of many people that the Greek authorities are thinking of abandoning Tsamouria. Confirmation of this seems to be given by the following facts. So far no troop reinforcements have been sent to the Albanian frontier; Nebil Dino, of the Fascist Higher Council, having gone to Preveza to make contact with his friends, has so far remained undisturbed in that locality.[4]

On August 27 another dispatch followed, saying *inter alia:*

> The Greek population is thinking of coming events with resignation, but also with the hope of a better future . . . the Greek population does not on the whole seem inclined to fight. . . . The military preparations in Tsamouria have hitherto been of little interest . . . in some quarters in Athens it is thought that in the event of an Italian attack there will be a show of initial resistance essentially for the purpose of telling the world that Greece tried to resist the aggression of the authoritarian states. . . . The Metaxas government is hated by many. The King is neither esteemed nor loved. . . . During his stay in Athens Nebil Dino had close contacts with that royal Minister.

It would not be easy to condense more false or tendentious information into a few lines. The Greek military preparations were active and intense, the Greek people were ready resolutely to resist aggression, and Metaxas enjoyed widespread popularity. In talking of resistance to authoritarian states the dispatch reaches the acme of absurdity. As if Greece were itself not an authoritarian state, though Fascist propaganda for its own purposes contemptuously equated it with the flabby and spineless democracies. The seed sown by Nebil Dino germinated in Jacomoni's mind. On August 28 he sent Benini an interesting urgent memorandum:

> With Nebil Dino of the Fascist Higher Council, who has returned from Athens, I have examined the possibility that influential per-

sonalities in Greece attached to him by sincere and deep friendship may in confidential conversations be willing to consider the future situation of Italy in the Mediterranean basin and the future relations of Greece with Italy. And this with a view to offering the Hellenic world an anchorage in the storm in the form of the vision of a free and sovereign Greek state within the framework of the Roman Empire . . . Nebil Dino's friends at Rome are neither few nor negligible. . . . In substance, he would try to persuade his authoritative friends to consider that Greece, having lost hope in British protection and faced with the pre-eminent position that Italy will have in the Mediterranean basin, a position now openly recognized by the supreme German hierarchy, has only to make an intelligent gesture: to come forward and meet Rome in the certainty of a better future.[5]

Jacomoni suggested that Nebil Dino should collaborate with Grazzi. The ministry replied by granting him authority to make this approach, but without making any contact with Grazzi.

Money must certainly have been sent to finance this operation. It should, however, be noted that, before the famous meeting of October 15 in the Palazzo Venezia, Nebil Dino sent Jacomoni a letter from Athens that was full of good sense. "I found here a general spirit much more unfavorable towards us than before," he wrote.

The principal causes of this state of mind would seem to be the following: the torpedoing of the cruiser *Helle* and the bombing of Greek ships—which in Greece are believed to have been operations carried out by us—and finally our continuous press and radio campaign. As a result Greece has carried out a 50 per cent mobilization, while in the Epirus area and in Macedonia and Thrace the mobilization is general. Your Excellency will understand how delicate is my task in these conditions. Our attitude is not intelligible in my modest judgment. In my view there are two alternatives: either it is intended to use political means or to carry out a military attack. In the former case I do not think that the Rome press and radio campaign is the right way to rouse a people's sympathy. In the latter case I do not think it opportune to give warning to and anger a people whom it is proposed to conquer.[6]

In other words, Nebil Dino's ideas had been clarified by his stay in Athens, he saw the situation as it really was, and realized the colossal mistakes made by the Italian government. But by now his fatuous previous impressions had taken root in Rome and grown into serious expectations that the Greeks would give in. It was a diffuse state of mind, but it had become irreversible. That is all the documentary evidence there is about the prospects of treachery on the Greek side; and, apart from some payments made for promises that turned out to be of advantage only to those who pocketed the money, the non-documentary evidence cannot have amounted to very much either.

In the Greek camp the alarm had been sounded and did not subside. Metaxas, who was always very well informed by his ambassadors, suspected that the German "veto" had been provisional rather than categorical. On August 26 Ribbentrop assumed a somewhat threatening tone towards Rankavì, the Greek ambassador in Berlin;[7] he complained about the pro-British attitude of the Greeks, stated that in future centuries Europe would be dominated by the Axis Powers and that the Mediterranean came within the Italian sphere of influence, and concluded by advising the Greeks to come to terms with the Italians. On the same day Churchill wrote to Metaxas from the other side of the barricade, saying that in the difficult times through which Greece was passing he desired to express his admiration for the firmness and ability with which Metaxas was controlling the crisis, which could be called the gravest in his country's contemporary history. The British, he added, hoped soon to be stronger in the Mediterranean.[8] Metaxas replied with a pretty anodyne letter of thanks.

On August 28 Metaxas wrote in his diary: "I place the problem of Greek dignity over and above everything else. I shall not bow my head to the Italians." So the result of Ciano's diplomacy and Italian propagandist and military activity was that a dictator of the

Fascist type, who tended by nature to be pro-Mussolinian, became ardently pro-British and anti-Italian; that Germany assumed the role of protector and savior of weak Greece against aggressive Italy; that the Italian press followed in the wake of the Albanian *Tomori* in an irredentist campaign that made no impact in Italy and hardly any in Albania; that the intended victim of aggression was put on her guard long enough in advance to enable her to await the attack in the most favorable conditions; and that the attack was delivered by inadequate forces in the most adverse conditions.

In September, as we have seen, Greece was dropped while Yugoslavia rose high on the horizon of Mussolini's plans. But there were several occasions on which the spotlight suddenly flashed on Greece again. The Duce's stubborn observations in conversation with Ribbentrop in Rome on September 19 were reported thus: "There remained the problem of Yugoslavia and Greece. Italy had half a million men on the Yugoslav frontier and 200,000 on the Greek frontier." (In reality there were far fewer; Mussolini was very ill informed.) "To Italy the Greeks represented what the Norwegians had represented to Germany before the operation in April. It was therefore necessary for us to set about the liquidation of Greece; particularly as, when our land forces had advanced farther in Egypt, the British fleet would be unable to remain at Alexandria and would try to seek shelter in Greek ports. However, the Duce agreed with Ribbentrop that the primary objective was the defeat of Britain."[9]

At the end of September the permanent secretary of the German Foreign Ministry, Weizsäcker, reported that when he accompanied Ciano to the station in Berlin after the signature of the tripartite pact, the Italian Foreign Minister "spoke once more of the Greeks with a note of anger; though I reminded him that it had been agreed in the discussions that a solution of the Greek question was not particularly urgent at the moment, Ciano insisted that something must be done to prevent the British fleet from taking refuge in the Greek islands when it had to leave Egypt."[10]

Hitler did not wish to disturb the peace in the Balkans, but Mussolini—as we saw in the quotation from his letter of August 24—wanted some action and took a different view. In July he had ordered the General Staff to prepare a plan for an offensive against Yugoslavia, a much easier operation than an attack on Greece. There were no major problems of communication or supply, troops and equipment would not have to pass through the bottleneck of two inefficient ports such as Durazzo and Valona, and the base for the major units would be on Italian national territory.

"All the forces available in northern Italy," Roatta wrote, "were gathered on the Yugoslav frontier between Tarvisio and Fiume. There were two armies side by side in the first line and a third in reserve. Altogether there were thirty-seven divisions, eighty-five groups of medium artillery, and all the special formations with corresponding services and supplies."[11] On this potential front the Italians were at any rate ready, though with all the limitations and defects of their military machine, which were not eliminable in a few months, or even a few years. But the strength available was impressive, and its impact on the Yugoslav army, which was equipped in an obsolete traditional manner, like the Greek, would have been great. Yugoslavia was governed by the pro-German Regent Paul, though the strong pro-Allied party was working underground. Hence the German hesitation to disturb an equilibrium which, though precarious, tended at the time to favor the Axis (which became tripartite when Japan joined it on September 27).

During the course of September, Contingency E (war with Yugoslavia) was filed away for reasons that are not very clear; indeed, there is not much that is very clear about the decisions made at that time. German opposition undoubtedly played its part, but German influence was certainly not responsible for persuading Mussolini actually to demobilize a large part of the army. Orders were given to release 600,000 reservists, many divisions returned to garrisons or depots (only twenty were to remain on a war footing), and many "veterans" were sent back to Italy from the major units in Albania and replaced by young men who had no experience of the country, were given no time to settle down with their comrades, and had had little practice in handling weapons. The demobilization was not completed, but when the decision to make war on Greece was made on October 15, 300,-000 men had been sent home. A grave blow was thus struck at the substance and efficiency of an army that was in any case basically weak.

In making this decision Mussolini was probably concerned with the "home front." He wanted to create a feeling of normality and encourage agriculture and industry. There might be excellent reasons for such a policy, but it was hardly consistent with aggressive intentions. A circular dated October 15[12]—the day of the meeting in the Palazzo Venezia at which the plan of attack on Greece was decided on—said that "the steps taken do not mean demobilization" and that "the necessity of using these establishments may arise again." With greater subtlety the General Staff spoke of "adjustment of the structure and strength of the army to the actual situation." The trouble was that the actual, or imminent, situation required a quite different structure and, if anything, the opposite kind of adjustment.

Because of the way in which General Staff orders "stuck," as mentioned previously, the three divisions promised by Roatta were duly sent to Albania. The transfer of the Parma, Siena, and Piemonte divisions was completed by the end of September. Badoglio knew nothing of the Duce's anti-Greek outbursts or, if he did, did not attach too much importance to them, because orders were normally followed by counterorders; General Armellini, who was attached to the High Command, once noted that he "changed his mind so many times, let us hope he will do so again."[13] On September 25, at a meeting of chiefs of the General Staff, Badoglio said: "Action against Yugoslavia is not probable, except in the case of internal upheavals (a revolution in Croatia); the present troop concentrations in Albania are sufficient to contain Greece, which has no intention of attacking; once the three divisions (then being sent) are in position, we shall consider the situation to have been stabilized, the Greek, like the Yugoslav, problem being one of those that are settled round the conference table."

A curious thing that happened was that the air commander in Albania, General Ranza, had informed Pricolo, that "the local army authorities are asking for reinforcements and air support for an early military operation against Greece, more particularly for the invasion of Epirus."[14] Pricolo replied in perfectly good faith by categorically denying any such project, "nothing official having ever been communicated on such an important matter, and thinking, I believe correctly, that, though preparations for a campaign can and should be made secretly, one of the three heads of the armed forces cannot be excluded from the secret." In the end it was only casually that Mussolini mentioned to Pricolo in the second half of October at the end of one of the usual weekly meetings that he had decided to attack Greece on October 26. "We must get there before Britain makes a springboard of it against us," he said. "Is there any evidence that Britain has such intentions?" Pricolo asked. "Certainly," Mussolini replied. "If anything, the island of Crete would be more valuable to us." "We shall take that too." "But we shall have to be given our directives in good time." "Of course."

At the beginning of October the General Staff, and Soddu, the undersecretary for war, still believed that there would be no more need to worry about Greece, at any rate for a long time ahead. Soddu was concerned with the "problem of wintering" the troops in Albania, and Roatta ordered Visconti Prasca to move back the Siena Division, which was too close to the frontier; it would be sufficient, he said, if it were ready in case of need to adopt an offensive poise "if orders are given."[15] It looked as if a winter of grumbling and discomfort, though a relatively peaceful one, lay ahead for the troops in Albania. Forty thousand men had been sent there between August and October and the deployment had been changed so that the greater part of the Italian strength now faced Greece instead of Yugoslavia. Meanwhile the Duce's eyes were riveted on Egypt, where the attack on Sidi Barrani (opposed by Badoglio and also by Graziani, but greatly desired by Mussolini) was being prepared. At a meeting of the chiefs of staff on October 11 Badoglio again observed "with visible satisfaction" that the so-called Greek campaign was definitely off and that no more was to be done about it.

Thus we come to October 12, 1940, described with good reason as the fateful day by General Emilio Faldella in his *L'Italia nella seconda guerra mondiale*. History sometimes has its ironies; the entry in Metaxas' diary under that date is chiefly concerned with family troubles. "This morning I tried to reach an understanding with her [i.e., his daughter Lulu], up to a certain point all went well, but then we quarreled again. It is impossible for her to understand me. I know who it is who is deceiving and inciting her. I actually forgot the meeting with Palairet [the British minister in Athens]. I stayed with her until midday. How sorry I am for her. And what a tragic girl she is. Lulu, Lulu, my beloved daughter. We fell into each other's arms and wept over our fate." This is followed by some political notes of no particular interest. Metaxas was completely wrapped up in his domestic troubles. Meanwhile the destiny of Greece was being decided elsewhere.

On the previous day, October 11, the Germans had informed Mussolini that, "in accordance with the Rumanian request," a German military mission was going to Bucharest, and that the Luftwaffe was to undertake the defense of the Ploesti oil wells.[16] German troops had actually begun installing themselves in Rumania on October 8. This was one of the countless military steps taken by Hitler without consulting his comrade of the Pact of Steel, and a further advance by Germany towards that absolute supremacy in Europe that Mussolini wished to prevent, so that the alliance should remain within the limits of a partnership and not be one of obvious German hegemony; and Ciano, pleased that chance, or rather Hitler, had unexpectedly brought grist to the mill of the war with Greece that he wanted, noted in his diary (I complete a quotation used in the Preface):

[Mussolini] is above all indignant at the German occupation of Rumania. He says that this has deeply and adversely affected Italian public opinion, because no one expected this result of the Vienna arbitration [on the division of Transylvania between Hungary and Rumania—*author's note*]. "Hitler keeps confronting me with *faits accomplis*. This time I shall pay him back in his own coin; he shall learn from the newspapers that I have occupied Greece. Thus equilibrium will be restored." I asked if he had reached agreement with Badoglio. "Not yet," he replied. "But if anyone finds it difficult to fight the Greeks, I shall hand in my resignation as an Italian." This time the Duce seems determined to act. Actually I believe the operation to be useful and easy.

Mussolini's hope that Rumania would ask for Italian troops had been disappointed. His troublesome ally had called off Operation Sea Lion, the invasion of Britain that was to lead to its rapid defeat, and was turning east and making an unwelcome appearance in the Balkan area. Mussolini was as nettled as an actor when a rival steals the show, and the consequences were grave. He decided on a war after the army had demobilized 300,000 men, at a time when the military formations on Italian soil were undergoing a reorganization that in many cases resulted in conditions bordering on chaos. The navy, having completed the transport of three divisions to Albania, believed itself to have been freed of an onerous task so that it could devote itself to safeguarding the communications with Albania; and the air force was transferring to Belgium squadrons that were intended to collaborate with the Germans in the Battle of Britain. Such was the state of the Italian armed forces when Mussolini gave his order.

He spoke to Ciano of his decision to invade Greece and, among the military leaders, to Soddu, the undersecretary for war, who was simultaneously deputy chief of the General Staff. Soddu informed Badoglio, who, on October 13, issued the following order: "At zero hour on the twenty-sixth all must be ready in order to be able to begin the operation foreseen (Contingency G)." Was Roatta immediately informed? According to Visconti Prasca, he was not. As I mentioned in the Preface, he states: "On October 14 I was summoned to Rome; in the morning I went to see Roatta, who told me that the operation against Greece was off.[17] But Soddu, who was better informed and more trustworthy at that moment, told me that operations were to begin on October 26. He added that Roatta did not yet know this. The latter sent for me during the afternoon and confirmed that the operation would take place on the twenty-sixth."

Roatta's ignorance is confirmed by the almost incredible inconsistency of two orders simultaneously received from the Air Staff on October 14.[18] The first, signed by Roatta, stated that "the implementation of Contingency G [Corfu] is postponed for the time being. Study of the subject will, however, be continued and kept up to date so that if the necessity arises it will be possible to implement it as quickly as possible. Please acknowledge receipt." The other, signed by Badoglio, said that "the twelve days required by the navy for the transport operations for the Corfu expedition run from October 14. Hence all must be in readiness at zero hour on the twenty-sixth to enable the operation foreseen in Albania [Contingency G] to begin. The organization of anti-aircraft defense must also be completed by that date. The Air Staff will make arrangements for the reinforcement of the air force in Albania and the deployment of units as planned."

Roatta was so much in the dark about the Duce's decision that when he was told to go with Badoglio to be received by Mussolini on October 14 he took with him the old Guzzoni-Pariani plan, which, as mentioned, proposed the use of eighteen or twenty divisions for the main purpose of securing a breakthrough to Salonika. Mussolini summarily informed the two men that Greece had grown so favorable to the Allied cause that she must be occupied. Obviously he gave no hint of his pique at the German affront to him over Rumania. He asked Roatta what forces would be necessary for the campaign, and in his *Otto milioni di baionette* Roatta states his reply: he considered it necessary to employ twenty divisions simultaneously, and to have a delay of at least three months in which to transfer the extra twelve divisions to Greece. Badoglio, he said, agreed.

At this point we enter a zone of mystery. Marshal Badoglio had issued an order stating that operations were to begin on October 26. Yet, after Roatta had indicated the necessity of three months' delay before the beginning of operations, he took leave of Mussolini without further ado. Perhaps the explanation is to be looked for simply in Badoglio's elastic delaying tactics, his hope of restraining Mussolini's intemperances by a kind of passive resistance; as already pointed out, he relied on the frequent changes of mind of the second "First Marshal of the Empire." The other First Marshal, Victor Emmanuel III, held his peace. On October 16, after the decision to make war on Greece had been made, he busied himself "with a proposal, said to have originated with Soddu, for the appointment of the Prince of Piedmont to be inspector general of the Army after the disbandment of Army Group West."[19] On the afternoon of October 14, Soddu spoke to Roatta on the telephone and, referring to the Greek operation, made the strange observation: "A lot of time will pass."

Jacomoni was in Rome too. He had hurried there, also on October 14, in response to a telegram from Ciano; and he maintains that he was so far from imagining the reason for the summons that he took with him a file concerning the granting of honors under the Order of Skanderbeg, as well as another relating to the order of precedence of Albanian dignitaries at the Quirinal.[20] Ciano received him immediately after his arrival and told him that it had been decided that the operation against Greece was to begin on October 26. In his "self-defensive" memoirs Jacomoni comments on the statement in Ciano's diary that he gave the Foreign Minister "very favorable information about the state of mind of the Tsamouriot people."

That was what I gave him [Jacomoni says] but he omitted to mention what I added, which was that what I was able to tell him about the state of mind of the Muslims in Tsamouria seemed to me to have little importance if it were no longer a matter of carrying out a political operation limited to that region. In reality it was a sense of anxiety that I felt when confronted with the new plan of action . . . I had believed that the intention was to induce Greece, no doubt by the exercise of decisive and energetic pressure, to accept a frontier agreement such as would satisfy Tirana's irredentist demands for Tsamouria. My sole concern . . . had been that, as a result of some mistaken assessment by our government or of impatience on the part of some hot-headed Albanian group, the operation might fail at the diplomatic level, causing us to embark on the slippery slope of military unknown quantities. But now Ciano revealed to me for the first time a completely different project: a genuine act of aggression to which the Greek Army would react energetically; a military adventure. . . .

As I have already said, this is unconvincing. What the Palazzo Chigi wanted of Jacomoni was not a plan for applying political pressure, but a plan of aggression, a Balkan Danzig, and that is what he supplied. It is perfectly possible, and even probable, that in his talk with Ciano he felt acutely aware of the lack of politico-military preparation, or at any rate of a balanced assessment of all the factors in the situation, and that, having himself contributed to putting things on the slippery slope to which they were now irretrievably committed, he was struck with belated remorse now that the vindictive Mussolini had taken the decisive step.

The forces at our disposal in Albania seemed to me to be insufficient to support diplomatic action to obtain Tsamouria. I said so at once to Ciano. He replied that that was not a Foreign Ministry concern, that at most it was a question I might have discussed with General Visconti Prasca. . . . In the afternoon I saw Visconti Prasca at the Hotel Excelsior. He confirmed that the operation had been decided on for the twenth-sixth of that month, i.e., in twelve days' time. Thus it could be carried out only by the troops already in Albania. He could tell me no more, and still less could he tell me about the operational plan. In all matters pertaining to the employment of troops he was not subordinate to me and must therefore adhere to the obligation of military secrecy. He added that his total reserve on the subject . . . ought to be intelligible and acceptable to me in view of the fact that the operation was now passing beyond the sphere of Albanian aspirations in Tsamouria.

Jacomoni's story reveals another aspect of Visconti Prasca's attitude. It should be recalled that at that moment he knew nothing definite yet, because Mussolini's *volte-face* was only forty-eight hours old; on the afternoon of October 14 Roatta, as we have seen, was still in the dark about the decision to make war. Nevertheless Visconti Prasca put up a façade of mystery, entrenching himself behind military secrecy instead of behind his state of total uncertainty. As he insisted in remaining in the ivory tower of his strategic secrets, Jacomoni consulted General Manlio Gabrielli, who was the officer "attached to the governor-general's office," and asked him for an outline of the military situation. That same evening General Gabrielli gave him a pretty clear one.

He stated that if Yugoslavia remained neutral and Bulgaria were allied to Italy, the Italians would have to face "a maximum of 150,000 Greeks, in addition to possible British air and naval support." If both Bulgaria and Yugoslavia remained neutral, the Italians would have to face "the greater part of the Greek army, which today, according to the General Staff, has about 250,000 men under arms." With Yugoslavia as an enemy and Bulgaria neutral, the Italians would have difficulty in facing a threat from the north while they were engaged with Greece. "The operation, if it is begun," General Gabrielli continued, "should be carried out in such a way as to give us possession of the greater part of Greek territory in the shortest possible time."[21] Jacomoni states that on the morning of October 15 he did all in his power to hand the report to Ciano, but succeeded only in submitting it to Filippo Anfuso, who was opposed to the campaign. Jacomoni also states that he exchanged a few words with the Minister when he was already at the Palazzo Venezia.

I told him that my conversation . . . with Visconti Prasca had further increased my concern that we should be running into the gravest difficulties, if not into disaster. Ciano replied that the decision about making war on Greece was not within my competence, nor was expressing an opinion on our military preparedness. I was therefore not entitled to make representations to him on the subject; my duty was only to supply the information required of me. He also said: "This is not an Albanian question, but a direct question between Italy and Greece. We need guarantees."

Jacomoni handed Ciano Nebil Dino's pessimistic letter from Athens. At that point Mussolini sent for them both, and at eleven o'clock the meeting began.

Mussolini presided, and those present were Badoglio, Roatta, Soddu, Visconti Prasca, Ciano, Jacomoni, and the secretary, Lieutenant Colonel Mario Trombetti. Faldella very rightly points out in his book that neither Cavagnari, chief of the Naval Staff, nor Pricolo, chief of the Air Staff, was summoned to attend, as if the matter to be discussed was not one that closely concerned them. Roatta arrived after the meeting had begun, having been hurriedly summoned on the telephone by Sebastiani, the Duce's private secretary; and when he came in, hearing that war with Greece was being discussed, he felt "convinced they were discussing a campaign to be carried out on the lines approved and decided on by the Duce twenty-four hours before. I soon realized, however, from the progress of the discussion, that something quite different was at stake, but I assumed that Mussolini's rapid and radical change of mind was the consequence of important circumstances mentioned at the beginning of the meeting at which I was not present."[22]

In this passage of his book Roatta performs a far more skillful disengagement maneuver to exonerate himself from responsibility for the war than any he was able to carry out as leader of the forces that had to oppose the Germans on September 8, 1943. There is no evidence that on other occasions he showed any extraordinary strength of mind in opposing hazardous or mistaken plans of Mussolini's. However, he hardly intervened on this occasion. The report of the meeting[23] can be said to constitute the basic document regarding the disastrous war on Greece. Attempts have been made to dispute marginal details (Visconti Prasca, for instance, later asserted that he had no memory of having used "the many optimistic adjectives that adorn the report"). But it is indisputable that they very faithfully record or summarize what was said at that meeting on the morning of October 15. All those present had *arrière-pensées* which they were afraid of declaring in the presence of the dictator, who notoriously disliked contradiction. Badoglio approved in order to obstruct, Roatta was opposed but did not make the fact very plain, and for every objection raised by Jacomoni he said yes 100 times. Ciano and Visconti Prasca were unreservedly in favor of the attack, and so of course was Mussolini. A strange cloud of reticence and equivocal silence surrounded these men. After the disaster each of them used it to exonerate himself.

4. Fateful Blunders

Mussolini, very sure of himself, very much the Commander-in-Chief, opened the meeting[1] by announcing that its purpose was to "lay down—in broad outline—the course of action I have decided to undertake against Greece." The first phase of the operation was to lead to the acquisition of the whole of the southern Albanian coastline, the occupation of the Ionian islands Zante, Cephalonia, and Corfu, and the capture of Salonika. "In a second phase, or concomitantly with these operations," Mussolini continued, the objective was "the total occupation of Greece, to put it out of action and ensure that in all circumstances it shall remain within our politico-economic sphere. Having thus defined the issue, I have also decided the date, which in my opinion must not be postponed even by an hour; that is, the 26th of this month. This is an operation that has been maturing in my mind for a long time, since many months before our entry into the war and even before the beginning of the conflict."

Thus since his meeting with Badoglio and Roatta on the previous day Mussolini had thought out an entirely new plan, divided into two parts: a first phase corresponding to Contingency G (what was left of the *coup de main* visualized by Visconti Prasca in August), and a second phase consisting of an all-out offensive basically inspired by the Guzzoni-Pariani plan, which assumed the use of twenty divisions.

In this hour that seemed the prelude to victory, Mussolini, with characteristic arrogance, assumed responsibility for all the decisions and the planning (the long preparation for the war dated back to a moment of pique forty-eight hours previously). Later, when reverses occurred, he blamed his generals, who, as usual, had "misled" him.

Passing to the political aspect of the campaign, the Duce stated that he did not foresee "complications in the north," from Yugoslavia, or from Turkey, "especially since Germany has established herself in Rumania and Bulgaria has strengthened herself." He undertook to invite Bulgaria to join in the operation—and later did so, as we shall see—offering her an outlet to the Aegean in return. This was yet another example of the Duce's and Ciano's frivolity. A factor as important to the success of the operation as Bulgarian co-operation, which would have pinned down the greater part of the Greek strength, was considered merely in passing. Jacomoni, who was called on to speak immediately after the Duce, spoke of Albanian enthusiasm for the war and of the "manifest indifference" of Greek public opinion.

To do him justice, however, he added a significant qualification. "From information supplied by our informants it appears that, while two months ago the Greeks did not seem inclined to put up serious resistance, now they seem determined to oppose our action." But Mussolini wanted reassurance—the members of the hierarchy knew well enough that he grew testy if he was disagreed with—and he persisted. "What is the state of mind of the Greek population?" he asked, and Jacomoni ended by telling him what he wanted to hear. "It appears to be profoundly depressed," he said. Ciano intervened to say that the great mass of the Greek population was "indifferent to everything, including the prospect of our invasion." Grazzi's and Mondini's reports from Athens were not mentioned, and neither were those of the General Staff.

Having disposed of the political and psychological aspects of the enterprise with this depth and thoroughness, the meeting turned to the military aspect. Visconti Prasca described the proposed operations in Epirus.

This theater of operations will enable us to carry out a series of rounding-up operations against the Greek forces—estimated to number about 30,000 men—which will enable us to occupy Epirus in a short time, ten or fifteen days. This operation—which might allow us to liquidate all the Greek troops—has been prepared down to the most minute details and is as perfect as is humanly possible. Its success would bring about an improvement in our position, give us a more secure frontier, and possession of the port of Preveza, resulting in a complete change in our situation. That is the first phase of the operation . . . The spirit of the troops is excellent, enthusiasm is as high as it could be. . . . The only signs of indiscipline among officers and men have been the result of excessive eagerness to go forward and fight.

Visconti Prasca, who in his mind's eye already saw himself promoted to full general at Preveza and to Marshal of Italy in Athens, attributed his own enthusiasm, hopes, and illusions to the troops quartered in the disconsolate Albanian countryside. The language he used was excessively untechnical and excessively unserious, and if Mussolini had not long since been hypnotized by adulation, by his followers' declarations of unshakable faith and iron will, he would have noticed it. But his sensibilities in the matter had inevitably been dangerously blunted. Visconti Prasca said that the Italian superiority in strength in Epirus was more than two to one, 70,000 to 30,000.

Mussolini mentioned the importance of Salonika, but here Visconti Prasca restrained him; a couple of months would be necessary for that objective, he said, and added: "The basis for everything, including the beginning of the march on Athens, is the occupation of Epirus and the port of Preveza," to which Mussolini immediately added Zante, Cephalonia, and Corfu. Visconti Prasca also said that the Greeks were not "people who like fighting" and referred to the organization of a frontier incident that would provide a semblance of provocation to justify the Italian action. "The incident will occur on the twenty-fourth," Ciano promised. Visconti Prasca undertook to deliver a shattering blow, Mussolini told him not to worry too much about casualties, and the commander in Albania brightly assured him that he had given orders that battalions were to attack, always attack, even if faced with a division.

Not till this point was reached did the aged Badoglio intervene. He did so ambiguously, with general support for the operation systematically qualified by criticisms. He suggested that, to prevent the British from landing troops in Greece when the attack began, they should simultaneously be engaged in Africa. He said that "stopping short in Epirus is not consistent with the situation," and that the occupation of Crete and Morea should also be planned. He agreed that the "operation worked out by Visconti Prasca is all right," but objected that to make it worthwhile the whole of Greece would have to be occupied, and "for this about twenty divisions are required, while in Albania we now have nine, plus a cavalry division." (The chief of the General Staff was mistaken; there were only nine divisions in Albania, including the cavalry division.) "In these conditions it is obvious that three months will be needed," he said, and Roatta backed him by saying: "The problem of the total occupation of Greece must therefore be studied at once."

Mussolini said: "The beginning of the operation having been fixed for the twenty-sixth, and the liquidation of Epirus being expected by about November 10–15, that gives us another month for sending fresh forces." But Visconti Prasca did not want too many divisions at once. "The sending of extra troops depends on how the operation develops, and they can be sent only to occupied Epirus," he said. Then the discussion turned to Athens, which was not regarded by Visconti Prasca as an objective very difficult of attainment: "A group of five or six divisions would be sufficient." When Mussolini asked how many extra divisions he considered would be necessary to occupy the whole of Greek territory as far as Athens, Visconti Prasca replied that he would be satisfied "during the initial period" with three mountain divisions. Mussolini summed up by saying: "Offensive in Epirus; observation and pressure on Salonika, and, as a second phase, the march on Athens." Those who took an active part in the meeting were Mussolini, Visconti Prasca, Jacomoni, and Ciano. Badoglio, Soddu, and Roatta tepidly agreed on plans that had the blessing of the Commander-in-Chief, who was also the infallible dictator—and also had the backing of the Foreign Ministry and the enthusiastic support of an ambitious general whom Pricolo was to describe as an *exalté*. When the meeting broke up with a great clicking of heels and Roman salutes the die was cast, and any eleventh-hour attempts to divert the course of events were doomed to fail.

The course taken by this fateful meeting requires clarification. Some points still remained obscure, and it seems unlikely that they will ever be fully cleared up. In the first place, why was Mussolini, who cannot have failed to appreciate that twenty divisions were necessary for the conquest of the whole of Greece, in such a hurry to attack, and why was he initially satisfied with the prospect of an only partial success? To that question there is only one possible reply. He was afraid that Hitler and Ribbentrop would sharply apply the brake and thwart him again as they had in the middle of August. This time he intended at all costs to confront his comrade and rival with a *fait accompli*. When he and Hitler met a few days later the point of no return had been passed. Mussolini was interested not so much in quickly gaining a decisive victory as in quickly beginning hostilities; the rest, he believed, would follow of its own accord; after Epirus, Athens, and then, Greece having been cut in two, Salonika would drop into his hands like a ripe fruit.

There is another question that can be answered—that of the odd behavior of Visconti Prasca. Why was he so reluctant to accept any serious reinforcement of the army under his command? Badoglio and Roatta insisted on the idea of twenty divisions and on the necessity of organizing the sending of reinforcements without delay, while Visconti Prasca obstructed this, insisting that extra troops could be sent only to "occupied Epirus," and that the three mountain divisions, in addition to those already under his command, would be sufficient to occupy the whole area up to Athens "during the initial period." (And what did this last phrase mean? If Greece were occupied all the way to Athens, it would mean complete victory.) And, finally, why did he say that "a group of five or six divisions would be sufficient" for the march on Athens?

Visconti Prasca always asked for very little; also it should be noted that his opinion was always asked on strictly military matters, independently of any political considerations. He was a lieutenant general low on the seniority list, aged fifty-seven, and he was afraid that if the army under his command grew too big the command would be taken away from him and given to someone else. He believed he had a hidden (though not so very hidden) enemy in Roatta, an office general who was a greater expert on the army list and procuring promotions than in maneuvering troops in battle. Roatta had given him clear indications of his hostility during the discussions on how the Albanian command should be organized at the beginning of September, when the invasion of Greece still seemed a pretty remote contingency.

"The operational studies," Visconti Prasca writes, "made it evident that an operation against Greece would involve the division of the front into two sectors, the Epirus sector and the Koritsa (or Macedonian) sector, separated by the Pindus massif. It was obvious that, as more than one division was involved in each sector, organizationally and tactically it was an army corps command. But the commander of two army corps is the commander of an army, and our regulations lay down that an officer who has commanded an army in wartime is thereby qualified for the rank of full general."[2]

It was this that was in Visconti Prasca's mind, and it was in Roatta's mind too. In a conversation with the commander in Albania, Roatta had exclaimed in alarm: "But in that case you would become a full general-designate ahead of Rosi." And Rosi was senior to Roatta. Thus Visconti Prasca seemed likely to be promoted over the heads of both. He had his way in regard to the division of the front into two army corps, in spite of Roatta, who took the line that there should be a single army corps in Epirus and a number of divisional commands in the Macedonian sector responsible directly to general headquarters in Albania. But he was obviously afraid that if his command were still further increased, he would lose it.

Evidence of his preoccupation on this score is provided by a letter he sent on September 30 to Soddu (a friend), in which he mentioned the arrival of other generals. "From the operational point of view in present circumstances," he said, "there is no need for their presence, which would constitute an obstruction rather than a help, though all those sent by higher authority for any reason will be welcome. . . . They will have their share of glory. . . . That having been stated, I have reason to assume that there is a desire to use this participation of other commanders in the Epirus operation as a concealed but direct diminution of my responsibility as commander."[3] In particular, Visconti Prasca was afraid that Gastone Gambara, who had the reputation of always managing to unseat his superior officers and take their place, might be appointed to serve under him. ("He is an outlaw, he does not recognize subordination and the chain of command, but communicates directly with everyone," General Armellini said of him.) Roatta was indeed opposed to Visconti Prasca's having the Albanian command, and "careerist" reasons probably mingled in his mind with technical reasons.

When he learned that the attack on Greece was imminent, he again proposed that the Albanian command should be put on a "proper footing," with Ambrosio or Vercellino in command and Visconti Prasca, Gambara, and Francisci in command of three army corps (to be organized after the sending of more divisions to Albania, which Roatta still believed possible on the eve of the meeting at the Palazzo Venezia).

On October 25 Mussolini wrote to Visconti Prasca in his own hand: "Dear Visconti, you know, and if you do not I am telling you now, that I have opposed all attempts to take your command away from you on the eve of the operation. I believe that events, and above all your actions, will justify me. Attack with the greatest determination and violence. The success of the operation depends above all on its speed." Mussolini was in a hurry because he was engaged in a race with time against Hitler, and Visconti Prasca was in a hurry because he was engaged in a race with time against Roatta, and the two things worked together hand in glove. Both general and dictator were motivated by what we may call "professional" interests and preoccupations. Mussolini did not want to be too obviously outdone by Hitler in his role of military adventurer, and Visconti Prasca did not want to lose a command that might take him like lightning to the top of the military tree.

This, reinforced by Ciano's and Jacomoni's assurances, was basically what made Mussolini press for swift action and Visconti Prasca do all in his power to ensure that the operation should begin with the forces already in the field. As the number of divisions under his command increased, so would he rise in rank, and there would never be a disproportion between the two. This interpretation, which is backed by facts and documents, will be considered by some to be malicious or harsh. The sad reality is that small, if not petty, human weaknesses and ambitions often underlie great events.

Then again there is the question of the pretty widespread belief in the corruption of the Greek generals and the expected inevitable collapse of the Greek army. At the Palazzo Venezia Ciano and Jacomoni made no mention of corruption; they confined themselves to vague hints about low Greek morale and the gap between a dominant "plutocratic class" and the mass of the Greek people. In his memoirs Visconti Prasca denies knowledge of any payments to Greek generals, "even though there was talk later of checks on a Rome bank payable to bearer to the amount of five millions"—five million lire then, of course, being equivalent to at least 5,000 million lire ($200,000) today. The figure vaguely indicated by Visconti Prasca is lower than the reality. The files of the Foreign Ministry contain references to an allocation of one million lire for Contingency G,[4] a fund of five million lire which was "running out," and a further allocation of five million lire "for the requirements of our operation against Greece."[5] Jacomoni justified the expenditure of these substantial sums by the necessity of creating "the circumstances, both on this and the other side of the frontier, necessary for a favorable development of events." But five or six days before the opening of hostilities these sums could not possibly have been used to buy Greek generals or politicians, who would have had to have been won over to the Italian side much sooner. They must have been intended for propaganda purposes in the areas into which it was believed the Italians were going to blitz their way, to be greeted there with acclamation, according to Jacomoni.

Grazzi, the minister in Athens, points out that "it is incredible that the information supplied by these informants (of the governor-general's office in Tirana), whether they were volunteers or hired, should have been accepted as biblical truth without any checking whatever, and should have been preferred, only because they were more favorable to the plan for aggression, to those supplied by responsible officials known for years to their superiors as serious persons."[6] He also states:

> It is incomprehensible that Count Ciano, who must have read my reports, letters, and telegrams, should have spoken of a sharp division between the people and the leading political and plutocratic class, and that he should have stated that, apart from this restricted class of bureaucrats, the rest of the Greek people were indifferent to all events that might take place, including an invasion by us. If there were good reasons for supposing that our information was so totally false as not to deserve so much as comparison with that supplied from other sources, only two hypotheses are possible: either we were complete idiots or we acted in bad faith. In either case the question arises why the government continued at great expense to maintain in Athens a diplomatic mission staffed by idiots or traitors.

In the course of his career questions of this kind had often crossed Grazzi's mind. When he was director of transoceanic affairs in the Foreign Ministry, for instance, he prepared a report on the danger of a growth of hostility of American public opinion towards the authoritarian powers, and therefore towards Italy, but Mussolini peremptorily dismissed the matter by blue-penciling in the margin: "America has no military importance"—the assumption of an ignorant provincial. The reality of the situation, as has been shown by Professor Guido Gigli in a study intended to defend Badoglio,[7] was that Mussolini and Ciano had their own informants, emissaries, temporary ambassadors. Jacomoni's recent revelations corroborate this. Members of the Fascist hierarchy traveling at state expense reported impressions often distorted by ignorance and inaccuracy.

Badoglio states that soon after the meeting at the Palazzo Venezia Ciano told him "that he had succeeded in winning over various Greek notables, some of them forming part of the present government, to overthrowing the government itself and bringing Greece over to our side."[8] He added that this had cost him a good deal, but that the expense had been justified by results. It seems strange that similar confidences do not seem to have been made to Visconti Prasca, who would have had every interest in the world in quoting them in his own defense. Badoglio states that he confirmed to Colonel Trombetti, who drafted the report of the famous meeting, that "politically everything has been done." This same officer had the impression that "a great deal of political work was in hand on the part of the Foreign Ministry and the governor-general's office in Albania to facilitate a possible invasion of Greece, and this by way of corruption of Greek leaders." But there is no documentation of this, apart from the maneuvers of Jacomoni, which, like everything he attempted—the fomentation of a rising in Tsamouria and organization of Albanian military support—produced nil results.

It seems clear that corruption played a part in Ciano's plans, but only as a marginal possibility; the hope of it was based on vague, flattering, unconfirmed rumors, and information that any serious, experienced statesman would have regarded with total skepticism. Statesmen and military leaders who on other occasions, when it was a matter of taking steps to save what could still be saved of the country's honor and prestige, made very cautious assessments of the favorable factors in the situation (the reader is reminded of the attitude of Badoglio and Roatta when faced with the American offer to send an airborne division to Rome for the defense of the capital on September 8, 1943), on this occasion pretended to accept as hard currency hopes and expectations so vague that Ciano did not even dare mention them explicitly at the decisive meeting. But on September 8 they were faced with the risk of paying in person. It might even be suggested—though it seems rather far-fetched, for at that time Mussolini, Ciano, and Visconti Prasca had no doubts about the success of the Greek project—that both politicians and the army were preparing alibis for themselves for history, the politicians showing that the army went into the campaign on the basis of purely military considerations, while the army took the line that the politicians counted on extra-military factors, on which they, the army, relied. But whichever way one looks at it, it was a mess.

Badoglio, as we have already pointed out, played a strange role at the meeting and during the days that followed. He approved but obstructed, obstructed but approved. He knew that the enterprise was misconceived, but was neither resolute enough to oppose it nor compliant enough unreservedly to accept it. Jacomoni relates that, having noticed the marshal's lukewarmness at the Palazzo Venezia, he was delighted to receive an invitation to lunch with him on the following day, October 16;[9] he thought this would be an excellent opportunity for threshing things out with him in a *tête-à-tête*. But "I was . . . painfully disillusioned. . . . I told Badoglio that what I had said at the meeting had been intended to pave the way for him to insist on the nature of the forces that were necessary for the invasion of Greece. . . . The marshal replied: 'You are right. The Greeks are good fighters. They showed that in their last war with Turkey. They were beaten, but they fought bravely.' Then he changed the subject, drawing my attention to an old diploma of his that was hanging on the wall."

Badoglio, with a guile typical of the time, tried to put off the prospect of a crazy campaign by dangling the prospect of a bigger and more alluring one. To prevent the invasion of Epirus he insisted on a march to Athens, with the result that he not only failed to stop the former but exposed himself to the charge of having encouraged the latter. Mussolini took no notice of him, and Ciano listened to him with forbearance. But a timely resignation by the chief of the General Staff—even of a chief of the General Staff whose prerogatives were frequently ignored or bypassed—would have created a sensation and strengthened the attitude of the King. As happened more than once, King Victor Emmanuel III saw the situation correctly, but let things take their course. He did not lift a finger.

"His Majesty," his aide-de-camp Puntoni noted on October 20, "allowed me to see the report of the meeting of the fifteenth inst., summoned by the Duce, at which there were present Badoglio, the undersecretaries of the armed forces [this was incorrect, because those for the air force and the navy did not attend], the chiefs of staff of the army, navy, and air force [this was incorrect too], General Visconti Prasca, Ciano, and Jacomoni. At this meeting the invasion of Greece was decided on for October 26 and is to take place in two phases. From the report it appears that there was a great deal of optimism that does not seem in any way justified when the strength of the forces now stationed in Albania is taken into account. Emphasis is laid on the necessity of a lightning stroke, the logical result of which would be the disorientation of the enemy. The *casus belli* is to be provoked on October 24."[10]

Victor Emmanuel III knew the Italian forces were totally inadequate, and so did Badoglio and the chiefs of staff of the three services. "Marshal Badoglio came to see me," Ciano noted on October 17, "and spoke to me very seriously about the operation in Greece. The three chiefs of staff are unanimously opposed to it. He said that the present forces are insufficient, and the navy does not believe it will be able to carry out any unloading at

Preveza, because the water is too shallow. There was a pessimistic note about Badoglio's whole speech; he foresees a prolongation of the war, and with it the exhaustion of our meager resources. I listened and did not argue. I said that from the political point of view the timing was right. Greece is isolated. Turkey will not move, and Yugoslavia will not move either. The Bulgarians, if they enter the war, will be with us. Militarily I am not qualified to judge. Badoglio should unreservedly tell Mussolini what he told me."

Ciano does not mention having said anything about the bribing of Greek generals, but, according to the sentence from Badoglio's memoirs which we quoted, it would seem that he did so. But one point that Ciano mentions should be noted. Visconti Prasca insisted on the necessity of overrunning Epirus before beginning a general offensive against Greece in order to ensure Italian supplies by way of the indispensable harbor of Preveza. But here we are told that this harbor was considered to be of little use because of its shallowness. Ciano was inclined to listen only to optimistic statements, such as those of Jacomoni and Visconti Prasca when they told him immediately after the meeting on October 15 that "in Albania expectations are high and keen" and that "there are now the most open demonstrations of enthusiasm on the part of Albanian youth, which has always been reserved in its attitude towards us."

Immediately after the meeting, while Ciano was talking to Visconti Prasca and Jacomoni, Roatta had a conversation with Soddu, who, as undersecretary for war and deputy chief of the General Staff, stood halfway between the political and military spheres and tried to steer a course enabling him to gain the greatest personal advantage from the Duce's cavortings and changes of mind. Roatta relates that he told Soddu he felt very doubtful, in spite of the "optimistic views" about the "expediency of attacking Greece so soon and with such few forces." "We were running the risk of a grave failure," he said. Soddu replied "that I should remain completely quiet in my mind; there were circumstances, particularly of a political nature, that gave the assurance of rapid and certain success, quite apart from the size of the forces employed. . . . Subsequently"—this is still Roatta speaking—"it was learnt in the corridors, in an indefinite but uniform and persistent manner, that this optimism was based on the certainty that some high Greek political and military personalities who were opposed to the Metaxas government and were anti-Allied and more or less in agreement with us were going to act in such a way as to force that government, or another that might succeed it, to accede to the demands that we should make before beginning operations. Consequently we should not meet resistance, or at most very feeble resistance."[11]

This was one more fatal blunder of the kind that was liable to arise in the confusion that existed in the Fascist government, to the vaunted efficiency of which some now look back nostalgically, and in the confusion between political and military leaders, between official ambassadors and secret emissaries, between serious informants and unreliable informers. But it was on this disastrous blunder that the whole campaign was based. Ciano wanted war, and it helped him to get it, and it helped Mussolini to try to grab the success that he wanted in his competition with Hitler without worrying about the opposition of the military experts. These continued to put up opposition, thus providing Mussolini with a kind of alibi. They wanted no campaign, no offensive, because they knew the Italians were weak everywhere. In North Africa Graziani was dragged by the hair into an offensive that ended in disaster.

When Italy entered the Second World War Badoglio's advice amounted in substance to the maintenance of total immobility. The truth of the matter was that Italy should not have entered it at all. The Italians did so to get their share of the pickings, and from then on every military move by Mussolini was the result of improvisation and pique, not the outcome of considered appraisal by experts. On this particular occasion Mussolini had an expert: Visconti Prasca, a "rebel" against the General Staff, who regarded everything as simple, easy, and straightforward, and afterwards had the honesty not to take cover behind the shield of alleged Greek corruption. He pleads other extenuating circumstances, which we shall examine. Mussolini and Ciano's "party" —Visconti Prasca, Jacomoni, and to an extent also the hesitant Soddu—knew at heart that Greek corruption was not a card to be relied on. They used it as a propaganda weapon, not against the enemy, but against the Italian General Staff.

On the morning of October 17, as we saw from the entry in Ciano's diary, the three chiefs of staff held one of their regular meetings. Badoglio's perplexities were powerfully reinforced. Pricolo and Cavagnari rebelled against the decision taken in their absence at the Palazzo Venezia. Cavagnari insisted that three months were necessary for the transfer of three more divisions to Albania, and Pricolo announced that he would not be able to deploy his forces before the beginning of November. Moreover, before this meeting with his colleagues, Pricolo had rushed to see Badoglio "to ask for further clarification, particularly in relation to the possible requirements of the undertaking, the contribution to it that would be required from an air force which at that time was scattered in Belgium, Sicily, Sardinia, Libya, the Aegean, and East Africa, as well as in the territory of the peninsula. The answer I was always given was that it would be sufficient to reinforce the air units that were already in Albania, because the campaign would not require an excessive commitment of forces."[12]

At the meeting on October 17 Roatta, who, as mentioned, was acting as army chief of staff in the absence of Graziani, renewed his objections. Mussolini was at Terni, so Badoglio went to see Ciano, to whom he made the statement summarized in the latter's diary. Badoglio had decided to ask Mussolini for another meeting at the Palazzo Venezia at which Pricolo and Cavagnari might express their views and another attempt might be made to restrain the Duce. That same evening this buzz of activity came to the knowledge of Soddu, who had accompanied Mussolini to Terni. Soddu was to some extent committed to the Ciano-Jacomoni-

Visconti Prasca clique in favor of the attack on Greece, and did some maneuvering on his own. He got into contact with General Armellini with a view to sidetracking the request for another meeting at the Palazzo Venezia, and next day, October 18, he went to see Mussolini early in the morning.

After Soddu had said his piece Mussolini received Ciano, and the Duce's state of mind is recorded by his son-in-law in some significant phrases. "I went to see the Duce. In the antechamber I found Soddu, who had spoken to Badoglio, who says that if the Greek operation takes place, he will resign. I reported all this to the Duce, who was already in a very ill humor because of the Graziani affair. He had a violent outburst of anger and said he would go to Greece in person to witness the incredible shame of Italians who were afraid of the Greeks. He intends to march at all costs, and if Badoglio hands in his resignation, he will accept it on the spot. But not only did Badoglio not submit his resignation, he did not even repeat to Mussolini what he said yesterday to me. In fact the Duce said that Badoglio insisted only on a few days' postponement, at least two." What had happened? Once more the leading role had passed to the indecisive, Hamlet-like Badoglio. On the previous day he had been determined to speak plainly to the Duce, even at the cost of provoking a crisis, but now he suddenly became malleable and accommodating. Soddu played a part in bringing about this *volte-face,* that is certain. Armellini notes that Soddu went to see Badoglio "in a rage" after protesting that the marshal "never kept him informed of anything."

The undersecretary of war, who was committed to the campaign, probably emphasized the complications that would ensue from a too outspoken opposition to the project; and it seems likely that he may have raised the specter of treachery by Greek politicians and soldiers. It was all settled very quickly, however, for, as Faldella mentions, Armellini told Roatta at 9:20 A.M. that there would be no meeting at the Palazzo Venezia. At 11 A.M., when Mussolini received Badoglio, it was all over; the only thing he got from the Duce was a postponement of the declaration of war from October

26 to October 28. Thus, when the Duce in his speech at the Adriano Theater on February 23, 1941, boasted of the "absolute agreement of all the responsible military elements"—the phrase is not exactly grammatical in Italian though the idea is readily intelligible —there was a certain adroit impudence about the claim. This absolute agreement was in fact obtained with a great deal of difficulty and with many reservations. The only military leader who wholeheartedly approved of the project was Visconti Prasca.

The view that the meeting at the Palazzo Venezia was prevented by Soddu is shared by Pricolo, who writes: "I, too, heard from well-informed sources that it was General Soddu, in his capacity as deputy chief of the General Staff, who 'torpedoed' the meeting; he was unwilling to tolerate what he called 'superfluous and belated obstruction' of a decision made by Mussolini. How many persons were in command? There were other reports later according to which the head of the government, who was to meet Hitler at Florence on October 28 or 29, wanted to confront him with a *fait accompli*. In any case, there was no more to be done." Emilio Faldella points out in his book, however, that the Hitler-Mussolini meeting was decided on not before October 24. Mussolini certainly wanted to confront his troublesome ally with an accomplished fact, but the choice of date was the result of fortuitous circumstances, which alone caused it to coincide with the anniversary of the March on Rome. Thus it came about that, after all the celebrations that took place on that date in Italy during the twenty-year history of Fascism, it continues to be celebrated to the present day, not in Italy, but in Greece, in memory of an act of aggression that resulted in a grave and humiliating Italian defeat.

Mussolini's aspirations for secrecy, which in any case accorded ill with the violent anti-Greek press campaign, were vain, however. Politis, the Greek minister in Rome, telegraphed to his government on October 23: "According to information from military sources, the action against Greece will begin in the period between October 25 and 28." The Greek envoy was not only aware of the imminence of the operation, but also had wind of the hesitations that caused the date to be fixed and then postponed; and Psarouda, the Greek minister in Berne, informed his government that "according to news from Berlin, the attack on Greece is a question of days." The secret was no longer a secret, at any rate to those from whom it should have been kept.

On October 16, twelve days before the attack, Mussolini busied himself with a major factor in the military and political situation which should have been settled a long time before, and no doubt would have been if the war with Greece had had roots deeper than a dictator's pique. This was the attitude of Bulgaria. At the meeting on October 15 the possibility of Bulgarian intervention had been incidentally mentioned, though in all probability it constituted the essential condition for the success of the attack. Only if Greece had been fully engaged on the Bulgarian frontier and thus had had to fight simultaneously on two fronts would the weak Italian forces have been able to carry out the otherwise senseless project of an invasion in two phases, first of Epirus only and then of the whole country.

On October 16, Anfuso left for Sofia to hand to King Boris a letter from Mussolini which arrogantly stated: "I have decided to begin the settlement of accounts with Greece during this month of October. A historic opportunity is presented to you and to Bulgaria to fulfill the old and just aspiration for an outlet to the Aegean. In informing you of my decision I have no intention of influencing yours or of soliciting the co-operation of your armed forces. You will do what your conscience and your royal responsibilities and the interests of your people dictate."[13] The tone of the letter is characteristic. Mussolini claims the right to make war as his personal prerogative and speaks in the first person, ignoring Victor Emmanuel III; he does not even propose an alliance or an intervention based on concrete political or military factors.

In Bulgaria German influence counted for much more than Italian, and if the Italians had acted with German support King Boris would probably have fallen into line. But once more the jealous Mussolini wanted to act on his own account, and fired his broadside into the void. Anfuso noted that in conversation Boris was "rather evasive" and showed nervousness about the Turks. The royal reply, written in French, was handed to Ciano's *chef de cabinet* in a sealed envelope. It declined Mussolini's invitation. "You have indeed divined . . . the specially delicate situation of Bulgaria," it said. "As a result of the unfavorable circumstances which have prevented and delayed a sufficient rearmament of her army, and surrounded as she is by neighbors that you know, she is obliged to act with a great deal of circumspection and prudence without, however, renouncing her sacred rights and historic mission. For the above-mentioned reasons Bulgaria is forced to refrain from armed action."[14]

To Mussolini this was a bitter pill. Once more it was borne in on him how little "weight" he carried. He vented his rage on Boris. "These gutless royalties will never do anything," he said. "We shall manage without him. Visconti Prasca's march will be so rapid that it will attract the Greek forces from the north to Athens, unless they disintegrate and all go home."[15] Here Mussolini's amateurism reached one of its peaks. For all the adulatory obsequiousness that the times required, the military leaders had made some fundamental facts clear on October 15. Even the adventurous Visconti Prasca had put some limitations on the prospects of an easy triumph. The situation as seen by the military leaders was this: a limited operation was to be carried out with the forces available on October 28; this was to be developed later with the arrival of reinforcements. The chances of success were favored by the prospect of Bulgarian intervention and perhaps also by the disloyalty of some Greek generals.

But Bulgaria did not move, and at any rate at the beginning of the war there was no disloyalty by Greek generals. The Italian army was in a phase of demobilization. The staffs of the various services had serious doubts about the operation and were opposed to it. Germany did not want it. The secret was no secret to the Greeks, who had mobilized and greatly strengthened their defenses. But Mussolini raved about an advance "so rapid" as to smash the Greek troops stationed in the North. Among other things, in spite of Mondini's thorough and painstaking reports from Athens, the Italian General Staff acted as if it believed the attack was going to be a surprise. Pricolo says: "I should have liked, taking advantage of civil air line flights, to have had some aerial photographs taken of the border and the most important places suitable for revealing possible Greek troop movements, harbors, railway stations, etc., but I was prevented, because this might have risked nullifying the famous surprise. But I believe that from the end of September the Greeks were perfectly conversant with our plans."

Mussolini, then, was convinced that he had done everything that a Commander-in-Chief, a skillful strategist, could and should have done to ensure victory. All he had actually done was to send Visconti Prasca the malicious letter we have mentioned, which made him fear he might be replaced; the object of the letter, to use Ciano's phrase, was to "spur him over the obstacle." While Italy was on the point of taking the plunge into a war full of unknown quantities, and doing so in a state of unpreparedness that a military expert could not possibly ignore, Badoglio went shooting at Perugia on October 20. On the previous day Mussolini had gone to Rocca delle Caminate, his *buen retiro,* where he proposed to tackle a grave problem. As we know, his great aim was to inform Hitler of the attack when it could no longer be halted. But, inhibited by inferiority feelings that Hitler did not reciprocate, he wanted to find a third way, to inform him without informing him, with Machiavellian cunning.

"Mussolini has returned," Ciano noted on October 22. "He has drafted a letter to Hitler on the general situation. He also refers to the imminent operation in Greece, but he does not mention either the strength to be used or the date, because he fears that we might be stopped again. There are many signs to show that in Berlin they are not enthusiastic about our going to Athens. The date is now fixed for October 28. Pricolo reports that Badoglio has given orders for very moderate air action. The Duce is not in agreement. He wants to strike hard, because he hopes that the whole thing will collapse at the first blow. If too much time is left, if too much breathing space and time for reflection is left, the British, and perhaps the Turks, will come, and things will become protracted and difficult. The Duce is very resentful of Badoglio, whom he considers a barrier between himself and the troops. I have begun drafting the ultimatum which Grazzi will hand to Metaxas at 2 A.M. on October 28. It is of course a document that leaves no way out; either they accept occupation or they will be attacked."

It is curious to note from this passage that it was Badoglio who suggested restraint in the proposed initial air attack; Pricolo's hesitancy and pessimism have already been noted. On the eve of this new campaign the shifting of responsibilities between the service chiefs—in order to gain the maximum benefit in the event of victory and suffer the minimum of damage to their reputations in the event of defeat became frantic. The attitude towards the Germans remained a problem. It is strange that in a city in which secrets are usually very ill kept, Mackensen, the German ambassador, did not obtain information about what took place at the meeting at the Palazzo Venezia on October 15 and did not even suspect that it had been held. Mackensen had noted the Italian irritation at the German occupation of Rumania (Ciano had received "without comment" the message handed to him by Bismarck, the German chargé d'affaires, on the evening of October 10) and believed an attack on Greece to be imminent. But, so far as the actual decision was concerned, he was groping in the dark.

In a dispatch to the German Foreign Ministry on October 18 he said: "Powerful forces, including Count Ciano, are working for a solution of the Italo-Greek problem. It appears from information from a reliable source that with a view to accelerating the matter Count Ciano has summoned the governor [i.e., Jacomoni] and the commander of the armed forces in Albania to Rome to listen to their views. Both are known at the Palazzo Chigi to be in favor of action." Mackensen did not know that the most ardent advocate of action at that moment was Mussolini.

Also on October 18 Mackensen complained in a letter to Weizsäcker, the secretary of the Foreign Ministry, that Italy had been tactlessly treated over Rumania. Next day he telegraphed that he had learned that the beginning of the operation had been fixed for October 23, and that the objectives were Athens and Salonika.[16] On the same day he was received by Ciano, whom he asked outright whether action against Greece were imminent. Ciano "shrugged his shoulders, saying that Italy had complete liberty of action in relation to Greece, as the Führer had admitted to the Duce." Mackensen was in a delicate situation. He had to act in his country's interests, but had always to bear in mind that if he acted with insufficient discretion Mussolini might at any moment go over his head, communicate directly with Hitler, and obtain his recall.

To reinsure himself against these pitfalls, the ambassador, legitimately annoyed at Ciano's evasive and almost arrogant reply, sought instructions from his ministry, suggesting that a "friendly request" for information about the measures intended against Greece might be officially addressed to the Italian government. Hitler—the interpreter Schmidt describes him as having been "beside himself" and determined to prevent "the crazy enterprise"—decided that no "friendly request" should be made. He probably already had in mind a meeting with Mussolini in the course of the next few days (the meeting at Florence on October 28 was in fact proposed by Ribbentrop on October 25) and intended to clear up the matter for himself. Another warning came from Mackensen on October 24: "There is no doubt that Italy proposes to launch an action against Greece in the next few days. The Italian government has given me no information about its plans." Von Rintelen, the German military attaché, like Mackensen, knocked in vain at the Italian door in the hope of extracting the secret of the date of the attack. On October 29, when the die was cast, he wrote a bitter memorandum:

> Marshal Badoglio informed me on August 23 that Italy would take no action against Greece unless she were forced to by Greek or British action. . . . The crisis again became acute in the middle of October, when German troop movements towards Rumania became known. An intensification of military preparations against Greece has been noted since that time. . . . On October 23 General Roatta denied to me that there was any intention of undertaking military action against Greece, while on October 24 Marshal Badoglio told me that all preparations had been completed for an offensive against Greece in the event of British violation of her neutrality. Obviously the highest authorities had been given orders not to tell the German military authorities anything about the initiative that . . . was to be undertaken at the end of the month.

Though anticipating events, let me add for the sake of completeness that von Rintelen showed himself to be a good prophet in this memorandum. "Since two of the nine divisions in Albania have to cover the Yugoslav frontier," he wrote, "the Italian superiority is probably not sufficient to fulfill expectations of rapid success if the Greeks put up serious resistance."

That was the view of Visconti Prasca's foolish and reckless plan likely to be taken by any military expert. If this reticence towards the Germans, this desire to give them tit for tat, had been swiftly followed by a shatteringly successful offensive, it would probably be worth no more than a psychological footnote after the passage of so many years so crowded with events. But Mussolini's rearings and cavortings were the prelude to bitter humiliations. In order to act on their own account, the Italians refused to confide in the Germans, and then were forced to beg for their co-operation.

At Rocca delle Caminate, then, on October 19, Mussolini drafted the vaguely informative letter[17] intended to provide him with a clever alibi in relation to the Germans. Information about the attack on Greece was buried in a broad, panoramic survey of the politico-military situation. The Duce, who had met Hitler on October 4 on the Brenner, began by asking Hitler for clarification of the relations between France and the Axis, and he introduced Greece under the general heading of "British positions on the Continent." The positions from which the British were to be shifted were no less than the following: Portugal, Yugoslavia, Greece, Turkey, Egypt, and Switzerland. "As for Greece," Mussolini wrote, "I am determined to stop dilly-dallying and to act very soon. Greece is one of the strongholds of British naval strategy in the Mediterranean. A British King, a British political class, a people that is immature, but brought up to hate Italy. Greece has set about mobilizing her forces, and has put air and naval bases at the disposal of the British since May, as is shown by the documents that von Ribbentrop courteously sent me after the finds at Vitry la Charité; during the past few days British officers have practically taken possession of all the airfields in Greece. In short, Greece is in the Mediterranean what Norway was in the North Sea, and must not escape a similar fate. I believe that Turkey, another pawn in the British game, will not move, particularly if you increase your occupation troops in Rumania, as you certainly will. As for Egypt, the resumption of operations is subject to a huge task of logistic preparation, similar to that which you have had to undertake in preparation for the landing in Great Britain. At all events, I hope to carry out operations simultaneously on the Greek and Egyptian fronts."

Mussolini's attempt to be crafty in this document is so obvious as to be pathetic. He declares himself to be determined to act "very soon," but without mentioning the date of the attack, though this had been decided on. He discusses the position of Turkey, but without confessing the rebuff that followed his request for Bulgarian intervention. He avoids giving any details about the immediate and more long-term objectives of the campaign. He behaves, in fact, like a small boy who has to show a toy to another, bigger and stronger boy because he cannot do otherwise; but he does so half-heartedly and reluctantly, fearing all the time that the bigger boy will take it from him. On October 23—in other words, without hurrying, and very likely the delay was deliberate—Ciano sent the letter to Berlin in an envelope attached to a letter to Zamboni, the chargé d'affaires. Zamboni was instructed to see that it was submitted to the Führer immediately. But Hitler was not at his headquarters; he had left for Montoire and Hendaye for talks with Pétain and Franco (which was worrying to Mussolini, who was jealous of any rapprochement between Berlin and Paris).

So the letter could not be submitted to Hitler immediately. Zamboni informed the Foreign Ministry in a telegram sent at 11:00 P.M. on October 24 that he had "handed the Duce's letter to Secretary Weizsäcker, who assured me that it will be sent by special air courier tomorrow morning to the Führer, who is still in the occupied zone." When Ribbentrop telephoned Ciano that evening from a small station in France to tell him about the Führer's conversations and the proposed meeting between the two dictators in Italy, he was not yet aware of the letter and was in no hurry and suggested no definite date. (According to other sources, Hitler had received news of the letter on the twenty fourth, but this seems to be refuted by Zamboni's telegram.) But next day he telephoned again, suggesting that the meeting might take place on October 28 at Florence. So Hitler reached Florence too late, a few hours after the ultimatum had been delivered.

The only excuse for the German dilatoriness in intervening is that the German government and the German diplomatists in Rome, inured to Mussolini's indecision and changes of mind, did not really believe in his preparations and warlike announcements but expected the order to be followed by the inevitable counterorder. Sure enough, the counterorder duly came, but it merely canceled the operation against Corfu and postponed the attack by two days. There is no other explanation for the German failure to halt the operation if they wanted to halt it, as indeed they did. By this time its imminence was common knowledge. The Greek diplomatists, as we have seen, were very fully informed about it; Metaxas was expecting it (on October 25 he noted, with surprise, in his diary: "No Italian attack today," and on the twenty-sixth he added: "Not today either"). A note by Puntoni, the King's aide-de-camp, on October 26, is significant: "The Minister Aquarone came to Pisa. During a conversation we had he told me that everyone in Rome is talking about the operation against Greece, giving today as the date fixed for the beginning of the operations [this was the date fixed at the famous meeting]. That is why the Germans tell us nothing in advance about their intentions."

But the die was now cast, and even Badoglio, in spite of his perpetual vacillations, seemed to have been won over to the campaign, so much so that in a letter to De Vecchi he spoke of a "punitive expedition" against the Greeks, who "will get the treatment they deserve";[18] and at a meeting of chiefs and deputy chiefs of staff on October 24 he actually outlined ambitious plans for launching divisions in the direction of Salonika and expressed the view that there was little likelihood of a Greek counteroffensive. This is strange. Badoglio and Mussolini were by now on bad terms, and their attitudes towards the conduct of the war were certainly very different; the *fronde* of the chief of the General Staff flared up every now and then, but sometimes he actually created the impression of being more Ducist than the Duce. He relied on fifth column and political action, which even Ciano did not mention in his diary on the eve of the operation.

The marshal's defenders seize on this point. He was certainly a difficult man to fathom. He was an indecisive character who generally kept his foot on the brake but every now and then unexpectedly transferred it to the accelerator. But on October 24, when the meeting of chiefs and deputy chiefs of staff took place, he knew that Bulgaria was not going to move and that thus one of the essential conditions for the success of Contingency G was lacking. One final grain of sand was thrown into the works on October 26, but failed to bring them to a standstill. General Francesco Rossi, who was sent to Albania on a tour of inspection, reported that the weather was impossible. This eliminated another essential condition for the success of the attack, namely, massive air intervention. "Atmospheric conditions particularly adverse without expectation of early improvement," Rossi telegraphed. "Supply and movement extremely difficult. Conditions for air force prohibitive. In my opinion date for beginning of operations should be fixed by commander on the spot. Bad weather hampering unloading of ships." Roatta passed the telegram to Badoglio, who mentioned it to Mussolini. It made no difference. October 28 had been decided on, and October 28 it remained, particularly as Visconti Prasca, probably still obsessed with the fear of being replaced, had confirmed that he would move on October 28. The weather was vile, but the morale of the troops was "very high," and that was enough for him and *a fortiori* for the impatient Mussolini.

5. Unarmed Goliath

If any anxiety about forthcoming events was felt at the Palazzo Venezia, Jacomoni quickly dispelled it, and when he returned to his own lesser palazzo at Tirana he set about "creating the most favorable atmosphere for the rapid and victorious development of our military operations against Greece."[1] In a report dated October 19 he referred, this time in more concrete terms, to an attempt to corrupt the Greeks, but only as a possibility, an aspiration, and limited in any case to border outposts. "It having been reported to me that Greek officers serving along the frontier line have shown an interest in the Italian treatment of their Albanian colleagues, I have asked his Excellency General Visconti Prasca to intensify contacts between officers of the two armies, relying on possible aid and support for Greek soldiers favorable to our cause. Effective action in this field might facilitate the initial effort of our troops. I have therefore put at General Visconti's disposal a fund appropriate to this purpose."

This was obviously a minor, last-minute effort, quite distinct from all previous assumptions about Greek corruption, disloyalty, or prospective surrender. Jacomoni also organized groups of Albanian saboteurs, who were to infiltrate into Greek territory, destroy telegraph and telephone communications, eliminate guard posts, disarm gendarmes, create confusion by opening fire behind the enemy lines, assassinate enemy generals, and incite the population to rebel. These "commandos" performed no acts of sabotage, disarmed no gendarmes, did not open fire, and incited no one to revolt. They merely pocketed the cash. Altogether there were 250 of them, and they carried distinctive marks of identification "known only to our operational troops," who, however, never had the opportunity of identifying any of them.

The governor-general took an active interest in the organization of the incidents which were to serve as "justification for our lightning military intervention in Greece"; the word "lightning" accords ill with what happened later, and above all with the acute "anxiety" about the military prospects he professes to have mentioned on the eve of the meeting at the Palazzo Venezia on October 15. The phoney frontier incidents were to consist of the dropping on the Albanian side of the frontier by an unidentified aircraft (which of course was to be Italian) of manifestos calling on the Albanians to revolt against the Italians and make common cause with the British and the Greeks; Italian agents on Greek territory were to open fire on Italian frontier posts and on Albanians going peacefully about their business; a bomb was to be exploded in the governor-general's office at Porto Edda (Santi Quaranta) as the result of a plot organized by British and Greek agents; and there were to be a popular demonstration and a violent press campaign protesting at all these Greco-British acts of provocation. These incidents were to provide the *casus belli;* as Mussolini put it at the Palazzo Venezia, the object was to "put up a bit of smoke" and create "an occasion for lighting the fuse." "No one will believe it," the Duce admitted, "but for metaphysical reasons it will be possible to say that it was necessary to conclude the matter."

The date originally fixed for the incidents was October 24, but that was when the attack was going to take place on the twenty-sixth. When Ciano informed Jacomoni of the two-day postponement,[2] the incidents were postponed for two days too, and he arranged the timing in detail.[3] He ordered the explosion at Santi Quaranta for the evening of October 25, the sham attack on an Italian frontier post in the Koritsa area for the morning of the twenty-sixth, and the dropping of leaflets for dawn on the twenty-seventh. He had now docilely fallen into line again. He reported to Rome that there were signs of Greek demoralization, and said that it was the opinion of many that "if our initial blow is violent, a disintegration of the Greek forces will take place," and confirmed what we already know from other sources, namely that "Visconti Prasca believes he will be able to carry out his task with the resources already at his disposal and those which are on the way." In the performance stage-managed by Jacomoni even the choral note was not lacking. "I shall summon a plenary session of the Fascist Higher Corporate Council. . . . Thus I shall enable the representatives of the Albanian régime to make . . . a solemn demonstration of jubilation and faith in our military intervention in Greece."[4]

So far as the border incidents were concerned, everything for once went according to the Italian plan. On October 26 Stefani (the Italian official news agency) announced that early that morning a band of Greeks had attacked an Albanian frontier post near Koritsa with automatic weapons and hand grenades, that the attack had been repulsed, that six of the Greek assailants had been captured, and that the Albanian casualties were two dead and three wounded[5] (sacrificed on the altar of a pitiless *raison d'état,* if this part of the announcement was true). The statement added that three bombs had exploded in the governor-general's office at Santi Quaranta. Athens promptly denied that there was any truth in these reports; according to the official Greek news agency, Greek frontier posts had heard firing, but had had nothing to do with it. With a certain naïveté Metaxas noted in his diary that the alleged incidents might have had some foundation in fact: they might have been not between Albanians and Greeks, but between Albanians and Italians.[6] On the afternoon of the twenty-seventh Greek and Italian officers met in the area at the Greek request for the purpose of inquiring into the incidents and establishing the truth. As the Italian officers were not of senior rank and therefore not competent to make any decision, and as the Greek officers included the local area commander, the latter asked to meet an Italian officer of equivalent rank. Nothing ever came of this, as that night Grazzi delivered the Italian ultimatum and the war began. At 9 P.M. Ciano handed copies of the ultimatum to Bismarck, the German chargé d'affaires, and to the envoys of the "friendly" countries, Spain, Japan, and Hungary, who were "rather surprised"[7] by it.

While Jacomoni was thus putting the finishing touches to his masterpiece of organization, Visconti Prasca was giving the last turns of the screw to the military machine. The euphoria induced by the atmosphere of Rome having subsided after his return to Tirana, he must have had second thoughts about what he had said at the Palazzo Venezia, and in particular about that significant statement of his: "The sending of extra troops depends on how the operation develops, and they can be sent only to occupied Epirus," and that other statement, referring to the march on Athens: "During the initial period three mountain divisions" which "could be sent to the port of Arta in a single night" would be enough. That is to say, he had made the sending of reinforcements subject to the overrunning of Epirus and possession of the Greek ports of Preveza and Arta. Perhaps, when he came to think over the matter at Tirana, he was worried by the imprudence of those words. Later, complaining about the inadequacy and slowness of arrival of his reinforcements, he stated that on October 15 and in later verbal agreements with Roatta it had been agreed to send him three divisions at once. We know what Visconti Prasca said to Mussolini on October 15; at the Palazzo Venezia the others had wanted to send more divisions to Albania, but he had refused them. The first sign of a change of heart on his part appears in a message to the Army General Staff on October 17.

He asked that there should be sent to Albania "as quickly as possible" four groups of mountain artillery, a motorized division (i.e., the Trieste Division), and a mountain infantry division (i.e., the Modena Division).[8] These were to land at Durazzo in the order indicated. The Modena Division was to co-operate in Macedonia with the Bulgarians if they entered the war, and the other division was to take part in the advance towards Arta-Missolonghi. In other words, they were intended for operations that would follow those of the first phase, or were more ambitious than the first, or in any case different. Visconti Prasca also suggested that there should be "equipped and held ready for possible transfer to Albania" two mountain divisions, another infantry division, and three cavalry regiments. Bearing in mind the general trend of the meeting at the Palazzo Venezia, it seems clear that all this was to have been intended for the second phase, that of the general offensive. Nevertheless the impression is created that he was beginning to see more clearly from the clouds of his overconfidence and was trying to make amends.

His mistakes do not excuse other, no less grave mistakes that were made in Rome. But he showed himself a bad loser in trying to shift responsibility for his failures on to the General Staff on the grounds that it did not send him reinforcements quickly enough. He himself refused those reinforcements, and in any case disaster overtook him so quickly that even if the extra divisions had arrived with drums beating and flying colors, it would have taken place just the same.

On October 20 the General Staff issued a directive signed by Roatta summarizing the broad lines of Contingency G.[9] This called for an offensive in Epirus, "active defense" in the Koritsa zone, and the occupation of Corfu by the navy and the Bari Division. That was to be the first phase. "As soon as sufficient reinforcements are on the scene" there was to be an advance from Epirus towards Athens along the lines Arta-Lamia-Atalandhi-Tanagra and Agrinion-Missolonghi-Athens. "As soon as possible this movement will occupy the southern bank of the Corinth Canal (Perivali zone)." The reinforcements foreseen in Roatta's directive were as follows. Before the end of October, twelve 20 mm. anti-aircraft batteries, one anti-aircraft group of Skoda 75s consisting of three batteries, one anti-aircraft group of 75 CKs consisting of two batteries, two 75/46 anti-aircraft groups each consisting of two batteries, four groups of alpine "valley" artillery each consisting of two batteries, one battalion of M13 tanks. The Trieste Division would be sent by November 15 and a mountain division would arrive later. Also "one or two mountain divisions are being made ready, one or two alpine divisions, and one mobile division. Of these four divisions, in view of your message to the effect that three are necessary for the advance from Epirus to Athens, two will, if possible, be landed in the Gulf of Arta or otherwise in the nearest Albanian ports . . . the other two will be landed at Durazzo and Valona."

The High Command behaved generously: it gave Visconti Prasca more than he asked for, at any rate on paper. It kept strictly to his plans and assurances, and it respected his timetable. Had he stated that the divisions at his disposal were sufficient for the invasion of Epirus? Very well, the substantial part of his reinforcements would reach him in November, but he would have to open the attack with his nine divisions (eight organized and one "scratch" division, the Littoral Group). These final instructions from the General Staff were translated by Visconti Prasca into a more detailed operational directive. According to this, the objective was the "occupation of Epirus, that is, the area between the Pindus and the Arta River and the sea."[10] It must be admitted that in his directive Visconti Prasca plainly foresaw how the enemy would react, by adopting "a defensive poise in the Epirus . . . and possible offensive action in Macedonia to threaten the rear of the Italian forces operating in the Epirus sector." The campaign began with both sides' cards on the table: Papagos knew Visconti Prasca's intentions, and Visconti Prasca knew Papagos'. So the problem reduced itself to making an accurate assessment of the opposing forces and using one's own to the greatest possible effect. In this respect Visconti Prasca made unpardonable errors.

His plan was simple and, from the local point of view, rational (from a wider point of view an attack on Salonika would have been sounder, but this would have been inconsistent with the irredentist campaign for Tsamouria and a short-term operation was necessary to satisfy Mussolini's whims). Since "the Epirus area is like a big triangular pocket formed by the Pindus, the river

Arta, and the sea and the Albanian frontier, and is traversed from northwest to south by a single road (Borgo Tellini [now named Kakavia]—Perati—Kalpaki—Yanina—Philippias [northwest of Arta])," and since "Greek troops can enter and leave the area only at two points, from the east by the Metsovon Pass (coming from Thessaly and Macedonia) and from the south through Arta and Missolonghi (coming from Sicily and Athens)," Visconti Prasca proposed to seize these two points and thus close the pocket.

The eastern arm of the pincer movement was to be provided by the Julia Division, which was to occupy the Metsovon Pass, and the western arm by the mobile forces of the Littoral Group (two cavalry regiments and one regiment of grenadiers), whose objective was the town and harbor of Preveza. The main body of Visconti Prasca's troops, consisting of the Siena, Ferrara, and Centauro divisions, was to advance frontally towards the Kalamas and attack the Greek line of resistance at the key point of Kalpaki and advance in the direction of Yanina. Visconti Prasca's plan was sound in theory, but in practice was based on feet of clay, undervaluation of the enemy, overvaluation of his own troops, and a vague belief that the enemy would give in or collapse without a fight. Roatta also made concessions to this fantastic idea. He said in his directive that "in the event of exceptionally favorable developments (grave internal Greek collapse and consequent elimination of resistance worthy of note), the advance from Epirus on Athens and the Koritsa operations will be begun without awaiting the reinforcements that would normally be required."[11]

Visconti Prasca's plan left the whole Macedonian sector to the Parma Division. The Arezzo and Venezia divisions were left to guard the Yugoslav frontier, and the Piemonte Division was in reserve. On October 24, four days before the attack, two army corps commands were set up. General Carlo Rossi was put in command of the Tsamouria Army Corps, consisting of the Ferrara, Siena, and Centauro divisions, which were to be engaged in Epirus; and the XXVI Army Corps (including the Parma and Piemonte divisions, responsible for the Macedonian sector) was entrusted to General Gabriele Nasci.

The Julia Division, at the point of junction between the two army corps, remained under Visconti Prasca's direct command, as did the Venezia and Arezzo divisions. Thus six divisions, plus one in reserve, were to engage in an offensive campaign on a 150-mile front. The command structure was set up at the last moment, it was not run in with the lower formations, the divisions were not up to establishment in equipment or transport animals, and the supply services were not functioning yet. Units had with them a five-day supply of ammunition for rifles and automatic weapons, seventy days' supply of fuel for the motor vehicles, and forty days' other supplies. In the whole of Albania there were 140,000 men (not 140,000 combat troops), including carabinieri, frontier guards, Fascist militia legions, and Albanian volunteers. A winter war was started without adequate mountain equipment.

In Rome the High Command had second thoughts too. At a meeting on October 24 it was decided that the invasion of Corfu was practicable only if it were found to be possible to make landings "at at least two points," and the Cephalonia operation was postponed *sine die*. Thus some of the sound assumptions underlying the operation envisaged by Visconti Prasca were knocked away, and in this respect there was substance in his complaints. The High Command, belatedly impressed by the weakness of the Italian deployment, also ordered one of the divisions covering the Yugoslav frontier to be sent in reserve to the Macedonian sector (the Venezia Division in fact set out at once and reached the front on October 30, where it was promptly involved in fierce fighting). The High Command noted that stormy seas were hampering the sending of reinforcements, but Mussolini, still afraid that Hitler might put a spoke in the wheel of his war, was unshakable in his determination that it should begin on October 28.

While the patient men in gray-green of the Venezia Division marched towards a harsh destiny of which they still knew nothing, and Visconti Prasca's general headquarters worked feverishly issuing final orders to the "columns" that were to move on the night of October 28, while Mussolini prepared to receive Hitler at Florence, and the frontier incidents duly took place and the bombs duly exploded to provide a *casus belli,* huge gray clouds concealed the jagged Albanian peaks, the bad weather spread, and a long period of rain was forecast. The Greek and Italian troops swore and cursed. The opposing forces faced each other in the static fluidity of waiting armies.

One of the most burning and most important of the questions that face one in reconstructing the Albanian campaign is establishing the strength of the Italian and Greek forces that faced each other at dawn on October 28, 1940. It is not an easy task. For different but convergent reasons both Visconti Prasca, the Italian commander at the beginning of the campaign, and Papagos, the Greek commander-in-chief, had an interest in inflating the strength of the Italian forces and deflating that of the Greek: Visconti Prasca in order to diminish his responsibility and cover up the recklessness with which he engaged in an offensive with nil chances of success; and Papagos in order to make the most of his generalship and the valor of his troops. The convergence of these two attitudes has led to the blame for the Italian disasters being attributed not to political and military leaders who were either reckless or pusillanimous, but to the Italian troops, who in spite of everything fought well and did what was possible to make good the fearful errors made in Rome and Tirana.

By a combination of circumstances that cannot be called inevitable, the operation began without the advantage of surprise, without massive air support, without Bulgarian intervention, and without any collapse of the Greek army from treachery within. All these things, though with curious ups and downs and periods of forgetfulness, had, as we have repeatedly indicated, played their part in expectations before the war began, and one after the other they collapsed. But now matters were no longer in the hands of diplomatists, intriguers, or spies; what now counted was the voice of arms. The Italians were about to take the plunge into territory which the enemy knew much better, where he was waiting for them, fully informed of their intentions. Behind him he had friendly territory, lines of communication which, though difficult, were far better than the void of the back areas in Albania, separated from Italy by sea lanes on which the British lay in wait. In the air, however, the Italians were distinctly the stronger, but the bad weather deprived them of this advantage. Meanwhile demobilization was taking place in Italy.

Let us now take a somewhat more detailed look at the disposition of Italian units from the coast to the point where the Greek and Yugoslav frontiers meet at Lake Prespa. On the extreme southwestern flank there was the Littoral Group, commanded by General Carlo Rivolta. It included the 3rd Grenadier Regiment (3,082 men and four pieces of artillery), and the 2nd Cavalry Regiment, consisting of drafts from the Aosta and Milano regiments (1,741 men), as well as a group of 105/28s, another of 77/13s "borrowed" from the Parma Division, two mule-drawn batteries of 65/17s, and a detachment of a few hundred Albanian volunteers. Next in the line came the Siena Division, under the command of General Gualtiero Gabutti, with 9,200 men and about fifty guns, and then the Ferrara Division, with 12,785 men, about sixty guns, and an auxiliary force of 3,500 Albanian volunteers. The Centauro Division, in the second line behind the Ferrara, had 163 light tanks (not all immediately serviceable), 4,037 men, twenty-four pieces of artillery and twenty-four light anti-tank and anti-aircraft weapons. The Siena Division was reinforced by a cavalry regiment, less a detachment lent to the Ferrara Division. A legion of Blackshirts was also attached to the latter.

The nub of the deployment was the strong Julia Division, which had 10,800 men and twenty guns. The forces allotted to the Epirus offensive totaled 55,000 men, 163 tanks, 268 pieces of artillery, sixteen 47/32 anti-tank guns, thirty-two 20 mm. light anti-aircraft guns. In the Koritsa zone the Parma Division in the front line consisted of 12,000 men, sixty field guns, four anti-tank guns, and eight anti-aircraft guns. The Piemonte Division (which, like the Venezia, was initially in the second line but was moved into the first almost at once) had 9,300 men, thirty-two field guns, four anti-tank guns, and eight 20 mm. anti-aircraft guns; the Venezia consisted of 10,000 men, with five groups of artillery. The Arezzo Division (mountain infantry), which was facing Yugoslavia, consisted of 12,000 men (including two Albanian battalions) and three groups of artillery, or thirty-two guns.

Altogether 87,000 men were deployed against Greece, while 12,000 were left on the Yugoslav frontier, or a total of eighty-four battalions and 686 guns, including those at the disposal of the High Command and the army corps commands. Approximately one hundred thousand men with their backs to the sea were about to invade a nation which was on the alert, had already mobilized and was still rapidly mobilizing, had been insulted and provoked, and was able to raise eighteen divisions. In Epirus the Greeks had deployed their 8th Division, reinforced by a brigade of infantry and artillery. They had three reinforced battalions between Mount Smolikas and Mount Grammos (Pindus zone), and between Mount Grammos and Lake Prespa they had the 9th Division and the 4th Brigade. Seven battalions of infantry were in the second line.

Visconti Prasca, with little charity to his country but great love of himself, states in his book that on October 28 "the Italian mobile forces deployed on the Greek front were more than double those deployed by the Greeks." This reckless statement is refuted by various (and therefore the more credible) Greek sources. The *Military History of Greece,* published by the Greek General Staff, states that on October 28 there were four first-line Greek divisions against six Italian (this calculation obviously includes the independent units), while on November 14 there were seven divisions against ten Italian, on November 30 eleven divisions against fifteen Italian, on December 15 thirteen against seventeen Italian, while not until January 15 were thirteen Greek divisions opposed by twenty-five Italian, thus reaching (according to this Greek source, though it is stoutly denied by others) the odds of two to one in the Italian favor that Visconti Prasca claims to have existed at the outset. But if one consults another authoritative Greek source, the monumental *Italian-Greek Conflict,* also published by the Greek General Staff, it appears that the front-line forces were even more equally balanced, and that in the Koritsa zone the Greeks were distinctly superior in strength at the outset. And that was the chief reason for the way the fighting went. I translate literally:

The opposing forces in the front line immediately up against the frontier were: in Epirus, against fifteen battalions, a reconnaissance unit and sixteen and a half batteries, of which one was a heavy battery, of the (Greek) 8th Division, there were twenty-two battalions, two reconnaissance units, three cavalry regiments, sixty-one battalions, eighteen of which were heavy batteries, and ninety tanks of the Tsamouria Army Corps; in western Macedonia against twenty-two (Greek) battalions there were three reconnaissance units, twenty-two and a half batteries, seven of them heavy, of the Western Macedonia Army Corps, there were seventeen Italian battalions, an Albanian detachment, twenty-four batteries, five of them heavy, and ten tanks of the XXVI Army Corps. In the Pindus, against two of our battalions, a mixed formation and one and a half batteries, there were five battalions, six batteries, and a squadron of cavalry attached to the Julia Alpine Division. . . . A comparison of these forces shows that in western Macedonia the Greek forces had a certain superiority over the Italian. The Koritsa-Florina-Salonika area was vital to Greece, and the Greek command was greatly concerned about its defense. . . . The Greek advantage in the northwest Macedonia section was increased by the existence of substantial defense works. In the Pindus zone the Italian superiority was great, both in infantry and in artillery, in the proportion of about two to one in the former and four to one in the latter. In the Epirus zone the superiority of the Italian forces was slight in infantry, crushing in artillery. The presence of ninety tanks greatly increased the strength of the Italian deployment.

We shall discuss these estimates again in a moment. Meanwhile
it is clear that the Italian forces, contained in the closed vessel of
Albania—in contrast to the Greeks, who were in a vessel with easy
communications to western Macedonia, where large forces were
stationed—began operations in conditions of numerical inferiority
on a broad sector of the front. It will be noticed that according to
the Greeks the number of the Italian battalions was considerably
fewer than the eighty-four which were in Albania; the explanation
is that on October 28 three Italian divisions (the Piemonte, the
Arezzo, and the Venezia) were not in the front line. The Venezia
and the Piemonte were thrown in almost immediately, but as soon
as it became clear that Bulgaria was not going to intervene the
Greeks brought up massive reinforcements too. But, while the
Italians had no more reserves available once they had thrown in
the Arezzo Division, the Greeks still had substantial forces to
draw on in the interior of the country and near the Bulgarian
border. And included in the eighty-four battalions were six
Albanian battalions, two garrison battalions, and six mobile territorial battalions of slight or no utility.

The Italian army was of the old type, but so was the Greek. It
was relatively rich only in light arms (Manlicher 6.5 and Mauser
7.92 rifles, Hotchkiss 6.5 light machine guns, St. Etienne and
Schwerzlose 7.92 machine guns, and Brandt 81 mortars); it was
deficient in tank and armored car units, weak in artillery, had
little motor transport, and what there was had been scraped together as best it could. The Greek soldier, like the Italian, is frugal,
not highly disciplined, patient; he fights well, particularly for a
cause that is close to him—his country, his family, his home. He
has a deep sense of injustice, to which he reacts with tenacity and
violence. The fighting spirit, the state of spiritual tension that
Visconti Prasca attributed to Italy's troops, was in fact widespread
on the other side, and it was natural that it should be so.

In some respects the poor Greek army was the more solid. The
"triple" Greek division, consisting, that is to say, of three infantry
regiments, was by that very fact more substantial than the Italian

"double" division, consisting of two regiments. A legion of Black-shirts, consisting of up to two battalions, was normally included in an Italian division, and this brought its average strength up to from six to eight infantry battalions, compared with the nine battalions of a Greek division. But the Blackshirt legions were summarily trained and lightly armed, with the result that their effectiveness was considered equivalent to that of a single infantry battalion. The Italian division had a distinct advantage in mortars —six of 81 mm. and fifty-four of 45 mm. against the four 81 mm. Brandt mortars used by the Greeks, though the latter were excellent and the men who used them were admirably trained. But it had half as many machine guns in comparison with the Greeks and fewer light machine guns. In artillery Greek and Italian divisions were more or less equally matched: each had nine batteries. Italy, which at the time was absurdly reducing the number of divisions it held ready for employment on national territory from forty to twenty, began the war on Greece with nine weak divisions.

The General Staff knew very well that they were weak. The innovation of the "double" division was "due more than anything else to the usual desire to bluff (increasing the number of divisions by one third by forming new divisions out of the third regiments set free)." The writer of those lines was Roatta, and he wrote them with the strange, critical contemptuousness characteristic of the Italian military leaders who, for some mysterious reasons, felt themselves to be totally devoid of responsibility for the defects of the army under their command, though if it had gained victories, it would have brought them honors, promotions, and financial rewards (which, incredible to relate, they sometimes managed to gain even after defeats). Mountain divisions normally differed from infantry divisions in that they did not automatically include a legion of Fascist militia, they had many more pack animals, and their artillery was entirely mule-drawn.

The typical Italian division had no anti-aircraft defense worthy of the name and, in spite of its strength of 10,000 men or more, its motor transport section consisted of twenty-four vehicles. Con-

sequently, in practice it was able to move only on foot, and so was
slow and unmaneuverable. To cope with this limited mobility of
the infantry, in 1941 the Army General Staff had a brilliant idea;
it laid down that infantry divisions must be trained to be able to
march twenty-five miles a day and 100 miles in five days. "This
order was conscientiously carried out and the desired result obtained," Roatta noted with satisfaction. But even if the Italian
division normally moved on foot, it could not be supplied on
foot. On October 28 Italian troops in Albania were short of lorries, and the back areas were short of them too. Those available
were few and old.

In October, on the eve of the attack, the War Ministry sent
Colonel Amioni, an expert, to Albania, and he estimated the requirements at 1,750 lorries. "Up to November 17 only 107 lorries
had been landed in Albania," Visconti Prasca complained, with
every justification. By one of those bureaucratic absurdities that
will forever remain beyond the range of human understanding, a
motor transport hire firm had sent back to them from Bari to Turin
a number of Fiat 666 lorries that had actually been on the way to
Albania. The order came from the War Ministry. But did Visconti
Prasca not know these things when he stated on October 15 that
the operation against Epirus "has been prepared down to the most
minute details and is as perfect as is humanly possible"?

There were two ways in which the Italians were superior. They
had armored formations and a crushing advantage in the air. The
divisions rather pompously called armored divisions—such as the
Centauro, for instance—consisted of a regiment of motorized
Bersaglieri, a three-battalion regiment of tanks (light three-tonners
armed with two 8 mm. machine guns), and a regiment of motorized artillery. They were not remotely to be compared with the
phalanxes of steel and fire with which first the Germans and then
the British, Americans, and Russians fought in Europe and Africa.
But they still had advantages as compared with the "king of battles," the infantryman, whose reign was actually over, though the
Italian General Staff seemed not to have noticed the fact.

These "sardine-tin" type tanks had a certain penetrative power if used on suitable terrain and in the right season. They were used in an area in which the rain caused the few roads that existed to be churned into a sea of mud, and they turned out to be of little use or none at all. On a number of occasions men of the Centauro Division fought on foot like infantrymen in the frantic effort to check the Greek counteroffensive.

The Italians had air supremacy. On about November 10—there were some additions between October 28 and the first few days of November, but not substantial ones—their air strength in Albania was as follows: eight bomber squadrons equipped with thirty-one S79s and twenty-four S81s; nine fighter squadrons equipped with forty-seven G50s, forty-six CR42s and fourteen CR32s; two reconnaissance squadrons with twenty-five Ro.37s. The fourth flotilla at Brindisi consisted of sixteen bomber squadrons with sixty Cant.Z1007bs, eighteen S81s, eighteen BR20s and twenty-three Cant.Z506s; two squadrons of dive bombers equipped with twenty German Ju.87s; four fighter squadrons with twelve Macchi 200s, thirty-three G50s and nine CR32s. There were about 400 aircraft in all, suffering from the congenital diseases of the Italian air force, the excessive variety of types, the age and inadequacy of some types (e.g., the CR32), and the limited efficiency of others. But on the whole, in comparison with a weak and even more ramshackle enemy force, the Italians' could be considered strong.

The enemy force, according to Greek sources, consisted of thirty-eight fighters, nine light bombers, eighteen heavy bombers, and fifty aircraft for reconnaissance and co-operation with the ground troops. These were the aircraft immediately available for action; the remainder were in the workshops. General Santoro quotes rather different figures: thirty-nine bombers, forty-four fighters, and sixty-six reconnaissance aircraft, but the discrepancy undoubtedly results from the fact that not all the aircraft theoretically available were immediately serviceable. The Greek aircraft were of British, French, and Polish types, and most were of little military value. In fact the Greek air force never gave the Italian troops serious trouble, and even when RAF units came to the

assistance of the Greeks, the Italians preserved their air superiority.

We have now seen what the opposing forces were, and we know
the Italian plans. The Greek operational plan, dated September
16—which shows how foreseeable the Italian moves were—was
extremely simple. Papagos organized his defense on two lines:
Line A, the closest to the frontier, followed the Kalamas River,
Elea (Kalpaki), Mount Gamela, Mount Smolikas, Mount Stavros,
Mount Psoriaka, Mount Flatsata, Mount Varba, and Laimos. Line
B followed the Arachthos River (referred to as the Arta River in
Visconti Prasca's dispositions), Metsovon, Mount Orliakas, the
Venetikos River, the curve of the river Aliakhmon, the Portas
Pass, the Hadovas Corridor, Mount Vermion and Kaimaktsalan.

> The task of the forces in western Macedonia [the Greek High
> Command declared] consists in protecting the defense positions of
> Line A and, if possible, gaining new positions in Albanian territory
> which will be used as a platform for launching operations against
> the plateau of Koritsa after the concentration of the necessary re-
> sources. The task of the forces in Epirus is to ensure at all costs the
> protection of the zone's communications, which are essential for
> the influx of reinforcements. In the battle to stop the enemy on Line
> A positions a wearing down of the forces in Epirus such as would
> imperil the achievement of their principal objective, i.e., covering
> and securing the lines of communication, must be avoided. . . .
> The destruction or excessive weakening of these forces must be
> avoided even at the cost of territorial losses. Therefore the opera-
> tions of the forces in Epirus must follow the principle of elastic de-
> fense. The directives given to the commanders in the field are that
> they must stop the enemy advance either on Line A, according to
> circumstances, or in positions further to the rear, or finally on Line
> B, the last line of defense.

Those are the circumstances in which the Greek campaign was
launched.

6. "So It's War"

On October 23 the Italian minister in Athens, Emanuele Grazzi, and the military attaché, Colonel Luigi Mondini, did not yet know that war was imminent. They were naturally aware of the change of atmosphere and knew what was in the wind. But no one asked them to corroborate the reassuring information on the basis of which the Italian Foreign Minister, and Badoglio and Soddu, seemed to think that Greece was about to drop into the Italian lap like a ripe plum. It was only thanks to indirect hints that Grazzi was able to gain clues to what was going on on the other side of the wall behind which the Italian diplomatic mission was kept. On about October 20, for instance, Curzio Malaparte, who belonged to Ciano's snobbish-bellicose set and was in Greece on a journalistic mission, called on Grazzi and, in a semiserious tone in perfect harmony with the semiserious manner in which Ciano dealt with politics, the fate of nations and the lives of the Italian soldiers, told him that the Foreign Minister had said to him: "Tell Grazzi he can write what he likes, I'm going to make war on Greece all the same."[1] Malaparte also told him that Ciano was thinking of making his triumphant entry into Greek territory at the head of the Albanian "bands" recruited by Jacomoni.

On the afternoon of October 23, which was a Thursday, Mondini, on telegraphic instructions from Rome, went to Athens airport to meet a military intelligence officer who was taking urgent dispatches to De Vecchi, the Governor of the Aegean.[2] This officer told Mondini that war might break out at any moment from October 26 onwards, and he added that, according to General Staff information, Bulgaria was going to attack simultaneously and that some representative Greeks had been "bought." De Vecchi confided to Mondini a year later that this officer had brought him a letter from a high military personality (this turned out to be Badoglio) foreseeing Bulgarian intervention and a Greek collapse as a result of treachery.

Events came thick and fast, and they did so in a strange atmosphere of reticence that entitled the Greeks to attribute to Italy all kinds of Machiavellian cunning, though it was merely a result of the personal politics and antagonisms that prevailed inside the Fascist government machine. The Italian attack on Greece was an open secret, the whole world was talking about it, but in the meantime lack of instructions and reliable information put the Italian representatives in Athens in an extremely embarrassing position. The legation was asked to send one of its members to Rome "for urgent secret instructions" but, the Ala Littoria air service being interrupted (another clear sign of the imminence of action), Grazzi was unable to send anyone. Then the arrival of a "courier" from Rome by special aircraft was announced, but even the emissary of the Palazzo Chigi failed to make the trip.

The Stefani agency issued its statements about the frontier incidents, but meanwhile the National Theater in Athens put on a special performance of *Madama Butterfly*. Giacomo Puccini's son, accompanied by his wife, arrived in Athens as an honored guest of the Greek government; Bottai, the Minister of Education, was evidently in the dark about Ciano's plans and failed to cancel this official visit by a distinguished personality. Celebrations were organized, and invitations were issued for a solemn reception to be held at the Italian legation on the evening of October 26. In accordance with Greek custom, the guests were to gather very late, at about midnight, after the performance, which the royal family and Metaxas were expected to attend. In spite of the chilly atmosphere that now surrounded the Italian colony in Athens, this program was carried out but the royal family and Metaxas did not attend the reception. Colonel Mondini has described how, while the guests were talking in the legation rooms—the tables were decorated with intertwined Greek and Italian flags and the words "Long Live Greece" were written on a cake—long telegrams in cipher started arriving from Rome with the text of the ultimatum. The nervousness of the legation staff unconsciously communicated itself to the guests; the secretaries engaged in deciphering the dispatch circulated among the guests in order not to create alarm but, in spite of the mask of impassiveness they assumed, their pallor no doubt betrayed their agitation.

This coincidence—the reception in progress during the transcription of the ultimatum—might seem a masterpiece of malicious cunning, though it was merely a coincidence. On top of it, by some mischance, the first part of the dispatch, stating the date and time of the attack, was transcribed last, with the result that poor Grazzi did not know until 5 A.M. whether he would have the disagreeable task of presenting the declaration of war while the reception was still in progress, or whether he would have to hand it to a Prime Minister to whom he had said good-by as an honored guest only a short time previously. However, the Italian minister was instructed to call on Metaxas at 3 A.M. on October 28 and inform him that he would have to accept the Italian demands by 6 A.M.[3]

On the morning of Sunday, the twenty-seventh—it was one of those superb warm autumn days in Athens—Papagos sent for Mondini to deny that the Greeks had been in any way involved in the shooting at Koritsa or the bomb explosions at Santi Quaranta. The Greek commander-in-chief knew well enough that these incidents were the prelude to an attack. He took the opportunity to point out to the Italian military attaché that the frontier was guarded "yard by yard" and was ironic at the expense of the Stefani agency's claim that the perpetrators were Greek or British agents. As their identity was unknown and they had not been caught yet, by what miracle were the Italians aware of their nationality?

On that same Sunday the anniversary of the March on Rome was celebrated at the Casa d'Italia in Athens one day in advance. Mondini recalls that the imminence of the attack was in the air

and, for all their acclamations of the Duce and their shouts of
a noi, the Italians in Athens were worried at the prospect ahead
of them. Many of these men had Italian passports, and frequently
were very Italian and very Fascist by sentiment, but by birth and
education they were Greek. Some of them could speak Italian
only haltingly, and their friends and interests were all in Greece.
What they had to look forward to now was the internment camp,
harsh treatment by the authorities, coolness or aversion on the
part of their friends, a period of hardship and deprivation of indeterminate length. They had good reason to be pensive. In Rome,
however, there was one man who was deliriously happy. Galeazzo
Ciano had got his war.

John Metaxas lived in a two-story villa at Kifisia, the well-to-do
quarter of Athens, which in the still very provincial, "oriental,"
penurious, and self-contained Athens of a quarter of a century ago
stood out more than it does today. It is full of pine trees, and its
fresh air, quiet, and atmosphere of prosperity mark it off from
most of the rest of the hot, noisy Greek capital. From Kifisia the
dictator went daily to the Prime Minister's office, escorted by a
coach full of police, but he was not a very ostentatious dictator,
as was shown, among other things, by his villa, situated in the
middle of a small garden at the junction of two streets, and built
in a style vaguely suggesting the Byzantine but with ordinary
middle-class furniture. By the standards of the Villa Torlonia* it
was very modest indeed.

Right at the corner there was an iron gate. At night the area
surrounding the villa was floodlit, and patrolled by guards. For
the unwelcome task of delivering the ultimatum Grazzi used
Mondini's car; the legation's Greek chauffeur had been allowed to
go home, so Mondini took the wheel. Grazzi and Mondini were
accompanied by the interpreter De Santo. They left the legation
at 2:30 A.M. "The sky was clear and calm, dotted with the
myriads of stars that make the sky of Attica so marvelous, and the
temperature was mild," Mondini has recorded. Up on the Albanian

* Mussolini's villa in Rome.

frontier the troops were waiting for the order to move, and a tense eve-of-battle atmosphere prevailed behind the lines. Perhaps Visconti Prasca was asleep, like the Prince de Condé on the eve of the Battle of Rocroi, but fate had no victory in store for him.

Mondini's car, with its diplomatic corps number plate and a small Italian flag on the radiator, drew up outside Metaxas' villa at 2:45 A.M. De Santo asked the guard commander, one Travlos, to inform the Prime Minister that the Italian minister wished to see him to deliver a highly important message.[4] This Travlos, who cannot have been exactly an eagle, rang a bell and then telephoned from his sentry box to another security guard inside the villa, and then spoke to Metaxas, who was awoken from sleep. He told him (in the artificial light he had probably mistaken the green of the Italian tricolor for the blue of the French) that the French minister wanted to see him. Metaxas, a man of the old style, used to sleep in a nightshirt. He was not in good health, and on the previous day had been informed of the unreassuring results of some analyses ordered by his doctor.

He slipped on a dark dressing gown with a pattern of little white flowers, put on his slippers, and went down to the door himself; a small, sad little man who had lived for weeks and months in expectation of what was now about to happen. Though physically at the end of his tether, mentally he was still alert. Greek statesmen are very unassuming and approachable in their ways, and to this day it is incomparably easier to secure an interview with a minister in Athens than with a minister in Rome. The dictator still preserved traces of these ways, the more so as he was a dictator of relatively recent date. He had not been given any title on the pattern of those that distinguished the Duce, the Führer, the Caudillo, the Conducator, etc. He appeared on the threshold of the service entrance.

"*Oh, monsieur le ministre, comment allez-vous?*" he exclaimed when he saw Grazzi, and took him to a small room on the ground floor full of mass-produced furniture and petty bourgeois trinkets. They sat down facing each other, Metaxas on a cretonne-covered couch and Grazzi on a leather armchair. Grazzi announced in

French that his government had charged him with handing over an urgent note, and he handed Metaxas a copy of the ultimatum. Metaxas slowly started reading the document—which was in French—shaking his head every now and then in token of denial. The note repeated the familiar complaints that the Greek government had transgressed the obligations of neutrality and openly supported the British. It then referred to numerous violations of neutrality—though the Italian authorities had never succeeded in substantiating any of their previous allegations of these—and spoke of provocations against Albania, which were truly spun out of thin air.

"All this," the note concluded, "cannot be further tolerated by Italy. . . . The Italian government has therefore decided to ask the Greek government, as a guarantee of Greek neutrality and of Italian security, for permission to occupy some strategic points on Greek territory for the duration of the present conflict with Great Britain. The Italian government asks the Greek government not to oppose such occupation and not to put obstacles in the way of the free passage of the troops that are to carry out this task. These troops do not come as enemies to the Greek people, and by the occupation of some strategic points, dictated by contingent and purely defensive necessities, the Italian government in no way intends to prejudice the sovereignty and independence of Greece. The Italian government asks the Greek government immediately to give the orders necessary to enable this occupation to take place in a peaceful manner. Should Italian troops meet with resistance, such resistance would be broken by the force of arms, and the Greek government would assume the responsibility for the consequences that would ensue."

The note was presented at 3 A.M. and the ultimatum expired at 6 A.M. To some extent it followed the style of the German ultimatum to Norway; in practice it permitted no alternative and allowed no time for reflection. The difference, however, was that the ultimatum to Norway was followed by one of the most consummate and deadly examples of the Blitzkrieg known to military history, while the necessary consequence of the Italian ultimatum was an operation that wavered between the concept of a *coup de main* and a large-scale campaign, with no trace whatever of any *Blitz*. Metaxas' hands trembled slightly as he read the document, and behind his slightly misted spectacles his eyes were wet with tears. Like other men who in some respects are hard and even cruel, Metaxas' emotions were easily roused, and in this instance he had ample justification. Grazzi was shaken too. He was aware of the injustice—and, perhaps even worse, the folly—of the cause of which he was compelled to be the spokesman, and, if he had known the full background and circumstances in which this winter war on a mountainous frontier was being undertaken, he would have been even more shaken.

Metaxas raised his eyes from the sheet of paper. *"Alors, c'est la guerre,"* he said. Grazzi, knowing that he was lying, and lying badly, replied that this was not so, that Greece could accept the Italian terms and thus avoid war. Metaxas replied that in the space of three hours it would be impossible to awaken the King, summon the Minister of Defense, Papagos, and get orders not to put up resistance to the most distant garrisons and units. Grazzi, still more embarrassed, insisted, and tried to argue that, though difficult, it was not impossible. "What are the strategic points that Italy wishes to occupy?" Metaxas then asked, and with a disconsolate gesture Grazzi had to admit that he did not know. He might have added, without in any way conflicting with the truth, that Rome did not know either. This was a war of pique and prestige.

"So you see that it is war, then," Metaxas said. Grazzi again protested weakly, and added that he would wait at the legation until 6 A.M. for a possible acceptance of the Italian terms, and with that the conversation ended. According to Grazzi's story, which there is no reason to doubt, the famous *ochi* ("no") with which Metaxas was believed to have replied to the ultimatum—it became a proud Greek slogan—was never specifically said, though Metaxas made his meaning plain enough. The ultimatum made "no" the inevitable answer, as it was intended to. This was the last thing that went according to the Italian plan.

Metaxas accompanied Grazzi to the garden door. *"Vous êtes les plus forts,"* were his parting words. Grazzi waited at the legation for a possible Greek reply, as he said he would, though he knew it would not come and that he was being unnecessarily scrupulous. Metaxas' diary has this laconic entry for Monday, October 28, 1940: "I was awakened at 3 A.M. It was Travlos. Grazzi had come to see me. War! I sent immediately for Nikoloudis and Mavroudis. I reported to the King. I called on Palairet and asked for British help. I summoned a cabinet meeting for five o'clock. Everyone confident, even Mavroudis. Everyone except Kirou. The King. Surveyed the situation with him. Incredible fanaticism of the people. Fighting on the Epirus frontier. Bombings. Sirens. We are beginning, and are getting busy. May God help us." An eyewitness, Ambrosios Tsifou, has left an account of that dawn cabinet meeting in Athens.[5] Tsifou was a close colleague of Metaxas', and his story may have been slightly "touched up" here and there in order to show Metaxas in as favorable a light as possible, but there is no doubt of its substantial correctness. I quote the most important passages:

As soon as the telephone woke me at 4 A.M. on October 28, I knew, even before lifting the receiver, that war had broken out. I was told to go immediately to the Prime Minister's office. As soon as I reached the entrance I was told by the doorkeepers that the Italian minister had just handed the Prime Minister an ultimatum, which he had rejected, and that the Italian army was already on the march towards our frontiers. When I entered the Prime Minister's office, the first of the ministers to arrive, I found him seated in an armchair, looking like a man from whose back an enormous burden had been lifted, a man who felt he had done his duty to his country and to himself. Meanwhile the others arrived. In a sepulchral silence, while agitation was written on the faces of all the others, the Prime Minister said that at 3 A.M. he had been told on the telephone that the French ambassador wished to see him. He had replied that he would receive him there and then, at his house at Kifisia. A few minutes later he opened the door, as he was, in his dressing gown, and was greatly surprised to find himself faced, not with the French ambassador, but with Grazzi. He realized at once what it was about. Grazzi, without explanation but with a great deal of agitation, handed him the envelope containing the ultimatum, which asked that Italian troops should be allowed to occupy some strategic positions on Greek territory until the end of the war. These positions were not specified. Among other things, the duration of the ultimatum was three hours, or until 6 A.M., which allowed no time for action whatever, even if it had been desired to accept the terms. . . .

As soon as Grazzi left, Metaxas telephoned the King and ordered that the Cabinet should be called immediately. On the way he stopped —by now it was 3:30 A.M.—at the British embassy and informed Ambassador Palairet what had happened, insisting that he should send a telegram immediately to Admiral Cunningham at Alexandria, asking him to send the British fleet full steam ahead to Greek waters in order to prevent the Italian fleet from taking action in regard to Corfu or the Ionian islands or making any attempt to land in the Peloponnese. Sir Michael Palairet wanted to send a telegram in cipher, but Metaxas insisted on its being *en clair,* so that no time should be lost in deciphering it. He also dictated a warm telegram to Churchill asking for immediate aid, particularly air aid. After telling us this Metaxas said: "The interests of the Axis are joint interests, and sooner or later we shall have to fight Germany too. So it is quite likely that we may have temporarily to abandon Epirus and Macedonia, and perhaps Athens itself and our homes and everything that we can leave temporarily, and withdraw to the Peloponnese or Crete. So the war we are facing today is a war only for honor. . . . The outcome of the world war will not be decided in the Balkans. . . ." The cabinet meeting was very brief, it lasted for only a quarter of an hour. Meanwhile the King arrived from Tatoi. A meeting of military leaders followed. . . . The capital had already assumed its wartime aspect and everyone was busy blacking out windows. The streets were full of military vehicles and motorcycles, the trams were crammed with young men who had already heard about the general mobilization.

Once more we see how the enemy overestimated Italy's strength
and attributed to the Italian High Command brilliant and auda-
cious ideas that never crossed its mind. Metaxas, with the greater
part of his army concentrated on the northern frontiers, was very
worried about Corfu and the other Ionian islands and, in spite of
all the indications that it was not going to happen, he feared the
possibility of a landing in the Peloponnese, which would have met
with only slight resistance. The German seizure of Norway showed
that the sea was anything but an insuperable obstacle, and the
main force of the British fleet was a long way away (the British
did not move into Suda Bay in Crete until two days later). The
reality of the situation was that the only Italian plan, apart from
that of attacking on a limited sector in a zone where the enemy
was ready and waiting, was that for an invasion of Corfu, and this
had been postponed *sine die.* Meanwhile Visconti Prasca started
a campaign of the traditional type, without exploiting in any way
the advantage he had by reason of the enemy's antiquated equipment; and, as if his total lack of strategic imagination (as distinct
from fantastic optimism) were not enough, he began it with inadequate forces.

The tone of the ultimatum demonstrated the same combination
of arrogance and unpreparedness. There were two alternatives. If
the sole purpose of the ultimatum was to lead to war, its tone was
a matter of indifference; all that mattered was that the blow that
followed should be shattering, quite independent of any political
action. Alternatively, if the intention was if possible to foster pro-
German, pro-Italian, anti-British trends the development of which
would have justified the assurances of Ciano and Jacomoni which
were half-heartedly accepted by the General Staff, these forces
should have been left with elbow room in which to act and develop.
Since the Italian war machine in Albania was insufficient for a
Blitzkrieg, or even for a decisive *coup de main,* it is obvious that
the ultimatum should have left a way open for the second
alternative.

If this second path had been cleverly taken, the possibility that the Greeks might have given way cannot be totally excluded. In his conversation with Grazzi, Metaxas himself hinted at a possibility of discussions, negotiations; and the reasons for this were that the only possible alternative to the resigned acceptance of the occupation of strategic points was a bravely fought but hopeless war, with the prospect of the abandonment of Greek territory within a relatively short time. Among other things, Metaxas did not know what Bulgaria would do, and he might well fear the imminence of a German attack. But the ultimatum, with its three-hour time limit and its failure to mention the strategic points that the Italians wanted to occupy, was couched in such a way as to block the path to any possibility of acceptance. That was the technique the Germans used towards Norway, Denmark, Belgium, and Holland, but it was applied without the German strength. Furthermore, the ultimatum promised that the territorial integrity of Greece would be respected; but it had been preceded by a violent Italian press campaign supporting Albanian claims to part of Epirus. Even if Metaxas had had any doubts in the matter—though after his conversation with Grazzi he had none—the King and the British diplomatists would have had no trouble in dissipating them.

The ultimatum was drafted by Ciano and revised by Mussolini without consulting the military leaders. Badoglio, Cavagnari, Pricolo were told nothing about it, and neither was Hitler. Mussolini, Ciano, and Visconti Prasca prepared their war "jealously," almost as if they feared that someone might rob them of it. When the two Axis dictators met at Florence on October 28 the campaign was a few hours old and, now that it was too late to stop it, Hitler, who must have been furious at the news, did not waste any time on criticism. Instead, he expressed his good wishes and his solidarity with Italy. The optimistic Ciano noted in his diary: "We are attacking in Albania and talking in Florence. In both places things are going well. In spite of the bad weather, the troops are advancing rapidly, though air support is lacking. In Florence the talk is of great interest and shows that German solidarity has not

ceased." From Ciano's point of view, things were perhaps going
well in Florence, but in Albania, in spite of Visconti Prasca's first
optimistic communiqués, they were not.

After the beginning of hostilities Grazzi, and all the members of
the Italian colony in Greece, had painful and dramatic experiences.
Italian aggression roused Greek popular indignation, which sometimes took violent forms. Italian schools and offices were wrecked,
and many Italians were arrested. In a dispatch to Rome sent via
the German legation, which assumed the representation of Italian
interests, Grazzi reported, among other things, a raid on the
Italian consulate at the Piraeus and the total isolation of consular
offices. Excesses occurred which, in the national state of mind at
that time, are comprehensible enough. They are of course to be
deplored, but it must be admitted that everything humanly possible
had been done on the Italian side to provoke them. On November
8, immediately after his arrival in Italy—he was repatriated together with his diplomatic staff in accordance with international
usage—Grazzi was received by Ciano.

By this time the situation in Albania was already deteriorating,
the Calvary of the Julia Division on the Pindus had begun, the
machine that Mussolini and Ciano had set in motion was showing
itself in its true light, a very dangerous one to anyone who handled
it, jeopardizing the prestige and good name of the Italian army.
But Ciano displayed an arrogant confidence. He hardly discussed
the situation on the Greek-Albanian border with Grazzi; instead,
he concealed his embarrassment by cutting him short or changing
the subject. He obviously wanted to avoid an objective, though
belated, discussion of events the sequel to which demonstrated
Grazzi's wisdom and foresight and his own frivolous recklessness.

Instead, he wanted full information about the ordeals to which
members of the Italian colony in Athens were being subjected. He
showed a lively interest in what Grazzi had to tell him on this subject, so much so that he got through on the telephone to discuss
it with Mussolini.

In the course of this conversation Ciano said: "Grazzi is here with me now, he too says that everything will be all right." As soon as Ciano put down the receiver, Grazzi objected that he had said nothing of the sort. "You'll see, you'll see," Ciano replied in confidential tones. "The General Staff has made a fool of itself, but now we are sending twenty divisions to Albania, and in two weeks it will all be over." Rarely has such an authoritative forecast been so wide of the mark, though perhaps it was not so much a serious forecast as a repartee intended to silence the indignant Grazzi. Subsequently Grazzi realized that he was being cold-shouldered; he had the feeling that he was put on a par with Badoglio in the Fascist hostility towards those responsible, or rather those who were made the scapegoats, for the failure of the attack. Because he did not meekly accept these veiled insinuations, but went about stating the truth of the situation and explaining where all the false information and reckless forecasts had come from, Anfuso gave him a half-threatening, half-friendly warning and advised him to leave Rome and take a holiday. He retained a profound distaste for the odious role that had been imposed upon him and a deep respect for Metaxas.

Later he learnt that several months afterwards, after the Greek Prime Minister's death, his widow received a caller who came to offer her condolences in the sitting room of the villa at Kifisia where the ultimatum had been delivered. The visitor was about to take a seat on an armchair, but Metaxas' widow stopped her. "No, not there," she said. "That's where Grazzi sat on the night of the declaration of war."

7. Forward through the Mud

For the first three days of the campaign the Italians' real enemy was the weather. The Greeks seemed to be disheartened, inert, resigned. During the night on which the Italian minister handed Metaxas the ultimatum the whole front, from the Grammos massif to the sea, moved forward. According to the Greeks, Italian troops crossed the frontier at 5:30 A.M., or half an hour before the ultimatum expired. Some units may indeed have done so, though the detail is not very important. The Italians had left their quarters in the squalid villages near the frontier and moved up to the frontier line several days previously, after an inspection by Visconti Prasca, smiling, calm, and confident.

Then the weather had been fine, and the lorries raised clouds of sharp, yellowish dust, which caused the troops great discomfort. To these men, banished to a remote and desolate spot, war still seemed a strange and distant prospect. Almost until the last moment leave had been granted normally, but had then been suddenly stopped. New officers arrived to whom the terrain was still strange, and others who were expecting to go home and see their families had their leave canceled, and resented the counterorder. Then the atmosphere became that of the eve of action, telephone operators at the various headquarters were continually transmitting and receiving messages, motorcyclists continually roared past companies on the march, authoritative and energetic generals came and went to the accompaniment of the sharp clicking of heels.

Visconti Prasca had first decided to establish his headquarters at Libohova, but then shifted them to Dervisciani, to be near the sound of the guns. The air commander, General Ranza, who was as portly as Göring, remained at Tirana, and there was no proper liaison between the two. Instead of allotting him properly qualified liaison officers, Roatta and Soddu, wishing to keep an eye on the ground commander in Albania—though they were his superiors they regarded him as a competitor—put men of confidence among his entourage whose duty it was zealously to watch and report on him. On October 26 the weather deteriorated, a leaden autumn descended on the frontier zone, torrential rain fell, and streams that in normal conditions were dry or at any rate easily fordable began swelling and pouring cataracts of water down into the valleys. The normally thin and meager Vojussa, Kalamas, and Sarandaporos turned into tumultuous rivers. Aircraft could not fly along the frontier line, and the prospective theater of operations was immersed in wet and gloom. General Francesco Rossi, as we have seen, wanted operations to be postponed, and sent a recommendation to that effect to Rome. But Visconti Prasca took the opposite view. "If it was inconvenient to us, the bad weather was just as inconvenient to our enemy," he wrote, "and by masking our advance it prevented him from making effective use of his weapons, particularly artillery, of which the Greeks make masterly use."

But the Italians had to advance through the morass, while the Greeks had only to remain where they were and wait. True, their artillery was hampered, but the Italian air arm was totally paralyzed. And how could Visconti Prasca tell beforehand that the Greek gunners were going to turn out to be so skillful that the poor visibility would benefit the Italians? The plan of operations laid down that they were to advance in columns, thin tentacles creeping along the few possible lines of penetration into Greek territory.

The columns moved forward in the dark under the driving rain. Boots sank in the mud, puttees were soon wrapped in a thick yellow crust, horses and mules kicked up showers of slush at every step. Each column was known by the name of the colonel in command. The Andreini column, belonging to the Littoral Group, consisting of cavalry and grenadiers, advanced along the coast; the sea, barely visible through the rain, was gray and covered with angry white horses. The Siena Division was spearheaded by the Gianani column, consisting of the 32nd Infantry Regiment and the Carloni column, consisting of the 31st. Further north the Ferrara Division was led by the Sapienza column, consisting of the 48th Infantry Regiment and the Trizio column, consisting of the 47th. Along the roaring torrent of the Vojussa the tanks and motorized Bersaglieri of the Solinas column, formed of elements of the Centauro Division, advanced towards the Kalamas, making for the Perati bridge and Kalpaki. There was a great silence in the valleys, broken now and again by a burst of fire. Sometimes a brief skirmish took place, but the thin network of Greek frontier posts was evidently withdrawing without resistance. Here and there Italians cautiously entered hutments abandoned by Greek customs men or police. On the walls there were incomprehensible notices in Greek and photographs of King George and Metaxas, and on the tables there were newspapers and the remains of meals. In the rear of the Ferrara Division other columns of the Centauro Division struggled through the mud; these were intended for the breakthrough towards the Kalamas and beyond. The advance was slow but steady.

In Florence Mussolini and Ciano, engaged in their conversations with Hitler, anxiously awaited news, but not till late afternoon did they learn from a telephone message from a Foreign Ministry official that the "air force has not been able fully to carry out the tasks allotted to it because of adverse atmospheric conditions," and that Visconti Prasca had telegraphed in his usual exultant tone: "Our troops proceeding with much enthusiasm beyond frontier with artillery in the van. Because of storms air force did not intervene."[1] On the Pindus, at the point of junction between the offensive deployment in Epirus and the defensive deployment in western Macedonia, the Julia Division was on the move.

This division, the sinews of which were provided by mountaineers from the valleys of the eastern frontier and men of the Aquila Battalion from the Abruzzi, had had its troubles before October 28 (as was pointed out, among other things, by Italo Pietra in an article in the *Illustrazione Italiana* in June, 1951).

The first of these troubles occurred in June 1940, when Rome ordered that all officers and men of Slavonic origin should be removed from the strength; and this applied not only to those from areas annexed in 1918 but also to those from areas that had been included in the Kingdom of Italy for more than seventy years; it all came to nothing, but left resentment and bitterness behind. The second trouble resulted from a directive by Roatta . . . ordering "the adjustment of the structure and strength of the army to the present situation"; the war on Greece had been decided on in the Palazzo Venezia that very day, and "adjustment" meant releasing classes, breaking up units, returning large-scale formations to their depots. But the men of the Julia Division in Albania had nothing to hope from this order, and the result was depression in the tents at evening. The third trouble, and the usual one, was that caused by certain Alpini who, while in transit towards the ports of embarkation, shouted anti-war slogans and came to blows with Fascist militiamen who were, or seemed to be, volunteers. The results were severe orders, inquiries, reports, charges, and officers under arrest.

In spite of these troubles, the Julia was a tough division, lacking in enthusiasm on the one hand but with no trace of bad morale on the other. It had with it five days' hard rations and four days' fodder for the mules, and in front of it was the Smolikas, one of the most towering mountains of the Pindus chain, rising to 8,640 feet or more. Two columns were to make their way round either flank of the massif and advance to Metsovon. The first, on the north, was the tactical group commanded by Colonel Dapino, consisting of the 8th Alpini and the Conegliano artillery group, with Albanian detachments in support; the second, to the southwest, consisted of the 9th Alpini, commanded by Colonel Tavoni and the Udine artillery group, as well as some Albanian detachments.

The 9th Alpini had the benefit of a bad road transformed into a river of mud, but the 8th had to force its way down forest tracks. As elsewhere, the enemy appeared only fleetingly and his activity was confined to putting space between himself and the advancing columns. There were five columns of Alpini, spread out like the fingers of a hand, consisting from north to south of the Tolmezzo, Gemona, Cividale, Vicenza, and Aquila battalions. October 28 was, in short, an uneventful day, and the Italian war communiqué No. 144 of the following day reflected the truth when it said:

At dawn yesterday our troops stationed in Albania crossed the Greek frontier and penetrated into enemy territory at various points. Our air force, in spite of adverse atmospheric conditions, repeatedly bombed the military objectives assigned to it, striking docks, wharves, and railway yards and causing fires in the port of Patras, installations along the Corinth Canal and the naval base of Preveza and airport installations at the base of Tatoi near Athens. All our aircraft returned to their bases.

All this was true, but these phrases were capable of rousing false hopes. The enemy had not yet shown himself, the battle had not yet begun, and both sides were still maneuvering. There were large gaps in the front, the slender Italian tentacles were testing out the ground, and all they came up against were a few enemy outposts.

On the twenty-ninth some hitches occurred, only hints, however, of graver things to come. The Army General Staff informed Visconti Prasca that "because of the state of the sea the Corfu operation has been postponed." This was bad news. The column moving along the coast would not have naval support, thus depriving him of one of the pillars of his overall plan. While the bad weather continued, some advanced units of the Siena Division and the Littoral Group reached the Kalamas, which was swollen and yellow, carrying along in its tempestuous course tree trunks, mud, the carcasses of sheep, and the wreckage of bridges blown up by the Greeks. For the greater part of its course the river was unfordable, and Italian resources in bridging equipment were slender; at all events they were inadequate for a campaign in a season of rivers in spate. While the Siena Division occupied the village of Filiates (the inhabitants watched the troops marching through with apathy) the Centauro Division got bogged down behind the Ferrara Division. The weather conditions prevented Colonels Trizio and Solinas from joining up as planned, and the Julia Division was having trouble with another stream swollen by the rains, the Sarandaporos. The 8th Alpini were late in relation to the 9th, their terrain was the more difficult, the supply lines were lengthening, and the Albanian scouts reported the approach of troops in brown uniforms, new Greek detachments.

The Tolmezzo Battalion, which was most exposed to attack from the north, received orders to take up a defensive position on the Furka; the Julia Division, which had spread out in the advance and was gradually approaching Samarina and Koniton, started closing up again; the Alpini had by now realized they were faced with anything but a picnic. But in closing up the division left a gap in its rear. Dapino and Tavoni continued moving cautiously forward; the Alpini of the Aquila Battalion made the acquaintance of the Vojussa, which was flooded and tumultuous too, at the point where the Julia Division sector joined that of the Ferrara Division. There was a tension in the air that ill accorded with the hope of a lightning seizure of Metsovon. Officers realized how slight is the strength of a division simultaneously engaged in a pincer movement taking in a huge mountain, gaining a great deal of ground, and guarding its flanks and rear and lines of communication. From the Grammos mountains to the sea the air force was eliminated by the weather, and the divisional artillery, which according to Visconti Prasca was in the van, could not keep up even with the slow march of the infantry, on whom the whole weight of the operation fell.

The Greeks, worried by the relatively deep wedge that the Julia Division was driving into their territory, began taking counter-measures; it would be a grave blow to them if the Epirus sector were isolated and communications with the Macedonian sector were cut off. As the hours passed and the columns approached the first Greek defense line, resistance became more lively; the loss of five officers and thirty men was reported to Visconti Prasca on October 31. But the fighting was still in the skirmishing stage. The weather was still appalling. Communiqués announced that "our troops have continued their advance" and later that "our troops have reached the river Kalamas at various points" and, on November 1, "that operations in Epirus are proceeding according to plan." The troops were drenched to the skin, the puttees round their legs weighed pounds, and in the case of the Alpini in the freezing temperatures of 4,500 feet and more, they gripped their legs as in a vice. Warm and sunny Athens was a distant dream, and even their primitive quarters in Albanian villages were a sweet memory. The men spent their few hours of rest taking advantage of the rare shelter available, and the arrival of supplies soon became irregular. The Julia Division was shortly reduced to hard rations: the biscuits were damp and swollen, and flaked like a leper's skin. On October 31 a column of the Ferrara Division was surprised by very well camouflaged artillery fire. War with the enemy began to be superimposed on war with the weather. At this point Mussolini thought it opportune to give another "taste of the spur" to General Visconti Prasca, who was now right up against his obstacle. He wrote:

Dear Visconti, I am satisfied with the development of operations in this first phase. General Ranza has also given me satisfactory impressions. For the purpose of reinforcing your strength, the Bari Division, which was to have occupied Corfu, will land at Valona tomorrow, November 1. In view of the attitude of Belgrade, you can move the Venezia Division south, or to the Koritsa sector. Meanwhile I have sent General Soddu to Rome immediately to accelerate the sending of the divisions requested on October 16, and all the lorries. I am convinced that you will continue to impress on the operation as a whole the rapid pace that events, even more than military theory, peremptorily require.[2]

Mussolini was then at Grottaglie, near Bari, and it is not clear whether he had gone there to be in readiness to inspect his victorious troops, or to be able to follow the operations more closely, or simply in order to have a "wolf's lair" of his own, after the manner of his colleague and rival, Adolf Hitler. Soddu and Pricolo went there with him.

Mussolini, Pricolo states, kept questioning Soddu about the operations and showed concern about the situation on the left flank of the army advancing in Epirus, i.e., in the Koritsa zone.[3] Soddu assured him that the Devoli and the bastion of the Morava constituted a solid defense, and said the Italians should be in Yanina within a week and in Preveza within three weeks. Pricolo was charged with delivering Mussolini's letter to Visconti Prasca, and he flew to Albania from Grottaglie on November 1. The Duce, who could not tolerate contradiction but sometimes had an animal instinct for sizing up a situation, sniffed a smell of burning. The dropping of the Corfu operation prejudiced the plan, and the Bari Division, according to Roatta, "at once found itself in the gravest difficulties because, in view of its original task, it lacked transport and had only very little artillery."[4] On the other hand these extra battalions, meager though they were, turned out to be invaluable in the anxious operation of plugging the gaps a few days later.

On October 30 and 31 Galeazzo Ciano went to Albania too. Like many members of the Fascist hierarchy, he was in a hurry to gather some laurels, and, in between his diplomatic journeys and games of golf, wanted to make an operational sortie that would earn him the ritual silver medal. But bad weather prevented him from taking off. However, at Tirana he was able to observe the first symptoms of the furious controversy, not excluding fisticuffs, that later broke out between Visconti Prasca and the General Staff. "I wrote a long letter to the Duce. There are complaints here about the ill will of the General Staff, which did not do all it should have done in preparation for the operation. Badoglio was convinced that the Greek question would be solved at the conference table and acted on that pre-assessment of the situation. . . ."[5] That Ciano should speak in such a detached tone of political "pre-assessment" of the situation, as if political assurances had not come from him and as if Mussolini's conduct of affairs had been totally rectilinear, is truly extraordinary; and he thus added another brushstroke of mystery to events and to human psychology.

On November 1—the date on which General Armellini's diary has the significant phrase "complete chaos"—the weather improved, and Ciano briskly took advantage of it for a "slap-up bombing raid" on Salonika, in the course of which a direct hit was very nearly scored on the building in which Italian nationals awaiting repatriation were concentrated. The improvement in the weather should have been a good sign, but instead it coincided with the opening of the Greek offensive in western Macedonia. Papagos had two objectives, one immediate and the other more remote: first, to reach the line of the Devoli, and then to gain possession of the Morava—in other words, the two physical features which, Soddu had assured Mussolini, provided a guarantee against enemy penetration. The Greeks, in khaki uniforms and British-style steel helmets, launched their assault at 8 A.M. on November 1. Behind the Devoli and the Morava was the plain of Koritsa, and if they succeeded in advancing into it, the whole Italian deployment in Epirus would be threatened with encirclement. The Parma Division was strung out along a huge front, but it had the support of the Piemonte Division, which was in reserve, and the Venezia Division, which, as we have said, had been withdrawn from the Yugoslav frontier.

The Greek attack caught a battalion of the 83rd Infantry Regiment of the Venezia at the awkward moment when it was taking up its position in the front line. It gave way, a gap was opened in the thin defense line, and enemy advance guards moved towards Treni and Verniku. They gained only a few miles, but the incident, trivial though it was, was a bad sign. The commander of the Venezia Division loaded the 84th Infantry Regiment into lorries hastily scraped together and sent them up in support, and meanwhile General Rodolfo Naldi, of the Piemonte Division, was ordered to hold himself in readiness to intervene. Treni was recaptured, but the recovery was brief. Some other villages were lost and some hill positions yielded. On November 3 the Greeks started exercising pressure on the Devoli. In their advance they did not follow the valleys but used the slopes and infiltrated over the mountains; and they made excellent use of mortars to bombard Italian positions. This sudden springing to life of an enemy who had not been expected to put up much resistance created a certain bewilderment among the Italian troops. The already massive Greek deployment in western Macedonia was strengthened by more battalions from the Bulgarian sector, and for the Parma, Venezia, and Piemonte divisions a relentless battle of attrition began.

The extent of the reliance that could be placed on the Albanian detachments which Jacomoni had taken so much trouble about was promptly made clear. At 9:30 A.M. on November 4 the Tomor Battalion, which was considered to be one of the best Albanian units, assaulted and took Hill 1289 in the Lapishtit Range. But under the shock of a counterattack it fell back in disorder and fled along the valley, and carabinieri had to intervene to stop the rout, whereupon the Albanians fired on the carabinieri. Efforts were made to round them up, but only 120 of a total of 1,000 were left, including the discomfited battalion commander.

The whole front had turned on its axis, pushed northwest by the Greeks advancing from western Macedonia and southeast by the Italians in Epirus. The Italians were on the Kalamas in Greek territory while the Greeks were on the Devoli in Albanian territory. The Julia Division, the pivot of the whole line, had moved too; but it had become almost detached from the two arms of the lever and was in an extremely dangerous position. On November

1, at a meeting in Rome with Badoglio in the chair and Soddu also present, the first belated and fragmentary steps were taken to reinforce the Italian front. The Duce's decision to redirect the Bari Division to the front was confirmed, it was decided to give absolute priority to shipments to Albania, and to send the Trieste Division there as a matter of urgency. The mythical idea of landing three divisions at Arta after it had been captured was not even mentioned.

While the Bari and Trieste divisions were on their way to Albania (it was feared that the Trieste Division would not arrive until November 20), Papagos ordered his 2nd, 3rd and 4th Infantry divisions, as well as a crack regiment of evzones, to Epirus. Meanwhile the offensive operations of the Siena, Ferrara, and Centauro divisions continued; the latter was delayed by minefields as well as by the mud. The main body of the Centauro was divided into two columns, commanded by Colonels Costa and Anzini. Because of an error in map reading Anzini believed, among other things, that he had reached the village of Sant' Attanasio on the Kalamas, though in reality it was another village. The divisional objective was "to break through the center of the Greek line between Policastro and Kalpaki and advance on Yanina," but the Greek lines at Kalpaki held firm. General Carlo Rossi, the commander of the Tsamouria Army Corps, complained on November 4 of the "failure of our bombers to intervene; this was promised daily but never happened."[6] He also noted that "fresh forces are needed for the attack, and a much larger amount of artillery, both numerically and in caliber . . . but it is no use thinking about either."[6]

The troops fought bravely in spite of the appalling weather, which was wearing both to body and mind. During this advance in columns regimental commanders exposed themselves in person, and one of the first to be killed was the leader of one of them, Colonel Gianani of the 32nd Siena Infantry Regiment. The Kalamas, more than 200 feet wide and ten feet deep, could not be forded in its middle reaches, but on October 28 was crossed near its mouth by men of the Littoral Group; the honor of having been the first to cross went to Lieutenant Riccardi Avati of the Aosta

Lancers, who was awarded the Gold Medal and was later killed in action. The citation states:

> The commander of the patrol, having established that the river could not be forded, after putting his horses under cover in a riverside wood, and, having found a suitable spot, took his horse, removed his clothing, and, with his pistol between his teeth, managed to reach the left bank. The patrol consisted of volunteers who were good swimmers and wished to go first, but Lieutenant Riccardi Avati would not permit this, wishing to spare the lives of his men and reserve the honor of crossing first for himself. The reconnaissance detachment caught up with the platoon and a rope was fixed between the two banks. A fragile raft only just capable of standing up to the rushing stream was the only means of getting the group headquarters and the three weapons of the machine gun platoon across to the enemy bank, thus constituting an embryonic bridgehead on a hill about 1,000 yards from the bank. At first light on the twenty-ninth the transport of the whole detachment to the opposite bank was begun. . . . Other troops of the group crossed as soon as the engineers had built a bridge of boats on November 5.

Lieutenant Avati was sent forward to reconnoitre in the direction of Igoumenitsa and was killed in an engagement with the enemy.

The lower Kalamas was also forced by the Siena Division during the night of November 4–5. The operation was carried out by the 32nd Infantry Regiment under the leadership of its new commander and cost thirteen killed and eighty-five wounded, but the regiment joined up with troops of the Littoral Group who were already on the other bank and succeeded in establishing a solid bridgehead. This local success might have been promising, but urgent distress signals were now coming from other sectors, and the Julia Division was in danger. General Nasci, the commander of the XXVI Army Corps, after noting "the aggressiveness and mobility of the Greek troops facing me as well as the strong support they have so far had from their artillery and mortars," added depressingly that "it is not possible to make contact with the Julia Division."[7]

The Julia Division was alone. On November 2, when Alpini

units reached the banks of the Vojussa, which was in spate, the first attacks on the rear of the division took place. An exhausted officer who had been in command of a column of pack animals which had been surprised and dispersed by a Greek patrol presented himself to Colonel Tavoni. His men had been taken prisoner, but he had managed to escape from the encirclement. He said that the Greeks were behind the Julia Division on the Sarandaporos, they had taken Samarina, and their strength was continually increasing.

Orders sent to his battalions by General Mario Girotti from his divisional headquarters did not always reach them. He asked army corps by radio to send him no more supplies. The Julia Division was isolated, it could count only on the rations and ammunition that the troops had with them, and there was no way of supplying them except by air. All the battalions from the Tolmezzo to the Aquila were now engaged with the enemy. On November 4 the pressure increased, the Cividale Battalion entrenched at Vovusa was surrounded by superior forces, and the necessity of a withdrawal began to grow clear. The Greek mountain cavalry, mounted on small, agile horses trained in the most difficult country, carried out damaging raids on the Alpini. But Girotti hesitated to give the order to retreat, which would indicate that the division had failed in its task.

General Nasci tried to remedy the situation. To cover the lines of communication of the Julia Division he sent forward to Konitsa a company of Bersaglieri motorcyclists, tanks and artillery belonging to the Centauro Division, and on November 6 ordered the Julia Division to withdraw to Konitsa and gather its remaining forces there. Because of the isolation of his headquarters and the malfunctioning of the radio communications, this order reached Girotti only on November 7. His troops had to fight their way through the Greek forces behind them. After an interval the rain had begun again; at high altitudes it turned to sleet. The tough men of the Julia Division from the Veneto and the Abruzzi, the mountaineers from the Carnia and the Val Natisone, had long beards,

reddened, deep-set eyes, scratched hands; their gray-green uniforms were covered with a thick crust of mud, their boots weighed
tons, and their black helmet feathers were frayed. The Vicenza
Battalion occupied the Cristobasile saddle to cover the division's
retreat. Ten days after the beginning of the campaign Italian troops
were held up on the Kalamas and in a critical position on the Pindus
and in western Macedonia.

The repercussions of the stormy wind blowing in Albania were
felt in Rome. Visconti Prasca was the only remaining optimist.
General Pricolo has left us some illuminating observations in this
respect. What must certainly be taken into account is that after
the end of the campaign a bitter feud arose between the two men,
because Visconti Prasca tried to put the blame on the air force;
he obsessively strikes this note on every page of his *Io ho aggredito
la Grecia*. Co-operation between the air and ground forces in Albania was bad, as it was on every front in which the Italians were
engaged in the Second World War. Ranza was in Tirana and
Visconti Prasca at his advanced headquarters.

Furthermore, a central role in the air war was allotted to the
4th Squadron, which was stationed in Apulia and, incredible to
relate, there was no telephone communication between it and
air headquarters in Albania. Until a submarine cable was laid, contact was maintained by coded messages and a liaison officer who
flew backwards and forwards between Tirana and Brindisi, and
it is easy to imagine how rapid and effective co-operation was in
those circumstances. According to Visconti Prasca, the air force
should have been everywhere, carrying out apocalyptic devastation,
and he complained that there was little air activity and that what
there was was not very effective. Requests for air intervention
soon became frantic and were formulated in ridiculous terms
("bomb Macedonian zone,"[8] for instance, which meant both too
much and nothing at all). Long-range bombing activity consequently rapidly diminished, aircraft were used piecemeal, and the

airfields became congested with transport aircraft moving troops. Taking all this into account, and its repercussions on the relations between Pricolo and Visconti Prasca, I nevertheless believe that credence should be given to Pricolo's story, which is corroborated both by documents and by events.

The undersecretary for air and air chief of staff went to Albania, then, to deliver the Duce's letter to Visconti Prasca, praising him and promising him reinforcements. At Visconti Prasca's headquarters at Dervisciani Pricolo found that the commander-in-chief was up in front between Dogliana and Kalpaki, which was almost the extreme point reached in their advance by the columns of the Ferrara and Centauro divisions. Visconti Prasca read Mussolini's letter with "visible satisfaction," and on the way back to Dervisciani had a conversation with Pricolo of which Pricolo remembered "even the most minute details." Here is what he says passed between them:

VISCONTI PRASCA: I am pleased with this order of the Duce's [for a swift, all-out offensive—author's note]. In any case, you can reassure him completely. With three new divisions or without them, I count on being at Yanina within three days and at Preveza within a week. The Greeks have put up little resistance or have run away, even leaving tables laid and hot food behind them.

PRICOLO: Very good. But forgive me if I put to you one or two questions that you may think out of place, but I do so solely for the purpose of being able the better to report to the Duce. Now you will have need of artillery and, as you see, the road is in very bad condition and there are big holdups.

VISCONTI PRASCA: It will soon be opened up again. Thousands of workers have been engaged. The most serious holdups will be dealt with by bridge-building equipment [it was subsequently learnt that this was still at Valona].

PRICOLO: Have you news of the Julia Division?

VISCONTI PRASCA: Not yet, but it is certainly on the way towards the Metsovon Pass.

PRICOLO: Actually it is rather strange that five days after the beginning of operations there should be no news of the division yet. Is there no radio communication?

VISCONTI PRASCA: Not yet, because there have been many violent storms that blew down the aerials.

PRICOLO: While I was at the airfield at Argyrokastron a reconnaissance aircraft landed. Perhaps we shall find news awaiting us on our return. On the way from Rome to Grottaglie the Duce repeatedly expressed concern for the protection of the left flank of our line, and the defense of Koritsa in particular. General Soddu said that steps were being taken in the matter. What can I say about this?

VISCONTI PRASCA: Tell the Duce that he can be completely reassured. Two divisions are being transferred from the Yugoslav front. But five days have passed, and now there is no more danger for Koritsa. The Greeks have not attacked yet, and now they will not. I am completely confident. The spirit of the troops is very high, and they have all gone into the attack. They all have orders to attack, always to attack, without worrying about their flanks. Every column must attack, even with only a single man.

PRICOLO: But that strikes me as excessively rhetorical, how can one attack with only a single man?

VISCONTI PRASCA: To give an idea of the spirit of our troops, you can describe this episode to the Duce, who likes these characteristic details. A fatally wounded young Albanian volunteer said before he died: "I am happy to die if only the Duce gets through."[9]

This conversation took place on November 2, i.e., before the most dramatic developments of the crisis. Those who have followed the development of events can judge for themselves whether a commander-in-chief in those circumstances has a right to have so many illusions and to be so full of facile optimism.

When Pricolo and Visconti Prasca reached the latter's headquarters at Dervisciani, the air chief of staff wanted to telephone the airfield, but either there was no telephone or it was not working. Pricolo returned that same evening to Grottaglie, where he talked to Soddu about his meeting with Visconti Prasca and expressed his puzzlement about the man. "Soddu rather brusquely interrupted,

saying: 'He is one of our best generals.'" On November 3 Pricolo
was summoned by Mussolini, who asked him what his impressions
of Visconti Prasca had been. "I firmly replied that he seemed to
me to be excessively sure of himself. I thought to myself that he
should be considered at least an *exalté*." Soddu went on protecting
Visconti Prasca; he had his son sent to Albania "as his advance
guard," as Visconti Prasca put it, not to take command of a combatant unit, but to work in the operations section of the General
Staff, "a job that he knows, having done it in Africa."

This highly recommended officer, who went from front to front,
collecting ribbons, was the bearer of a message from his father.[10]
So far from showing any signs of undermining Visconti Prasca's
position, Soddu promised him nine more divisions ("I shall send
you on request three at a time"). But Visconti Prasca, that "rebel"
against the General Staff, was about to be disgraced. Badoglio and
Roatta, who did not like him, were working against him, and they
had an excellent case. There was a strange and ambiguous paternal
note in a telegram the marshal sent him on November 4. Badoglio
referred to himself as his "former superior officer," a curious inaccuracy in view of the fact that he was his immediate superior
at that moment. "It is my principle," he patiently explained, "to
be firmly anchored at one point during the battle. For you this
point is the Koritsa sector. . . . Please tell me exactly and frankly
how you see the situation."[11]

The old fox realized that the Italians had fallen into a trap which
Visconti Prasca had neither foreseen nor coped with in good time.
The Greeks were beginning to mass where the Italian front was
thin. Visconti Prasca's reply, which was not lacking in grotesquely
obsequious telegraphic salaams ("Your Excellency is still my immediate superior and master") tried to display a confidence a great
deal of which he must by this time have lost.

My ideas correspond to your Excellency's. Can be confident of
solid defensive cover Koritsa area in order maneuver offensively
Epirus. Koritsa area situation delicate particularly first period when

considerable Greek forces massed and defense could count only on Parma Division. With employment on Koritsa front Venezia and Piemonte divisions after marching respectively two and three weeks for lack motor transport situation greatly improved and will further improve with landing Bari Division and forthcoming employment Arezzo Division. Consider situation not disquieting and arrival forces from Italy increasingly favor war objectives. Total mobilization Greek army necessitates prompt arrival new forces from Italy and availability motor transport essential both for defense and offense. Massive air intervention more than ever necessary in this first period solely for tactical objectives supporting troops. Repeat my confidence final outcome in spite of temporary difficulties essentially due transport and bad weather.[12]

Visconti Prasca had the honesty, or the imprudence, to quote this illuminating telegram verbatim in his memoirs. Nothing could better illustrate his improvidence and reckless optimism. The campaign was a week old, and already he had to admit that the Italians were running risks because of the Greek superiority in the Koritsa area, as if this were something extraordinary, the result of an unaccountable vicissitude in the fortunes of war; and he asked for new forces to be sent immediately because the Greeks were mobilizing to the last man—as if they could have been expected to do anything else.

To Badoglio he did not use the argument with which he made such play later, namely, the delay in sending him three more divisions; and he had good reason to keep quiet about it, because at the Palazzo Venezia meeting it had been the Badoglios and the Roattas who had been worried about reinforcements and not he; he had been going to do everything by himself, and the advance to Preveza had been going to be a walkover. The language he used would have been legitimate if it had been used by Papagos, i.e., a commander-in-chief facing an attack, not one aspiring to imitate a German Blitzkrieg. The shortage of motor transport was grave and inexcusable, but there was nothing new about it, it existed on a national scale and was well known to everybody, and the specific shortages that existed in Albania must have been very well known to Visconti Prasca. Had he really believed he would get many more lorries, divisions, and weapons in the period between October 15 and 26? And how does this fit in with his claim that the operation had been planned and made ready in every detail?

The general who had been going to sweep the Greeks from Epirus in a few days now described the situation as "not disquieting," and "not disquieting" of course meant its opposite. Athens radio announced the capture of five officers, men, and weapons on the Julia Division front, and Visconti Prasca, to whom Rome sent a request for information, forwarded it to the division—all regular contact with which, as Pricolo testifies, was cut off. The Rome request, according to Visconti Prasca, was absurd, for it failed to take into account the "fluctuations of modern fronts and the consequent big or little pockets that arise." The fact remains that the incident was typical of a situation that was going from bad to worse. Little more than a week after Grazzi had delivered the ultimatum, ominous news was piling up in Rome and Tirana. Ciano, who in his "long letter" to the Duce had said that Greek resistance was going to be "soft," realized that no glory would be accruing to him from this campaign, and Mussolini began to appreciate that he was faced with yet another failure to emulate Hitler's military triumphs. For Visconti Prasca it was the beginning of the end.

On November 6 the General Staff decided to organize the troops in Albania into four army corps. A note to the General Staff from Mussolini laid down that the Ninth Army should consist of the Piemonte, Arezzo, Parma, and Venezia divisions in western Macedonia, the Julia and Bari divisions on the Pindus, and the Tridentina Division in reserve. This army, failing a Bulgarian intervention, was to remain on the defensive throughout the winter. The Eleventh Army (the Ferrara, Centauro, and Siena divisions) was to be reinforced by four more divisions in order to resume the offensive. Three divisions were to be held in reserve in Apulia. The new deployment was to be completed by December 5.

This order by the strategist Mussolini can be said to have begun the desperate and frantic search for an offensive that the Italian High Command pursued like a fleeting phantom for the whole six months of the Greek campaign without ever succeeding in catching it. The General Staff started deluging Visconti Prasca with warnings. "The operational situation on our left wing (the Koritsa area) must be considered with great care. Your Excellency will wish to take all the necessary measures to complete the defense of the central redoubt."[13] This central redoubt was a series of mountain positions enclosing in their midst Tirana and the harbors of Durazzo and Valona, which were difficult of access not only to the Greek army, but also to the Italian, because of the lack of good roads and motor transport.

The change in the command structure did not coincide with Visconti Prasca's dismissal, but this was in the air. Soddu offered himself as his successor. "If I could be given a command, I could answer for the steps to be taken," he said to Mussolini, according to Pricolo, and added: "I ask you, Duce, to send me to take over the command of the armed forces in Albania." On November 7 Soddu, on a tour of inspection in Albania, had talked to Nasci, the commander of the XXV Army Corps, and his impressions must have been extremely pessimistic and were reflected in a pessimistic telegram to Rome. The undersecretary for war asked Nasci to hold out at least for another five or six days while emergency steps were taken. When it decided on the reorganization of the army in Albania the High Command simultaneously ordered that the Taro and Tridentina divisions should be made ready to be sent to the Koritsa sector, and that the 4th Bersaglieri, who were in Apulia, should be sent there by air. As usual, the order was followed by a counterorder, and the 4th Bersaglieri left by sea on November 7. Instead, the Morbegno Battalion of Alpini belonging to the Tridentina Division was sent by air on November 8. It can be stated that from now until March the sending to the front of units detached from their divisions, lacking in transport and services, and put under the command of colonels and generals whom they did not know, practically never ceased; and this was one of the worst troubles of the Greek campaign and one of the basic causes of the Italian failures.

The beginning of the Greek war caught the War Ministry while the "adjustment" of the army, ordered on the day on which the Duce decided on the Greek campaign in the Palazzo Venezia, was still in progress. The system of working in watertight compartments, characteristic of bureaucracies, reached almost incredible extremes in this case. But both the "adjustment," i.e., the release to civilian life of hundreds of thousands of men, and the war on Greece were such high-level decisions that they necessarily reflect on the supreme Commander-in-Chief, Benito Mussolini himself, and they are a sufficient demonstration of his irresponsibility. The process of putting divisions on a peacetime footing had to be put into reverse, and the slogan of "adjustment" had to give way to an anxious call to arms. I quote from Visconti Prasca's book this account of the remarkable vicissitudes of the Modena Division, which had to "go into reverse" before many others, because it was decided to send it to reinforce the army in Albania. Though it had the advantage in this respect in comparison with other divisions which were flung into the furnace in the anxious, almost panic-stricken first ten days of November, it was never restored to full establishment throughout the campaign.

In about the middle of October the Modena Division was at Vittorio Veneto. It had been transferred there from the western frontier in August, after taking part in the offensive against France. Between August and October it perfected its equipment and training in expectation of a campaign against Yugoslavia. During September, at the conclusion of its training and to demonstrate the standard reached, it carried out maneuvers on the Cansiglio plateau that were completely satisfactory in spite of climatic and service difficulties. Such being the situation in the middle of October, the division received orders to return to its ordinary station (Savona), but first to carry out a big reduction in its establishment (officers and other ranks); this was practically complete and the establishment was reduced by 50 per cent. This reduction, which was practically a demobilization, was begun at once, and had been in progress for several days when the division received orders to return to full establishment because it was going to Albania. This order arrived on about October 20. The division was not reconstituted by recalling the officers and men who had been sent home, but by transfers from neighboring divisions. The order to leave (ports of embarkation Bari and Brindisi) arrived on about November 10. The reconstitution of the division, which was troublesome enough, was still in progress. Some officers, including the commander of the 41st Infantry Regiment, joined their units when they were already in the train. The first detachments of the division reached Albania (Valona) between November 15 and 20. As the various units arrived they were sent off towards the front in the Argyrokastron sector, with the exception of the 41st Infantry, which was sent to the Klisura sector and did not return to the division until March 1942. I recall distinctly the arrival of detachments piecemeal, not up to establishment in transport animals, particularly for the artillery, or in infantry weapons or in materials for the engineers, which were left at Bari or at the port of disembarkation. When some of this material arrived it was sent to other divisions, and the same happened with the transport animals. For the routing operations (troops, weapons, materials, transport animals) still in progress at Bari, a special office was set up with a senior officer and other personnel that reached Albania only in March 1942.

The 5th Alpini, who landed in Albania in the first two weeks of November, had similar troubles. "Nearly all the transport animals were left at Brindisi and reached the regiment belatedly, as they were used temporarily to help other infantry and artillery units who were without transport animals," Aldo Rasero writes in his history of the regiment.

This was chaos, or something very like it. Mussolini frantically telephoned, interfered, gave orders, appealed, rebuked, praised, tried to clear up the situation with words and telegrams. At 10 P.M. on November 9 Visconti Prasca was set on the slippery slope that within a few days was to end with his being put on the retired list (this, however, was preceded by a strange promotion to "full general-designate"). Soddu was appointed commander-in-chief, and Visconti Prasca was put in command of the Eleventh Army.

The story of this relegation of a commander-in-chief to a subordinate role (Rome had actually been thinking of downgrading him to the command of a corps of the Eleventh Army) has been told by Visconti Prasca himself in his usual pungent style. Soddu went to see him at his Dervisciani headquarters on November 5 and merely told him that the task on which he was engaged was accelerating the transport of troops from Italy. With that he left the perplexed Visconti Prasca and went off to the Koritsa zone, where he had a clear impression of approaching disaster. Next day Soddu, who in the meantime had been sending alarming telegrams to Rome, as we have mentioned, was more explicit. He had not come on a tour of inspection or to encourage or admonish, but was the new commander *in pectore,* and would soon take over officially. Visconti Prasca had failed, the more so as his friend Soddu had said to him: "You see how well we shall work together. Both of us will become full generals and then marshals of Italy."

Visconti Prasca, with his enormous capacity for self-deception, was still able to believe that he had in his hands the tools for his Epirus *coup de main.* He went on cherishing offensive plans while elsewhere the Italian front was bending almost to breaking point and the Julia Division was being harried by the Greeks like a wounded boar by a pack of hounds; and his illusions were suddenly fed by a brilliant action by cavalry detachments of the Aosta and Milano regiments belonging to the Littoral Group. As we know, this formation, together with the Siena Division, had established a solid bridgehead on the left bank of the Kalamas.

The cavalry, after advancing to Igoumenitsa Bay, with its green coastline surrounding calm waters and the little village clinging to the hills above, had pushed on to Paramithia and Margarition farther to the south, making a bold and pretty deep penetration. They did not meet any solid resistance. Visconti Prasca, with a

sudden burst of enthusiasm, wrote to Soddu, now his immediate
superior (the letter is dated November 10), saying "that a push
from the lower Kalamas might yet be practicable and profitable"
and that "it might pave the way to the collapse of the fortified
camp of Kalpaki on the road to Yanina." He added that this
operation "should be carried out without delay, taking advantage
of the period of crisis through which the enemy seems to be passing
and denying him time for recovery."[14]

He therefore asked that all the Alpini battalions and mountain
artillery units arriving in Albania should be sent to the Epirus
sector. With the resources at his disposal the objective of the offensive could only be limited, but with the reinforcements he hoped
for, "perhaps . . . we shall open the gates of Yanina." Visconti
Prasca was writing to a commanding officer who as undersecretary for war had been very friendly to him. The rebuff, dated
November 11, that came in reply, was couched in official language,
did not use the intimate second person singular, suggested a schoolmaster reading a lesson to an unruly pupil, and was the more significant for that reason.

The operations of the two cavalry regiments were truly brilliant
but they must of course be considered in their true context. It is
necessary to be realistic. All the ideas indicated by you, your Excellency, are first rate, but it is not good ideas on which successful operations are based, but the possession of adequate resources with
which to carry them out, aided and abetted by favorable lines of
operation. Improvised operations, using forces piecemeal, do not
and never will have successful results. . . . You ask me for all the
troops now arriving from Italy to plug the many gaps in our line
that exist in the face of an enemy whom you yourself did not consider to be of superior strength, and in the meantime you suggest
to me new operations that would seem to be somewhat hazardous.
. . . I cannot see how the idea that the enemy is in a state of crisis
and that an attack should be made on his flank can be reconciled
with the assertion that even if the units asked for are obtained it
will not be possible to think of offensive possibilities but only of

better stabilizing the sector. . . . In substance I note a fundamental difference of approach; and I therefore ask you, your Excellency, to inform me outright whether or not you feel yourself able to collaborate with me on the basis of identity of outlook.[15]

Visconti Prasca had no need to reply. On November 11, the radio announced his replacement in command of the Eleventh Army by General Carlo Geloso (which was a kind of revenge for the latter). On November 30, by a decision of the Council of Ministers, Visconti Prasca was released from the active list and put on permanent leave. Such was the inglorious end of the career of a general who was both culpable and a victim. These extracts from Armellini's diary for January 15, 1941, are significant:

> General Ricagno came to see me . . . he is Visconti Prasca's former chief of staff. We talked about Greece, of course. He agrees that Visconti Prasca was more or less taken for a ride by everyone, Ciano, Jacomoni, and Soddu, who then dropped him, after promises and flattery. It had been worked out in advance that Soddu was to succeed him, and both were assured of the rank of marshal if things went well. That explains the speech made to me by Soddu, and his anger at Badoglio when the latter succeeded in persuading the Duce to send a full general to Albania in Visconti Prasca's place.

Visconti Prasca refused to resign himself and humbly accept the lesson given him by facts even before it was given him by Mussolini and Soddu. He kept bombarding the War Ministry with pleas, and in April 1943, when the overthrow of Mussolini (which was to take place on July 25) was already germinating in the minds of politicians and statesmen, Ambrosio, the chief of the General Staff, was obliged to deal with the Visconti Prasca "case" and to remind the restless general who had attacked Greece that, by the Duce's orders, consideration of all appeals had been postponed until the end of the war.[16]

Mussolini, who cannot be said to have treated him harshly (to Pricolo, who suggested more severe measures against him, he said one should not be too hard on people such as that), did not have occasion again to return to the matter. But Visconti Prasca, claiming service with the resistance and the merit of having been imprisoned by the Germans, came forward in the postwar period, when Luigi Einaudi was President of Italy, and demanded an inquiry into the Greek campaign. He wanted "the truth to be ascertained." Well, many years have now passed, and a great deal of the truth, at any rate that part of it which refers most directly to him, is now in the public domain, and it still condemns him. The career of this meteor in the sky of the Albanian campaign was as brief as it was catastrophic. The ambitious "rebel" who wanted to go over the heads of the General Staff paid, not for his ambition, but for his incompetence, and thousands or tens of thousands of others who were blameless paid too.

Visconti Prasca, however, was not substantial enough to provide a satisfactory alibi for Mussolini. It was impossible to admit that the infallible, unsleeping dictator had made a bad choice of man, time, place, and enemy. If a scapegoat had to be found in those dark days, it had to be one big enough to excuse the Duce's blunder. In view of the fact that Ciano was for the time being still untouchable, this could be none other than the chief of the General Staff, a personality of Badoglio's caliber. The latter was meanwhile preparing the evidence for his future defense. This was his second Caporetto, from which he again wished to emerge, if not with promotion, at any rate in the position of an accuser rather than of an accused. So on November 10, commenting in his own hand in the General Staff diary on Mussolini's attribution of responsibility for the failure of the offensive to Jacomoni and Visconti Prasca, he described as follows the part he played at a meeting of Chiefs of Staff at which the Duce was present:

Mussolini spoke, giving an account of the operations in Greece and stating that the forecasts of Jacomoni and Visconti Prasca about a rising in Tsamouria had turned out to be completely unfounded. The opposite having occurred, the forces now engaged were evidently insufficient for the operation. He believed it necessary to send another seven triple divisions, to bring those already earmarked for Albania up to nine battalions, and to hold another three divisions in a state of readiness in reserve in Apulia. These steps should be completed by December 5. I intervened and said: "On October 14 you summoned me and General Roatta and asked us how many divisions were necessary to occupy Greece. Our answer was twenty, which meant sending another ten divisions to Albania, adequately equipped. On the following day you again summoned us to a meeting at which their Excellencies Ciano and Jacomoni and Visconti Prasca were present, and without consulting us further you gave orders to attack on the twenty-sixth, which later became the twenty-eighth. The facts are as you have stated, but neither the General Staff nor the Army Staff can be held responsible for them. As for attacking on December 5, unless a repetition of what has happened is desired, I do not believe it is possible. An accurate estimate must be made of the time necessary to enable the reinforcements to arrive and preparations to be completed, and the necessary decisions can be made only on the basis of the results." The Duce agreed, giving me the task of setting in train a study of the transport plan by the royal army and royal navy staffs.

That is what Badoglio said. A certain basic consistency can be discerned in his ideas and attitude on this occasion. His mistrust of Visconti Prasca's plan had been evident enough, but he cannot be credited with an outspoken consistency of outward attitude which would necessarily have expressed itself in definite opposition. Badoglio spoke out clearly to Mussolini only after the real face of the campaign had been revealed and, the chapter of wild illusions having been closed, a new chapter of desperate remedies, sometimes bordering on panic, had opened.

8. Soddu's Telephone Message

While Badoglio compiled evidence for his defense and Visconti Prasca retired from the scene, the Julia Divison was still isolated, pinned down by mud, snow, and hunger, and harried by the pack. The advance along the flanks of the Smolikas had been tough, but the retreat towards Konitsa was, as we have said, an inferno.[1] "The whole movement of the 8th Alpini tactical group from the Armata and Konitsa area," General Girotti later wrote, "took place by various paths that lead from Armata to the Cristobasile saddle under intense artillery and machine-gun fire. Our columns crossing the Eleuteron depression were attacked by enemy infantry, with which the civil population joined. The troops, though exhausted from lack of food for the past week or thereabouts and nearing the end of their tether, reacted with indomitable energy and succeeded in forcing their way through in various places in battles lasting up to seven hours in which the batteries of the Conegliano group were heavily engaged, firing at point-blank range to the last round. In this tremendous situation heavy casualties were suffered by officers and men, and a large proportion of the transport animals were killed. . . . If rations had not run out after the fifth day, the struggle could have been continued."

Thus, when the Julia got back to the Perati bridge, it was a ghost of the fine division that had moved against the enemy at dawn on October 28. "Several days fighting in mountainous country in rain and snow," an official Greek history states, "had greatly reduced the strength of the battalions of the Julia Division and notably affected the morale of its men. In spite of the excellence of the human raw material and its training, and the high spirit with which they entered the struggle, ten days after the invasion began these battalions had lost a great part of their fighting spirit."² It had lost in killed, wounded, and prisoners a good fifth of its strength; and the remainder were exhausted.

The Greek way of attacking "from above," of infiltrating from the rear and laying ambushes, the consequences of which were likely at best to be capture and a prisoner of war camp, became an obsession with the Julia Division, just as it later took its toll of the morale of all Italian units during the weeks in which the "wall" was formed. The initial Italian reverses had an enormous influence on the rest of the war because, coming on the heels of Visconti Prasca's reckless optimism, they inspired the Italian commanders at all levels with a spirit of caution, a pessimistic, sometimes overpessimistic, approach to the situations with which they were faced. The morale of the army in Albania had been shaken once and for all. The Julia Division, on its return to its old position on the Perati bridge after so many vain sacrifices, was the most obvious victim of the failure of the offensive.

On November 10 Neville Chamberlain died. On November 12 British torpedo bombers attacked the Italian fleet at Taranto and severely damaged two battleships. In a sense the Second World War went its own way while the Albanian "sideshow" continued. The Taranto attack was indirect British aid to the Greeks. Britain, though in no position to be openhanded, had sent air reinforcements to Greece in the first few days of November. A squadron of Blenheim fighter-bombers landed at Tatoi and Eleusina, near Athens, on November 3, and in the course of the next few days more squadrons of Blenheims, Gladiators, and Wellingtons followed. These forces were under the command of Air Commodore J. H. d'Albiac, and they went into action with a raid by three fighter-bombers as early as November 5.

In order to avoid provoking Germany, which, though hostile, was still neutral, Metaxas did not allow these squadrons to be based in Macedonia; and d'Albiac, who wanted to concentrate on attacking Italian ports of disembarkation in Albania, had, like the air commanders on the other side of the barricade, to deal with the requests of ground commanders who wanted constant and massive air intervention in the front line. On November 16, 2,200 officers and men of the RAF with 310 vehicles landed at the Piraeus, followed by 2,000 anti-aircraft gunners with 400 vehicles. The nature of this British military aid became plain at once: specialized units, a great deal of material, at any rate by Greek or Italian standards— and relatively few men. Italian air supremacy, which was crushing at the beginning of hostilities, was not wiped out, but undoubtedly began to be eroded.

Though chronologically it is anticipating events, this seems an appropriate point at which to comment on Mussolini's speech to the provincial hierarchs of the Fascist Party in the Palazzo Venezia on November 18.[3] The speech was written several days in advance —Ciano saw it on November 12—and it did not take into account the Greek offensive launched on November 14. It was a sequel to the stormy meetings that Mussolini had had with Badoglio, who was now in disgrace, and with Roatta, who, however, refrained from excessively exposing himself. The speech was arrogant and full of lies; Mussolini spoke like a man trying to shout down his bad conscience to prevent it from becoming manifest to the world. Not that any trouble was to be expected from his audience, which was guaranteed to applaud whatever he said.

"After being patient for a long time," the dictator said, "we have torn the mask from a country guaranteed by Great Britain, a subtle enemy, Greece. It was an account overdue for settlement. There is one thing to be said which will perhaps not fail to surprise some out-of-date Italian classicists: the Greeks hate Italy as no other nation does. It is a hatred that seems at first sight inexplicable, but it is general, deep, and ineradicable in all classes, in the towns, the villages, at the top, at the bottom, everywhere. The reason for it is a mystery." After this profound psychological diagnosis, based on Mussolini's notoriously vast experience of Greek life and character (its purpose was to provoke an equal hatred of the Greeks by the Italians), the Duce passed on to a survey of the military situation. He spoke of the documents that had been found at the station at Vitry la Charité, which indeed made clear the Greek trend during the last few months preceding the campaign to seek British and French support (Italy having done everything possible in heaven and earth to push her in that direction), and then went on: "The rugged valleys of Epirus and their muddy roads do not lend themselves to Blitzkriegs, as those incorrigibles who practice the easy strategy of sticking pins into maps would claim. No act or word of mine or of the government promised this."

This was a shameless lie. There had been no resounding public statements promising a lightning advance, but the documentation we have quoted demonstrates how firmly convinced the Palazzo Venezia, the Palazzo Chigi, and Tirana had been that the campaign would be a walkover. It is sufficient to point out that before the opening of hostilities General Ranza, the air commander in Albania, asked not for more fighters or bombers, but for torpedo bombers with which to attack British shipping after the swift occupation of Greece.[4] Not content with lying about Greek hatred and the soundness of his government's forecasts, Mussolini continued in the same vein.

> I do not think it worth the trouble to deny all the news spread by Greek propaganda and its British loudspeakers. The Julia Alpine Division, which is said to have suffered enormous losses, to have run away, to have been pulverized by the Greeks, has been inspected by General Soddu. After the conclusion of his inspection he telegraphed me on November 12: "Having this morning inspected the Julia Alpine Division, I must inform you, Duce, of the magnificent impression created by this superb unit, which is prouder and stronger than ever with its granite-like Alpini."

About the valor of the Julia Division there is no doubt; nor is there any doubt that in spite of its fifteen days' Calvary it was still able to fight. But there is also no doubt that it had been caught in the millstone of the Greek mountain infantry and cavalry that had harassed it with murderous mortar and machine-gun fire, and that it had had to beat a rapid retreat, leaving many dead, wounded, and prisoners behind. While Soddu was sending his bombastic telegram, the Julia Division was trying to put itself in order again, having temporarily handed over responsibility for the Pindus sector to the Bari Division, which had been originally intended for the occupation of Corfu. But the Bari Division's entry into the line was singularly unfortunate; its advanced units, lacking artillery support, were assaulted and overwhelmed by massive Greek forces, and the result of this unhappy episode was the bad reputation that clung to it for the rest of the campaign. It was called the "runaway division" by the Alpini of the Julia, who were compelled to remain in the line because of the way in which the Bari broke. As a fighting instrument Girotti's division was now of limited efficiency; it was in urgent need of rest and reorganization, but the threatening situation permitted neither. Soddu, when he inspected its remnants, should, if anything, have denounced the incapacity and recklessness of those who sent it into the Greek trap, instead of composing rhetorical telegrams. While the Duce was speaking the Julia was again in the height of the fray, engaged in checking the Greek offensive. Meanwhile the unsleeping dictator continued with his blustering:

Is there anyone among you, comrades, who remembers the unpublished speech made at Eboli in July 1935, before the Ethiopian war? I said then that we should break the Negus' back. Now, with the same *absolute* certainty, I repeat *absolute*, I tell you we shall break the Greek back. Whether in two months or in twelve does not matter. The war has barely begun. We have men and resources sufficient to eliminate all Greek resistance. British aid cannot prevent the fulfillment of our determination in the matter or save the Greeks from the catastrophe they asked for and have shown that they deserve. Anyone who thinks or suspects anything else does not know me. Having once chosen a path, I do not slacken to the end. This I have already shown and, whatever happens or may happen, I shall show it again. The 372 killed, 1,081 wounded, and the 650 missing in the first ten days of fighting in Epirus will be avenged.

Mussolini had coined one of his "historical" phrases: We shall break the Greek back. But he failed to do so until the Germans intervened. He owed this to the troops who put up a resistance that neither he nor his aides in the preparation of the campaign deserved. In Albania the Duce was faced with the possibility of total defeat.

As soon as he assumed command, Soddu issued some directives which Visconti Prasca describes as being "rather textbook and academic" in nature,[5] and so indeed they were when they spoke of "maintaining a combative attitude with frequent harassing actions and *coups de main*," for maintaining a combative attitude is the least that can be asked of troops in battle. But basically Soddu's directives reflected the reality of the situation. In the Epirus sector, he said, "on the right flank the Kalamas bridgehead will be held and organized in such a way as to ensure its retention, and the coast will be carefully watched; on the left the Konitsa-Stracani area will be strongly defended with a view to providing flank support and a center of reaction against enemy operations in the Perati-Klisura direction."

The Koritsa sector was to be organized for defense, and in particular steps were to be taken to ensure "the inviolability of the left flank." By now the Italians were very conscious of the threat to that weak flank. Visconti Prasca argues that the changeover from an offensive to a defensive deployment led to the creation of a "thin, linear" front, the weak patches in which were a source of grave danger. But the change in deployment was dictated not by General Soddu, but by circumstances, and this Visconti Prasca ended by forgetting.

Reinforcements began arriving in Albania at a rate which, though rapid, was insufficient to meet the situation. On November 10, 11, and 12 the Val Fella, Val Tagliamento and Val Natisone battalions of Alpini arrived at Valona and the Edolo Battalion of the 5th Regiment arrived at Tirana by air. The Tirano Battalion, also belonging to the 5th Regiment, reached Albania by sea, and the landing of a medium tank battalion began at Durazzo. But when the names of units are mentioned it must not be assumed that they were up to establishment, fully trained and equipped, and ready to fight. "Battalions," Colonel Aldo Rasero has written, "were hurriedly sent to unknown and not well-defined positions, where they sometimes had to find out at their own cost in which direction the enemy lay."[6] When in Greek accounts of the campaign the presence of a division at the front is assumed because one of its battalions was in the firing line, it is a serious distortion of the truth. Divisions had practically ceased to exist as such, and in the case of troops put in as reinforcements, regiments had often practically ceased to exist too. The typical unit was the battalion, thrown in to fill a gap in some sector under an unfamiliar command.

On November 14 and 15 Field Marshal Keitel had a meeting with Badoglio. Their conversation could not be very fruitful, because Keitel was talking to a man lacking in authority, out of favor with Mussolini, hesitating between a decisive step such as resigning and delaying tactics that might allow him to gain time. Keitel was hard, almost contemptuous. He expressed his disappointment at the situation, and added that Germany considered necessary "the total annihilation of Greece, which was being transformed into an important air and naval base for the Allies" (an idea which was to be repeated in a letter to Mussolini from Hitler on December 31). Badoglio put the blame on the politicians. While the two marshals were discussing the military situation and Mussolini in a conversation with General Armellini was forecasting the capture of Preveza and Arta by December, the Greek offensive began. The opening shots were fired at dawn on November 14, 1940, an especially unhappy day for the Italians.

After October 28 strong Greek forces arrived in western Macedonia; the 10th, 11th, and 7th divisions reinforced the 4th Brigade and the 9th Division already in that sector. The army commander was General Pitsikas, and one of his corps commanders was General Tsolakoglou. I mention these two generals now because they played an important role in the days of the Greek capitulation. Tsolakoglou, after being one of the artificers of the victories of the Greek western Macedonia army and later of those of the Epirus army, became a quisling in Greek eyes, the head of a collaborationist government.

On this front the strategy of the two armies was to a large extent imposed by nature. The Italians, after a first withdrawal, as we have seen, dug themselves in on the Devoli for a good part of its length. Behind their backs was the Morava massif, wild and precipitous mountain country, with no villages, cultivation, or roads, full of great crags, crevices, and ravines. It was a bastion, but also an obstacle through which supplies could not pass.

To the north of the Morava the Devoli enters a wide valley beyond which there stands, as solitary and forbidding as a castle of legend, Mount Ivan, rising to a height of 5,500 feet. Not far away, still farther to the north, is Lake Prespa and the Yugoslav border. An offensive could not be launched directly at the Morava; it would have to bypass it, either by way of the Devoli Valley to the north or by the pass between the Devoli and the Pindus to the south. Here, in the Erseke zone, was the point of junction between Geloso's Eleventh Army and Vercellino's Ninth.

Papagos gave orders for the preparation of the offensive on November 5. Fortunately for Soddu, planning it took longer than the transfer of troops to the area. The Greek commanders were by no means in agreement. While the divisional commanders agreed with the High Command directives and were anxious to attack, Pitsikas hesitated; he feared having to meet an Italian counterattack without reserves and consequently made difficulties and in practice obstructed the orders of the High Command. Not till Papagos settled the argument by giving definite orders did the Greeks move to the assault. The frontier separated the Devoli Valley from the Tsangoni area, and the Greek troops' fighting spirit was given an extra spur by the memory of Greek claims to this border zone, which the Greeks believed to be Greek. They had twice occupied it during previous wars, and had twice had to give it up again under the peace treaty.

By now it was winter on these mountains. Mount Ivan was wrapped in cloud and whipped with snow, and the Morava was thick with mud. The height of the Albanian mountains is relatively not so very great, but their peculiarity is a freezing north wind that causes the thermometer to plunge many degrees below zero. The Greeks attacked along the whole Macedonian front, their major effort being to the south of the Morava, though they also exerted heavy pressure on the pass between the Morava and Mount Ivan. The ultimate objective was of course Koritsa, which lay down in the plain beyond the mountains, a precious goal, a paradise in comparison with this inferno. The 10th, 9th, and 15th divisions were in the first line of the Greek advance—in that order from south to north. The 15th Division was the first to move, at 6:30 A.M. on November 14, from a starting line on the isthmus that divides the two Prespa lakes. The assault was violent, and the Italians were soon in a critical situation. Enemy penetrations took place more or less everywhere and endangered the back areas. No total disintegration of Italian units took place, but there was confusion and loss of contact between units. Nasci, who was still in command of the sector, pending its take-over by Vercellino, was immediately alarmed at the crumbling of his front, and on the fifteenth he telegraphed to the High Command to report the deep and dangerous breaches opened by the Greeks and to ask that "everything possible" should be sent immediately.

On the same day he conferred with his front-line commanders, those of the Venezia, Piemonte, Arezzo, and Parma divisions, and decided to retreat to a line of resistance running along the ridge of the Morava massif, but a withdrawal in the Erseke area made it evident almost immediately that it would be impossible to carry out this intention. This was an incident of considerable importance and plainly demonstrated the disorganization of the command structure. Erseke was a key point, held by the 1st Ber-

saglieri, commanded by Colonel Azzaro, who withdrew to positions in the rear, creating a dangerous gap on the left of the Bari
Division, which had no warning of this disengagement maneuver
and was left with a completely open flank. A court of inquiry was
held into Colonel Azzaro's conduct, and he maintained that he
was ordered to withdraw by General Nasci. The latter stated that
in a telephone conversation with Azzaro he might well have indicated the advisability of a withdrawal to better positions, but
that he had no authority to give him orders because the 1st Bersaglieri belonged to the Eleventh Army and not to his. Azzaro replied that until the evening before Erseke had been in the Ninth
Army area, and that he had received no information about any
transfer. The romantic and improbable suggestion was even made
that a phoney order had been given by a spy, imitating Nasci's
voice.

The colonel must have had a very good case, because no disciplinary action was taken against him; it turned out that the unfortunate 1st Bersaglieri had alternately been assigned now to one
army, now to the other, which certainly did not facilitate its commander's task. The truth was that chaos prevailed in the rear and
at many headquarters. What with the rain and wind-driven snow,
the situation was nightmarish. The 81 mm. shells caused horrible
wounds; field hospitals, bandages, lint, drugs were lacking; the
wounded were operated on and tended under lorry tarpaulins or
in the debris of cottages. Uniforms were tattered and torn, the
thread broke at the seams, the cloth turned as hard as parchment
and weighed heavily without providing warmth or protection. Many
Italian units fought furiously; others were stunned, as it were, by
the swift change of fortune; the supply services were improvised
and erratic, and the back areas were chaotic.

A single hammerblow had sufficed to throw into confusion a
haphazard organization based on the comfortable assumption of a
continuous offensive. Reinforcements were flung straight into the
heat of battle almost before they realized they were anywhere near
it. There were infantrymen on the way to the Morava massif who

rounded up stragglers from the front and took them forward again only to be wounded by mortar fragments and taken to the rear without having fired a shot. There were Alpini who landed at the Koritsa airfield after Greek 151 mm. guns had begun shelling it, were wounded while disembarking from the German Junkers which had been hurriedly thrown into service to reinforce the Italian air lift, and were sent back again in the same aircraft to hospitals in Italy. The wounded soon numbered hundreds, and then thousands; officers of the supply services, such as Second Lieutenant Franco Sampietro of the Morbegno Alpini Battalion, Gold Medal, had to take command of units that had lost their officers. Men belonging to the mule trains were involved in the fighting, regimental commanders set many examples of personal valor, and the commander of the 84th Infantry Regiment, Colonel Luigi Zacco, was killed on November 18 in a bayonet counterattack.

The Taro Division, commanded by General Gino Pedrazzoli, and the Vestone and Verona battalions of the 6th Alpini were rushed to the front, but the Greeks threw into the line the K Group, consisting of the 10th and 11th divisions, and still had a distinct superiority in strength. Misunderstandings and mistakes also occurred among the Greek commanders in those hectic days. The commander of the 13th Division was relieved of his command for ordering a withdrawal that risked exposing the flanks of other advancing units. Vercellino, after assuming command of the Eleventh Army, declared the situation to be untenable in spite of the bastions of the Morava massif and Mount Ivan, which were about to be encircled. On the night of November 19 Soddu decided that there was no alternative to a withdrawal in depth to new positions. The bulwarks for the defense of Koritsa, of which he had spoken to Mussolini with so much confidence and optimism, had to be given up.

The withdrawal visualized was of about thirty miles in depth from the original Italian positions, and it implied the abandonment of Koritsa. Soddu proposed to "build up the second position with arriving units" and not to "exhaust excessively the units in the line." Badoglio declared himself to be in agreement, but with some detachment. At 10:30 on November 20 Soddu went to Pogradec and, after a final conference with some of his commanders, decided that the withdrawal should begin that same evening, but then postponed it until next day. On November 21 he tried to cover himself by securing specific authority for the abandonment of Koritsa either from Mussolini or from Badoglio. When Soddu asked him for instructions the old marshal, according to Pricolo, confined himself to quoting "a military maxim which says that in difficult circumstances one must have the courage to make quick, if painful, decisions in order not to be too late."[7] All that he got from Mussolini was an invitation not to rush matters but to think it over. To the Duce the decision to abandon a large slice of Albanian territory to the Greeks was a bitter pill to swallow. That day Ciano had brought him a letter from Hitler,[8] whom he had met at Berghof on the occasion of his visit to Austria for the formal adherence of Hungary to the Tripartite Pact (Rumania and Slovakia joined it a few days later).

To Ciano Hitler had been sharply critical of the attack on Greece, and he adopted a similar tone in his letter to Mussolini. In fact the Führer rapped the Duce over the knuckles. He said that he would have preferred to have delayed "the operation a little if possible to a more favorable season, but in any case until after the election of the American President," and he had been proposing to explain these ideas at their meeting in Florence. The Italian initiative had had "displeasing psychological consequences" and the "military consequences" were "very grave." The Duce had to swallow these rebukes, the justice of which had been demonstrated by events, and he answered in conciliatory tones, saying "yes" to everything that Hitler suggested and attributing to pure mischance the fact that his letter of October 19, in which he had informed the Führer of the impending attack on Greece (though without mentioning the date) had not reached him in time. He meekly attributed the initial Italian reverses to the weather, to "the almost complete defection of the Albanian forces," and to the attitude of Bulgaria, and he announced that "Italy is now preparing thirty divisions, with which she will be able to annihilate Greece"; and he concluded by saying: "I too have had my black week, but now the worst is over."[9] Three weeks had sufficed to quench the aspirations to rebellion of the second-class dictator who had wanted to confront Hitler with an accomplished fact.

The responsibility for the decision to retreat was left to Soddu. He laid down that the new line was to be Mount Cytetit–Ferit–Haxhiut–Bregu i Bresave–Valomone–Lenijes–Mali Haisht–Nikolara–Gostanghes–Mali Velusces. During the night of the twenty-first all the easily transportable supplies of arms and equipment were gloomily evacuated from Koritsa, and the 4th Bersaglieri rearguard left Koritsa at 7 A.M. on November 22. Contact with the enemy was broken off. To all Italians war communiqué No. 168, dated November 22, had overtones heavy with defeat.

> Our covering troops consisting of two divisions which at the beginning of hostilities were entrenched on the defensive on the Greek-Albanian border at Koritsa have withdrawn after eleven days' fighting to a line west of the town, which has been evacuated. Bitter fighting took place during this period. Our losses were considerable. Those of the enemy were the same, or perhaps greater. Our reinforcements are concentrating on the new line.

According to Greek aerial reconnaissance reports, one column of retreating Italians was more than twelve miles long. The whole Greek front moved forward into a void. The Italian retreat was sufficiently orderly, though a great deal of material had to be abandoned and the troops received supplies irregularly and their equipment was worn out. They marched through desolate, deserted villages, the Albanian battalions had disintegrated completely, and on the faces of the few Albanians to be seen there was a kind of

resentment against this army which they had believed to be strong
and was now retreating before the Greeks. Even the Albanian
puppet government barely concealed its resentment. The wounded
could not be given proper attention; the wife of Jacomoni, the
governor-general, who worked as a volunteer nurse, told Pricolo
that many wounds became gangrenous because of lack of dis-
infectant.

Badoglio went on accumulating evidence for his defense, and
on November 23 wrote in the High Command diary:

> Reinforcements in Albania are arriving slowly because of the inade-
> quate equipment of the ports of disembarkation. It cannot be stated
> with confidence that we shall have time to fortify the chosen se-
> curity line. The Duce gave me to read two reports by a carabinieri
> officer and an officer of the General Staff in which it is stated that
> Nasci did not think it necessary to withdraw. In my opinion the
> withdrawal has been a sound step, because it provides an opportu-
> nity for strengthening the defense. However, stabilization of the
> situation in Albania will in my view require the whole of De-
> cember.

In fact, in the last hours before the retreat, Nasci regarded the
situation with more confidence than Vercellino, but he was now the
commander of the Alpini Army Corps, not of the whole Macedonian sector. This change made in the command of the most crucial
sector of the front while the crisis was at its height was probably
yet another mistake. It should, however, be pointed out that, while
it might have been possible to hold the bastions of the Morava and
Mount Ivan with fresh and determined troops, the wave of ap-
prehension that spread through all ranks, from the infantrymen
in the line to the top command level, deriving from the feeling that
they were inferior to the enemy even numerically, made it a doubtful and hazardous enterprise.

In Greece the jubilation that followed the capture of Koritsa was
indescribable. Koritsa was a name and a symbol, a town seized
from the hated aggressor, from a Great Power humiliated by a

small country. Metaxas spoke on the Greek radio, sternly replying to Mussolini's boasts and threats of four days previously.[10] Lord Halifax expressed admiration for the Greek achievement in the House of Lords. With singular untimeliness, the Italian radio on the same day put out a broken-winded commentary claiming that General Soddu was continuing his preparations for the conquest of Greece, and that there would be no more hope for that country once the Italian High Command began carrying out its plans.

The crisis on the Macedonian front necessarily had repercussions on the Epirus sector, where the Julia, Bari, Centauro, Ferrara, and Siena divisions and the Littoral Group, with grenadiers and cavalry as well as two regiments of Bersaglieri, were deployed between the Pindus and the sea. On November 16 Geloso officially succeeded Visconti Prasca in command of the Eleventh Army, but on the previous day, by Soddu's orders—Visconti Prasca having by this time, as we have seen, become a culprit rather than a commander—the troops in Epirus had begun making their way back along the roads they had followed in the first advance. The Littoral Group, the Siena and the Ferrara divisions withdrew, and the Centauro Division had to leave many of its small tanks behind in the mud. The Greeks patched them up and put them back into service, and officers of the British expeditionary force saw them in use in the spring of 1941.

On the night of the seventeenth the withdrawal in the Erseke area, which opened the valley of the Ossum to the Greeks and exposed the left flank of the whole Eleventh Army, added drama to an already serious situation. So grave was the threat that General Geloso formed a tactical group of a battalion of customs guards and two battalions of Blackshirts to plug the gap suddenly opened on the flank of the Bari Division. The latter—the command of which had been taken over from General Zaccone by General D'Havet, another swapping of horses in midstream—was in trouble; its headquarters were isolated both from the units under its command and from corps headquarters. The Julia Division, which had not been allowed a moment's respite, had to be thrown into the sector which the Bari Division was no longer able to hold, and to hold the Perati bridgehead. It had now been assigned to the newly constituted VIII Army Corps commanded by General Bancale. On the night of the nineteenth Bancale ordered the Aquila Battalion, which was holding the bridgehead, to cross to the right bank of the Sarandaporos, making the river its line of resistance. But Geloso disagreed with Bancale and insisted on the bridgehead's being held; and so, while the commanders vacillated, we come to November 20, when the bridgehead was assaulted by massive enemy forces.

The retreat was now general, the whole of the line from the Yugoslav frontier to the sea was on the move, the Italian commanders were in the grip of a catastrophe psychosis, and their cries of alarm multiplied. Mario Vercellino, installed at Elbasan in a dilapidated villa that was the headquarters of the Eleventh Army, surrounded by miserable hovels, gloomily noted: "We are without communications and almost without motor transport. Information reaches us only by way of messengers. . . . I have nothing but mountainous mule or sheep tracks by which to supply the new line; and there are very few mules." On the eleventh, Geloso, who was abandoning Epirus in order to hold a line that would enable Argyrokastron to be held, was in a similar mood of black pessimism. He stated that when the retreat had been completed he would have left "no reserves worthy of the name," because "the sorely tried Bari and Centauro divisions needed to be taken back into the second line for reorganization, the Ferrara Division was reduced to a handful of men, and the Siena Division was in a similar state." Geloso had yet another cause for concern: on November 23 the Greeks made a landing behind Italian lines. The infiltration was eliminated, but it caused alarm.

On November 26 Geloso pointed out to Soddu that the new line "was chosen in the hope of avoiding the loss, even temporarily, of Santi Quaranta, Argyrokastron, and Permeti, and would be tenable only in the event of the availability of two complete, newly arrived divisions. These not being available, the question of the loss of these places becomes a secondary matter in comparison with the necessity of maneuvering so as to be able to gather our forces and reorganize them in order to be able to resume the initiative. Since our forces are exhausted and their efficiency is reduced by 70 per cent and the newly arrived forces amount only to five battalions of the Modena and two of the Pusteria divisions [the latter alpine division was under the command of General De Cia and was disembarking], it becomes necessary to choose a shorter and more easily defensible line."

This new line was to run from the Logora Pass to Tepeleni to Klisura to Quari Mortes. Geloso in fact asked for a blank check, for authority to occupy this line "as soon as the situation made it advisable." From a strictly military point of view, Geloso's proposals were sound enough; a withdrawal to the full extent suggested by him would have resulted in a much shorter and more easily defensible line. But it would have involved the abandonment of Albanian territory, including territory in the Eleventh Army sector, to a depth of dozens of miles, would have put Mussolini in a very difficult political position, and would have been another severe blow to the morale of the troops. It would have been a confession of defeat.

Pricolo, who went to Albania partly as chief of Air Staff on a tour of inspection and partly as Mussolini's personal informant, stated in a report dated November 23 that "the various headquarters seem little informed about the situation either from the tactical point of view or from the logistical and geographical," and that "the commanders have many doubts about the fighting spirit of troops who are tired, mixed up in different units and sometimes disorganized. . . . One reason why the morale of the troops already tried in action is anything but good is that they have the feeling of having been badly used and badly supported, and in particular they are depressed at having suffered the humiliation of defeat at the hand of the Greeks." Starace, another "secret informer" in his capacity as chief of staff of the Fascist Militia, told Ciano that the troops had not fought well; and De

Vecchi, the Governor of the Aegean, a stubborn and arrogant supporter of the attack on Greece, handed in his resignation, threatening a personal strike if he were not given much more braid or the rank of a marshal of Italy. Another old man, De Bono, got to work behind the scenes with a view to succeeding Badoglio. While the disheartened troops marched back—furious fighting occurred when they were engaged by Greek advanced units in the Epirus sector—Soddu, in accordance with his nature, alternated between moments of ephemeral optimism and long periods of profound discouragement, according to whether the disorganized and fragmentary news that reached him from the front was encouraging or depressing, sometimes excessively so in either case.

If Soddu was in grave trouble, Papagos was tormented by doubts. Greece was jubilant, but Papagos was perplexed. The directives he issued were correct. "We appreciate the tiredness of our troops, but the situation of the enemy is worse. We must not give him the chance to reorganize or organize his defense." But he hesitated to order a resumption of the all-out offensive, fearing that he in turn might excessively lengthen his supply lines and fall into a trap. His army was not capable of rapid movement, he was a soldier of the old, solid school, and he liked advancing with his flanks and rear well protected. He was not a Rommel. The Greek intelligence services tended to exaggerate the solidity and efficiency of the enemy forces (the Italian intelligence services had a similar tendency, though on the eve of October 28 no one in a position of responsibility took much notice of them). Gian Carlo Fusco, in his lively little book on the Albanian war, mentions the belief of one Colonel Gerothanassis that the stretches of road towards Valona, Elbasan, and Berati abandoned by the Italians were infested with thousands of tons of mines.[11]

The Italians were not equipped for measures of that kind, and in the confusion of the retreat there were other, more urgent tasks to see to. Badly organized as they were for an advance, they had no way of covering their retreat other than by the fire and self-sacrifice of their troops. General Tsolakoglou, whose army corps was on the extreme right wing in western Macedonia adjoining the Yugoslav border, helped to some extent to resolve Papagos' doubts by suggesting that, to avoid giving the Italians any respite, a group of four picked infantry battalions with strong artillery support should make a drive for Pogradec. This was a precious Italian defense bastion, and its loss would increase the threat of encirclement of the Ninth Army on the left, while seizure of part of the shore of the Lake of Ochrida would enable the Greeks to attempt landings behind the Italian lines.

It was now snowing heavily on the Albanian mountains, the battalions of the Ninth Army were often isolated, and three centers for dropping air supplies had to be organized to ensure troops engaged in a bitter battle at least of their rations. The interruption of contact between the Ninth Army and the Greeks lasted for only three days, from November 21 to 24. On November 24 the task force designated for the Pogradec operation tested the Italian line, and on the following day other units were brought up to it. The decisive part of the operation was carried out by Greek mountaineers who followed the narrow, rugged course of a small stream, the Tseravas, running between precipitous rocks. By this arduous route the Greeks succeeded in carrying out an infiltration that threw the defenders, who had only just settled down in unfamiliar positions, into confusion. The battle was hard, the troops of the Venezia Division fought, but on November 28 Pogradec fell. The consolidation of Soddu's new front was undermined by the loss of one of its essential pillars.

Mussolini stormed and raged. To the head of military intelligence, General Cesare Amé, who was summoned to the Palazzo Venezia on November 15, he declared: "I want the truth, because I am going to have various heads blown off by a firing squad." No one was shot by a firing squad, but the temporizer Badoglio, who opposed the Greek campaign but had sudden outbursts of enthusiasm for it, and objected to Visconti Prasca's fantastic plans but then resigned himself to them because he believed, or pretended to believe, that the politicians had arranged everything, was sacked. On November 23 Roberto Farinacci, the ambitious and vulgar deviationist Fascist and fanatically pro-German boss of Cremona, attacked the marshal in his personal newspaper, the *Regime Fascista.* "Mussolini," he announced, "has spoken plainly. Mussolini has proclaimed that the modern Carthage will be defeated and that Greece will end with her back broken. We are convinced that all this will come about, even if lack of foresight and shilly-shallying by the General Staff has enabled Churchill to enjoy a stupid diversion. But all evils do not come to harm us. The reaction will be the greater, and the defeat of the enemy the more shattering."

The attack was certainly inspired, if not by Mussolini and Ciano in person, at any rate by individuals who circulated within the orbit of the Palazzo Venezia and the Palazzo Chigi, and it was by no means displeasing to the Germans. Badoglio asked for an audience with Mussolini and rejected the charges; and he did so in terms so humiliating to Farinacci that, according to Ciano, he would have preferred dynamiting the presses of the *Regime Fascista* to listening to it. Badoglio himself relates that "Mussolini said that Farinacci could not stand me, and that this had been at his initiative, and that he would summon him to Rome in order to confer with him." Badoglio also tried to have an article defending the General Staff printed in the Rome daily *La Tribuna.* The article was wordy, but not without sound arguments. It never saw the light, however, because it seems that on the day *La Tribuna* printed it, all copies of that newspaper were confiscated. Cyclostyled copies of Badoglio's article were sent to the military commands.

Badoglio cannot be blamed for rejecting a charge that ignored the parts played by Visconti Prasca, Jacomoni, and Ciano and attributed all the responsibility for the defeat to him. He took four days' leave and went to his country house in Monferrato to do some shooting and reflect. Meanwhile he submitted a letter of resignation. He probably counted on an intervention by the King but, as on other occasions, Victor Emmanuel III preferred to see nothing and hear nothing. Puntoni, to whom General Armellini, a close colleague of Badoglio's, wrote a letter in connection with his resignation, remarked in his diary that "there are many obscurities about Badoglio's conduct"; as the worthy Puntoni was incapable of forming independent opinions of his own, it seems safe to assume that this was a reflection of the royal view. Next day, November 27, he wrote: "Mussolini is postponing his decision whether or not to accept Badoglio's resignation. His Majesty is not completely informed about the Duce's intentions. He reported to the King that there are complaints at the General Staff that the Minister of Popular Culture gave instructions to the press with a view to persuading public opinion that the Albanian failure should be attributed exclusively to lack of military preparation, and that the army leaders are therefore exclusively responsible." On the same day, November 27, Badoglio returned to Rome and went "a trifle reluctantly" to see the Duce. The news from the front was better that day, and Mussolini, according to Armellini, said to him: "And now that things are going better do you want to go?"

On November 28 Armellini went to the Quirinal, stated that "Mussolini has lost confidence in Badoglio and Badoglio has lost confidence in Mussolini," and proposed a strange compromise, namely that Badoglio should remain chief of staff but that a deputy chief should be appointed who would deal directly with Mussolini. On November 29 Mussolini informed the King by letter of Badoglio's resignation, and the King promptly acquiesced. "It should not be thought that Badoglio is irreplaceable. On the contrary, I am convinced that not all evil comes to harm us." (How many people were there in Italy at that time, from the King to Farinacci, who were ready to believe that, no matter what happened, not all evil came to harm them?) Later, after receiving the marshal in audience, Victor Emmanuel was even more specific.

"Badoglio made a disastrous impression on me. Physically he is a ruin and intellectually he is blunted. He said he was going to see the Duce tomorrow to withdraw his resignation." This was on December 3, and by now Badoglio had gone into reverse, but the King dropped him without compunction; the part that Badoglio was to play on July 25, 1943, when Mussolini was deposed, certainly had its roots in the circumstances of his resignation. Not only did Victor Emmanuel not defend Badoglio, but he actually informed Mussolini through Acquarone that he considered him a wreck.

When Badoglio saw the Duce on December 4, the latter made him a humiliating speech. He said that Cavallero had gone to Albania to see whether Soddu's nerves were standing up to the strain. If they were, Cavallero was to take Badoglio's place. Otherwise Cavallero would remain in Albania, and the marshal would remain chief of staff. "I cannot wait for Signor Cavallero to make up his mind," the marshal replied. "Very well, from now on you are at liberty," Mussolini replied.

It was after a great deal of indecision that Mussolini chose Ugo Cavallero to be Badoglio's successor. He seems, according to Ciano, at first to have inclined towards Orlando or Pintor. Pintor was killed in an air crash after the choice had settled on Cavallero, and Orlando's name was dropped. Puntoni says in his diary: "We spoke of Cavallero—and his agitated past. The King intimated that the story of Cavallero's past life did not have much importance and, incidentally, that the Duce was of the same opinion." Thus ended the story of Badoglio's dismissal from the conduct of the war. This time the man who had seemed always to be protected by a lucky star came out as loser; and when he was fished up again in 1943 it was not to win any more victories but to carry out the tragic liquidation of a bankrupt situation.

Cavallero's enemies, who were many, called him the "profiteer general" because of his frequent transitions between military posts and positions in industry or the para-political sphere. His management of the Ansaldo concern became the subject of an inquiry.

He was a man of unusual intellectual distinction. He had a degree in pure mathematics, was a translator from German and English, came first at the School of War, was promoted general at the age of thirty-eight, and spent his whole career in positions of command. He moved easily in non-military circles, was Jacomoni's father-in-law, and his outstanding characteristic was optimism. This was what Mussolini needed at a time when he was surrounded by discomfited and quarreling generals and ministers and was trying to restore good relations between the army and the party, which became stormy after the Badoglio incident. The fact that Cavallero and Badoglio, both natives of Monferrato, had detested each other for many years did not do any harm either. Cavallero was summoned to the Palazzo Venezia on the afternoon of December 3; at the Council of Ministers that morning the Duce had delivered a tirade against Badoglio, whose dismissal, though not yet official, was already a reality. According to Cavallero's memoirs, Mussolini said to him: "I wish to give you a job." Then he added: "The Badoglio crisis is irremediable, you are to be his successor."

The only strange thing about all this, if Cavallero's report of the interview is correct, is the use by Mussolini of the formal *Lei* in addressing him instead of the familiar *tu*. With characteristic lack of modesty, Cavallero added that when Mussolini discovered how well informed he was about the Albanian situation, though he had hitherto had nothing whatever to do with the conduct of the campaign, he could not believe his ears. "But he knows Albania as well as if it were his own home!" the Duce is said to have exclaimed in astonishment. At home, according to his son Carlo, Cavallero said: "We are back again at Caporetto, and as at that time I have to remedy Badoglio's mistakes as I did then." Apart from the Badoglio crisis, December 4 was also a day of crisis at the front. Enemy pressure on the Eleventh Army sector was intense, and Geloso proposed to Soddu an immediate withdrawal to the line he had previously suggested north of Santi Quaranta and Argyrokastron, but Soddu refused to agree to this extreme course. The consequence was a sequence of partial withdrawals, depending on how threatening enemy penetrations became at one point or other of the front. On December 1 the Julia Division was subjected to violent flank attacks, and a gap was opened on its right flank near Mali Micanit, separating it from the 41st Regiment of the Modena Division, which had been sent in disorderly fashion into the line. On December 2 a serious situation arose in the Permeti sector, when the way to the Klisura Pass was left open.

There was not a single stretch of the front which, in Badoglio's words to Visconti Prasca, was "solidly anchored" and could be used as a pivot for maneuver. The whole line was unstable, enemy blows and territorial losses took place now on the extreme left, now in the center, and now the Greeks had achieved a real breakthrough at a highly sensitive spot. Soddu, a man of volatile character and unstable morale, paled when, after the arrival of the first news about the breach opened by the Greeks, his chief of staff, Colonel Salvatore Bartiromo, said to him with singular untimeliness: "I think that your Excellency's name will be connected with the gravest defeat in our history." This was just what was needed to plunge Soddu into panic. December 4 was consequently a highly dramatic day. In a telephone conversation with Roatta, Soddu described "the critical situation in which operations are taking place, the precarious physical, numerical, and moral state of the troops as well as the deficient state of the services, and concluded by saying that the situation thus created and the rate of arrival of reinforcements did not allow the possibility of an equilibrium, let alone a recovery, to be foreseen." In another telephone conversation on the same day with Guzzoni he spoke of the advisability of "reaching a political solution to the conflict." This phrase, to which Mussolini replied by ordering that "ground must be held to the last," caused a cataclysm.

On the morning of December 4 there was an agitated discussion of Soddu's proposal at a meeting of ministers in the Duce's antechamber. Mussolini unburdened himself to everybody. To

Ciano he said: "There is no more to be done. It is absurd and grotesque, but that is how it is. We shall have to ask for a truce through Hitler." Ciano's comment was: "Impossible. The Greeks' first condition will be the Führer's personal guarantee that nothing else will ever be done against them. Rather than telephone Ribbentrop I shall put a bullet through my head. But are we really beaten? Is not the situation that the commander has laid down his arms before the troops have?" It should not be overlooked that there is some suspicion that this part of Ciano's diary may have been altered or at any rate cut, but the general impression that it records is genuine. To Pricolo Mussolini said in consternation: "Have you seen Soddu's telegram? [It was not, as we know, a telegram, but a telephoned statement transcribed for Mussolini.] He proposes that we should actually ask for an armistice. Rather than ask Greece for an armistice it would be better for us all to go to Albania and get killed on the spot."

There has since been discussion whether Soddu really intended to suggest asking for an armistice and was not in reality merely suggesting German intervention; whether, that is to say, the words transcribed really represented what was in his mind. I cannot see the fundamental difference that others see between the two alternatives. In either case Mussolini, Ciano, and Jacomoni would irretrievably have lost their war, would have been forced either to end it themselves with a grave defeat or, thanks to the Germans, with a German victory. In either case the Italians were bound to emerge severely humiliated, as they ultimately did.

Cavallero entered on a bankrupt legacy. Ciano summed him up acutely. "The man is much talked about, opinions about him differ widely, but no one says he is stupid." He was redeemed by his death; his suicide gave him moral stature in bitter days for Italy, when very few others showed resolution or contempt for life. He was one of the very few Italian generals who in any way or for any reason performed a proud gesture in those tragic times. Stories were current about him that cast doubt on his reliability and even his honesty. This is not the right place for a biography,

or even a biographical sketch, of Cavallero. Pricolo attributes to
Amedeo d'Aosta an extremely harsh judgment on him.

> I had to dismiss him [from the command of imperial troops during
> the Abyssinian War] for lying and propose that he be sent on leave.
> One fine day he put himself in command of a reconnaissance col-
> umn consisting of picked men borrowed from the subordinate gov-
> ernors; and, on his way through various areas in the neighborhood
> of Lake Tana, he sent numerous reports about alleged operational
> activities. He spoke of bitter fighting, suppression of revolts, captur-
> ing prisoners, etc. I had serious doubts, and had his movements
> checked, making use of aircraft, among other things. The findings
> made it clear that his reports were false from beginning to end. All
> this to gain promotion.

Whatever his faults may have been, he confronted the situation
in Albania with an optimism which was his way of life and was as
natural to him as breathing, and at any rate contributed to extracting Soddu and the whole general headquarters in Albania
from the gloom in which they were plunged. On that same morning of December 4 Mussolini sent for him. "Your aircraft is ready
at Littorio," he said. In the afternoon Cavallero was at Ninth
Army headquarters at Elbasan. With him were Soddu and Vercellino, the Ninth Army commander. That afternoon the "double
command" period of the war in Albania began, with Cavallero
there in his capacity of chief of the General Staff and Soddu as
the military commander. This did not last long. Soddu was too
weak; he was totally inadequate in the situation. His ascent to
the top of the military tree showed how defective was the method
of selection. Doctrinaire, desk-bound officers, possessing exceptional intelligence, perhaps, but altogether lacking in character
(the primary quality of a soldier) succeeded in making their way
to the top, leaving behind real soldiers and men of action who
might not be able to write brilliant reports, but were capable of
handling men in action. Soddu had willingly stepped into Visconti
Prasca's shoes because he had hoped quickly to rectify the situa-

tion. The faintest hint of good news led him to express unjustified optimism, as when he summoned the Albanian notables and promised them that Koritsa would be retaken before Christmas. Bad news shattered him. At that time he was the wrong man in the wrong place.

9. Cavallero's Hour

While Soddu succumbed to panic, the atmosphere in the Palazzo Venezia was a combination of impotent rage and frenzied desire for action. The demobilization order had been followed, too late, by counterorders. Divisions on reduced establishments in winter quarters were hurriedly and fragmentarily reorganized and sent to the snow and mud in Albania. In a fit of futile anger the Duce ordered the air force to "raze to the ground all places of more than 10,000 inhabitants,"[1] an operation that would have been criminal if it had not been technically impossible. The chaos in the organization of reinforcements has been vividly described by Roatta, who ascribes sole responsibility for it to the Duce, who "wanted to concern himself personally and in detail even with the transport of reinforcements, interfering several times a day, and even at night, and urging everybody only to hurry."[2]

As soon as any means of personnel transport was available, whether warship, merchant ship or aircraft [Roatta writes] men were put on board, often piecemeal, and off it went. Heavy arms, radio transmitters, field kitchens, blankets, baggage, medical equipment, ammunition, transport animals and vehicles, however, followed as soon as possible by the appropriate means of transport. Consequently, when the men landed, they had only their light arms and personal equipment and ammunition. Units arriving in Albania were units only in name. They were totally lacking in the equipment necessary to occupy a sector properly and fight; while at the same time they were exposed to all the rigors of the season and—unless they could rely on more fortunate neighboring units—were condemned to hard rations and cold food. . . . The consequence was that on the Albanian front there was an incredible mixture of units, with an enormous preponderance of infantry, while guns, transport animals, vehicles, and heavy material accumulated at the ports of embarkation in Italy waiting for a passage. At one time we had more than 30,000 transport animals, with their drivers, waiting in Apulia. To sum up, the General Staff never succeeded in landing a single regiment in Albania with all its arms and equipment. Complete plans of course existed for the organized transport of everything that was necessary, from men to material for improving bridges and road-building machinery, but these were continually upset by orders from the Palazzo Venezia.

It is obvious, of course, that Roatta is talking here to suit his own ends. He would like to contrast the picture of a cool, efficient, smooth-working General Staff with that of a Mussolini who threw everything into confusion. It is probable, it is indeed certain, that the interferences of the amateur strategist Mussolini made matters worse. But any Italian who spent any time in a combatant or noncombatant unit in wartime knows perfectly well that the picture of a rational and all-wise General Staff is a product of Roatta's retrospective imagination, and that the officers at the top level of the Italian military hierarchy calculated correctly only in such matters as the timing and allotment of promotion, jobs, and allowances. Mussolini, who felt he had been "torn with daggers," tried to meet the situation in Albania by frantically sending troops to plug gaps, troops who were ill armed and ill equipped and would have been suited to a war of the age of the Risorgimento but were more or less helpless against even an old-fashioned army such as the Greek.

On the afternoon of December 4, then, Cavallero, as mentioned above, was at Elbasan with Soddu and Vercellino. The strategic problem was this: if the line at the river Skumbi bridgehead (the Skumbi cuts Albania in two, running almost from the Lake of Ochrida to the sea) were not held, the way to Elbasan would be open to the enemy, and it would be necessary to look for a line of resistance still farther back, this time near Tirana. General

Scuero, responsible for the supply services, handed Cavallero a memorandum describing the state of supplies in Albania. This was it. Reserve rations, nil. Equipment, minimal. Woollen clothing, zero. Infantry ammunition, none. Artillery ammunition, insignificant. Arms and artillery, all supplies exhausted. Engineering equipment, practically nil. Medical equipment, inadequate.[3] The only notable thing about the document is the variety of ways in which it says the same thing, i.e., that in Albania there was practically nothing at all.

Meanwhile the temperature was falling, the winter was turning out to be extremely severe, and the Italian troops were facing it in terrifying conditions. Vercellino described the situation to his superior officers in gloomy terms: "The most tragic situation is at the Skumbi bridgehead, where we are one against five and have no artillery, because the 105s were dismounted today. There is some light artillery, and that is all. The III Army Corps has not much artillery support, but fortunately it has regained Mount Sareces thanks to a reserve battalion of the Venezia Division. . . . The air force is a sham, it limits our objectives and intervenes belatedly. It ought to help our troops more and not worry about remote objectives."[4] Soddu said that the Eleventh Army was retreating towards Klisura and that, in the absence of a line of resistance, it was having to carry out the maneuver slowly because the enemy had engaged its rearguards, and the Siena Division in particular. As for the Ninth Army sector, it was decided that a further withdrawal to the line of the Skumbi would give the troops a week's breathing space, which would be useful if substantial reinforcements arrived in the meantime. Cavallero actually spoke of the possibility of establishing an entrenched camp at Tirana and bridgeheads at Valona and Durazzo. That was the state to which the Italians were reduced.

That evening Cavallero and Soddu telephoned Mussolini, making frantic appeals for properly organized reinforcements. Soddu actually managed to work a bit of shameless sycophancy into a conversation of extreme gravity. "Duce," he said, "today I inspected the 42nd Blackshirt Battalion, which received your name with acclamation." He also announced that he was going to be stricter in his demands in future; he had ordered a court-martial on Colonel Manai, the commander of the 41st Regiment of the Modena Division (which had given way and left open a disastrous gap), and he had also relieved a divisional general of his command. If the news from the Ninth Army was worrying, that from the Eleventh was hardly better. Two days later Geloso told Cavallero that "the grave losses of men and material and the great shortage of mules, lorries, and ammunition, have put the army in a condition in which it will not be able to hold out for long, a week or a little more, unless the situation changes."

The 8th Alpini Regiment of the Julia Division had lost 80 per cent of its effectives, the Dari Division had been almost wiped out, and one of its infantry regiments, the 139th, had had to withdraw because it had no more ammunition, the stores had run out of hand grenades, and the luckier units were reduced to one day's supply of other ammunition. Girotti, the commander of the Julia Division, on December 1 declared that the state of his troops made it "absolutely essential that the division should be withdrawn to the rear for complete reorganization." The orders issued in this situation by Soddu on December 5 consequently seemed somewhat inadequate, creating the impression of an orderly maneuver being carried out on the instructions of higher authority while in reality the course of the battle was dictated by enemy pressure. Soddu radiotelegraphed to the Eleventh Army in the following terms:

> In view of the situation of the Ninth Army and in particular that of the Tridentina Division, which is spread over a wide front, I think it necessary to accelerate the completion of the known movement of your right and center to make possible a more economical front and consequently create the possibility of reinforcing your left, which must constitute an obstacle to enemy efforts in the direction of Val Tomorritsa and the left of the Devoli.

The "known movement" was the withdrawal to the north of Argyrokastron of the Eleventh Army, a sad epilogue to the advance in Epirus begun on October 28. War communiqué No. 185, dated December 9, announced this in the following terms: "The Eleventh Army has completed without loss of men or materials its withdrawal to a line to the north of Argyrokastron and adjoining localities." The completion of this movement reduced the length of the Eleventh Army front from seventy-five to forty-five miles as the crow flies. This might have been considered satisfactory if it had been the sequel to a Greek act of aggression and not of a war that Italy had declared and wanted. According to Italian official estimates, between November 9 and December 7 nine Italian regiments in Epirus were opposed to as many as twenty-three Greek regiments. These figures are not accepted by the Greeks, who, I repeat, maintain without foundation that the Italians enjoyed continual numerical superiority.

The confusion and the way in which men of different Italian units were mixed up makes an objective estimate extremely difficult. Italian General Staff studies point out that the enemy did not attain his strategic objectives, Berati, Tepeleni, and Valona, but that is a very modest consolation.

On December 7 Mussolini and Cavallero summarized their objectives in phrases of disconcerting obviousness and banality:

> The problems that as from today require immediate solution are two: *Tactical:* At all costs to prevent a breach of the line held by our troops and finally to stop the enemy advance; to resume the offensive as soon as possible in order to defeat the enemy, drive him back over the frontier, and pursue him into his own territory. *Logistical:* Urgently to transfer from Italy the new forces and resources necessary to sustain and reinforce the present deployment, completing and strengthening it.

It was only at this period that the rate at which landings took place in Albania begin painfully to quicken. The transfer of the

Taro, Modena, Pusteria, Trieste, Tridentina divisions was completed, and the landing of the Acqui and Cuneense divisions began. As the result of the construction of new wharves, cargoes unloaded daily gradually increased from 1,500 to 5,000 tons. But the appetite of the front for men, arms, and equipment was such that it still remained unsatisfied.

The situation of the Italian troops was considered so critical, and hence the political and moral position of Italy in the face of world public opinion so embarrassing, that Ribbentrop felt obliged to give German envoys in foreign capitals instructions about the attitude to be adopted by them if conversation turned to the awkward subject of Albania. In a circular dated December 11 their attention was directed to the following points, on which their comments were to be based:

(1) Italy undertook her operation against Greece for the purpose of gaining purely local control of some areas that are providing the British with secret bases against her, particularly for naval purposes. (2) The operations were begun with weak forces and have now reached a phase of immobility chiefly due to the season. Since the operations came up against superior Greek forces, they resulted in a withdrawal and Italian losses, which are limited in extent. (3) Italy is now engaged in stabilizing the front by sending new forces; it is her intention to improve her front-line positions during the winter as soon as sufficient reinforcements reach Albania. (4) The Italian retreat is a passing phenomenon; a military episode of the kind that frequently occurs in war.[5]

If on the Italian side the consternation was great, on the Greek side the official optimism concealed persistent anxieties. Metaxas remained levelheaded. He was a soldier, and did not exult at the Greek victories. The notes in his diary remain sober and realistic. He noted the Greek successes, but "I do not see a way out," he added, for he knew that his country's efforts, though magnificent, were vain. There was also some friction between

him and Papagos, who, put in a strong position by his military
achievement—by the end of November the Italians had been
driven from Greek territory and the Greeks were now dozens
of miles within Albanian territory—showed a certain dictatorial
tendency himself and behaved almost as if he were a rival of
Metaxas' rather than his subordinate and colleague. Also Metaxas
(who was highly suspicious by nature) expressed some doubts
about the loyalty of some senior officers on the General Staff.
Some of his diary notes have a pathetic quasi-poetical note.
"Sweet Greece, forward," he wrote on December 21. The bombing of Corfu on Christmas Day raised his indignation. "On this
day of all days, the blackguards," he noted in his diary. He was
ill and tired, and showed an increasing tendency to facile emo-
tionalism. That winter the weather was cold even in Athens, and
this distressed him. "Who knows how my poor soldiers are suffering," he wrote. It would be pleasing to the Italians if Mussolini
had ever expressed any consideration of that kind.

On the last day of the year Metaxas was deeply depressed. He
knew that his life was nearing its end and that the Greek victories
could not last. There were the Germans, who were annoyed and
angry, and also rather bewildered at the contradictoriness of the
information and requests they received from Italy; first, Alfieri
appealed to Hitler for immediate aid, and then Cavallero talked
to von Rintelen, who went on a mission to Albania on December
10, about forthcoming offensives. At this phase, however, Hitler's
aid did not go beyond sending about fifty transport Junkers to
help in the airlift of reinforcements.

Cavallero put his finger on the chief source of trouble, the chaos
with which reinforcements were arriving, and he devoted his efforts to the organization and acceleration of the transport system,
and he had more workers and tugs sent to help in the handling
of ships at Durazzo and Valona. His industrial experience had
at any rate taught him that it was useless to devise strategic or
tactical plans in the absence of an orderly supply system. But,

in spite of all his efforts, he did not succeed in bringing about a proper reorganization of the complicated and fragmentary mosaic of Italian troops. On December 15 Geloso sent him a message saying:

> The loading at Bari and Brindisi must be carried out with more foresight and judgment. The 8th Machine-Gun Battalion has landed its personnel with its weapons still in cases at the bottom of the hold. The same has happened with other battalions. It should be remembered that the object is not to embark personnel, transport animals, and material as they are doing now, but complete units that are required for immediate use.

In his telephone conversations with Mussolini, Cavallero—who from December 10 to 17 was in Albania officially on a "tour of inspection"—emphasized that he was engaged on a major job of reorganization, but also insisted on the dangers of a situation that perhaps still seemed so acute more because of a certain inferiority complex on the part of the commanders than because of the enemy's real penetrative capacity. Papagos' operational aim was essentially the prevention of a resumption of the Italian attack. He attached great importance to the Italian tanks, those "sardine tins," the threat of which kept him from making use of the plains and dissuaded him from "a large-scale exploitation of offensive actions, though opportunities presented themselves that might have yielded notable results."

Let me again recall that Papagos insisted on the numerical inferiority of his troops.

Italian estimates of strength were very different. On the afternoon of December 18, at a meeting in Rome at which all the armed services were represented, Cavallero stated the situation in Albania to be as follows:

> The front is 150 miles long, held by 160,000 men, of whom 100,-000 are in the line, and it has retreated but not yielded, though it has been reinforced only in dribs and drabs and has had to sustain

the onslaught of the Greek forces daily. It is only a thin veil of men, but every enemy effort to break it has been broken. The great danger was that of a separation of the two armies, which, however, did not take place, because of the stubbornness of our troops' resistance.

The nature of the terrain imposed itself both on defenders and attackers; action necessarily followed the watercourses, and when possible, as we have mentioned, attacks were delivered from above. The Dhrino, Vojussa, Ossum, and Tomorritsa valleys, flanked by snow-covered peaks, became the theater of operations. Italian troops based their positions on the massifs, and at the point of junction between the Ninth and the Eleventh armies the new line of resistance was on the Tomorrit. The Italians had been forced back to the northern edge of the famous "central redoubt." Bancale, the VIII Army Corps commander, stated that his troops no longer had "any capacity for reaction," and Carlo Rossi, of the XXV Corps, said that the "new position does not permit further withdrawals." Soddu's orders were rational, though obvious. On December 15 he announced that "the defense of individual sectors must always be conducted in such a way as to wear down the enemy forces to the greatest possible extent, while for our part we must try firmly to retain possession of the key points in our line, even if infiltrations and pockets develop." On the Ninth Army front the Greeks attacked rather wearily; the cold was now intense at high altitudes and affected the troops on both sides impartially, and it was difficult to get supplies through. Men with long beards and torn and tattered brown uniforms swarming with lice delivered attacks on men in equally tattered gray-green uniforms and broken boots who furiously defended themselves. The Tomorritsa Valley towards the north and the Klisura sector farther south became the critical points in the line. One position in the Tomorritsa Valley was successfully defended by 700 customs guards; the unfortunate Julia Division, which no one dared withdraw from the line for a decent period because it would have left an unfillable gap, was still being harassed, though from time to time it still showed some relics of vitality by mounting a counter-attack. But it was broken, and discomfiture increasingly affected the "veterans" of the advance of six weeks earlier. In reply to the suggestions for local offensives sometimes nourished by Cavallero and Soddu, who was now in better spirits—both had now been promoted to the rank of full general—General Nasci, the commander of the Alpini Army Corps, described the reality of the situation in a telephoned message:

This is the situation which has been developing in the past few days as the result of climatic conditions and circumstances in the line held between Mount Mietes and Mali Velusces by the remnants of the battalions of the Piemonte Division and the 3rd Battalion of Customs Guards. Twenty cases of men frozen to death and several dozen cases of frostbite have impaired the last moral energies of men who for more than a month have slept in the open in temperatures which in the last few days have dropped to several degrees below zero. Against these defenders the assailant, operating in a friendly environment in which every house constitutes a refuge, every mountaineer a guide, and in which every help is given him, is free to choose his place and time of action, with few worries about supply or finding his way and with a numerical preponderance of strength that enables him continually to vary his offensive patrols. The two battalions of customs guards who recently arrived should have retaken the Tomorritsa bridgehead, attacking the enemy's flank from above. The conditions of the road, on which there are several fords which have to be waded through with water up to one's waist, while for mile after mile it is nearly knee-deep in slush, brought about a deterioration among men who are not used to such efforts (the 1st Battalion of Customs Guards took ten hours to cover the first stretch of one mule track, which is normally covered in three hours by Alpini units in the area). In these circumstances the offensive action proposed for the recapture of Gostanghes has no prospect of success.

General Nasci's statement about the help given to the Greeks by the local population was a disappointing thing to have to acknowledge. Was this not supposed to be friendly territory, inhabited by the dear, good Albanians who, according to Jacomoni, were so keen to co-operate with the Italians in their Greek adventure?

Except in the coastal zone, the whole front was now manned by mountain troops. General Mario Arisio, the commander of the III Army Corps, wanted to send back to Italy three battalions of Sicilian and Calabrian Blackshirts who had shown no trace of fighting spirit. The Italian troops were depressed. Even in what were considered crack units incidents took place that pointed to a deep demoralization. On December 20 the Greeks, after taking Porto Palermo, attacked Himara on the coast, an important stepping-stone towards Valona. The battalion of grenadiers that was holding the position gave way after a brief engagement, and its commander was taken prisoner. The whole Siena Division was in a state of crisis. This incident was celebrated in Greece as a major success; also it took place after a few days' inactivity, and went to show that the Greeks were still on the offensive. During the days of relative quiet the Siena Division was the victim of a disastrous mistake. Some Italian aircraft, thinking they were attacking a Greek headquarters and troops, strafed Italian troops. The casualties were forty killed and many wounded.[6]

The bad state of morale of the Siena Division was reported by the carabinieri, and Mussolini sent Cavallero a furious telegram:

According to carabinieri report, rout, I repeat rout, of Siena Division was caused by infiltration few Greek patrols. Result was expulsion from Himara followed by order in Greece to put out flags for three days. This only further encourages morale Greek people and army. . . . More than ever necessary to reverse situation now exclusively one of morale.

It was, however, not exclusively a question of morale. A division that on paper had twenty-four armored cars never had more than twelve available when it wanted to use them, and of these only six, when they finally got going, reached divisional headquarters. It was the same in every field. The commanders had a defensive mentality because they realized that when an attack was attempted the machine did not work properly, and perhaps the machine did not work properly when it might have done so because the commanders had a defensive mentality. Units were continually shifted from one command to another, and the points of junction between the various sectors were always the most sensitive. The setting up of a special army corps under the command of General Messe for the defense of the Sciuscizza Valley strengthened a stretch of the line, but in the process of reorganization misunderstandings arose with General Carlo Rossi's XXV Army Corps. The text of a conversation between Cavallero and General Emilio Bancale, the commander of the VIII Army Corps, throws light on the psychological attitude of the commanders in the field.

> CAVALLERO: If you had an infantry regiment, where would you put it?
> BANCALE: I should use it to connect the Chiarista Regiment with the line of strongpoints.
> CAVALLERO: What, you would not attack?
> BANCALE: In that case I should put it behind the Chiarista and then attack to gain some elbow room.
> CAVALLERO: And if you had a division?
> BANCALE: I should gather it together and then go down to Permeti. But it would have to be a complete division. . . .
> CAVALLERO: If you had a machine-gun battalion, what would you do with it?
> BANCALE: I should put it in the strongpoints and collect the forces in them to counterattack.[7]

These questions and answers make it evident that even the commanders of large formations were living from hand to mouth, thinking of reinforcements here, a minor counterattack there. The large- or small-scale *coups de main* dreamt of by Visconti Prasca were being carried out by the Greeks; they had ceased to form part of the real prospects of an army whose fighting spirit had been blunted. Mussolini blamed it all on the Italians. He talked of a future in which he would make an Italian professional army, "skimming the cream of ten or twelve million Italians of the Po Valley and part of Central Italy"[8] (this last concession was probably due to the fact that he himself came from the Romagna). The rest of the nation would manufacture arms for this aristocracy of warriors. "I must admit," Mussolini added sadly, "that the Italians of 1914 were better than those of today. This is not a happy outcome for the régime, but so it is."

Cavallero was a permanent optimist, while Soddu was optimistic only on the telephone to the Duce. But each of Cavallero's optimistic prognostications was normally followed by some small kick from the Greeks. Ciano acutely summed up Soddu's psychology.

> When he talks to the Duce he expresses himself in one way and when he talks to Sorice [*chef de cabinet* to the War Minister] he expresses himself in another. To him the important strategy is not that in relation to the Greeks; it is that towards the Palazzo Venezia. . . . The jealousies between generals are worse than those between women. You only have to read the transcriptions of what Soddu says on the telephone to Sorice. He demolishes them all. Geloso has grown soft, Perugi is a disaster, Trionfi a failure. Today by chance he spoke well of Vercellino. What he said verbatim was this: "Poor Vercellino! He is such a dear man. He came to see me and wept."

Also it seems that Soddu spent his free time, even during the most anxious hours in Albania, composing film music. Thanks to some kind informant on the General Staff, this came to Mussolini's ear and contributed to Soddu's final disgrace at the end of December, when he was relieved of his command, "for health reasons."

Shortcomings had been shown by officers and men, and the commander of the Modena Division had been induced by some unpleasant incidents to issue an order, addressed to officers only, threatening that those who did not show sufficiently vigorous leadership would be shot. But below the high command level, at regimental and battalion level, and still lower down, at that of small parties sent out to hold inaccessible positions in the mud and the snow, at any rate the sad music of personal jealousies, careerism, and ambition was stilled. Many senior officers were killed leading their men. I have already mentioned the death of Colonel Luigi Zacco of the 84th Infantry, killed at Qifarishtes in a bayonet counterattack. On November 7 (still in the phase of the first ephemeral advance) Lieutenant Colonel Adalgiso Ferrucci of the 47th Infantry was killed, and on December 1, after the first hurried retreat, the commander of that regiment, Colonel Felice Trizio, suffered the same fate. At Qafa Gallina on December 8 Colonel Rodolfo Psaro of the 7th Alpini, Pusteria Division, was killed in a counterattack; with the Feltre and Cadore battalions he had closed the breach that the enemy had been opening in an unstable front. Colonel Gaetano Tavoni, of the 9th Alpini, Julia Division, was fatally wounded after Christmas on Mali Topojanit; he and his men had been through sixty days of unbroken, relentless fighting, because the Alpini of the Julia Division, though grumbling, broken, decimated, still represented a strongpoint in a line in which some units turned out not to be tough enough to stand up to a remorseless winter war against a spirited enemy made exultant by his early successes. Lieutenant Colonel Umberto Tinivella, commander of the Val Tagliamento Battalion, was also killed. On December 14 Lieutenant Colonel Adolfo Rivoir, commander of the Edolo Battalion of Alpini (5th Tridentina Regiment), was seriously wounded in the Koritsa zone.

The Fascist Party, which vented its rage on the "traitor" Badoglio—though Mussolini as usual vacillated between fits of harshness and fits of moderation—undertook to set a good example in the crisis. While the women—too late—knitted woollen garments and sent Christmas presents to the front, the members of the hierarchy were indiscriminately mobilized and sent to Albania.

Some undoubtedly went willingly, motivated by genuine patriotism and sometimes also a sense of something like remorse—remorse for the disastrous course taken by a war that was Mussolini's
war, a Fascist war, fought in spite of the General Staff. Others
went off to this new adventure knowing that, so far as they were
concerned, it would last just long enough to enable them to say
afterwards that "they were there," and that it would procure them
another silver medal at a minimum of personal risk. Various divisional headquarters were adorned by the presence of Major
Dino Grandi of the Alpini, Lieutenant Colonels Renato Ricci
and Achille Starace of the Bersaglieri, Captain Carlo Alberto
Biggini, of the infantry, and Major Giuseppe Bottai, of the Alpini.

Ciano, Pavolini, and Raffaello Riccardi (the Foreign Exchange
Minister), who were reserve officers in the air force, were drafted
to bomber squadrons in Apulia: Ciano and Pavolini to a squadron
of S79s and Riccardi to a squadron of Cant.Z1007bs, in which
the Duce's sons were also serving. An order by Mussolini laid
down that members of the Fascist hierarchy at the front should
not have batmen or luggage. Commanders of air units who had
"political" authority acted on their own account, as Pricolo has
admitted. They varied objectives to suit themselves and showed
great enthusiasm for bombing Corfu, perhaps because the antiaircraft defense was weaker there and the distance shorter.

Ministers who occasionally put on uniform claimed favored
treatment. Riccardi protested at Ciano's bombers always having
fighter protection while his did not, though it must be granted
that the S79s were weakly armed and hence in a situation of excessive inferiority if attacked. This mobilization of hierarchs certainly made no serious contribution to the military effort, but it
enabled these men cheaply to assume a halo of selfless valor.

After the capture of Himara by the Greeks, the front became
more or less stationary. The new Italian defense line was attacked
here and there, in the Tomorritsa Valley near the Klisura Pass,
and at the bridgehead in the Sciuscizza Valley on the coast. But

the penetrations were slight; the severity of the winter contributed to diminishing the Greek élan. On the night of December 21 Cavallero, Soddu, Vercellino, and Geloso held a conference at which it was decided that the period of gravest crisis had passed. There were solid reasons for taking this view, but it opened the way to premature hopes. On December 22 Soddu issued an order that the troops should maintain "an aggressive attitude with a view to improving our positions and giving the enemy the feeling that an offensive on our part was in preparation." During the days that followed Soddu gave orders for the recapture of Himara by the Cuneo Division, commanded by General Carlo Melotti, which was just arriving, and for the rectification, in Italy's favor of course, of the Tepeleni-Klisura line. The object was to create elbow room round Valona, which was only twenty-three miles from the front in the Sciuscizza Valley. But the Cuneo Division, after assembling for the projected offensive in January, was almost immediately broken up again to help units desperate for reinforcements, the attack on Himara did not take place, and a memorandum by the High Command stated that "the enemy initiative was essentially due to his better organization" and that "our fundamental weakness lay in having to fight in non-organic groupings."

When Christmas came it snowed in Rome, and Mussolini was delighted. "This snow and cold are fine," he remarked triumphantly in the well-heated Palazzo Venezia. "They will kill off the weaklings and improve this mediocre Italian race. One of the principal reasons why I wanted the reafforestation of the Apennines was to make Italy colder and more snowy."[9] Perhaps that explains a great deal. As Italy did not have enough cold and snow, perhaps the raving dictator went to Albania to look for them. At all events he found plenty. He also tried to explain that he had started the campaign in autumn to avoid the risk of malaria, but that was a puerile excuse; we have seen the circumstances in which war with Greece was begun.

Frostbite worked havoc among the men of the Ninth Army, who spent months at the highest altitudes, sleeping in the open without proper winter clothing, often living in undrained trenches amid the mud and snow, with no climbing boots or change of warm clothing, and often without medical services. By the end of December the victims numbered thousands; eventually a total of nearly 13,000 was reached. Among these long-suffering troops, fighting for reasons unknown to them an enemy they did not hate, the dreaded "dry gangrene" or "white death" started insidiously to spread. Its onset was painless. Legs swelled above the ankle, all feeling disappeared from the foot, the flesh changed color, turned purple and then blackish. Then there was the agonizing journey to overcrowded field hospitals of men who often had to be carried bodily by their comrades because of the lack of stretchers, and were then loaded on to lorries that caused agony at every jolt on the appalling roads to Valona or Durazzo or Tirana, where they awaited transport to Apulia.

Surgical intervention was often necessary; men who had set out for a "walkover" against Greece found themselves condemned to physical disabilities that compromised the whole of their future lives. It snowed and was cold, and the man in the Palazzo Venezia was delighted. There was no Christmas truce; in fact on Christmas Day the Greeks launched a furious assault in the Ossum Valley, and the Feltre and Cadore battalions of the Pusteria Division gave way. Fortunately the Ossum River was unfordable, with the result that the Greeks were unable to exploit this serious symptom of exhaustion on the part of troops who normally stood firm. On Christmas Day Mussolini drafted another of those messages of his that were intended to galvanize the troops and their commanders. He telegraphed to Cavallero:

It is evident that the enemy has two strategic objectives: one in the center, to divide our armies and try to surround them, and the other on our right, to meet the British desire to occupy Valona. In any case it is easy to see what the loss of Valona would mean. The possibility of British troop reinforcements cannot be excluded. Your directives seem to me to be adequate to the situation, that is to reinforce the center to frustrate any enemy effort and provide elbow room for Valona. The best way of attaining this last essential purpose will be to take the initiative, based on strongpoints equipped with men and material, and strike as hard blows as are possible. The enemy initiative, which has lasted too long, cannot be stopped in any other way. . . . The reorganization of the old divisions, which I consider of fundamental importance, can be carried out gradually, beginning with the Ninth Army, which, in view of the season, will enjoy a certain tranquillity, at any rate for two months. All concrete, I repeat concrete, measures to keep the morale of the troops high are excellent; this morale will rise tremendously as soon as the troops from north to south realize that the direction of the wind has changed and that a first hammerblow has been struck at the Greeks.

But this blow was still to come, and in Italy deep pessimism spread. In Africa Graziani had suffered a heavy defeat, and the news from Albania went from bad to worse. The retreats, the ravages of frostbite, were now common knowledge, and the legend or illusion of Italian military strength had gone up in smoke. Young men wanted to have nothing to do with a war that promised to send them to the slaughter without the componsation of the prospect of victory or the pride of fighting in a good cause. Three thousand candidates offered themselves for an air force competitive examination for the selection of 150 officers for airfield duties.[10] Nearly half the pupils at the military school at Parma chose to be sent to the carabinieri. Buffarini Guidi, the undersecretary of the interior, Serena, the party secretary, Bocchini, the Chief of Police, supplied discouraging information to the Palazzo Venezia. Mussolini's appearance on the newsreels was greeted with an oppressive silence; the enthusiasm and eloquence of radio speakers talking about the war made no impact on a grim-faced, depressed, or resentful people. The country was disillusioned, while on the mountains of Albania the troops grimly consumed the contents of the few food parcels that got through the chaos of the back areas and reached the front line wrapped in paper stiff with frozen snow. And it was Christmas.

If the relative stabilization of the front can be considered as a success, at the end of 1940 it had been attained. Different, though not excessively disproportionate, figures are given by Italian and Greek sources about the strength of the opposing forces at the beginning of the period of positional warfare early in December. According to Papagos, the Italians had fifteen infantry divisions and one armored division deployed against eleven (three-regiment) infantry divisions, two infantry brigades and one division of Greek cavalry. According to the Italian General Staff, the Italian forces consisted of nine infantry divisions, two Alpini divisions, one armored division, several battalions of Blackshirts and Bersaglieri, three cavalry regiments, and one regiment of grenadiers, while the Greeks had thirteen infantry divisions, one cavalry division, and two infantry brigades. The latter were deployed as follows: four divisions in the Koritsa zone, three divisions plus one infantry brigade in the center, three divisions in the south, and three infantry divisions plus one cavalry division and a brigade of infantry in general reserve.

Papagos emphasizes the numerical superiority of the Italian artillery, which Italian experts deny. The Italian General Staff has estimated that there were from 100 to 105 battalions of Italian infantry and Blackshirts against from 130 to 135 Greek. Final agreement will never be reached on these figures, but it can be definitely stated that even according to the Greek sources the Italians at best attained numerical parity only at the end of the year, though not an effective parity in strength and organization of units (and the morale of the Italian troops was low). It appears from the figures of the supply services that on January 1, 1941, there were in Albania 10,613 officers, 261,850 other ranks, 7,563 motor vehicles, and 32,871 transport animals. The "wall" that Cavallero was trying to build was beginning to gain solidity, but his and Mussolini's persistent dream of a major or minor, immediate or delayed, offensive refused to come true.

Soddu was now out of it. He was got rid of by a kind of strata-gem. On December 29 he was summoned to Rome "for a conference," and he never returned to Albania. On December 30 Cavallero assumed command of the troops in Albania in addition to his post as chief of the General Staff. Mussolini continued to act the strategist by telegraph. He informed Cavallero on December 28 that "the Cuneo and Brennero divisions will soon have been completely assembled in Albania" and that they must not be "dismembered in any degree or for any reason whatever," but "left absolutely intact, employed complete, and deployed with a view to meeting the now evident enemy intentions to attack." These orders were very right and proper, but they conflicted with the usual desperate emergencies and panic of many commands, who competed furiously for newly arriving units, with the result that in spite of the Duce's veto the Cuneo Division, which, as we have seen, was intended for the recapture of Himara, in the course of the next few days underwent the fate of other units.

Thus the New Year opened with little movement taking place on the front, though what there was was to the disadvantage of the Italians. The two High Commands went on "playing with their cards on the table." Both Cavallero and Papagos basically knew what their enemy intended to do and how he was going to do it. But on the basis of this knowledge Papagos succeeded in counter-maneuvering, and Cavallero did not. This is not just an impression; it is confirmed by the documents. Papagos decided to break off major offensive actions and employ his II Army Corps—which had been practically inactive for two weeks—for the capture of Klisura. This would be another step towards Valona and Tirana.

One of the differences between the two commanders was that Papagos could afford to ring the changes with his troops. The Greek 17th Division, which had fought admirably in the Pogradec sector but had suffered heavy losses, was sent to eastern Macedonia on the Bulgarian frontier and its place was taken by the 13th Division, and similar steps were taken with other units that had suffered heavily. The movement of Greek troops, hampered but not paralyzed by the Italian air supremacy, was free of the bottlenecks at the ports, and the ability to send tried and tested but tired units to the Bulgarian border to reorganize was a precious safety valve. No Greek division suffered the fate of the Julia Division, which in the middle of January was reduced to 1,000 men with fifteen serviceable machine guns and five mortars. It had lost in action 153 officers and 3,844 other ranks.

Cavallero cautiously prepared two plans, one for an advance and the other for the contingency of another defeat. The latter provided for the setting up of two separate operational sectors, one to defend Valona and the other to defend northern Albania. Six divisions would occupy the Valona redoubt and thirteen the Tirana redoubt. The High Command would continue to function; the Eleventh Army would be deployed round Valona and the Ninth would defend northern Albania, together with a new army to be set up. This planning accorded ill with the aggressiveness that Mussolini was frantically trying to instill, and was yet another symptom of a demoralization which was as widespread at the top as it was among the troops.

Simultaneously, however, Cavallero issued his "directive No. 8" for an operation, to take place on January 5, in which the Italians were to attack from the sea in the direction of Tepeleni and advance to their old positions beyond Himara and Porto Palermo. The offensive was to be undertaken by the newly arrived Legnano Division, commanded by General Vittorio Ruggero. Cavallero was at the same time proposing to assemble in the Berati zone a reserve army corps consisting of the Pusteria, Lupi di Toscana and Siena divisions in order to have massive forces available to meet enemy attacks. Most of this ambitious staff work turned out to be a waste of time, however. The plans for the two separate "redoubts" fortunately did not have to be carried out, but those for an advance were not carried out either.

A "memorandum" laid down lines for a reorganization of the front. No longer were there to be about seventy battalions in the front line consisting of exhausted men from different units, but nine properly organized divisions, with twenty battalions as local reserves, and eleven divisions in the second and third lines. Four Alpini divisions and the unattached Alpini regiments were to be assembled in the mountainous sector of the front (Devoli, Tomorritsa, Ossum). The cavalry, the Bersaglieri, and the Trieste Division were to form a mobile army corps. This reorganization was to be completed by the end of February, immediately after which an offensive was to take place in the Koritsa zone which would be the "prelude to the final offensive."

Mussolini continued bombarding Cavallero with exhortations. In his New Year letter, after informing him that "German military and political circles are following our fortunes in Albania with extreme interest" and that "the condition of their intervention is that the present line should be held at all costs," the Duce went on to give more detailed instructions. His continual hammering away like this was so anxious and futile as to be pathetic. One thing should be stated, however. Mussolini, who bore the primary responsibility for the Greek adventure, inclined though he was to indulge in private in denunciations, as disgraceful as they were ungenerous, of the soldiers whose lives he was sacrificing and the country that he was sending to ruin, at least shared in the anguish of those days. There is nothing to indicate that this state of mind was shared either by Ciano, whose attitude remained coldly political, or by many of the military leaders, who trembled for their personal misfortunes more than for the blood that was being uselessly spilled.

Here is the text of the letter in which those characteristics of Mussolini's temperament, the phoney toughness, the glibness, the blind confidence in his "star" that in the past had seemed never to fail him, and the belief that he possessed an unfailing magnetism appear plainly:

Dear Cavallero, before the day fixed by you for the operation summon all the corps and divisional commanders involved and tell them this: (a) The decision to attack can and must transform the situation, particularly from the point of view of morale. After sixty days of being the anvil, we become the hammer; (b) this operation, which must be begun and carried through with extreme energy, must eliminate all reason for world speculation about Italian military prestige, of which I have been, and shall be the most jealous defender; (c) Germany is ready to send us a division to Albania while it prepares an army with which it is proposed to attack Greece from Bulgaria in March. My desire, my trust, is that, thanks to your devotion and the valor of your troops, German aid on the Albanian front will be superfluous; (d) the Italian people is anxiously waiting for the wind to change. There is no more to add except this: on the eve of the operation you will go to the front to the most suitable place for following it and you will remain there until the operation is concluded. The battles of modern armies are too complex to be directed from a distance.

Words, words, words. They were carried away in the wind, just as Cavallero's plans were. The Greeks again seized the initiative. In the Klisura sector, where the road towards Berati lay through the Desnizza Valley between the Trebescines and the Mali Qarishta, the Greek infantry was once more faced with the Julia Division, of which more miracles could not be expected. Girotti had been promoted to the rank of major general in recognition of the valor of his Alpini, but the division had not been restored to full strength. The Italian front from the Lake of Ochrida to the sea was constituted as follows at that moment. On the left, in the Ninth Army sector, there was the III Army Corps, consisting of four divisions (Piemonte, Taro, Arezzo, and Venezia) and the XXVI Army Corps (the Tridentina, Parma, and Cuneense divisions). On the right was the Eleventh Army, with the IV Army Corps commanded by General Mercalli (Pusteria, Pinerolo, Bari, Julia, Lupi di Toscana divisions), Bancale's VIII Army Corps, which was intended to go into reserve with a single division (the Siena) at Berati, the XXV Army Corps consisting of the Brennero, Centauro, Ferrara, and Modena divisions, and the Special Army Corps commanded by General Messe (Special Alpini, Acqui, and Cuneo), which had the specific task of barring the road to Valona and was also being held in readiness for the projected offensive aiming at Porto Palermo, and finally a division responsible directly to the High Command at Rrogozhine. Altogether there were twenty divisions and one special unit of varying grades of efficiency. The beginning of the movement towards Berati of the VIII Army Corps had created a gap in continuity between the IV Corps and the XXV.

Italian troop movements were based on the plan for an offensive between Tepeleni and the sea, and the Greeks caught the Italian command on the wrong foot. Their attack in the direction of Klisura was violent and, though it could and should have been foreseen, it was initially successful. The Julia Division gave way, and so did the 140th Infantry Regiment. The two army corps commands overlapped, and Emilio Bancale, the commander of the VIII Corps, who was just leaving the front line when the Greek assault began, and the newly arrived Mercalli, both sent orders to the Lupi di Toscana Division, which was being brought up by forced marches to plug the gap. The first contact of the Lupi with the enemy was not brilliant, there were instances of disorderly retreat, and Greek propaganda made play with the weaknesses shown by this unit, and, with a lack of generosity provoked by ill humor, Italian "veterans" also laughed at its misfortunes; for a time it enjoyed the nickname of Lepri di Toscana ("hares of Tuscany" instead of *lupi,* wolves).

Weeks later an officer of this division told Pricolo what happened. "After a march of more than twenty miles the division was sent to occupy the positions assigned to it at night, with no officer accompanying it and with a promise that the troops would find a hot meal awaiting them. After several more hours of difficult climbing, the troops reached the places marked on the map, but they were not easily identifiable and some were already occupied by the enemy. The hot meal was of course only a dream. The division, without being able even to complete its deployment, had to meet violent enemy attacks first thing next morning and all the following day in an unknown area with no possibility of air support because of the bad atmospheric conditions."[11] The elements of the Lupi di Toscana division that reached the line were only infantry battalions, without mortars, artillery, or engineers. In these conditions a counterattack was bound to fail, and did.

The attack at Klisura forced Cavallero to cancel the plans for an advance towards Porto Palermo and induced him to send the VIII Corps back into the line. Rome insisted that he must not give up the offensive, but he dug in his heels. He sent Mussolini a message that was intended to be reassuring:

> The enemy offensive on the Klisura front was expected by us and the local commander took appropriate steps to stand up to the offensive blow. But the Lupi, who were sent in as reinforcements, though they were taken some of the way by motor transport and made forced marches by night as well as by day, could not get into position before today (January 9). That being the case, the troops on the spot had the task of holding out until reinforcements arrived. The huge forces thrown in by the enemy, who is here making his greatest effort, led to the Julia giving ground, which involved other units in doing the same, with the result that Klisura itself is in danger. Yesterday afternoon I personally confirmed to the commander of the sector the order that Klisura must be held to the end, informing him that our counterattack will be put in tomorrow.

The counterattack failed, and on the evening of January 10 Colonel Vincenzo Carla, commanding the 140th Regiment, withdrew four miles from Klisura towards a valley defense position to avoid encirclement with his 6,000 men. Carla was court-martialed, but General D'Havet, the commander of his division, the Bari, unreservedly defended him, and he was acquitted. D'Havet, however, paid the consequences for the loss of Klisura; he was relieved of his command a few weeks later. On the heels of yet another of countless failures—this one, unlike its predecessors, was hushed up by the Italian war communiqués, which limited themselves to mentioning "local attacks"—Cavallero to his chagrin had to receive von Rintelen, the German military attaché in Rome, at Tirana on January 11. The previous day's events were an unhappy prologue to their conversation. Von Rintelen referred to the projected sending of a German mountain division, acknowledged the extreme difficulty of the terrain, and appreciated that the resolute action of which Mussolini talked still lay a long way ahead.

The enemy had not only cut off the Klisura pocket but had actually made a dent in the Italian line, and once more the Italian High Command had had to take desperate countermeasures. Cavallero sent this anxious message to the commander of the Julia Division:

> The Julia has done its duty. We are satisfied even if it has withdrawn. New forces are moving up today and a part of them are already at Berati. The gap must be closed at the cost of one's own life. If they break through, we shall not be able to hold out. Our country requires this. Even at the cost of death, and I should come and die with you. Make this last effort, I appeal to you in the name of Italy. I am confident that in a few days you will be content, because later we shall be victorious. Reinforcements are on the way and you will be given a rest. We shall rebuild a fine Julia Division, but now you must hold on.

Cavallero's language was very different from that of the strategist who had been talking a few days previously of building up reserves and making countermoves. It was the language of a desperate man, whose "wall," built up with such trouble, was in danger of collapse. Mercalli, the IV Corps commander, whom Cavallero called a strong man, was similarly anxious. In a message on January 16 he said: "I am being attacked all along the line. Communications have been completely interrupted. All my officers are going about re-establishing communications. I appeal for urgent air intervention to relieve enemy pressure."

The capture of Klisura was the last Greek success of any importance, the last to which a name could be given. Three American journalists who followed the operation from the headquarters of the Greek 1st Division made it re-echo round the world. Cavallero was again condemned to remaining anxiously on the defensive. The enemy did not oblige the Italians by falling in with their plans, but consistently upset them. The following comment may seem humorous, but it was made by Cavallero: "We have already employed the four divisions that have reached us in a situation different from that planned. Indications that the Greeks were exhausted have been falsified. I conclude that operations will continue, and in the meantime we must reorganize the Alpini units for the offensive at the end of February." This was the Koritsa offensive which was never carried out.

10. "Put an End to this Passivity"

Mussolini, who said that the trust he had put in Visconti Prasca had been the one unpardonable error of his life, had an increasing itch to play the part of Commander-in-Chief in earnest. He had chosen for his headquarters a modest-looking peasant's house in the country not far from Bisceglie in Apulia, refusing the luxurious Villa Ciardi which had been chosen for him. He wanted to be a soldier, to some extent sharing, or imagining he was sharing, the hardships of his troops. That is the only possible explanation of the choice of this remote headquarters, to which he kept paying visits. As the crow flies it was nearer to Albania than to Rome, but because of the lack of communications it was extremely badly situated in relation to both.

A frequent visitor to Bisceglie was Ciano. The Duce's son-in-law was fighting hard to retain his position as Foreign Minister. All Italy now knew that the Greek war was Ciano's war, and could not forgive him for an act of frivolity that it would indeed have been hard to forgive. Away from Rome Mussolini subjected himself to a timely reassessment. The infallible, unsleeping dictator who had filled Rome and Italy with eagles, fasces, pennants, and skulls, pompous phrases and arrogant claims, no doubt meditated in this peasant's house about the fallibility of his plans and the dark prospects that now faced him in the "quick and easy" war that he had engaged in only for the sake of the pickings.

After von Rintelen, other German staff officers went to Albania to study the ground with a view to the employment of a German contingent that Mussolini both wanted and did not want and ended by refusing. For "Operation Cyclamen" Hitler's headquarters

at first examined the possibility (by order dated January 11)
of the employment of an army corps, including the 1st Mountain
Division and armored forces.[1] A few days later, following conversations at Salzburg between Mussolini and the Führer, the size
of the proposed expeditionary force was reduced to a single mountain division. Then the project was dropped.

The Germans had in mind attacking in the north on the hard-
frozen Ninth Army front, that is to say, attempting a breakthrough towards Florina and Salonika to join up with a German
army coming down from Bulgaria. They made one condition,
however: that this division of theirs, though it was only one as
against twenty Italian, should bear the brunt of the offensive, leaving the Italians a supporting role. If the Germans had had their
way and all had gone according to plan, all the glory would have
gone to another Rommel, whose exploits would have totally
eclipsed those of poor Cavallero. Considering all things, perhaps
it was better that the Albanian war, with all its agonies and casualties and heroism and setbacks, at any rate remained an Italian
war, and that writers on the subject at least have continually to
refer to the Italian army instead of reducing the campaign—as
when outsiders write about the war in North Africa—to a duel
between the Germans and the Allies, leaving the Italians with the
ungrateful role of not counting when things went well but being
held responsible when things went badly.

The Duce wrote, the Duce telegraphed, the Duce telephoned,
the Duce spoke. He never tired of repeating the same phrases,
and his listeners never tired of promising what he asked. The title
of "your Excellency" was never omitted in conversations with
those who had a right to it. Otherwise it was like a dialogue between deaf men. On January 14 Cavallero went to Foggia with
Vercellino and Ranza, and they, with Guzzoni, were received by
Mussolini in the drawing room of the Duce's special electric train;
and that evening Mussolini again received Cavallero in the presence of Guzzoni alone. "All the problems relating to the war with
Greece," Cavallero noted, "were examined in depth, so that when

I left for Bari the main lines of the future development of operations in Albania had been laid down."[2]

The main lines were an offensive in the Koritsa area, "the indispensable basis, barring an enemy collapse, for the ensuing final victory." But meanwhile the Greeks were tirelessly attacking in the snow, in a white landscape in which orientation had become exceedingly difficult. There were cases of isolated detachments in mountain positions being surprised by the enemy while in a sort of daze, and officers sending back false information to headquarters about the capture of positions because in the universal whiteness landmarks were difficult to identify. Some high altitude areas were held by Alpini skiers—the Monte Cervino Battalion, consisting of only 300 men, who tirelessly patrolled the snowy wastes and performed miracles.

Plans were made, but nothing went according to plan. This is demonstrated by the following conversation in the void that took place on January 18 between the Duce and Colonel Salvatore Bartiromo, Cavallero's deputy chief of staff. They were discussing the salient the Greeks had created by their Klisura offensive.

MUSSOLINI: The Greeks now have a ten-mile salient. The salient maneuver I have been hearing about for such a long time must be carried out without delay. We have got to maneuver.

BARTIROMO: Orders have already been given.

MUSSOLINI: We have got to start maneuvering, engaging the enemy's attention, we must put an end to this passivity.

BARTIROMO: Yes.

MUSSOLINI: But the maneuvering I have heard talked about has never resulted in our counterattacking in any direction.

BARTIROMO: Unfortunately it has never been possible to assemble the forces.

MUSSOLINI: But you have divisions.

BARTIROMO: They are not complete.

MUSSOLINI: Are there many prisoners?

BARTIROMO: We have no news of the 77th Infantry; I think some have been lost [on January 16 the 19th Battalion of the Greek 15th

Division had surprised the 77th Regiment belonging to the Lupi di Toscana Division and had taken about 300 prisoners].

MUSSOLINI: Bartiromo, there is only one way out. Attack, attack! I have been saying that for two weeks.

BARTIROMO: I know that that is his Excellency Cavallero's intention, but something has always been lacking, in particular, ammunition.

MUSSOLINI: They tell me that shiploads of ammunition left yesterday.

BARTIROMO: I have been informed that something has left.

MUSSOLINI: Bartiromo, we must counterattack, we must break the spell that for the past ninety days has been making us lose ground, position after position. If it goes on like this, we shall find ourselves in the sea, and there will be no more positions. The Greeks will soon reach the Skumbi, which they are making for.

BARTIROMO: There is no time to lose.

MUSSOLINI: In short, forces must be assembled on the right principles. We must maneuver and avoid this passivity.

BARTIROMO: That is what we are doing and have always been trying to do.

MUSSOLINI: I am going to Germany. The first question they will put to me is whether I shall be able to hold the present line. What am I to answer?

BARTIROMO: His Excellency Cavallero told the German colonel that he was confident he would be able to hold on.

MUSSOLINI: There is only one way out. Attack!

BARTIROMO: That is true, and it is his Excellency Cavallero's intention.

MUSSOLINI: Report what I have said to his Excellency Cavallero.[3]

There was a specific reason for Mussolini's half-violent, half-imploring appeal. After his meeting with Cavallero in Apulia he remarked irritably that "the military sector has completely failed" and that the campaign, "a political masterpiece," because Greece had been obliged to fight Italy alone, had turned into a military failure.[4] That it was a military failure was true, and that it was a political failure also was sufficiently shown by the failure of Bulgaria to intervene. Mussolini desperately wanted some good news to take to Hitler, but such was the Greek pressure that Cavallero could not accompany him to Salzburg.

After his conversation with Bartiromo, Mussolini left the Palazzo Venezia for Salzburg. Ciano noted:

> Grim-faced and nervy, he is shaken by the news from Albania. Nothing dramatic has happened, but again we have withdrawn and left many prisoners in the enemy's hands. The most serious thing is that the unit concerned was the Lupi di Toscana, a division of excellent reputation and great traditions, recently arrived in Albania, on which great hopes were based. He talked at length about all this; he reiterated his pessimism about the Italian army and people. He cannot explain the reason for things. He repeated several times: "If on October 15 anyone had predicted what has actually happened since, I should have had him shot."

At Salzburg Mussolini had to listen to a monologue by Hitler. The Führer was cordial ("there are no hidden condolences in the air," Ciano noted), but he behaved like a schoolmaster explaining things to a child. He did not emphasize the Italian setbacks in talking of the attack on Greece, and succeeded in impressing Mussolini without humiliating him. The Duce returned to Rome obsessed by a single thought—the necessity of gaining a success before the Germans intervened; and once more he kept repeating that the Italians must attack, attack, attack. Unfortunately Cavallero had to record on January 22:

> The enemy has occupied Qafa Sofiut. A height has been lost in the sector of the Siena Division. . . . The Val Chiese Battalion gave ground. The battalion commander assumed command on the ship and landed with the battalion still to be organized. The companies had still to be formed, a fact which has only just come to my knowledge. We used it at once, because when detachments arrive it is already late.[5]

In spite of this depressing information, Cavallero, goaded by Mussolini, still pursued the mirage of an offensive and organized it in every detail on paper. His operational memorandum No. 4 of January 16 stated some basic facts about the situation. By the end of February there should be twenty-five divisions in Albania, ten of them "in a state of satisfactory efficiency" (at the time there were twenty-two—the twenty-one divisions previously mentioned having been increased in the meantime by the arrival of the Legnano Division—eight of them in a good and fourteen in a battered condition). The regaining of the Koritsa area, according to the memorandum, would require about ten days, and it was desirable that the operation should be completed before the German intervention, which at that time was assumed to be going to take place at the beginning of March (it actually did so about a month later). After the regaining of the Koritsa area the Italians would attack in Epirus, this time concomitantly with the German offensive.

On January 20 another memorandum by Cavallero, No. 5, still hinged on the Koritsa offensive. Cavallero insisted among other things on a close understanding with the Germans, acutely observing that "if Germany continued in her attitude of not clashing with Greece and the latter eventually received German troops who maintained a non-hostile attitude, incalculable damage would be done to our situation and military prestige." The planning of offensives, both immediate and eventual, went on, but nothing came of them.

On January 21 Geloso issued orders for an assault on two mountain bastions, the Groppa and Bregianit, in the sector of the XXV Corps, on which the chief responsibility for the defense of Tepeleni lay. The object was to open the way to the recapture of Klisura. But on the twenty-fifth, just before the Italian assault was due to begin, the Greeks, as on countless other occasions, got their blow in first. Thus the two objectives were reduced to one, and the outcome was meager. The Duce stormed and raged, and informed Cavallero that fifteen reserve battalions were on the way (they reached Albania by February 5), but admitted that their training had been "summary or nil." This was no novelty, and was not confined to reserve battalions. Cavallero himself complained to Mussolini in a detailed memorandum dated February 1 about the limited efficiency of divisions that had recently been sent to him, the Lupi di Toscana (General Bollea), the Cagliari, the Forlì (General Giulio Ruggiero), and the Legnano, all of which were not up to the tasks that faced them. It was therefore decided to make another attempt to recapture Klisura only when "the Sforzesca and the Cagliari (commanded respectively by General Ollearo and General Giuseppe Gianni) had reached a sufficient state of preparedness."[6] With the loss of Klisura the front had been stabilized.

In February the Greeks stubbornly opened an offensive against Tepeleni—another name that would have brought out the flags in Greece if they had captured it—but they failed to reach their objective. The position of Tepeleni was delicate. The front formed a kind of loop round it, and the temptation to the Greeks to remove the protuberance was great. They advanced in strength from the east towards the bastions that protected the town—to the southeast the Golico and to the northeast the Scindeli and the Trebescines. The Crete Division, which traditionally possesses great fighting spirit, advanced towards the Scindeli. Various heights were taken, lost, retaken and lost again. The Greeks made some slight progress, but nothing very serious. To prevent the Eleventh Army front from breaking, the Julia Division had been brought up again; with the arrival of reservists it had been brought up to its normal establishment of about 350 officers and more than 10,000 other ranks. The veterans of the march on Metsovon and of the heroic resistance at the Perati bridge told the new arrivals about these things which had happened only yesterday, so to speak, though it seemed a hundred years ago. Colonel Michele Camosso had taken over the 8th Regiment and Colonel Achille Billi the 9th. The artillery continued in the hands of Colonel Gai.

The divisions were now on the whole up to establishment again, and reinforcements were arriving sufficiently quickly, even though the improvement in communications and increase in motor transport did not keep pace with the arrival of so many new divisions. With the usual curious mentality of many generals of "poor" armies such as the Italian, who prefer getting the last ounce out of what they have available rather than drawing on home reserves, Cavallero had ordered Lieutenant General Ingravalle, the commander of the medical service, to repatriate only the sick who were totally unfit for future service.[7] The remainder were kept for "laboring" work. Thus the back areas were populated with discontented and unfit men. Many field officers, nearly all reservists, arrived from Italy to take the place of the dead, wounded, sick, and victims of frostbite. A large proportion of these majors and lieutenant colonels came fresh from civilian life. They had forgotten what they might once have known about tactics and were unfamiliar with their men's weapons. They were thrown entirely unprepared into a country that no one had told them about, faced with an enemy about whom they knew nothing, and were put in charge of men whom they now saw for the first time.

While Mussolini went on repeating his slogan of "attack, attack," and Cavallero continued to think out offensives that never happened, and Hitler (Operation Cyclamen having been shelved) put in hand the planning of Operation Marita, i.e., the invasion of Greece from Bulgaria, the British and the Greeks started discussing the problems of a collaboration that was never without friction and grew more and more thorny as the inevitable German invasion grew nearer. Mussolini's headstrong decision to invade Greece alone, without prior agreement with the Germans, created difficulties both for the Greeks and for the British. A simultaneous attack by the two Axis Powers would, at any rate from that point of view, have simplified the situation, for Greece would have been totally and indisputably on the British side, and Britain would have fought in Greece, or at any rate for Greece, the total war she was conducting in the English Channel, in Africa, and on the high seas.

A paradoxical situation occurred, however. While Italian troops invaded Greek territory and then defended themselves on Albanian territory, Prince Erbach, the German ambassador in Athens, maintained relations with the Metaxas government which were formally correct, however ambiguous they might have been on the real level. He alternated declarations of solidarity with Italy with counsels of moderation, but made it clear that Mussolini's rashness had not been shared by Hitler. Metaxas for his part made every effort to convince the Germans of his desire to maintain good relations. On December 20, for instance, he had assured Erbach that he had no expansionist aims in spite of the Greek advance into Albanian territory, and he had persuaded the King to send Hitler his good wishes for the New Year (the Führer thanked him for these but deliberately refrained from reciprocating). There is, however, no confirmation in the documents for the rumor, reported by the American chargé d'affaires in Germany, that the Germans offered to mediate between the Italians and Greeks about the middle of December.

The Germans had troops in Rumania, as we know. To attack Greece from the north they would have to concentrate divisions in Bulgaria. In November and December 1940, no such operation seemed imminent. It is true that the first directives for Operation Marita[8] were issued by Hitler's headquarters on November 12, 1940, and foresaw the employment of ten divisions. But these were long-term, largely hypothetical directives (there was a vague indication that the operation might be carried out in the following March), and obviously they were unknown to Papagos, who in any case had no choice in the matter. He almost denuded his frontier with Bulgaria, leaving there only three of his weakest divisions. His war, his country's war, was being fought in the Albanian mountains. As for the rest, what would happen would happen.

Churchill was immediately fascinated by the prospects in the Balkans and the Mediterranean offered him by this extension of the war, which he did not want but which was in some ways very welcome to him. The Balkans were a long-standing special interest of his, as was shown again in the final phase of the war, when he proposed an operation in the Balkans that would have checked the spread of Russian arms all over eastern Europe. For the time being he concentrated his strategic attention—or imagination—on one point: "One salient strategic fact leaped out upon us—CRETE! The Italians must not have it. We must get it first—and at once."9

After the Italian attack the Greeks put Suda Bay in Crete at the British disposal and accepted the aid of an air contingent under the command of Air Commodore d'Albiac. Metaxas—after a highly secret meeting with the German ambassador—immediately informed d'Albiac that his bombers must be based in southern Greece, not near Salonika. So long as British air aid was so restricted, the Germans would not consider it a provocation. British fighters, however, could use bases near the Albanian border. What mattered to the Germans was that there should be no British bombers within range of the Ploesti oil wells.

This was a compromise that could not last, and foreshadowed war with Germany too. But neither the British nor the Germans (let alone the Greeks) were in a hurry to put their foot on the accelerator; and they tolerated a nebulous status quo in relation to each other in which airmen of the country which was engaged in a struggle to the death with Germany and was also an ally of Greece lived side by side in Athens with German diplomatists, who observed and took notes.

At the end of November 1940, Churchill, who complained of the lack of first-hand news from the Albanian front, replaced General Gambier Perry as head of the British military mission in Greece by General Heywood. Both were severely hampered by the restrictions to which their movements were subject, the secretiveness that surrounded all their meetings with Greek personalities, and Metaxas' anxiety to avoid any action or statement that might lead to German protests. The British commanders in the Middle East—Sir Archibald Wavell, Admiral Cunningham, and Air Chief Marshal Longmore—took the view that this German immobility would not last long and that Metaxas' demonstrations of good will towards Hitler were pointless. Let us not take the initiative, the British said, but at least let us move with a certain freedom in order to prepare to meet an attack that will surely come and is being delayed, not by Greek moderation towards Germany, but because Hitler wishes to act at the moment of his own choice and with the forces that he considers necessary.

The argument was sound enough, but it was also motivated by legitimate British self-interest. The threat of an invasion of Britain was still in the air. Even after Hitler had given up the idea and was turning to the attack on Russia, the British were still haunted by Operation Sea Lion. Any extension of the conflict, though it created new problems, also gave them breathing space, engaged the enemy in distant areas. Wavell's successes in Africa at the end of 1940 and the beginning of 1941 enabled the British to consider aid to Greece beyond air support, lorries, and arms; it became possible to consider sending an expeditionary force. But this was an extremely complicated undertaking if its organizers had to adapt themselves to innumerable prohibitions and taboos in order to avoid offending Prince Erbach and his colleagues.

On January 13 General Wavell and Air Chief Marshal Longmore flew to Athens, where they stayed for four days, and had conversations with Marshal Papagos and Metaxas, whose ashen features already showed that his end was near. It was inevitably a meeting of very divergent mentalities and points of view.

Wavell was responsible for a vast area of operations, stretching from Northern Rhodesia to the Balkans; to him territorial gains and losses were events to be evaluated in relation to the whole politico-military situation. Metaxas and Papagos had their minds not so much on a distant final victory as on the defense of their country, the protection of its frontiers from invasion, above all the safeguarding of their Albanian victory, to Greece a matter of immense national pride. Thus there was a clash of two conflicting "sacred egoisms." Metaxas opened the proceedings with a firm declaration that Greece would resist a German, or German-Bulgarian, attack with the same resolution as that with which she had met the Italian attack. Then Papagos produced his ideas for

British aid. Wavell should send to Greece nine divisions, with adequate air support. Airfields and depots would be made ready for this impressive expeditionary force, the real objective of which would remain secret while it was being assembled. The Germans would be given the impression that the nine divisions were being made ready for the North African campaign.

Papagos and his General Staff had worked well to prepare their plan, which for their purposes and from their point of view made excellent use of British resources, or of resources that they attributed to the British. Technically they had done a good job, but a useless one; it was an academic military exercise that did not take into account the total politico-military situation and over-estimated British strength and Greek organizing capacity. The plan put Greece in the center of a world conflict in which it represented an important, but secondary, sector. Because of its theoretical nature Papagos' plan had an affinity with some of Cavallero's, showing that at bottom not only the two armies, but also the two general staffs resembled each other, and that Papagos won because he was the more efficient in a war conducted in the most traditional of ways. Ambitious plans such as Papagos' could be afforded several years later by Eisenhower, but for the time being Britain was trying to cover too big a bed with too small a blanket, and could not let her strategy be guided by Marshal Papagos, though granting him and his army all the merits that they possessed.

Meanwhile Wavell, with a typically British, distracted air was polishing his spectacles, and when Papagos had finished his exposition his laconic comment was: "I see." Then he began speaking with the cold, dry courtesy of a man who had been thinking that the exposition had been a fine academic exercise, but it was now time to get down to the hard facts. All that he could send at the moment was a regiment of artillery and a mechanized unit with about sixty tanks. This Metaxas refused, and for excellent reasons. That modest force would provide the Germans with an unnecessary but useful pretext for the invasion of Greece, and would provide no substantial aid for the defense of the country. Churchill was disappointed at these conclusions. He realized that a German invasion would put the Greek forces in Albania in an untenable position. "Destruction of Greece will eclipse victories you have gained in Libya, and may affect decisively Turkish attitude . . ." he wrote to Wavell.[10] It was these considerations that had persuaded him to seek the Athens meeting. Since it failed to result in agreement, he and the War Cabinet turned their attention to a new offensive in Africa intended to take the Eighth Army beyond Benghazi.

Success made Churchill's mind gallop ahead. He was both a dreamer and a realist, always tending to make grandiose plans and then refashion them under the pressure of reality. His messages to his commanders suggested operations everywhere; Operation Mandibles indicated a proposed attack on Pantelleria, and Operation Workshop and Operation Influx referred to other projects relating to Pantelleria and Sicily. Metaxas' hesitations and Papagos' dreams were a delaying factor, but probably did not change the history of those months. Greece was thinking of the Albanian front, and d'Albiac wanted airfields. The Greeks and British had agreed that air bases should be built by the end of January at Araxos in the northern Peloponnese and at Agrinion on the Gulf of Corinth, but the Germans entered Greece before they were ready;[11] thus in this campaign disorganization and delays were not confined to the Italians. Meanwhile new events were maturing. One of them that occurred in Greece, though it did not change the inevitable, nevertheless, in a way, marked the beginning of the end.

Metaxas was dying. His troops were fighting on Albanian soil, his army had won victories that filled his country with exultation. But this hour of hope and pride was nearing its end. On January 15, after confiding the substance of his talks with Wavell to his diary, he noted: "Tired. I have done my duty. . . . If the British had only had available five divisions with substantial armor . . . but they have nothing." On January 16: "Oppressive melancholy."

The diary ends with this entry on January 17: "The British are insisting on landing at Salonika with small forces of artillery. . . . I told them that they will not get to Salonika before the Germans cross the Danube [i.e., enter Bulgaria]. Heaven knows that it will not work. I worked till late at night. Nana is better."

Thus there ended on this humble family note the diary of John Metaxas, a dictator in bedroom slippers, a man who, all things considered, was a mediocrity, but nevertheless attained dignity and courage in his country's time of need. Mussolini's and Ciano's reckless arrogance greatly facilitated his task. Without the Albanian campaign he might well have been overthrown in some putsch and his name buried in recrimination or perhaps even in a wave of execration, but as it is, it is associated with the finest hour of modern Greek history. His life ended finely, and the melancholy he felt, his sense that these intoxicating victories were built on sand and were a strange and ephemeral gift of destiny, give his death an especially poignant note. He died on January 29, 1941. The bulletin signed by twelve physicians stated; "The Greek Prime Minister was affected ten days ago by a phlegmon of the pharynx which degenerated into an abscess. In spite of immediate surgical intervention and the appropriate post-operational care, blood poisoning with complications set in. The Prime Minister died at 6 A.M. today."[12] With incredible bad taste Fascist propaganda started talking of the "mystery" of his death, hinting at sinister British intrigues.

11. The Spring Offensive

Mussolini wanted a spring victory, a weight, never mind how small, to throw in the balance when the Germans began their Blitzkrieg in the Balkans. On February 23, when he made his speech in the Adriano Theater in Rome to the Fascist hierarchs of the capital, he did not explain how it had come about that he had not yet broken the Greek back, but eulogized the troops and the march of the Julia Division.[1] "The Italian prisoners who have fallen into Greek hands," he said, "are a few thousand, and most of them were wounded; the Greek successes have not gone beyond the tactical sphere and have been grossly exaggerated by megalomaniac Levantine rhetoric; the Greek losses have been very heavy, soon it will be spring and, in accordance with the season, our season, the fine weather will come. I tell you that the fine weather will come, and at all four points of the compass."

It was easy for Mussolini to prophesy: he knew that the Germans were nearly ready and that their invasion was a question of weeks. Cavallero, carried away by this speech, immediately sent him this telegram: "The fighting troops on the Greek-Albanian front, commanders, officers, other ranks, listened to your words with emotion and pride, animated by a single spirit, the spirit of self-sacrifice, and an implacable determination to win." A general who had seen the bloodshed and sufferings of his troops at first hand might well have spared himself this obsequious rhetoric. He now had twenty-five divisions at his disposal, and was still thinking about an offensive. Up to the middle of February 497 officers and 5,239 other ranks had been killed in action. In the course of that month Bancale was replaced by Gambara and Vercellino by Alessandro Pirzio Biroli. The fifty Italian regiments, plus about twenty unattached battalions, were opposed to forty-two Greek regiments. The Italians had real superiority at last.

The Germans were informed of the Italian intention to break through the Greek front, and they looked on with ill-concealed skepticism. Von Rintelen reported to the German Foreign Ministry as follows: "General Antonio Gandini, on behalf of General Guzzoni, has given me the following information about the intentions of the Italian High Command. The Italian armed forces wish to defeat the Greek army before peace is made. This is necessary for the prestige of the Italian armed forces, and the Wehrmacht certainly understands that. In reply to a question of mine, Gandini said that the Duce was aware of this communication."[2] There is a disarming naïveté about this admission by Mussolini to the Germans, whom he had hoped to "bypass" and score off by the Greek campaign. It was a confession of humiliating failure and of a desire belatedly to get his own back after all. But fortune did not favor him.

Not content with an offensive, he wanted to take an active part in it himself. He decided to go to Albania on a tour of inspection, imagining that his troops, animated by his presence, would reverse the fortunes of the campaign. First, he transferred himself to his usual headquarters near Bisceglie, where he conferred with Cavallero and other generals, including Guzzoni, the undersecretary for war and a specialist on Albania, who, it will be recalled, had been in command of the troops there before Geloso, and his successor, Visconti Prasca.

There was a difference of view between Cavallero and Guzzoni. The latter favored an offensive on the Ninth Army front in the Pogradec sector, which, if successful, would take Italian troops into a sector vital to the Greeks; also it would become one of the two arms of a pincer movement of which the advancing Germans would later provide the other. A considerable part of Papagos' army would be caught in the pincers. Guzzoni, in short, still adhered to the theory of an offensive in the Koritsa sector. Cavallero, however, now wanted a limited attack in the Desnizza Valley on the Eleventh Army front; that is, towards the valley between the Trebescines and Mali Qarishta which opens out towards Klisura. His aim was the recapture of Klisura instead of the recapture of Koritsa. This operation offered no opportunity of further development; its importance was purely local; its result would be merely that the Greeks, who were pretty active in this sector, having their eyes on Tepeleni, would be forced back on the defensive. Cavallero gained the day, and chief responsibility for the operation was given to General Gastone Gambara, the hero of the war in Spain, who was not very highly regarded by the most supercilious representatives of the General Staff, who were apt to look down on him as risen from the ranks, a practical man lacking in the higher subtleties of his craft. But they remembered him in times of difficulty. Gambara was on excellent terms with the Fascist hierarchy, and this may have been one of the reasons that influenced his selection, unless, as some maintain, he personally applied to the Duce for the job.

Carlo Cavallero, the marshal's son, who was in Albania in his father's suite (Badoglio set the example of making his son Mario his secretary in the Ethiopian campaign, and it became a habit of Italian senior commanders to put their sons on their staff), has defended the decision to attack in the Desnizza Valley instead of in the Koritsa zone in his book *Il dramma del maresciallo Cavallero*. He wrote:

The offensive in the Desnizza Valley, the value and prospects of which were denied by the table-top strategists, had the definite aim of relieving the pressure on the defense in the adjoining Valona sector, not by making our maximum effort at the enemy's weakest point, which is the classical aim of every offensive operation, but by striking him where he was strongest in order to wear down his strength. . . . For obvious and appropriate political reasons the Head of the Government was urging on my father an offensive in the grand style and with major objectives. The starting point of this would, of course, have been the most advanced sector of our line, that is, the Koritsa area, aiming at the rear of the enemy positions, as in fact was done later in the battle of Epirus. But in March my father was opposed to such a project, still having vividly before his eyes the tragic beginning of a hundred days earlier and knowing what trouble he had had in reorganizing in Albania an Italian army that was then nonexistent. . . . The continuation of an offensive undertaken in Mussolini's presence would have resulted in dramatic conditions if, our reserves exhausted, our line had been assaulted on the flank and in the rear by the Yugoslav surprise.

Cavallero's son's argument is questionable. It is hard to see why using forces in the Desnizza Valley instead of in the Koritsa sector would make any great difference if the Italians were subjected to a surprise attack. Implicit in the argument there seems to be a fear that the Italian advance might be so rapid as to become "unbalanced"—a contingency that previous experience of the campaign rendered somewhat remote. Still less is one able to see the tactical brilliance of knocking one's head against the strongest part of the enemy's barrier instead of seeking out a spot where it was weaker.

In reality it was a different matter. Cavallero had at last constructed his "wall." He had taken over a bankrupt situation and had managed to stave off total disaster. Having succeeded in that, he relapsed into the defensive mentality of Italian generals, always overcautious and terrified of risking their epaulets by an all-out attack. There was one Italian general who had the impulsiveness of a Rommel, and that was Visconti Prasca, but impulsiveness was the only quality of Rommel's that he possessed. The other generals, almost without exception (or at any rate without noticeable exceptions), liked good, solid fronts, massed with men—not with materials, which were always short—fronts which collapsed as soon as a mobile enemy made a breakthrough at any one point, as happened in North Africa. Cavallero was opposed by a good army, but not a mobile one, a good general, but one of the old style. When Italian military technicians enumerate the causes of the Greek success against them they mention, among other things, the technique by which the observers who directed the Greek mortar fire took up positions a long way away from the firing point and close to the enemy lines, which resulted in their mortars being used with great accuracy and effect. Such details are important, but do not go to the heart of the matter. Both sides now had their "walls," and the war had entered a static phase. There might be shifts in favor of one side or the other, but Cavallero intended to ensure that no catastrophe happened to him.

Gambara completed his plan for an offensive of limited scope in the last ten days of February, and he did so on questionable lines. The enemy was to be engaged by three army corps, the XXV to the southwest of the valley, the IV to the northeast and the VIII in the center; the latter was Gambara's own corps, which was to bear the brunt of the operation. The two corps on its flanks were intended not primarily to gain ground, but to pin the enemy down; it was intended that the breakthrough should take place into the Desnizza Valley, which wound its way through the mountains like a furrow. The Greek line formed a kind of salient in this sector, and the idea of attacking it head-on instead of trying to cut it off at its base seems open to criticism. Gambara would have liked to have had the Julia Division, but Cavallero and Geloso did not let him have it. In the front line he had General Giuseppe Gianni's Cagliari Division, General Alberto d'Aponte's Puglie Division and General De Stefanis' Pinerolo Division, with the Bari Division in the second line and three legions of Blackshirts in army corps reserve.

Gambara's plan was simple. It involved a converging attack on the Desnizza Valley from the heights of the Spadarit to the north and from the Trebescines to the south and a breakthrough to the center of the valley. The objectives along the valley were Suka and Klisura. Taking into account the activity of the two corps on the flanks, twelve divisions were to be engaged in the operation. Gastone Gambara wanted his VIII Corps to be very strong indeed in order to be able to make a breakthrough at a point where the

Greeks were not only strong but aggressively poised. The military instrument at his disposal was, however, a mediocre one. General Staff documents show that the corps called on to spearhead the offensive had "shortages of transport animals and materials, artillery, medical equipment, and general supplies." True, it had 200 small-caliber guns on a six-and-a-half-mile front, or 300 if the artillery of the neighboring units, the Sforzesca Division, an Alpini detachment, and the 41st Modena Infantry Regiment belonging to the XXV Corps on its right flank is included, as well as that of the Cacciatori delle Alpi and the Pusteria Division in the IV Corps area on its right.

While Cavallero was preparing Mussolini's offensive at the end of February, Papagos wanted to continue with his own offensive. The Greeks advanced stubbornly, with a kind of fanatical exaltation, to the assault of the positions covering Tepeleni, beyond which lay the plain and an uninterrupted descent towards Valona. The Golico, the 2,500-foot Scialesit, and Monastery Hill, the last of which was to acquire a tragic fame in the Desnizza Valley offensive, were stormed, some other hills were lost, and the Julia Division was again committed to battle (it took the place of the exhausted Legnano Division). The Greek élan was, however, diminishing. The grimness and futility of the struggle in the snow that led to slight territorial gains at the cost of heavy losses began to spread discouragement in the enemy camp too.

A reflection of this appeared at the beginning of March, when General Drakos, the commander of the Greek Epirus army, went to Athens for a high-level conference attended by the King, Papagos, the new Prime Minister, Alexander Koryzis, and the Minister of the Armed Forces.[3] Papagos wanted Greek pressure on Tepeleni to be continued. Drakos replied that, if the government and the High Command wanted his army to continue with this exhausting and expensive offensive, three tried and tested but exhausted divisions must first be rested, and withdrawing and replacing them would take from twenty to twenty-five days.

The Epirus Army would therefore not be able to resume its large-scale efforts before the end of March.

The sole result of these representations was the replacement of Drakos and two of his corps commanders. On March 6 General Pitsikas was transferred from the command of the army in western Macedonia to that of the Epirus army, and his previous command was taken over by General Tsolakoglou. After the Italian March offensive had begun, the Greeks were still attacking the Scindeli and the Trebescines, a huge spur to the east of Tepeleni, and the valley of the Dhrino and the Golico. The grenadiers, the Ferrara Division, the Susa and Cividale Alpini battalions on the Golico, and then the Julia and the Sforzesca divisions in the neighboring sectors, were at the receiving end of these last Greek hammerblows, which gave them possession of some more heights and some stretches of the Vojussa Valley, but did not enable them to debouch on Tepeleni. At dawn on March 9, 300 guns which were preparing the ground for the assault started their fearful symphony behind the backs of the infantrymen of the IV, VIII and XXV army corps.

Mussolini left Bari for Albania on March 2. He "personally piloted" a three-engined S.79, and was escorted by two more S79s, two 2-Cant.Z506 seaplanes and twelve Macchi 200 fighters.[4] The Duce was in the gray-green uniform of a First Marshal of the Empire, over which he wore a flying suit during the flight. He was silent and grim, or more worried than grim. He did not know what reception might be awaiting him. He feared that the attitude of the troops towards him might be cool or even hostile; that he might see reproach and bitterness in their eyes because of the useless ordeals imposed on them; that they would guess that his presence among them meant that defeat in a prestige war was to be followed by more bloodshed in a prestige offensive. In the cool, fresh morning air at the Tirana airfield Cavallero, Ranza, the air commander, and Jacomoni, the governor-general, were waiting for him, with faces radiating pleasure and optimism;

also present, with a smile that probably concealed many secret thoughts, was Verlaci, the Albanian Prime Minister.

Mussolini hastily returned their greetings and almost flung himself into the waiting car, accompanied by Cavallero and Pricolo, who had traveled with him. When a detachment of infantry of the Bari Division came marching towards them with their packs on their backs his expression became hesitant and anxious. The men recognized him, and unexpectedly, though not excessively so to those familiar with the psychology of crowds and the resilience of the Italian character, they cheered him loudly. Further on Mussolini was cheered again by scattered detachments, as when he reviewed the Siena Division at Roskovezza. These incidents raised his morale again, for he was exceedingly sensitive to applause, which made him forget his responsibilities, his failures, the useless casualties, the unnecessary victims of frostbite. Members of his retinue recorded a number of historic remarks. "You'll soon get better," he said to a wounded man, who bravely replied: "The important thing is to win."

From his car Mussolini was able to see something of the war traffic. He traveled along a recently reconditioned road on which marching men, lorries, mule trains, slowly made their way. The atmosphere was extraordinarily similar to that which the Bersagliere Mussolini had known in the First World War. The static nature of the Italian military organization and equipment, the antiquated conservatism of its military machine after twenty years of bellicose Fascist tirades, was the most obvious condemnation of the régime's military policy. The absence of danger from the enemy air force allowed all this busy traffic to take place in broad daylight, and hutments, stores, transport parks were totally unconcealed.

Mussolini's car and those of his escort—which was reduced to a minimum—stopped among the little houses of Rehova, and the party entered Gambara's headquarters; Geloso, the commander of the Eleventh Army, was also present. In a big, bare room Gambara, short, thickset, and energetic, described his plan of attack in stentorian tones. Pricolo, who was present, summarizes it as follows:

> While the IV Army Corps (Mercalli's) strongly engaged the enemy, the Cagliari Division was to break through, drop down to the Desnizza Valley and assault it from the rear. Simultaneously the Puglie Division (making for Mount Rapit) and the Pinerolo Division (making for Qafa Lusit) were also to force their way into the Desnizza Valley. Strength of opposing forces: ours, about 50,000 men; the enemy's was estimated at from 26,000 to 28,000 men. We had superiority in artillery and total mastery of the air.[5]

Gambara needed another four or five days to complete his preparations. Mussolini listened attentively, protruding his thick lips and rolling his eyes. He refrained from interfering in technical details, but attentively watched the faces of the others for signs of doubt or dissent. Since there was none, and everyone seemed perfectly satisfied, he gave his approval. Meanwhile the news of his presence in Albania had spread, and when he continued on his way in the afternoon he was enthusiastically cheered whenever he passed a camp. Latin exuberance exploded, and enthusiasts who wanted to cling to the bonnet and doors of his car had to be physically restrained. Instead of regarding these volatile changes of mood as a sign of the psychological frailty of part of the human material on which he relied, Mussolini was delighted.

Late that evening, after a drive that because of its slowness seemed interminable, an endless switchback of dismal hills, he reached Lahatun, five miles north of Valona. Two or three small houses lying in a thick wood that stood out in the inhospitable countryside had been prepared to receive the Duce and his suite for the night. He was awaited by General Alessandro Pirzio Biroli, Roberto Farinacci, talkative and arrogant, wearing a kind of hunting suit, and Ciano. The Duce went to bed straightaway, while the others stayed up talking in an atmosphere of ostentatious and loquacious good-fellowship.

Achille Starace, joking about his startling ups and downs in the military hierarchy, was the star of the evening. As chief of staff of the Fascist Militia he had recently held the rank of lieutenant general, which, however, he had lost on being called up in his army rank, like other members of the hierarchy. In the army he was a lieutenant colonel, and he had vainly sought employment at that level. But no one dared entrust a battalion to this lieutenant colonel of the Bersaglieri. Now he was trying to get back his rank of lieutenant general in the Militia, and soon afterwards he succeeded. The full colonels whom for a few days he had saluted then had to salute him.

Next morning Mussolini, who seemed in a much better mood, called at Demblan, the headquarters of General Carlo Rossi's XXV Corps. Then he reviewed a regiment of the Lupi di Toscana and another belonging to the Legnano Division. The troops were in clean uniforms, the wounded whom the Duce saw had clean bandages, and several bridges on which work had been advancing at a snail's pace had suddenly been completed with lightning rapidity. Demonstrations of enthusiasm, no doubt decreasingly spontaneous and increasingly organized, continued. The Duce nodded gravely when troops rushed towards him shouting, presumably on instruction: "We want an offensive! Give us the order, Duce!" It was difficult for those present to remain immune to the mob emotion, but there were some who did. Pricolo, who was an attentive observer of those few days, quotes a significant example.

Among all those hundreds of shouting troops my attention was attracted by a solitary individual who remained apart on the slope of the valley along the roadside and went on quietly eating. He looked no longer very young, was powerfully built, and had a strong growth of beard. While raising his spoon to his mouth he kept gazing at his excited fellow soldiers, and every now and again his hand stopped over his messtin as if he were dumbfounded by a scene that was obviously incomprehensible to him. Suddenly he noticed that I was looking at him with excessive curiosity; he went on eating for a moment, and then began slowly backing into the bushes and disappeared from my sight.[6]

At Demblan General Carlo Rossi, the commander of the XXV Corps, described his own and the enemy's position—the Bersaglieri and the tanks blocking the way from Klisura to Tepeleni, and the Greeks high up on the Bregianit, where they were now held up. Mussolini listened gravely, and then he and his escort went down into the Vojussa Valley, from where the rumble and stutter of artillery and mortar fire could be heard distinctly. "The Greeks now fear our mortars," someone said. "War consists of the clash of two psychologies," Mussolini declared, and then, struck by a new idea, he added: "Don't you think it would be appropriate to issue a press statement about my visit to the front?" "Of course," Cavallero replied. "The soldiers will hear of it at once on the radio, and a visit from you and your praise will be their most sought-after reward and greatest encouragement. And, if you agree, in due course I shall mention that you are going to take command yourself."[7] Others pointed out that it would be wiser to wait and see how the offensive went before making a press announcement. The result was that no one in Italy knew about Mussolini's visit, at any rate officially, until May, and he never took command because the offensive failed to make any territorial gains of the slightest importance.

Mussolini attended firing practices, talked to the principal commanders, and visited military hospitals, and as the tour progressed the stage management became increasingly assured. Everything was in order, everything was fine. But when he inspected a detachment of the Lupi di Toscana and asked when it had had its first firing practice, he was told that this had taken place on the previous day. He also inspected a detachment of Albanians. Jacomoni still tried to present a picture of a solidly Fascist Albania. Had he not informed the King a month earlier that "the Albanians are very loyal and well integrated, their morale is good, and when they are used the results are excellent. The situation that came close to disaster has been resolved by Cavallero, who will go down in history as the savior of the Greek front. Now we are at a standstill, but in a month at most the reinforced Italian armies will possess a superiority that will enable us victoriously to resume the offensive."[8]

A month had passed, and the offensive was about to begin. From Lahatun Mussolini went to the so-called Tactical Position No. 34, among a group of houses belonging to Agip, the Italian state oil concern, not far from the airfield at Devoli. Mussolini emerged from his night quarters at Tactical Position No. 34 at 4 A.M. on March 9. It was pitch dark, and while the cars made their way along the dusty road they were surrounded by all the familiar back-area noises, the panting of horses, the restless trampling of mules, the metallic clink of messtins, the hoarse voices of men still sleepy and cold. At 6 A.M., Mussolini left his car and, assuming a springy and youthful gait and followed by a large retinue, started climbing the hill leading to the observation post on the Komarit. The dawn of a cold but fine, clear day was breaking; the air force would be able to strike with the necessary vigor. Mussolini, looking corpulent and slightly awkward in his heavy gray-green greatcoat, looked around with anxious, inquisitive eyes. Next to him walked Starace, who, overlooked for a long period, had at last managed to secure a place in the foreground again. "What do you think of the morale of the troops?" Mussolini asked. The reply was the classic: "Excellent, Duce, all are keenly awaiting the signal to attack."

The observation post was at a height of about 2,500 feet, and before it lay a panorama of mountains and precipitous ridges, the grim valley of the Desnizza: a landscape in some ways reminiscent of the Carso,* with its fiercely contested heights and innumerable dead. The observation post itself consisted of a brick

---

* The rocky plateau northwest of Trieste, the scene of fierce battles between the Italians and the Austrians in the First World War, in which thousands of lives were lost.

and concrete pillbox in front of which there was a small open space protected by sandbags and boarding. It was crowded that morning, which, it was hoped, would mark the first success in a campaign strewn with failures. Geloso, the Eleventh Army commander, stood next to Ranza, who looked plump, almost stout, in his flying uniform. Gambara wore a short cloak of the Bersaglieri type; he explained that this non-regulation article of clothing had brought him luck on other important battlefields, but on this occasion it failed to do so.

Visibility was excellent. Cavallero assiduously pointed out the snow-capped ridges of the Trebescines and the Scindeli, where Italian blood was still being spilled, the Desnizza Valley, which in the summer would be dried up but was still covered with green, the Vojussa, beyond Klisura, the waters of which were glittering. The barrage started up along the whole front. Orders had been given that the artillery should be very active in sectors not concerned with the offensive, including the Ninth Army and coastal sectors, in the hope of confusing the enemy. But Papagos knew all about the Italian plan. An Italian officer had been taken prisoner with the orders for the offensive in his possession, and the troop movements noted by enemy observation had all been concentrated behind the three army corps involved.

In a couple of hours 100,000 rounds were fired off. While the ground reverberated, a bare, rugged hill was pointed out to Mussolini, the recapture of which was considered highly important for the protection of Berati. It was known as Monastery Hill, because of the ruins of a monastery that had used to stand on its summit, together with some other wretched buildings; it was one of the first objectives. Mussolini examined it carefully through a pair of binoculars, nodding his head to Gambara's explanations.

Aircraft with the tricolor emblem flashed through the sky. The Italian air force had been reinforced; an additional forty-six fighters and eight bombers had been sent to Albania, and in Apulia twelve Macchi 200 fighters had been added to the strength.

At 8:30 A.M. the artillery increased its range, dive bombers followed each other in succession over the Greek lines, and concentrated in particular on Hill 1308 of the Trebescines massif, on which murderous artillery and mortar positions were known to lie, and the infantry began to move forward. The first messages from the whole sector of the IV, VIII and XXV corps were satisfactory.[9]

0900 hrs. The Feltre Division has occupied the village of Spadarit, the 52nd Infantry Regiment has occupied Hill 700 on Bregu Guilici; the Puglie Division is approaching Monastery Hill, 731. 1015 hrs. The Sforzesca is advancing from Marizai towards Arzo di Mezzo. 1030 hrs. Our troops 100 yards from Qafa Mezgoranit, Hill 731 taken. Pinerolo Division now climbing towards Qafa Lusit. 1500 hrs. Hill 1615 on the Golico retaken. 1510 hrs. Qafa Lusit twice taken and twice lost. 1545 hrs. The Puglie Division has passed Hill 731 and is advancing on Sorgente.

These messages might have created the impression of a definite, though not shattering, advance, but nothing could have been further from the truth. The Italian troops were advancing slowly and suffering bloody losses. Most of the positions taken were lost again in immediate counterattacks, the news of the capture of Hill 731 was overoptimistic, the determined infantry of the Puglie Division had taken Hill 717 and set foot on Hill 731 but did not succeed in establishing themselves on it. A bitter and bloody struggle raged in which the chief weapons were those used in the Carso in the First World War, the bayonet and the hand grenade. There was no irresistible drive behind the offensive, because it was badly planned and ran into a real enemy "wall."

The first assault wave consisted of 3,000 men. General Giuseppe Gianni, the commander of the Cagliari Division, which was allotted one of the key roles in the operation, was ill, and the artillery had fired off a large number of rounds, but without obtaining noticeable results. In spite of the optimism still displayed by some of the generals around him, Mussolini realized that things were not going well. "If an offensive has not succeeded after two or three hours, it does not succeed at all," he said to Pricolo. On the way back to Devoli that evening he was in a very bad humor. "These generals who are taken ill on the day of an offensive make one wonder," he complained. "Don't you think that these generals show little spirit, little élan, and above all have little initiative? Look at Rommel, who is restoring the situation in Libya with a single division and a reconnaissance group." The responsibility for the failure to capture Mount Rapit as planned was thus in a way attributed to the unfortunate General Gianni, who had the misfortune to fall sick on March 9. But General Alberto d'Aponte's Puglie Division had also failed to capture Monastery Hill in spite of heroic sacrifices.

Next day's fighting followed an exactly similar course—minimal territorial gains, enemy counterattacks, heavy losses. The Bari Division, which was in reserve, was gradually inserted between the Puglie and Cagliari divisions to reinforce the front line, but this injection of fresh troops was insufficient to give penetrative power to an offensive that met stubborn resistance from an enemy established in strong positions. The only success of any importance was gained in the IV Corps sector. The 11th Alpini Regiment of the Pusteria Division assaulted and took Mali Spadarit, but the success was short-lived. The positions seized by the 11th Alpini formed a wedge the flanks and rear of which were uncovered, and furious attacks from all sides forced them to withdraw.

After the failure of its frontal attack on Hill 731 the Puglie Division maneuvered to surround it, but this operation had also been foreseen by the enemy and was repulsed. Mussolini stayed at the observation post on Mount Komarit from morning till late afternoon, conferred with Geloso, Gambara, and Mercalli, telephoned to the divisional commanders, and kept himself very busy, but his mood was grim. His offensive was failing; he was gaining neither the prestige card he wanted to play against Hitler nor the moral alibi that he no doubt wanted. Meanwhile the weather had deteriorated, it began to rain, and low-level air strikes to help the infantry became impossible. Once more the troops were laboriously plunging through that plague of the infantryman, the clinging Albanian mud, less dangerous than the enemy mortars or frostbite, less tormenting than the lice, less humiliating than the dysentery, but physically terribly exhausting. The dirty war in dirty Albania went on.

By next day, March 11, the Italian offensive had, so to speak, become routine, a bloody, heroic, desperate routine, a kind of furious knocking at a door that refused to open instead of a blow with a battering ram that knocked it from its hinges. On March 12 Mussolini paid a visit to Pirzio Biroli's headquarters at Elbasan and then returned to the Eleventh Army sector and gave Geloso his parting instructions:

> It is absolutely necessary to persist. The operational plan cannot be changed after four days. Hill 1308 on the Trebescines and its eastern slopes must be neutralized, and then the attacking columns must go forward. We must attack tomorrow, otherwise the troops will begin to get rooted to the ground and think the operation is over. The Greeks must be kept under fire all day. The answer to the mortar is rapid movement. We must insist on the plan as laid down. A military victory before the end of the month is absolutely essential to the prestige of the Italian army. I have always done everything in my power to keep the reputation and prestige of the Italian army high, but now a breakthrough is absolutely essential. I have instructed his Excellency Guzzoni to send here all the ammunition there is in Italy, because the Italian army is here, the war is here, and it is here that we must win.

While Mussolini raged like a child who cannot have a sweet it wants, the Greeks recovered their breath and attacked on Mali Spadarit, and the Alpini of the Trento Regiment held them off with difficulty. The final do-or-die Italian blow was now to be delivered on the afternoon of March 13. At the Komarit observation post Mussolini listened to Gambara saying: "The artillery preparation for the imminent operation is very accurate. There will be flanking fire and a moving barrage in front of the advancing infantry." The Duce read through the operational orders, several times nodding his big head in assent and holding his forage cap straight with his marshal's baton. Then he called Cavallero, who was at the observation post of the Bari Division,[10] on the telephone and said to him: "I have read Gambara's document. It is very detailed and exhaustive. The divisional commanders have only to apply it. Tell Negro that I have a high opinion of him and count on him. Tell him that the greater the dash, the smaller the losses."

General Matteo Negro was the new commander of the Bari, that is to say, the division which, if the Greek campaign had been carried out according to the original plan, would now be on garrison duty in Corfu, but had now been selected to take the place of the Puglie Division in the furious battle for Hill 731. It advanced from Hill 717 towards Hill 731, but did not succeed in taking it. Meanwhile the corpses were piling up. Mussolini distributed praise. To Negro he said: "They tell me you are conducting yourself well. I commend you and exhort you to continuo in the same way." To Guido Lama, the VIII Corps artillery commander, he said: "I commend the gunners for the great help they have given the infantry; carry on until you see the Greeks wavering." To Cavallero he said: "Things have gone very well today. I think the Greeks wavered, as I said they would, because the operation was carried out with extreme energy."

On the evening of the thirteenth Mussolini returned to Devoli. During the night Bari Division infantry took Hill 731, but were compelled to withdraw again by a hurricane of fire. The behavior of the Italian troops, even the best of them, was characterized by tenacity and resolution, a kind of resigned courage, rather than by aggressive dash. Basically there was something gnawing at the minds of these men. To cheap pragmatists, the basic wrongness of a war, the lack of a strong motive, may seem negligible factors, but the evidence of the Greek campaign, on the Greek side as on the Italian, seems to me to show how far from negligible they are.

On the afternoon of the fourteenth another assault on Monastery Hill, 731, failed. The slopes of the mountain on which the Komarit observation point stood were machine-gunned by a couple of enemy aircraft. Mussolini behaved courageously and entered the air raid shelter last. He was never in real danger, as the enemy fire was a long way away. After a brief revival of hope on the previous day, the Duce had decided that his breakthrough was not going to take place. For lack of anything better, he consoled himself with a report which alleged that the King of Greece was very anxious that the war should end, because of the heavy Greek casualties. To Cavallero Mussolini put a direct question. The troops had sacrificed themselves, he said, they had attacked, but what had been gained?

This was the moment of truth. Cavallero replied that he thought "our troops not suitable for making a break in the front of the enemy, who has used the time that we used in forming the front to build up a very effective defense system. Facing a well-consolidated defense system with centers of fire, troops are necessary who are capable of using infiltration tactics and are well supplied with officers. We do not have those conditions and therefore, instead of using infiltration tactics, we apply weight and wear the enemy down. If between now and tomorrow we see that there is a breakthrough, we shall be able to follow up the operation with the greatest intensity. Otherwise we shall have to give it up."

"And then what?" Mussolini said with dismay.

"If success is not in sight, we must not continue to feed the struggle, but break it off."

Cavallero's views were unexceptionable, but why had he not expressed them before? And why, to use his own phrase, had he applied weight in the place where the enemy was strongest? A divergence of view was appearing among the officers responsible for the offensive. Gambara, disappointed, wanted to break off the operation, while Geloso wanted to carry on. Losses had been heavy. The VIII Corps casualties were 5,000; the XXV Corps, 5,000; the IV Corps, 1,800—an average of 1,000 per division, though some divisions had hardly suffered and others had suffered severely. This tribute of blood might have been justified if the result had been victory, but 12,000 casualties were a shocking price to pay for an offensive that had not gone beyond its starting line, and it had been paid solely to satisfy Mussolini's ambitions.

On March 15 he seemed to be feeling better—these ups and downs of his, and a kind of amnesia about even his most humiliating failures, were characteristic of him—and he started giving orders again.

The following exchange took place in a conversation with Gambara, Geloso, and Cavallero:

> MUSSOLINI: How is the morale of the troops?
> GAMBARA: It cannot be said to be very high, but it is still good. The losses, the nil gain of ground, the few prisoners, are not positive factors. But it is not such as to prejudice their employment.
> MUSSOLINI: We have in progress an effort engaging the IV, VIII, and XXV army corps. This corresponds to the concept of a war of attrition, in so far as we are engaged with an enemy in a strong position. On the other hand, the only area of the Eleventh Army front on which a success of ours could be given a name is that of Klisura. If we reach that objective, the result will be a collapse of Greek morale. Consequently Tepeleni must be held at all costs and Klisura must be taken at all costs. We have an operation that has already been mounted and is in progress. We have chosen an objective convinced that on the day when it becomes known that we have captured Klisura the Greek army will collapse. Hence we must persist in the Klisura-Tepeleni operation. The operation of cutting off the Scindeli salient must be prepared immediately.[11]

These phrases echoed Cavallero's "lesson" of the day before. The offensive had failed, and the Klisura objective was unattainable. The Italians had fought with vigor and tenacity, though certainly not with enthusiasm. On the afternoon of the fifteenth a rather gloomy Mussolini went to Valona to see his daughter Edda, who had been serving as a nurse in the hospital ship *Po,* which had been struck by an aerial torpedo in Valona harbor during the previous night. Countess Ciano was in the water for a long time before she and others were rescued.

While Mussolini was at Valona, Cavallero, Geloso, and Gambara held a conference at Devoli. They discussed the situation in realistic terms. They agreed that "no positive result had been obtained from the operations, which, apart from causing us really substantial losses, notably lowered the level of the troops' morale." What, then, was to be done? Notwithstanding Mussolini's slogan of reaching Klisura at all costs, continuing the offensive was out of the question. There could be no thought of an advance on Koritsa, because "operations in that direction would require a considerable time for organization, while time was short." The way out of this dilemma chosen by the three generals was a decision to resume the Klisura offensive at an early date still to be decided.

Orders to break off Mussolini's offensive were accordingly given on March 16. On the same day Cavallero, in tones expressing arrogance and frustration, said to Pirzio Biroli:

> We have saved Italy from collapse, and now we are saving it from disgrace. On the seventh, eighth, and ninth [of March] we had a violent attack on Tepeleni and we stood firm, though with 5,000 casualties. The only positive result of the operation just completed is that the troops fought well. But we did not break through. The country requires that, having made our wall, we show we are superior to the Greeks. But time is short. The Germans will be entering Greece on April 1, and in the interests of the country the Duce does not wish that to be the factor that settles the conflict. Alpini must be massed for the offensive.[12]

How many things those few sentences left unsaid. Italy had not been "saved." The phrase would have had meaning only if she had been saved from the blows struck her by the man who had led her into the abyss by means of this campaign, that is to say, Mussolini. But Cavallero refrained from saying this, or even implying it; and it is hard to see what offensive he was now talking about, i.e., genuine "Italian" offensive, as distinct from an inglorious advance on the heels of a German breakthrough. Nevertheless the High Command in Albania obstinately went on planning another useless and bloody frontal attack on the Klisura sector. Directive No. 12, of March 19, laid down that the Eleventh Army should resume the attack on March 28. Fortunately for the troops, however, the coup in Yugoslavia led to the dropping of this ill-considered project, which would certainly have led to the futile waste of thousands of more lives.

Cavallero, optimistic by nature and by self-interest also, did not emerge well from the test of the offensive. But, thanks to his confidence and his promises, he succeeded in retaining Mussolini's favor until January 1943, even though he may not have retained his esteem to the very end. During the four more days that he spent in Albania Mussolini spent his time going from unit to unit, from sector to sector, always the condottiere, sometimes imperious, sometimes smiling and gracious, surrounded by tail-wagging hierarchs and obsequious generals, perfectly aware of the fact that he had been deceived, was being deceived, and liked being deceived. By now his "tour of inspection" had become a completely routine affair. The man who inspected regiments, smiled at the wounded in hospitals, opened bridges, talked to workmen building roads, watched the march-past of singing units of the Corps of Foresters, no longer believed in advances; he was the Duce accustomed to organized mass demonstrations and impeccable reviews, to the half-truths that were officially told him and the half-truths of his own speeches.

But before leaving Albania he at least on one occasion told his generals some disagreeable home truths, rebuking them for their excessive anxiety about promotion and their insufficient anxiety about graver problems, their excessively flourishing appear-

ance and deficiency in fighting spirit. "He has taken a load off
our shoulders," someone remarked, but there were no arguments
by which anyone could take the load off his shoulders.

At 7:45 A.M. on March 21 Mussolini's aircraft, with an escort
of twelve fighters, left Albania. He stopped at Bari, and at 10:30
A.M. was at the Roman camp at Centocelle. To Pricolo, who had
returned from Rome to Albania on the previous day, the Duce
had confided with a melancholy air before taking off: "I am dis-
gusted by this environment. We have not advanced one step.
They have been deceiving me to this very day. I have a profound
contempt for all these people. Last night I sent a detailed report
on the situation to his Majesty." The Duce had remembered the
existence of the King—which he was liable to do at serious moments, as has been pointed out. At the beginning of the offensive
his attitude had been different. On March 10 Guzzoni, on Mussolini's behalf, had asked for an immediate audience with the King
to deliver this extraordinary and almost insolent message:

> On behalf of the Duce, who is in Albania, where an offensive has
> been in progress since yesterday, I must inform your Majesty that
> the Head of the Government will not send special news about the
> operations in progress, because the official communiqués will reflect
> the truth of the situation. On the first day the outer shell of the Greek
> resistance has been cracked at some points. The Greeks are desper-
> ately holding on. The morale of our troops is very high.[13]

Mussolini did not keep his promise, for the official communiqués
did not reveal the truth. True, they refrained from claiming nonexistent successes, but they did not mention the ambitious offensive
or its failure.

There was a profound historical justice in the disappointing
outcome of the March offensive. It would have been too convenient for the Mussolinis, the Cianos, the Jacomonis, the Visconti Prascas, if the slate had been wiped clean of their disastrous
errors by a victory paid for with the blood of the humble; if a

triumphant advance had enabled them to bury in amnesia, as if with a drug, all thought of those who fell victim to frostbite because of unpreparedness, those who were killed because of unpreparedness, the humiliations inflicted on an army and a whole nation because of the reckless folly of their leaders. There is a sense in which it was a painful necessity that when the German operation began the Italian army should still be on Albanian soil, testifying to the incompetence of a leading political and military class that had for twenty years boasted of its bellicosity, of sleeping with its head on its knapsack, always with a rifle at hand as well as a book.*

When Mussolini went back to Italy the hierarchs began to return there too. The "total mobilization" farce petered out as pathetically as the tour of inspection of the Commander-in-Chief of the armed forces, who confessed with disarming naïveté that he had always been given false information on which his wrong conclusions had been based. On the mountains of Albania the snow began to melt, and from under the white blanket there began to emerge dead bodies, helmets, water bottles, the carcasses of mules, scraps of rotting paper still bearing traces of unfinished letters, illegible phrases spattered with blood.

* The slogan *Libro e moschetto* (book and rifle), which referred above all to students, was one of the most commonly quoted Fascist phrases and was sometimes extended to: *Libro e moschetto—fascista perfetto.*

12. How They Lived and Died

The men who fought in the campaign have reacted in very different ways over the years. Some have forgotten; perhaps they have unconsciously wiped out those pages from their memory. All that remains in their minds is a fragmentary succession of pictures, a collection of snapshots, so to speak; a succession of white slopes, the spatter of earth caused by the burst of a mortar bomb, a snowy trench, a stinking hut, a frantic dash to avoid encirclement after going out on a fighting patrol. Where? When? How? You ask, but they do not remember. They saw the war at the time, and even more remember it today, like a detail on a printed page seen under a powerful magnifying glass. The page as a whole disappears, leaving a letter or half a word swollen out of all proportion.

Others have wrapped their war memories in emotional pathos. The war, even the dirty Greek campaign, was their youth, it had an exhilarating quality which it will never lose. Those who try digging into the memories of the men who fought in Albania thirty years ago come up with a great many quotations from the daily or military press of that time. It is obvious that from the innumerable letters that were found in the uniforms of the dead, together with photographs of mothers, wives, children, fiancées, only those expressing optimism, hope, warlike spirit, and loyalty to the government's cause were published. At most this carefully selected correspondence revealed the feelings of a minority who were ardently Fascist, or naïve, or addicted to literature of the traditional patriotic type, or of a type that found an outlet for their adventurous spirit in war, even a war as absurd and agonizing as this. It certainly does not reflect the state of mind of the majority: of the infantrymen or Alpini who grumbled and waited for a change of wind that never came. However, the letters that were published then, and those published later, but not for propaganda purposes, in addition to the testimony of the men who remember and those who tried to forget, build up into a total picture of the Greek campaign, as revealed in the following accounts by Italian soldiers. Having reached a point in the story at which the most agonizing months were over and the army in Albania as a whole had become more organized again and the men in the line had at any rate a minimum of creature comforts, I propose to make a quick survey of what our soldiers had to say.

On the eve of the attack on Greece Genserico Fontana, an officer of the 3rd Grenadiers, which formed part of the Littoral Group, was waiting with his men in their assembly positions.

We lit the last fire in the dark and rainy night. Tomorrow the war will be here too. The captain is rather agitated, and wipes the lenses of his spectacles too often. He, too, is a volunteer. He could have had his discharge, but wanted to be here with his grenadiers. We are under canvas about 500 yards from the frontier. Silence prevails, the atmosphere is similar to that of a sacred rite. Tomorrow we shall hope for the favor of Mars. They have told us that we shall have to strike sparks, because we are only a few divisions, and the declaration of war could not be postponed. Though we are only few, we are not afraid. Our pockets are full of hand grenades, which have the advantage of being light. It is two hours since we flung ourselves to the ground under a slow, penetrating rain. Here is the gloomy and silent dawn. No one moves. A senior officer with his greatcoat collar turned up looks around through his binoculars. It is still very misty. At last the first gun is fired.[1]

Genserico Fontana became a captain of carabinieri and was killed at the Fosse Ardeatine. Here was a man who was clearly obeying the call of a genuine patriotism and had confidence in the Duce's wisdom ("the declaration of war could not be postponed").

The first setbacks did not diminish his ardor, but a sense of failure began to appear. On November 10, 1940, he wrote:

> We must be strong. Events are not such as our enthusiasm foresaw. We must hold on. We must give time for new troops to arrive from Italy and consolidate themselves on a defense line in the rear. Time will be needed. There are no roads. The harbors are inefficient. Winter is imminent. Rain has been tormenting us for a month. But we are disputing ground with the enemy inch by inch. He will pay dearly for his audacity.

There was a strange logical twist in the mind of this intelligent man, who was to be wounded at the beginning of December. He saw clearly the many reasons for the failure of the offensive. All of them were the fault of the Fascist government and the military leaders, but he turns them into reasons for hating the enemy.

He continues to note the toughness of the struggle. On November 24 he wrote:

> These are days of great efforts and great heroism, we have entered into a delicate phase of the war . . . it would be disastrous if the enemy broke through, Albania would be in peril. . . . Torments of the flesh fail to make us murmur or complain.

During the same period Captain Fernando Campione, attached to the propaganda department, was with the Siena Division. He too shared in the illusions of the first advance into Greek territory in Epirus against a fleeting enemy, when the Italians moved forward in a mood of mingled exultation and mistrust, because—apart from the vileness of the weather—it seemed too easy; and he too, though in less idealistic terms, describes the first withdrawals.

> Cavalry, mingled with the infantry, withdraw along the slopes of these rugged mountains, and this sudden and unexpected retreat is not understood by these valiant men, who cannot understand the rea-

son for this change of direction. Another infantryman is lying on the road. His hands are contracted, a shell splinter tore open the right side of his stomach, where the clotted blood has formed a huge dark filthy stain on his jacket. He will be buried this evening, probably beside the river at the foot of a small isolated mountain.[2]

On November 21 the withdrawal of the Siena Division grew hastier and less orderly, assumed the tragic and grotesque aspects of all war episodes.

A soldier who had managed to scrounge some alcohol, swaying and staggering in his drunkenness, was carrying in his arms a tin of tuna fish weighing several kilograms: another soldier on horseback, perhaps he was a shepherd or cow-boy, was guiding a herd of sheep in front of him with a long pole. . . . In spite of the behavior of a few undisciplined men, the troops as a whole are maintaining order and have fought well.

On November 29 "some soldiers are dragging themselves along limping, others have put their knapsack, rifle, cartride pouch on a mason's pushcart. . . . They are marching heavily, slowly." On December 2, "what with killed, wounded, missing, sick, etc., we have more than 2,000 men out of action."

We have now reached the period of the desperate plugging of gaps, and the Siena Division was suffering severely. On December 4 Campione wrote: "The sight of our retreating troops is sadder than ever, because of the painful sight of long columns of tired, tattered soldiers slowly dragging themselves along." On December 14 he noted that "more than ninety mules are lying along the road, either singly or in groups of two or three at various intervals; they collapsed from exhaustion and were abandoned on the spot with all their load." Here is a description of the remnants of a battalion returning from a mountain position:

The major in command drags himself along with his feet affected by the beginning of frostbite. His serious, emaciated, livid face be-

trays the tragedy of the days and nights passed in the cold and snow.
He coughs continually, and in spite of his state of obvious exhaustion, his serenity is admirable.

The Siena Division was approaching the peak of its sacrifice. On
December 17:

> Signs of disintegration in units of the 32nd Infantry Regiment
> create panic and alarm at headquarters. There are no reserves, there
> is nothing to fall back on. So we had to turn to the divisional cara-
> binieri and a guard company consisting of older men recalled to the
> colors. Mule drivers, lorry drivers, everyone available has been
> thrown into the defense, the whole garrison of Himara has been col-
> lected under the command of a colonel. . . . In the area where the
> snow is, it is said that forty men are frozen to death daily. . . . It is
> not the fighting that kills, but exhaustion that brings terror and hu-
> miliation.

Two days later the coastal front broke, and the way lay open
for the Greeks (General Geloso was later to write that heaven
knows how far they might have gone if they had exploited the
gap).

> The remnants of the grenadier battalion mingled with infantrymen
> gave way, leaving the extreme right wing and the only road open to
> the enemy. In its withdrawal under enemy pressure the 32nd In-
> fantry Regiment was threatened with encirclement and disintegrated.
> There is only vague news about the 31st Infantry, which was sub-
> jected to a mass attack. In its retreat it lost guns, weapons, rations,
> ammunition, and the small handful of survivors remained to deny
> the enemy the Sciuscizza Valley.

Next came the bitter sequel, threats of disciplinary action and
worse against these men.

> During the withdrawal to Drimades a battalion of the motorized
> 17th Infantry Regiment came down from the road in close columns,
> with motorized Bersaglieri machine gunners, to block the enemy's

path north of Himara. . . . . The machine gunners had orders to fire on anyone who withdrew. . . . . Threats of court-martial and the firing squad were made. It was desired to put the blame on heroic, exhausted and sick fighting men. . . .

The unfortunate Siena Division, which had advanced towards the Kalamas with so many illusions, had been practically wiped out after two months' fighting, and with it the grenadiers. One of the latter, Lieutenant Giulio Venini, the son of Captain Corrado Venini, Gold Medal, killed in the First World War, wrote to his mother: "If my country requires of me the ultimate sacrifice, that of my life, believe me, I completely accept it, feeling as father did; and I am convinced that in this end of ours you will find a source of pride and strength to support the far greater sacrifice that our country will have required of you." Giulio Venini was killed during the struggle to fill the gaps opened on the extreme right of the line towards the coast.

While the divisions used in the first advance were being ground to pieces, reinforcements were being hastily thrown in. Having learnt that things in Albania were going badly, that Badoglio was in disgrace, and that they had been called on to carry out a difficult and ungrateful task, the morale of these reinforcements was often very low. After the first setbacks, men in the alpine valleys were recalled to the colors a few days after being discharged in accordance with the so-called "adjustment." The 1st and 2nd Alpini regiments of the Cuneense Division landed in Albania after an exhausting journey by troop train from Piedmont to Bari, without hot food, and crossing the Ionian Sea on the deck of a ship with the icy wind cutting their ears. The Albanian harbors were a chaotic inferno, with men working feverishly in the blackout; one officer noticed while he was supervising the landing of his platoon's equipment that a man in uniform who was helping and encouraging him was a general (actually he thought he was a marshal). If the enemy had had an effective air force, the result would have been disastrous.

The 1st and 2nd Alpini landed, then, and the journalist Italo

Pietra, a lieutenant in the Mondovì Battalion of the 1st Alpini, described the experience in an article in the *Illustrazione Italiana* in September 1955:

It was December 1940. In the evening a cold wind swept the mole at Durazzo, raising clouds of white dust; stores, offices, and quays were full of ugly rumors about the front; the Alpini of the Mondovì Battalion, who had only just landed, were drawn up in ranks in front of their haversacks in the small square between the sea and the Doges' Hotel, waiting for orders to proceed to their quarters for the night. . . . A captain came hurrying from the town to announce that the chief of the General Staff was coming. "He'll be here in a few moments, and he wants to talk to the officers for a few minutes," he said, and, sure enough, soon afterwards Cavallero, accompanied by a small entourage, appeared from a corner of the square and marched smartly towards us. He embraced the battalion commander, Major Annoni, an old acquaintance from Abyssinia, shook hands with all the officers, finding a question and a smile for each, and said he wanted to have a look at No. 9 Company, which he had commanded before the First World War; and he concluded by announcing that the battalion was needed immediately to stop a small torrent of Greeks up there in the mountains. . . . His tone was right, and his serenity in that black hour was notable, but the impression he left behind was modest; short in stature, stout, and with short legs, his voice, his pince-nez, and green sash did not help him much to appear what he was. . . . Half an hour later a long line of lorries began carrying the battalion away through the long, snowy night to the other side of Gramshi; at dawn, after crossing the Devoli on a footbridge, we started climbing the paths of the Tomorritsa Valley under falling snow, sinking in the mud almost up to our knees at every step. Then, after going on like this for many hours, a brisk wind blew away the clouds and froze the earth; a great silence hung over the valley between the sublime white peaks of the Tomorrit and Mount Korbiet. The line at that time was neither continuous nor very well known, but by now the rearguards of the 5th Alpini, and the Greeks, must have been pretty near. From the top of a path that looked like a frozen mountain stream we saw coming down towards us an Alpino with his arm covered in blood and his feet wrapped in blankets; he looked very lonely in the snowy desolation, he must have been very young, his wound was bleeding, and his frostbitten feet looked like potatoes. When I saw his red tassel I said to him: "Courage, the Tirano Regiment." He answered: "The Tirano Regiment doesn't need anyone's courage," and off he went, swaying and struggling at every step.

It was touch and go for the 5th Alpini, but the mountaineers from Lombardy held firm. They had discovered ways of surviving in conditions more severe than those that the Americans now impose in their survival courses. One man going up to the line with reinforcements noticed one of them with his helmet stuffed with still steaming animal brains. They used hatchets to smash in the heads of mules dying of exhaustion and withdrew the soft, warm brains. They also used to urinate on their helmets, which were excellent targets when shiny, and then smear them with earth, thus producing a primitive but effective camouflage effect. These men, in torn uniforms, with heavy beards swarming with lice, went on fighting because they knew that in war fighting is often the best way of remaining alive. A medical officer with the Julia Division, Second Lieutenant Antonio Cantore, wrote:

At school they had heard that it was a fine thing to die with a bullet in one's heart kissed by the rays of the sun. No one had thought that one might fall the other way up with one's face in the mud. Also there is the dirt; there is no hope of washing; beards are long and thick with mud, and uniforms are torn to shreds.[3]

The Cuneense Division was split up immediately on landing, as was the rule at the time. The 1st Regiment was sent towards the Tomorrit, and the 2nd in the direction of Valona. At the Tomorrit the 5th Alpini, as we have mentioned, were retreating. It was the last line of resistance in this sector; if the positions on the Tomorrit, the Bregu i Math, and the Guri i Topit gave way, the Greeks would pour down into the plain. "I met Lieutenant Pasini of the 5th with about forty Alpini," an officer of the Cuneense wrote home. " 'Is this your company?' I asked

him. 'No,' he replied, 'it's the Edolo Battalion.' The battalion commander, Lieutenant Colonel Adolfo Rivoir was lying not far away,
having been hit by two machine-gun rounds. Red bubbles were
forming at the corner of his mouth."

And so the Cuneense was in the line, entrenched in the snow—
though, because of the mud, things were not much better at lower
levels—and at night the cold was fierce. A survivor relates that in
mountain positions a bit of wire was attached to outlying sentries
which was pulled at intervals from inside the main position, and
the sentry was expected to pull the wire in reply. Sometimes,
when there was no reply and a man was sent out to see what had
happened, he would find that the sentry was a block of ice, frozen
to death. Everywhere it was the same story: the cold, uniforms
that fell to pieces, rations that did not arrive, and continual Greek
pressure on a thin and unsubstantial front line. Those who went
out on patrol risked death or capture, but at least they had a sense
of freedom and adventure that was rare in a war that turned into a
war of position.

Second Lieutenant Silvano Buffa, of Trieste, who was to be
killed in March on the Spadarit, got lost behind the Greek lines
on the night after Christmas, was captured, but managed to escape
from the enemy soldiers who were taking him towards a house.

> They chased me, but I found a torrent down which I rolled and tum-
> bled headlong so that they should lose my footprints. Then I stopped
> in a thicket and waited motionless for two hours. For a time I heard
> the voices of the Greeks looking for me, then silence. I emerged
> from my hiding place and cautiously moved away in a wide circle.
> Then I started climbing the snow-covered mountain; I did not know
> where I was going, but on the mountain I could hope for safety. I
> walked for a good part of the night, sinking in the snow up to my
> knees until, exhausted by hunger and weariness, I flung myself down
> in a mountain hut half covered with snow. After resting for a while
> I noticed that one of my feet was beginning to freeze. I took off my
> boots and drenched socks, and for an hour I rubbed my feet with
> snow before they began to come back. . . . I spent the rest of the
> night shivering with cold and with my teeth chattering.[4]

That time death spared Silvano Buffa; it was waiting for him at Mali Spadarit.

Gradually the front was consolidated and the "wall" was built. The deficiencies of the Italian military organization were always appalling—no lessons for Albania were learnt from the western front, no lesson for Russia was learnt from Albania. The puttees that slowed down the circulation might have been specially devised to encourage frostbite, the model 91 rifle would not fire at twenty degrees below zero because the bolt jammed—but at any rate the period in which it seemed that nothing could be saved at last came to an end. Second Lieutenant Peppino Antolini, of Rimini, class 1914, of the Morbegno Battalion of the 5th Alpini, Tridentina Division, was sent into the line after his regiment had been somewhat consolidated again, and he kept a laconic diary.

January 1, 1941. At Sqimari. I have now been at the front for a week. Sqimari is a group of five or six houses, a tiny Albanian village that is now in the front line. There are no Albanians there. Half a mile away, beyond some small valleys that are peaceful in the daytime but highly treacherous at night, there is a small red house. In it there is a Greek advanced post. On our right the Tomorrit is covered with snow. We are rather low down, there is frost here, but so far no snow has fallen. January 4. Last night I was out on patrol with eight Alpini, all from the Lecco district. We are all from No. 45 Company, commanded by Captain Bellotti. Being on patrol is exhausting, particularly to the spirit. The total darkness is oppressive, and so is the thought that one might run into the Greeks at any moment. We are all rather weak, because we have little to eat. Galbussera and Vassena have told me of the terrible things that happened before I was sent up into the line.

January 25. For some days I have been the commander of the commando platoon. The captain said to me: "Do you want to join the Commando? But don't you think about your fiancée?" I have a fiancée and I think about her, but I am happier with these men. I think I can be more useful, do things a little more my way. January 27. I have been on patrol for the second night running. The cold goes down to twenty degrees below zero. We have been given white

jackets for operations in the snow. Last night we actually fired, but
without any results; we did not catch the Greek patrol. I managed
to sleep pretty well in my hole. We are not in trenches, but have dug
foxholes on the slope of Sqimari hill, and with a bit of straw on the
ground we are quite comfortable. But we look like beggars, the Alpini's boots are in a pitiful state.

From Sqimari Antolini and his unit were moved to Guri i Topit,
which was to be the center of their lives until the day of the
armistice.

February 10. The transfer from Sqimari to Guri i Topit was murderous. From Sqimari to the Devoli the mud was almost up to our
waists. Fortunately we were able to sleep more or less in the dry, on
the stones of a cemetery infested with enormous rats. At Guri i
Topit, where we are now, there is at least half a yard of snow. The
Greeks are on Guri i Topit and we are below them. It is not a good
place to be in. I think that the Greeks cannot have many weapons at
their disposal, otherwise they would have thrown us all out. The
conditions get more and more appalling, the clothing is bad, last
night's gale caused such huge snowdrifts as to prevent supplies from
coming up. We are on reduced rations. March 10. My detachment
is protected by Captain Adriano Auguadri's No. 44 Company;
Auguadri is a librarian at Como whom I should like to talk about
for a long time, because he is the most complete soldier I have ever
met. He attacked Hills 2109 and 2110 on Guri i Topit. The Greeks
were taken by surprise. I was slightly wounded by hand-grenade
fragments, and my sergeant got a bullet on his forehead, fortunately
diverted by his helmet. So he got away with a streak on his hairy
head. A Greek leapt at me with his bayonet, which cut the sleeve of
my white wind-jacket without hurting me. I fired my pistol, and my
wind-jacket was reddened with the poor devil's blood. We also took
about ten prisoners. Incredible but true, we were then ordered to
leave the positions we had gained. So the Greeks reoccupied the
two heights. I am sure we shall pay dearly for that crazy order.

By now it was March, the month of the unsuccessful offensive,
but also of the "wall," which had at last become too solid for the

Greeks to break through. The Italian strength in Albania was much greater now, but the events of the past months had left their mark on the most tried and tested troops, and above all on the Julia Division. Their state of mind has been described by the journalist Egisto Corradi, who was a second lieutenant in that division:

It has been stated many times that the war was not *felt*. In relation to Greece, I agree. The experience of my first night at the front on the Vojussa made me understand this at once. . . . This attitude, one felt distinctly, derived from something totally different from fear. . . . The evidence of this, and I had personal experience of it many times, was the incredible bravery and great effectiveness of the Alpini in defense. . . . I may be mistaken, but I believe that incidents of more or less open resistance to attack, similar to that which I tangibly experienced, took place in large numbers on the Greek front in March and April 1941.[5]

Nevertheless, in the minds of some enthusiasts, confidence in the High Command and in Mussolini persisted. One of these enthusiasts was Vincenzo Ambrosio, an infantry lieutenant and an ardent Fascist and in peacetime a civil servant, who was killed on March 10. He was a young man of unusual courage. The letters he wrote to his father were filled with a propagandist fervor which in retrospect is melancholy to contemplate. He seemed to feel it his duty while in the front line to explain why this war, which the "home front" thought senseless and most of those engaged in it detested, was just and right. On February 28 he wrote:

The war, now that I have had direct experience of it, presents itself to my mind and heart in the same essential terms as those that made me argue about it, often as if I were representing the interests of a minority. It is a war in our own interests if there ever was one, a war in which the real and constructive efforts of the Italian people converge (and with every day that passes the sense of this becomes more widespread among everyone). I am sure you will be pleased to hear that, thanks to good organization, all the troops now get their rations regularly, as well as extras, besides having good clothing and boots, wine, and regular distributions of cigarettes. . . . By that I do not wish to imply that the troops have no discomforts to suffer. . . . But the bad weather will pass, and the courage and spirit of the troops, who have and are still putting up magnificent performances in adverse conditions, will then be quite different; and I refer in particular to those first few months, the thought of which, I do not conceal from you, makes my heart weep.[6]

To the pure everything is pure, and enthusiasts always think everything is for the best, even though they are intelligent enough to have seen that everything had gone wrong, and that it was only after four months of war that the troops in Albania were at last assured of the most elementary comforts. On March 4, in another long letter, Lieutenant Ambrosio wrote:

We have just heard that Mussolini is only a few miles away at the headquarters of . . . Corps, to which we belong, where he is meeting the generals; if this news is true, it might perhaps be a sign of great news, which we should receive with enthusiasm. I have seen the text of our skillful helmsman's last speech; you will have noted in it many of the ideas that used to crop up in our arguments with Uncle Luigi. This is our country's great springtime, dear papa. . . .

Poor Lieutenant Ambrosio, who lost his life in Albania. His letters preserve his illusions. Perhaps in some ways it was for the best that he did not survive to see their collapse.

The bad weather, the mud, the snow recur on every page written about the war. One Riccardo Crespi, who, like Ambrosio, had no doubts, but was cruder and less reflective in his ardor, devotes nearly a whole chapter to the mud in his book of stale propaganda, *Squadristi in Albania*. Everything was fine for his Milanese militiamen, so far as he was concerned. His Excellency Galbiati was splendid, his Excellency Starace was the essence of masculinity, and his Excellency Farinacci was sturdy and bronzed. He actually burst into doggerel:

> *Fra poco tocca a noi*
> *Squadristi di Milano,*
> *E sfonderemo il fronte*
> *Pugnale e bombe a mano.*
> *Il Duce ha garantito*
> *Che adesso viene il bello,*
> *E i greci assaggeranno*
> *Il nostro manganello.**

These militiamen had reached the front very late, when "the Head of the Government was at the front, and his car was going backwards and forwards between army headquarters and the various headquarters in the line." The exultant Riccardo Crespi also wrote:

We sleep in short snatches. Turning over in bed to change position is normally done without waking completely, and in any case does not interrupt one's rest. But turning over in the mud is an entirely different matter. One's body, which in its wet clothes has made a warm hollow for itself, suddenly comes into contact with the rest of one's cold, wet clothing, unless something still worse happens and it comes into contact with the pool of mud which has formed at one's side.

These were slight discomforts compared with those that the "veterans" had suffered. In their animosity Alpini and infantrymen who saw these bold and fearless volunteers in black shirts marching by actually regretted that the season was now too advanced for them to taste the real pleasures of the Duce's winter war.

* "Soon it will be our turn, Fascists of Milan, and we shall break through the front, dagger and grenades in hand. The Duce has guaranteed that a good time is coming, and the Greeks will have a taste of our cudgel."

Corporal Peppino Caramuta, of the 139th Regiment, Bari Division, at the outset had complete faith in Mussolini's enterprise, and his first letters home were enthusiastic. But before he was killed in action he wrote these bitter words, dated April 8, to a cousin who had been sent to Albania later than he:

> As you know, I have been here for five months, and so I am more tired than you; the sufferings, hardships, and privations are indescribable, as you are already noticing, to say nothing of the danger that is everywhere, particularly from the famous Greek mortars, which have taken the lives of thousands of young men; the sound of them is continually in my ears. We must resign ourselves, dear Peppino, and put faith in God that we shall return to our homes safe, sound, and victorious.[7]

All this correspondence recalling the bloodshed, the snow, the mud, the heroism, the lice, and the hunger in Albania fails to answer one burning question—the question why. The letters of Lieutenant Ambrosio, who tried to give the answer in his letters to his father by echoing Fascist propaganda and the arguments of Fascist "political philosophy," fail to give it. Rapid victory after the October attack would have provided an answer, however questionable. When the prospects of victory faded, the retreats, the casualties, the ordeals, the humiliations, and the frostbite left nothing in the minds of the best of the survivors, except a sense of having done their duty. Major Sandro Annoni, the commander of the Mondovì Battalion, Cuneense Division, who had never been promoted to colonel because he was a bachelor and did not possess a party card, before leaving for Albania spoke gravely to his men and their families. "I do not promise you victory," he said, "but I promise that we shall conduct ourselves honorably. I am taking your sons to war, and I assure you that I shall expend their lives like a good father of a family." More than that could not be said to the humble soldiers to explain the necessity that took them to that war. They conducted themselves honorably. The men on the other side of the lines, however, had a powerful and splendid reason for fighting: the defense of their country—and that explains a great deal.

13. The Wall Moves

It had been clear both to the Greeks and to the British in February that only minor movements were going to take place on the Albanian front, though Mussolini, encouraged by Cavallero, went on nursing the illusion that an Italian breakthrough might yet be possible. In practice Papagos managed to cope with the increase in Italian strength by further mobilization and transferring troops from the now almost defenseless Bulgarian frontier; he thus maintained an equilibrium sufficient for his purposes without, as we have seen, sacrificing all offensive aspirations. To the Greeks it was a matter of understandable pride to have fought unaided in Albania, but they had denuded their other frontiers. The German threat was faced with a void. There was nothing to stop Hitler's formidable divisions.

The Greek attitude was simple. We have kept Italy at bay, they said in effect to the British: now it is up to you to put us in a position to face Germany. Thus a heavy responsibility was placed on the shoulders of the British, who were faced with a grave dilemma. Were they to leave Greece to its fate and concentrate all their efforts on the prosecution of the offensive in North Africa (where Rommel's Africa Corps was now landing) from Benghazi towards Tripoli, or were they to try to parry the German threat to the Balkans? Which was the more important, Athens or Tripoli?

Churchill, making one of his characteristic decisions that cut through the usual red tape, sent Anthony Eden, the Foreign Secretary, to the Middle East in the second half of February, with the widest freedom to evaluate and make decisions. His task was to listen and to look, but the War Cabinet would obviously be decisively influenced by what he reported. Churchill's instructions to him were: "Do not consider yourselves obligated to a Greek enterprise if in your hearts you feel it will only be another Norwegian fiasco. If no good plan can be made please say so."[1] Among other things, Churchill wanted to send the British 6th Division to seize Rhodes, but Admiral Cunningham pointed out that the protection of convoys put such a heavy burden on the British Fleet that it would be very difficult indeed for it to protect and supply such an operation.

On February 22 Eden was in Athens with Sir John Dill, the chief of the Imperial General Staff, Wavell, and Longmore. Every hour was precious to him, and he wanted an immediate discussion with the Greek and British military experts. Instead, the Greeks insisted on taking him immediately to the royal palace at Tatoi,[2] which was more like a big country house than a palace and was surrounded by a magnificent wood of a kind extremely rare in the neighborhood of Athens. The King asked Eden to agree to a private meeting with Koryzis, the Prime Minister. He wanted to discuss military rather than political matters, but in view of the royal insistence he had to give in.

The Greek motives were anything but obscure. Koryzis wanted to read to Eden a solemn statement that Greece would fight the Germans as resolutely as she had fought the Italians. He also pointed out the uncertainty that prevailed, for the British and the Germans alike, about the ultimate intentions of Yugoslavia and Turkey, and he hoped that Eden might be able to clear up this vital question. This political prologue was intended to pave the way to a military agreement. Greece needed British aid, but it had to be powerful aid, making it possible to put up solid resistance to the Germans.

For all its frankness, however, this prelude was to lead to misunderstandings that left bitterness in the minds of the Greeks and the British, traces of which remain in the accounts written by representatives of both sides. The Anglo-Greek conversations lasted for forty-eight hours, and each party interpreted the out-

come in its own way. Eden said that in his opinion, in the
event of German aggression against Greece, Yugoslavia and
Turkey in all probability would not intervene on the Greek and
British side. Turkey would defend her own territory, but that
was all, and Yugoslavia, under the weak guidance of the Regent,
Prince Paul, was wavering between pro-British demonstrations
and promises to the Germans, thus causing increasing perplexity
in both camps. This was the external reflection of a highly confused domestic situation, which—as Eden might have hoped, but
could not know—was soon to end in a resounding upheaval.

Eden and Papagos agreed that, failing a Yugoslav intervention
on the Greek side, the only defensible line was that running along
three mountain massifs, Kaimaktsalan–Vermion–Olympus. This
would involve the abandonment to the enemy of Salonika and
all Greek territory to the east of that city and would mean stopping
the enemy on the river Aliakhmon and the natural bastions of
central Greece.

Consolidation on this line would involve immediate withdrawal
of the Greek right wing in Albania. It was also agreed at these
meetings on February 22 and 23 that a telegram should be sent
to Sir Ronald Campbell, the British ambassador in Belgrade, asking him for clarification of the Yugoslav attitude.[3] In the event
of Yugoslav intervention on the lines that Eden and the Greeks
desired, the Greeks and the Yugoslavs would be able to link up
and establish a line passing to the east of Salonika, thus retaining
possession of that city and port, which would be invaluable for
the landing of reinforcements.

It should be noted that at that time the three weak and incom-
plete Greek divisions on the Bulgarian border were deployed in
the pillboxes and defense works of the long "Metaxas Line," i.e.,
in positions close to the frontier line. These field defenses, which
might have been effective against an enemy of the caliber of the
Bulgarians, would be negligible obstacles, or at any rate would be
swiftly obliterated, in the event of attack by troops having the
tremendous striking and penetrative power of the Germans.

So far both the Greek and the British versions of the conference decisions agree; that is, that there should be a retreat to the Aliakhmon Line, on which the British expeditionary force was to be deployed, though another defense line farther to the north was to be adopted in the event of a Yugoslav intervention. The controversial point lies elsewhere. Was the movement of Greek troops from Albania to begin immediately, so that it could be completed within about twenty days, or was the question to remain undecided until the British ambassador in Belgrade had replied to the telegram? The British maintain the former and the Greeks the latter. According to the Tatoi agreement, Wavell was to send to Greece as early as possible 100,000 men with 240 field guns, 202 antiaircraft guns, 32 medium-caliber guns, and 142 tanks, in other words, the Australian I Army Corps, the British 1st Armoured Brigade, and a brigade of Polish infantry.

Papagos relates that in the days that followed he daily asked the British liaison officer attached to the Greek headquarters whether a reply had been received from Belgrade, but none came. There was a very good reason for this, namely that neither Campbell nor anyone else could clarify the Yugoslav situation. The Regent Paul was pro-German, the young King Peter was pro-British, everyone was terrified of the Germans, and in the general confusion no such thing as a Yugoslav policy could be said to exist. Eden and Sir John Dill returned to Athens on March 2. Meanwhile the crisis was coming to a head. On March 1 the German divisions crossed the Danube and entered Bulgaria, with the consent of the Bulgarian government, which had mobilized its army.

The British Foreign Secretary and General Dill were alarmed to discover that the Greek withdrawal from the Metaxas line and the positions in Albania had not even begun. Papagos said that this was because no reply had been received from Campbell in Belgrade.[4] The only rational and possible step now, he said, would be to send British units to the Metaxas Line, i.e., to a long front behind which there would be nothing to stop the Germans if they once broke through. Eden and Dill would not even consider this project, which was in flagrant disagreement with the February decisions, and they sent a telegram to Wavell, who hastened to Athens from his headquarters in Cairo on March 3. The argument with Papagos was resumed; the Greek commander-in-chief actually appealed to the Greek King to induce the British to accept his proposal.

As often happens on these occasions, the disagreement was patched up by a compromise that proved disastrous. There were three possible alternatives: British divisions could be sent to the Metaxas Line (it is very doubtful whether in practice they would have reached it in time to take up their positions); the British could organize a defense line on the Aliakhmon, supported by three Greek divisions made up from units in Thrace and the interior of the country (in other words, twenty-three weak battalions instead of the thirty-five agreed on on February 22); or aid to Greece could be renounced altogether. The first of these would have been military folly, for the forces strung out along a long thin line would have been able to offer only limited resistance to Field Marshal List's army. From the military point of view (particularly in view of the fact that the fortunes of war in North Africa were about to be radically changed by the intervention of Rommel), the third alternative would probably have been the most sensible. But Churchill and Eden were reluctant to acquiesce in the serious political repercussions that would have ensued from leaving the Greeks to their fate. That left open only the second of the three alternatives. An additional reason for settling on this one was that Wavell took the mistaken view that there would not be a German-Italian counterattack in North Africa until the end of the summer. The three efficient Greek divisions deployed in the fortifications of the Metaxas Line or other defensive positions were to remain where they were, the Albanian front was to be moved, and three scratch Greek divisions were to join the British in facing the Germans in the decisive battle. It immediately became clear that this compromise, the only one possible in view of Papagos' obstinacy, was an unhappy one.

Eden sent Churchill the text of the Athens agreement, and he replied, after consulting his military advisers, with a message that was full of doubts and reservations and seemed to prelude a disavowal of the agreement, a refusal to send aid, at any rate on the scale promised.[5] When Sir Michael Palairet, the British ambassador in Athens, a man with the courage of his convictions, was informed of Churchill's message, he sent a telegram to Eden, who had returned to Cairo, saying: ". . . How can we possibly abandon the King of Greece after the assurances given him by the Commander-in-Chief and Chief of the Imperial General Staff . . . ?"

Meanwhile Operation Lustre (which was the code name for the sending of the British forces to Greece) had begun, and the first convoy sailed from Egypt to the Piraeus. There was also in Greece a Mr. Watt, to be seen in ordinary civilian clothes. He was none other than Major General Sir Henry Maitland Wilson, more familiarly known as "Jumbo" Wilson. He had been one of the chief figures in the war in North Africa, where he was commander of the forces in the Western Desert, but had now been removed from that vital theater of operations (where his place was taken by General Neame) to take charge of an enterprise that began in the most inauspicious circumstances. There was also a Mr. Wilson, who worked in close co-operation with Mr. Watt; he was none other than Patrick Wilson, the general's son— keeping jobs in the family was not confined to Italian senior officers.

British diplomacy made one last bid to bring Yugoslavia and the Cvetkovic government over to the Allied camp. On March 5 Campbell, after conferring with Eden, returned to Belgrade, bearing a letter from the British Foreign Secretary to the Regent Paul. He, however, was not there, having gone secretly to Berchtesgaden to confer with Hitler in his "eagle's nest." This did not prevent the Yugoslav Colonel Perescitch from flying to Athens three days later on a very obscure mission, disguising himself as a Mr. Hope.[6] He discussed the possibility of British aid to Yugoslavia, but in extremely vague fashion. These complicated events had a confused and dramatic sequel on the political plane, and by repercussion on the military plane. On March 25 Yugoslavia joined the Tripartite Pact between Italy, Germany, and Japan (Bulgaria had signed it on March 1). Two days later, on March 27, the Regent Paul was deposed by a coup d'état; Peter II, who was a minor, was put on the throne, and power was put in the hands of General Dušan Simović. It was an obviously anti-German putsch, and that was what it was taken to be by the crowds that demonstrated in the streets of Belgrade and other towns, cheering Peter and the British. Simović hesitated to put himself resolutely on the British side, but the Balkan knot was about to be cut in the most brutal manner. It was done by a lightning flash of the German sword. After so much bloodshed, agony, and humiliation, Italy was about to be relegated to a secondary role.

At this point in the story it is worth noting that the Greek hesitations about giving General Wilson a free hand went *pari passu* with desperate Greek approaches to the Germans. Evidently the pro-German party was pressing its case. Erbach stated in a dispatch dated March 9 that the general view was that, if the Germans attacked, resistance would be "hopeless but necessary for reasons of national honor."[7] In Athens the view was that "the war conducted successfully for so long against the hated Italians was now lost." A way towards an accommodation with the Germans was sought by devious means. The German consul at Salonika reported on March 12 that a Colonel Petinis had called to see him, and on behalf of a senior military commander in the north had suggested "a cessation of hostilities on the Albanian front if the place of Italian troops were taken by German troops . . . and if the Italians were excluded from negotiations between Greece and Germany on Albanian territorial questions."

This local initiative was evidently a prelude to the April surrender. Other contacts were attempted on March 16; and on March 21 some unknown personality in the government (which subsequently denied having taken any steps of this kind) sent to Admiral Canaris, the German secret service chief, a highly confidential document to be submitted to Hitler. Evidently it contained proposals for an accommodation. An official in the Wilhelmstrasse named Ritter, in whose hands the document ended up, tried to submit it to Ribbentrop, who refused to receive it, and then to Keitel, who did the same.[8] No one in Germany at an official level was willing to agree, even if only formally, to the principle of negotiations with the Greeks. The war machine had been set in motion and it had its own momentum. The document was finally returned to Canaris.

The failure of the March offensive was yet another blow to Mussolini's illusions. Normally he recovered quickly on these occasions, but this time the blow rankled. He returned to the Palazzo Venezia in a grim mood and insisted at all costs on "finding those responsible for the loss of face" that had been imposed on him. Badoglio, who had his feelers out for all the news that was going, even the most trivial, tried to return to the footlights, but too soon; his time was not to come again until two and a half years later. He asked Acquarone to inform the King that he was ready to resume office.[9] He also had in his pocket an operational plan that, in his view, would restore the situation in Albania; this was to attack in the North, in the Ninth Army sector (this was the plan advocated by Guzzoni, which Cavallero had opposed).

The Duce submitted an account of his Albanian trip to the King. According to Puntoni, who mentions it in his diary, he did not seek to minimize the difficulties in Albania or conceal the failure of the offensive. On the contrary, he claimed to have foreseen it, without, however, explaining why, in that case, he had launched it. He stated that "the morale of the troops is very high from divisional headquarters down, and this I personally confirmed in spite of stage management which could well have been omitted." The first of these statements was incorrect. The troops fought, but their morale was not high. Finally the Duce promised another attempt to break through "with a single division supported by tremendous artillery fire towards the end of the month. It is hoped to force a breach and drive a wedge through it capable of throwing the enemy line into confusion." This was a fantasy on Mussolini's part, totally detached from the realities of the situation. In any case, because of the Yugoslav coup, nothing came of it.

When Hitler was informed of the Belgrade *volte-face* on the morning of March 27, he at first believed it to be a joke. Then, in one of his attacks of hysterical rage, he summoned his closest collaborators, Göring, Keitel, Jodl, and Ribbentrop, announced that preparations must be made for the obliteration of Yugoslavia as a military and national entity, and gave orders for the plans for his Greek campaign to be revised in light of the new situation. He immediately wrote to Mussolini in friendly terms, which, however, revealed the mistrust roused in him by the Greek adventure.[10] He warmly appealed to the Duce "not to begin further operations in Albania in the next few days" in order to permit the Yugoslav-Albanian frontier to be reinforced, and he asked that the most complete secrecy be maintained and that only those whom it was absolutely essential to inform should be informed of the imminent German offensive. Mussolini replied next day, informing the Führer that his pending offensive had been called off and that another seven divisions were being sent to join the seven already in position together with 15,000 frontier guards on the eastern Alpine frontier, and assuring him of absolute secrecy.[11]

Meanwhile Hitler's plans were being revised by that highly efficient instrument, the German General Staff, which in 1941 was as close to technical perfection as is humanly attainable. Between March 27 and the dawn of April 6 the German generals organized the operation against Yugoslavia, co-ordinated it with Operation Marita against Greece, and issued directives to their Italian and Hungarian allies. It was inconceivable that in that same brief period a country torn by internal dissensions as Yugoslavia was could make preparations to face the menace it had somewhat recklessly provoked by its change of partners.

Cavallero, who resembled his master in possessing remarkable powers of recuperation, flung himself into studying the complications created by Yugoslav hostility and the situation of open war with Yugoslavia which would result from the German onslaught. Units preparing to resume the assault on the Greek positions in the martyred Desnizza Valley sector were transferred to the Yugoslav border; on the eve of making an attack, the Mondovì Battalion of the Cuneense Division learnt with immense relief that it was being sent elsewhere. On March 27 Guzzoni had sent Cavallero a telegram directing him to suspend all offensive operations and to "provide adequately for the protection of the border with Yugoslavia by appropriate movements of troops, particularly those not forming an organic part of infantry divisions"; and on March 29 Mussolini sent him his personal directives:

It is clear that Yugoslavia, on entering the war against the Axis and hence uniting its military forces with those of Greece, will try to attack our rear and flanks. It is therefore urgently necessary to prepare our defense and to hold out for the time necessary for Germany to attack from the east and join up with us. This is expected to take from ten to fifteen days. While sending you the Messina Division as a matter of urgency, I suggest that you remove two divisions from the southern front so as to bring up to six those deployed on the northern front in addition to the formations not organized in divisions, which you will increase if possible. It is a delicate step, but a necessary one. The stronger front must help the front which is weaker and most threatened in the actual situation. Above all it is necessary that everyone from the highest to the lowest ranks should be determined to hold out to the limit, i.e., until the arrival of German co-operation resolves the situation.

Once more the Italians were called on to hold out. Guzzoni had suggested that the Italian troops in northern Albania should temporarily withdraw in order to have a better defense line behind the Drin, thus abandoning Scutari to the Yugoslavs. Mussolini actually agreed and signed an order to that effect, and at first Cavallero agreed too. "Renunciation of Scutari simplifies defensive task," he telegraphed. "Am adjusting my actions in accordance your directives." But then Cavallero decided that it was impossible for the Italian army to make yet another withdrawal, and resolved to hold on to all his positions, including Scutari. "Reconnaissances undertaken by me reinforce my firm intention to hold Scutari," he announced. "I have given this order: Scutari must be defended at all costs, even if surrounded and besieged." "I believe I am right in wanting to hold Scutari. A commander, besides acting on the basis of facts, is also guided by his subconscious"; "we are taking various steps with a view to not letting Scutari go. This because I think it necessary for the honor of the army that while the Germans are on the point of entering Uskub [i.e., Skoplje] we cannot concede the Serbs a name like Scutari."[12]

Cavallero's decision was justified by events. According to General Cesare Amé, the head of the intelligence services, a stratagem used by the Italian espionage service on the outbreak of hostilities made a decisive contribution to preventing a Yugoslav offensive against Scutari. The intelligence service, with its knowledge of the Yugoslav codes, broadcast to the enemy divisions in that sector an order to withdraw into the interior; this worked, and when the deception was discovered the movement had already been begun. Before countermeasures could be taken the Yugoslav army was crushed by the Germans and by General Ambrosio's Italian Second Army advancing from the north. I believe it can be truthfully claimed that this intervention by General Amé's men had an effect on the fighting spirit and co-ordination of Yugoslav units that were already demoralized, were not very efficient, and had little desire to fight. The decisiveness with which Cavallero countered the Yugoslav aims, or alleged aims, at last gave him the feeling of having devised and carried out a brilliant and successful maneuver.

While Cavallero was kept in a state of anxiety by the prospect of an attack by superior Yugoslav forces, Papagos, possessed by a now futile will to win, persisted in giving his troops orders for bloody and useless assaults. The Greeks were still aggressive in the Tepeleni salient, and two days before the German invasion there was a fierce battle with the 5th Alpini for the possession of Guri i Topit in the Ninth Army sector.

On the eve of his Balkan operation Hitler sent Mussolini a message—which the Duce hastened to send on to Cavallero—declaring that "the first condition of success" was that the Italians should hold out in Albania.[13] Mussolini was treated like the faithful servant of his lord and master, who had to intervene to clear up an awkward situation after the former had mishandled it, but did not wish to disavow his unskillful subordinate in the face of the world, and to comfort him, Hitler sent him an expression of his esteem. The Fascist newspapers—whose polemical level was not very high, their insistence on Eden's "Jonah-like" misfortunes being one of the most piquant and persistent ingredients of the propaganda sauce—noted in all solemnity that the snow was melting on the heights round Tirana, and that the disappearance of the white blanket had revealed the word *Dux* in huge letters on a mountainside. This was a sure omen of victory.

Three large formations of the "imperial" expeditionary force in due course landed in Greece: the British 1st Armoured Brigade, commanded by Brigadier H. V. S. Charrington, the New Zealand 2nd Division, commanded by General B. C. Freyberg, and the Australian 6th Division, commanded by General Sir Iven Mackay.

Lieutenant-General Sir Thomas Blamey was to take command of
the Australians and New Zealanders—the 1st Australian Corps—
which was to be named the Anzac Corps by Wavell in April in
commemoration of their famous predecessors. Between March 21
and April 2 the armored brigade and the New Zealanders took
up their positions on the Aliakhmon in good time for the battle.
The other formations—delayed by bad weather and also by the
outcome of the naval battle of Cape Matapan—were still moving up
or were at sea when the German attack was launched. Until the
last moment General Wilson, the commander-in-chief of the
strongest section of the Greco-British army, had to remain in
civilian clothes because, in spite of the now obvious imminence
of the German attack, the Greeks somewhat naïvely wished to
foster even the slenderest hope of escaping Hitler's fury by avoiding anything that might provoke him. The Yugoslavs were affected by the same anxiety. Sir John Dill, who visited Belgrade
in the brief interval between the overthrow of the Regent and
the German invasion, found a distinctly pro-British state of mind,
but enormous confusion and indecision.

In the war memoirs written by the British there are slightly
derogatory descriptions of the Greek troops put at General Wilson's disposal. They were the last scrapings of the Greek mobilization: from Thrace, where they had been used for guard duties,
and from the interior—distinctly inferior both in spirit and in
training to their comrades fighting in Albania. The British were
dismayed by the 19th Motorized Division, to which Papagos
attributed considerable potentialities against parachutists. This division consisted of a heterogeneous collection of civilian motorcycles, private cars, captured Italian tanks that had been put back
into service, and aged lorries. Wilson decided to put the Greeks
in positions that best corresponded with their potentialities, and
he deployed his infantry and artillery in the gorges and on the
plains; also he deployed his strategic reserve of tanks on the plain.

His directives were technically unexceptionable, but they were
desperate directives in a desperate situation. According to a Greek

General Staff estimate, the opposing forces were as follows: Field Marshal List's Twelfth Army consisted of five panzer divisions, two motorized divisions, three light and mountain divisions, and three SS Regiments of the Adolf Hitler Division; the British and the Greeks had seven tank battalions against eighteen German tank battalions (or 176 tanks against 1,907), seventy infantry battalions against seventy-two, 427 guns against 1,086, 228 anti-aircraft guns against 1,549, 445 mortars against 1,080, and 45 aircraft against 1,000. These figures may in some respects be doubtful and liable to correction (the Greek and British aircraft, for instance, were at least double the number stated); but the disparity of strength was enormous, in the striking power of the German formations even more than their number. The British medium and light tanks of the A9, A10 and A13 types could not stand up to the German tanks. "They were inadequately armored, poorly armed, and of very limited mobility in the heavy soil conditions which were to be expected at the end of winter."[14] The W Force, as the army under Wilson's command was called (Wilson was at any rate nominally under the command of Papagos), was born of compromise, reticence, and lack of confidence. It is sufficient to say that when Admiral Sir Andrew Cunningham made his plans for sending the British expeditionary force to Greece he simultaneously gave orders that plans should be made for its evacuation.

A great deal depended on the Yugoslavs, whose army consisted on paper of 800,000 men. Papagos—somewhat carried away by his successes in Albania—worked out a grandiose plan for the concentration of the Yugoslav army in southern Serbia, involving the abandonment of a large part of the country to the Germans and the Italians but making possible a better organized defense. In other words, in the name of efficiency and good sense he wanted the Yugoslavs to make a sacrifice of territory such as he had not brought himself to carry out in Greece by abandoning the Metaxas Line and withdrawing troops from Albania. The Yugoslav divisions were strong, in Papagos' view, because they were numerically strong. In reality they were weak, reflecting the situation of a country torn by divergences of view and internecine hatreds.

The effectiveness of the Yugoslav army was shown by the resistance it put up to the Axis armies (the Italians and Germans were joined by the Hungarians), which lasted altogether for twelve days. In drawing attention briefly to the connections between the Italo-Greek campaign and other events, I must linger for a moment over the Anglo-Yugoslav-Greek meeting that took place on the night of April 3–4, forty-eight hours before the German attack, at the railway station of Kenali on the Greek-Yugoslav border. Those present at this dramatic nighttime encounter were Wilson, Papagos, and Janovitz, the deputy chief of the Yugoslav General Staff, accompanied by the Colonel Perescitch who, it will be recalled, undertook the mission to Athens, which had been as unfruitful as it was obscure.

The meeting lasted from 10 P.M. to 2 A.M., and each of the participants was the mouthpiece for his own and his country's preoccupations. Janovitz insisted on the defense, at all costs, of Salonika, the only port that could save Yugoslavia from total isolation; Papagos, still clinging to his dreams, wanted the mass of the Yugoslav army to be concentrated in southern Serbia; and Wilson pointed out that the British expeditionary force was still on the way and that the only formations immediately available were one armored brigade and an infantry division. Janovitz exclaimed in alarm that in Belgrade Sir John Dill had spoken of an armored division, not an armored brigade. No basic understanding was reached on a joint deployment against the German attack and, even if one had been reached, it would have been impossible for the slow-moving Yugoslav divisions to redeploy in the new positions in the few hours that remained before the opening of List's offensive.

Papagos and Janovitz quickly agreed, however, on an all-out offensive against the Italians in Albania.[15] Wilson listened indifferently. He realized that this diversion, psychologically tempting to the Greeks and Yugoslavs though it might be, could not affect the final outcome. Cavallero and Guzzoni erred greatly in over-estimating the Yugoslav threat, but Papagos and Janovitz went just as badly astray in aspiring to "liquidate" the Italians in Albania. Janovitz undertook to commit four divisions against the Italians along three different lines of attack all aiming at Tirana. Papagos stated that his armies in western Macedonia and Epirus would launch two attacks, one along the line Koritsa–Elbasan–Tirana and the other on the line Berati–Tirana. When the Germans were on the point of attacking, he dreamt of driving the Italian divisions into the sea, and it is significant that the Italian High Command believed that to be not impossible. Simoni, a diplomat at the Italian embassy in Berlin, has described the nervousness, bordering on panic, revealed by dispatches from Rome.

Cavallero feverishly reinforced the Albanian-Yugoslav frontier, and noted:

I am proceeding immediately to cover the left flank of the Ninth Army by sending to that sector the Firenze Division as soon as it lands and the Intra Battalion of Alpini. The Cuneense Alpini Division and the Milano and Aosta cavalry regiments are establishing themselves in the Dibrano area. The Puglie Division, reinforced by some battalions of carabinieri and customs guards and the Diamanti group, have been given the task of blocking an advance from the Dhrino direction. I am concentrating the Centauro Division in the Scutari sector.

Only a week after Mussolini's departure Cavallero was again building a "wall," and all offensive intentions seemed remote. As we have seen, the Germans assigned an exclusively defensive role to the Italian forces in Albania, at any rate at the outset. List's army was to advance on Salonika, cutting off the Greek troops in eastern Macedonia with one decisive blow. Then, advancing westwards from Salonika, the German infantry and tanks were to join up with another invading column, which, from its starting point in Sofia, was to cross the river Axios and then turn south;

Greeks and Yugoslavs were to be caught in this pincer movement, and the two armies were to be deprived of any possibility of contact.

General Maximilian von Weichs' German Second Army, consisting of nine divisions, was to be hurled at Yugoslavia from its bases in Austria and Hungary, its principal objective being Belgrade. The assembly of Weichs' army from divisions which, at the end of March, were still stationed in Germany, France, and Czechoslovakia, was a model of organizational efficiency on the German part. They adopted the "flying start" principle, that is, of opening the battle with the units available, on the morning of April 6, subsequently committing others as they arrived. Hitler wanted no further delays.

Only five months had passed since the fateful October 28, 1940, and Mussolini had abandoned all hope of an Italian success before the German intervention, adopting the "static" role that Hitler asked of him. This situation was underlined by the German "inspectors" who called on Cavallero. On March 31 Lieutenant Colonel Speth confined himself to inquiring how long the Italians could "hold," and Cavallero replied: "At least a month." Von Rintelen suggested abandonment of the Tepeleni salient, but Cavallero pointed out that this would cause too much of an international stir. In any case, the German view was that the Italians should remain where they were. The privilege of mobility was reserved for the lords of war. Even in the air the Italian contribution could not be very great, for the air force had been worn down by the struggle. Ranza had informed Cavallero that he had only seventy fighter pilots left out of 130.

To sum up, then, on the eve of Hitler's offensive the situation was as follows. The Greek and British forces were split up into three practically independent sectors. There were three divisions on the Metaxas Line; three more Greek divisions, plus the British contingent, on the Aliakhmon Line; fourteen Greek divisions and one brigade on the Albanian front, opposed to twenty-one Italian divisions (fewer than in the first ten days of March, because some had been moved towards the Yugoslav frontier). The Ninth Army, consisting of the III and XXVI army corps, had the Taro, Forlì, and Venezia divisions in the former and the Tridentina, Piemonte, and Parma in the latter. The Eleventh Army had the Pusteria and the Cacciatori delle Alpi divisions in the IV Army Corps, the Pinerolo, the Cagliari, and the Siena divisions in the VIII Corps, the Brennero, Legnano, Sforzesca, Julia, Lupi di Toscana, and Ferrara divisions in the XXV Army Corps, the Acqui and the Cuneo divisions in the Special Army Corps and the Casale and Bari divisions at the disposal of army headquarters. On April 6, when the German attack began, the Duce expressed his confidence to Cavallero that "the Italian front in Albania will hold firm in any circumstances." Another "wall," in fact.

Hitler's armies moved against Greece and Yugoslavia at 5:30 A.M. on Sunday, April 6. The Führer was superstitious; he had moved against Poland, Norway, and France on Sunday too. The declaration of war that Prince Erbach simultaneously handed to Prime Minister Koryzis was brief. It offered no terms, but merely announced the beginning of operations, accusing Greece of having subjected herself to the British and being incapable of independent decision. The impact of the German armies was shattering. Some forts on the Metaxas Line put up a brave and determined resistance, but the German spearheads infiltrated between them and the armor broke through towards the sea, forming deep pockets crowded with Greek troops, who were left to be mopped up later.

At 8 A.M. on April 9 the Germans entered Salonika, ready to wheel immediately towards Florina, Kastoria, and Kalabaka so as to take the Greek divisions in Albania in the rear. General Bakopoulos, commanding the eastern Macedonia army—he was responsible for the defense of the Metaxas Line—offered his surrender to the Germans. During the preceding days this officer had adopted an attitude of open disagreement with the British, refusing to consider abandoning the Metaxas Line (probably exercising a strong influence on Papagos in this respect). He had also submitted an insolent memorandum to the Greek High Command. What he said in substance was: Have you considered what you are doing in agreeing to the concentration of British and Greek troops on the Aliakhmon Line? And are you really confident of an ultimate British victory? Papagos had replied that the Greek government were firmly convinced of the latter, but he could not have answered in any other way.

In his memoirs the Greek commander-in-chief insists on the extraordinary tenacity with which Greek troops in eastern Macedonia resisted the Germans. The truth of the matter is that three days' fighting was not a great deal. This is said not to disparage the Greek performance, but only to point out that, when faced with an enemy fully equipped with modern weapons, they suffered exactly the same fate as the Poles, the Norwegians, and the French —and the Italians on September 8, 1943. It could be argued that the mass of the Greek army was in Albania. But the divisions that the Germans would have had to meet if they had committed themselves in the Balkans in the previous October and made an unexpected attack simultaneously with Mussolini's would probably have been the same as those which originally faced the Italians —a negligible obstacle to Hitler's armor. The Greek army shone in Albania as a result of Italian weakness. When put to the test of Hitler's Blitzkrieg its limitations, like those of the Yugoslav army, were exposed.

When Papagos claims that the Metaxas Line was considered by the Germans to be superior to the Maginot Line, he does no service to the troops of his who held out on it for only seventy-two hours. There is also the consideration that the Greek formations in eastern Macedonia, ill armed and not up to establishment, were not sustained by the hope that animated their comrades in Epirus and western Macedonia when they discovered the lack of power behind the Italian punch.

While the German tide advanced remorselessly, Papagos, a skillful strategist and tactician in "conventional" warfare against the Italians, was rash and lacking in foresight in the type of operations by which the Balkans had now been set alight, and he increasingly lost contact with reality. On April 8 his troops in Albania, facing the Italian Ninth Army, began some attacks that were supposed to coincide with vigorous Yugoslav pressure from the north and east. The Yugoslavs actually moved halfheartedly in the direction of Scutari, but there was no drive or conviction behind them, and a resolute Italian counterattack gained a substantial number of prisoners.

In his first telephone conversation with Cavallero after the opening of hostilities with Yugoslavia Mussolini showed some strange preoccupations. "I should like to send you those three battalions of young Fascists. They have had a lot of war training. They are tremendous," he said. "Send them," Cavallero replied. "We shall make the best possible use of them. I shall put them in the best possible position to yield advantageous results." The Germans kept the Italians informed about their progress and, as the Yugoslavs were being sliced through like butter, they wanted the Italians in Albania to move too. So did Mussolini, who on April 10 ordered them to operate "in the southern direction by the roads to the east and west of Prespa Lake, making for Bilishti and Zveshoda for the purpose of co-operating in the German operation to envelop the right wing of the Greek line facing us." So the Italians began to move forward, the Arezzo Division towards Lake Ochrida and the Cuneense and Firenze divisions towards the Dibra depression. These operations were against the Yugoslavs. In spite of Mussolini's pressure, on the Greek front the Italians were not yet ready to move; Geloso, goaded by Cavallero, needed three days' "breathing space." While the Germans took Salonika and Maribor, Cavallero stormed and raged, wanting his divisions, which for the most part moved on foot, to engage in an unequal race with the armored and motorized Germans. "I telephoned to Pirzio Biroli. 'Get everything together and move forward,' I said. 'We've got to get to Struga. Your Ferroni [this was General Ernesto Ferroni] has not got the necessary drive. The

Germans will be at Struga this evening, or at latest tomorrow. We have to hurry to prevent them from getting there first.' " In fact the Italians took Struga and Dibra. The link-up with the Germans took place at Lake Ochrida.

Major Annoni, of the Mondovì Battalion of the Cuneense Division, Gold Medal, died leading his men in the attack on Dibra. He had previously occupied the heights dominating the town, which were still covered with snow though it was April, and was killed by a shell while observing the Yugoslav positions. His men carried him with them on a stretcher so that this hero of the last offensive should not be deprived of the gleam of light that was beginning to appear after so much darkness, as were all those killed in the last few days, when pens were already being poised to sign the armistice agreements.

The Cuneense Division took 1,500 prisoners, including three generals and fifty officers; the Yugoslavs fought, but with little conviction. Meanwhile the Greek-Albanian front was still stationary; Papagos was torn with anxiety about whether or not the Yugoslavs were moving their arm of the pincers. On April 9 he sent a trusted officer, Major Theodosios Papathanassiadis, in a British aircraft to get firsthand information from General Simović's headquarters at Sarajevo, but Papathanassiadis was pursued by ill fortune. The aircraft had to make two forced landings because of bad weather, and then another at Bar, in which he was hurt, and, more serious, suffered a shock that deprived him of the power of speech. He did not reach Sarajevo until 10 P.M. on April 11. There he was immobilized during the daytime by German bombings, and not till the morning of April 13 was he taken to Simović's headquarters, which were concealed in a wood about fifteen miles from the city.

Simović told him outright that the Yugoslav army was broken, the Croats were rebelling against the Serbs, and the end was near. The return journey to Athens was at any rate quicker, and on April 14 he reported to Papagos that nothing could be expected of the Yugoslavs. Their country was on the point of collapse—

and it surrendered on April 17. The Italian Second Army on the eastern border was on the march, and General Ambrosio's troops had occupied Ljubljana. (Victor Emmanuel III had hurriedly decided to go to the zone of operations, and a villa belonging to the Pirzio Biroli family at Brazzacco, about nine miles north of Udine, was put at his disposal.)

On the morning of April 12 Papagos ordered the withdrawal of Greek divisions in western Macedonia and Epirus. The order was belated, but necessary; it was a last-minute attempt to avoid German encirclement. To the Greek troops in Albania it was a shattering blow: when it finally reached regimental and battalion level it provoked incredulity, protest, even mutiny; some said it was a trick by the German fifth column in Athens. The troops' refusal to obey was encouraged by the divisional commanders, who, for reasons of prestige and pride, rebelled against abandoning territory won at the cost of so much blood and sacrifice. Papagos was compelled to intervene and give orders personally, which were reluctantly accepted. He wanted the divisions that began evacuating Albanian territory, at first in good order, to establish contact with the W Force, but in the face of the lightning German advances his command structure was now acting in a void. To gain ground more rapidly, German motorcyclists and tanks actually used railway tracks. Papagos was faced with an ever greater reluctance of his subordinates to obey his orders. The armies in Albania did not break, but a spirit of humiliation and impotent rage spread among the troops.

On the day before he ordered the withdrawal from Albania, Papagos met General Wilson at Farsala. Conversation between the thin, olive-complexioned Greek commander-in-chief and the pink-cheeked, moustached Briton was not easy. The British did not tire of reproaching their Greek allies for the stubbornness with which they had insisted on holding indefensible positions at the expense of organizing a strong defense line, and the Greeks suspected—not entirely without foundation—that the British were now thinking more about re-embarkation than about putting up

serious resistance to the Germans. After the war Greeks and British exchanged charges and recriminations about the events that
followed the meeting at Farsala, the rights and wrongs of which
were equally divided. In their withdrawal from Albania the Greeks
failed to provide protection for the left wing of W Force, while
for his part General Wilson set about coolly rectifying his positions, which the Germans were now beginning to reach. After
reaching Florina in their advance west, they wheeled again and
turned south.

On April 12 Wilson ordered the abandonment of the Kleidi
Line. In his memoirs Papagos sharply criticizes this move, which
exposed part of his 20th Infantry Division and the whole of his
12th Division to destruction. As usual in such moments of crisis—
it was a bitter experience shared by the Italians in North Africa—
the army equipped with the better transport looked to its own
safety, leaving unprotected the slow-moving Greek formations
hampered by mule-drawn baggage trains. On April 13 the Italian
front in Albania at last began to move. The harsh truth was that
it did so because the enemy had begun to retreat and could not
do otherwise. The Germans surged forward towards Kleidi, and
at the Klisura Pass (not, of course, the Klisura in Albania), threatened the link between the Greek troops in western Macedonia and
Epirus and W Force. By now Papagos was hardly able to get
his orders to his divisional commanders, and in Athens Wilson
(at last in uniform) remained out of contact for hour after hour
with the British, New Zealand and Australian detachments.

Cavallero sent infantry, Alpini, and Bersaglieri to follow up an
enemy who still resisted stoutly but tended only to allow his rearguard to be engaged. On April 13 Bersaglieri entered the plain of
Koritsa, where minefields and roadblocks forced them to dis-
mount from their lorries and follow on bicycles. On their way they
found traces of what positional warfare had meant on the other
side of no-man's-land, and discovered that the Greeks had suffered
the same hardships and had recourse to the same ingenious and
pathetic expedients to diminish the terrors of the Albanian winter.

The air force had destroyed the Perati bridge. The Pusteria Division advanced on the Eleventh Army front and the Tridentina on the Ninth Army front. When engagements occurred the Greeks still fought vigorously, but these were obviously only delaying actions. The exhilaration of the Italian advance was only superficial; it concealed sadness at this belated success scored over a defeated enemy. Only the generals, beginning with Cavallero, took pride in maneuvers that did not impress the ranks. Even a child could see that they consisted of keeping up with a retreating enemy.

At midday on April 14 infantrymen of the Venezia Division made their way along the avenues of Koritsa, followed by mistrustful Albanian glances. The "wall" went on moving while Cavallero hurried to Scutari to accept the surrender of a Yugoslav general, and Farinacci took to the air with Ranza, the air commander, in order to play his part in the glorious advance. But the aircraft developed a defect, a fire broke out on board, they made a forced landing at Pogradec, and had a narrow escape. Mussolini sent a telegram to Cavallero saying that "Hitler wishes to go on delivering blows to Yugoslavia to the end." (The verb he used, *legnare,* literally, to beat with a piece of wood, was one of his favorites, perhaps because it reminded him of the cudgels swung by the Fascist gangs.) He had, however, been obliged to have the blows delivered by a third party, and this distressed him somewhat.

The VIII Corps was at last able to enter the Desnizza Valley, which had so long and so vainly been struggled for during the March offensive, and it rapidly approached (the Albanian) Klisura. Monastery Hill, 731, was taken. It was still covered with the unburied bodies of infantrymen of the Puglie and Bari divisions. On March 22, after the end of the offensive, the Italians had asked for a six-hour truce to bury the dead. Three chaplains with a white flag had gone to the Greek positions on Hill 731, in front of which the dead were strewn. "Dreadful, dreadful," one of the chaplains exclaimed, burying his face in his hands. Agreement on a truce had not been reached, however. The Italians wanted a local cease-fire, while the Greeks insisted that hostilities should cease all along the line, so the dead remained where they were. On Monastery Hill the Italians discovered that the Greeks had five lines of trenches. When they were attacked they withdrew from the first trench, sprayed the attackers with automatic weapons and then counterattacked to reoccupy the positions evacuated.

On April 18 the Eleventh Army reached Argyrokastron. Meanwhile the Germans were nearing Larissa, one of the Adolf Hitler regiments was approaching Yanina, and the encirclement of the Greek armies that had fought in Albania was nearly complete. Papagos had lost control of the situation. Mussolini seethed with excitement at the prospect of going to Albania to savor his triumph, but then dropped the idea. Meanwhile Cavallero decided on the formation of the regiment which was to have the honor of entering Athens with the Germans. The Italians marched at a prodigious rate; the Venezia Division covered seventy miles in four days, carrying haversacks and machine guns, though they had several times to open fire on the way. The Greek troops were now retreating in increasing disorder; their morale, which had held out for nearly six tremendous months, had suddenly collapsed.

General John Pitsikas, commander of the Epirus Army, wanted an armistice, and wanted it quickly; he had indicated this on April 12, before the retreat began. On April 15 King George in person, and Papagos, had sent him messages stating that it was essential to hold out to the end, on the ground that giving way would have been interpreted as cowardice by their British allies. Pitsikas' object was to cease hostilities while his troops were still on Albanian soil, in order to avoid the bitterness of having to continue fighting until the Italians had recovered all the territory lost in the first few weeks.

On April 16 he sent to Athens a message in catastrophic terms: "In view of the situation that has developed political intervention is absolutely essential. The situation is deteriorating from hour to hour." Not content with that, on the same day he sent his deputy chief of staff to Athens by air to plead that an armistice should be sued for. This officer, Colonel Grigoropoulos, had three agitated conversations with Papagos. The commander-in-chief hesitated between holding out as long as possible and accepting the necessity of an armistice and recommending a rapid British re-embarkation, which would free Greece of obligations to her ally. The message with which Pitsikas' emissary returned to Yanina amounted to asking the Epirus Army to hold out for at least a few more days, pending further developments. Pitsikas sent a message to his subordinate commanders calling on them above all to hold their troops together. Total disintegration threatened.

14. The Long Armistice

General Wilson's W Force withdrew under the German pressure. D'Albiac with his eighty aircraft did what he could, which was not a great deal, particularly after the destruction in a ground attack of sixteen Blenheims and fourteen Hurricanes, which was an irreparable blow. He hastily withdrew the remainder of his force to airfields in the Athens area, where it was more secure but less able to give adequate support to the ground troops. The British, Anzac, and what was left of the Greek detachments forming part of the W Force evacuated one position after another. First they tried to establish themselves on Olympus, but were threatened with encirclement there, and then hastily tried to organize a defensive position in the pass of Thermopylae (southeast of Lamia).

If the German bombers had concentrated on the retreating W Force instead of being dispersed in attacking secondary objectives, the whole British expeditionary force would probably have been stopped before reaching that historic site. The weather was bad: a light but troublesome rain was falling. The unpaved roads all the way from Epirus to Thermopylae were as muddy as they had been at the start of the Italian war in the Balkans. The columns of retreating men and vehicles wound their way along them amid scenes characteristic of every retreat.

Wavell had telegraphed to London that Papagos was suggesting a British evacuation, and Churchill replied, perhaps with relief: ". . . We cannot remain in Greece against wish of Greek Commander-in-Chief, and thus expose country to devastation. Wilson or Palairet should obtain endorsement by Greek government of Papagos' request. . . ."[1] The situation was actually not so clear-cut. Papagos, as we have seen, was wavering, and the government was uncertain, particularly as the Prime Minister, though a man of the greatest probity, lacked the gifts of authority and decision required by a national leader in wartime, and in a desperate situation.

On April 18 a conference took place in the royal palace at Tatoi at which the King, Prime Minister Koryzis, General Wilson, Palairet, Papagos, d'Albiac and Admiral Turle were present. Papagos described the situation in very black terms. He said that the British would not be able to hold out at Thermopylae, and the position of the Epirus army was desperate. The British forces would not be able to re-embark at the Piraeus, which had been devastated by bombing and was still subject to incessant attacks.

No decision was made at that meeting. During the afternoon Koryzis held a cabinet meeting, and Papademas, the deputy war minister, was even more pessimistic than Papagos. Among other things, he read a telegram from the commander of the II Army Corps, George Bakos (a subordinate of Pitsikas), which said:

I have already reported and report again that the situation is rapidly deteriorating. Disorder, disobedience to orders, and the abandoning of posts are spreading in spite of rigorous measures taken, including shootings. I appeal to you in the name of God immediately to make a decision that will avoid our having to weep over ruins with no to-morrow. Let anyone who believes himself able to bear the cross of martyrdom better than I take it over and come and weep at the catastrophe, because our tears have dried.

Papademas had the reputation of being pro-German. This was borne out by a strange decision he took in that turbulent period, when he granted two months' paid leave to soldiers who applied for it. The fact is that after the hour of glory the hour of pettiness had struck; something of the sort happens to all nations in defeat, and the Greeks were no exception. Violent argument took place at that cabinet meeting. Some ministers suggested the abandonment of Athens and the transfer of the government to Crete, giving the generals of the Epirus army authority to act as seemed best to them, which would have meant abandoning the British expeditionary force to its fate. This was the line taken by Papademas, but the opinion that the struggle should be continued prevailed. Koryzis was shattered by events and, torn between the two opposing factions, could not bring himself to support either. This intelligent, courteous, but irresolute man of aristocratic appearance went home and took his life with two pistol shots. He was the second head of a government to commit suicide in that dramatic month. On April 3 Count Teleki, the Hungarian Prime Minister, faced with the necessity of deciding whether or not to line up with the Axis, had chosen the same fate. A few days later Hungary threw in her lot with the Axis and joined in the invasion of Yugoslavia.

Wavell arrived in Athens on April 19. He was a tired man, feeling the strain of having to sustain exhausting battles on distant fronts, and was now faced with Rommel in North Africa. He attended another conference with the King, General Wilson, and Papagos.[2] He put a definite question. Were the Greek forces in a position to protect the left flank of Wilson's divisions on the Thermopylae Line? Neither the King nor Papagos was able to give this assurance. The Germans were approaching the rear of the Metsovon Pass, blocking the Greek way of retreat; and the Greeks were in no position to stop them.

The Epirus army as a fighting force had ceased to exist. The King, with the agreement of General Alexander Mazarakis, the Prime Minister-designate, and Papagos, gave his consent to the evacuation of Greece by the British imperial forces. This was what Wavell wanted. Before the gloomy meeting ended he expressed British admiration of the Greek effort and said that the British had no complaints against their ally. This was a notable example of British fair play. In fact, the Greeks and the British had never reached satisfactory agreement on the organization of a rational defense line with all the forces at their disposal.

Disorder and dismay were now general in the Greek armies of Epirus and western Macedonia, and senior officers were in a state of nervous crisis bordering on hysteria. A strange note crept into messages to the High Command, which began to contain melodramatic appeals rather than concrete information. A message from Pitsikas, dated April 18, ended with the plea: "In the name of God save the army from the Italians." In a telephone conversation to the new Prime Minister he frantically urged the government to make a decision that same day, and the government undertook to do so. Italian troops were on the point of crossing the Greco-Albanian border, and the commanders of the two Greek armies maintained that to reinflate his pride after the humiliations he had suffered, Mussolini would refuse an armistice. This assumption was not very far from the truth. Pitsikas was also under pressure from the Orthodox Metropolitan of Yanina, who feared reprisals and the total destruction of the town.

As Pitsikas, the senior army commander, definitely wanted an armistice but refused to oppose the government and the High Command, the other army commander, Tsolakoglou (who was in command of the western Macedonia sector while Pitsikas was in command of the Epirus sector), and the corps commanders, George Bakos and Panaghiotis Demestikas, decided to go over his head. They met on the evening of April 18 and agreed on a draft of what amounted to an ultimatum to be sent to the government and to Papagos. It said:

The situation of the army does not permit further fighting, even defensive fighting. We have done what was possible to obtain victory and, recently, to reach some sort of solution. We repeat that the situation offers no way out. To avoid the dishonor to our glorious army of a surrender to the Italians, whom it defeated, to avoid anarchy and national disintegration in the event of disintegration of the army, which may take place at any moment, negotiations for an armistice with the Germans must be begun. In full consciousness of the importance and gravity of what we have stated, we appeal to you to prevent the imminent catastrophe. Failing this, the Epirus army will assume historical responsibilities in the face of God and the country.

This certainly amounted to a pronunciamento. There have been plenty of military putsches in Greek history, but if there was ever justification for one it must be admitted that it was here. What it amounted to was that the Greek commanders were willing to surrender to the Germans but not to the Italians, and for this purpose they were willing to set up an independent government at Yanina under the leadership of the Metropolitan. However, because of the objections of the divisional commanders, the telegram was not sent. Instead, a still graver decision was reached. Setting aside Pitsikas, the commander of the Epirus army, the corps commanders declared Tsolakoglou to be the commander of both armies. It was also agreed that the military commanders should set up a provisional government headed by the Metropolitan of Yanina.

On the morning of April 20 a party of officers set out to make contact with the Germans with a view to negotiating a surrender. The conditions that Tsolakoglou and his colleagues proposed were: (1) an immediate armistice; (2) the Germans to retain the territory they had occupied and give authority over the rest of Greece to the provisional government. Failing German acceptance of this, they could occupy Epirus and consider the Greek army their prisoners. But there would be no surrender to the Italians.

When Pitsikas was informed by Tsolakoglou that he must consider himself relieved of his command, he made no protest; basically he was in agreement with the others, but did not dare stick his neck out.

After the party had set out to make contact with the Germans, news arrived from Papagos' headquarters that he was sending some officers to Yanina to investigate the situation. Meanwhile the corps commanders gave orders that "the frontiers should be held against the Italians until a decision had been reached." At

Yanina there was great confusion. Pitsikas, who was preparing to leave for Athens ("washing his hands like Pontius Pilate," so Papagos said), informed Papagos at midday that the armistice mission had left on Tsolakoglou's orders, and cautiously suggested that the government should take the whole thing in hand. When Papagos' emissaries, General Gialistras and Colonel Kanellopoulos, reached Yanina by car at 2 P.M., they found Pitsikas in a state of profound discouragement. "You've come very late," he complained. The troops were throwing away their arms and deserting, officers could no longer secure obedience to orders, and the commander of the Epirus army was a poor old man who had been deprived of his job.

Gialistras telephoned to Tsolakoglou, diplomatically asking him to return to the Yanina headquarters. Tsolakoglou, who was awaiting the return of the armistice mission elsewhere, behaved arrogantly. He could see no reason for meeting Gialistras, he had nothing to say to him, and he was awaiting the German reply. Perhaps he might come to Yanina after receiving it. That same afternoon, at Botonasi, where Tsolakoglou had established himself, he and General Dietrich, the commander of the SS Adolf Hitler armored division, signed a provisional armistice agreement which was quite definitely anti-Italian in effect.

It laid down that hostilities between Germany and Greece would cease at 1800 hours on that same day, April 20, and that, as a result of intervention by the German military commander, hostilities between Greece and Italy would cease a few hours later. German troops would take up a position between the Greeks and the Italians. The German army, through its commander, Field Marshal List, was to give instructions next day for the following: (a) the withdrawal of Greek troops within ten days up to (but not behind) the old Greco-Albanian border; (b) demobilization of the Greek armies of Epirus and western Macedonia, the troops to hand in their arms and then go home; (c) retention of their personal arms by officers, who were not to be considered prisoners.

This document contained more than one humiliating smack in

the face for Italy. It proclaimed that the Greeks were still on Albanian soil; it did not call on them to retreat beyond the frontier, and it permitted the Germans to dictate the terms of their surrender. The offensiveness of this document to the Italians persuaded Field Marshal List, who had arrived at Larissa, which his troops had taken, on the evening of April 20 and set up his headquarters there, not to approve it. He pointed out that the Athens government and the King had reaffirmed the Greek determination to continue the struggle, and therefore all that he could agree to was an unconditional surrender of the armies of Epirus and western Macedonia.

The next document, signed next day, was much sterner. It laid down that the troops of the two Greek armies were to be considered prisoners of war, though with the prospect of speedy release, and officers were permitted to keep their personal weapons. It acknowledged that the Greeks had fought bravely and in accordance with the laws of war, and it postponed delimitation of zones of influence until agreement had been reached with the Italians. There was no mention of withdrawal by the Greeks to the Albanian border, or of the prospect of an early suspension of hostilities by the Italians.

When Papagos was informed of the armistice he promptly disavowed Tsolakoglou, though this had no influence on events. He also issued orders, though these were no longer enforceable, that troops that could be scraped together in the area of the Greek capital should be sent against the Germans to provide as much protection as possible for the British re-embarkation. Tsolakoglou's troubles were by no means over, however. He tried hard to avoid the bitter cup of surrendering to the Italians, but in the end had to drink it.

When Mussolini was informed on April 21 of the armistice signed by List's representative at Yanina he was seized with a paroxysm of rage. He peremptorily ordered Cavallero, who was on a tour of inspection, to return to Tirana, and the Italian commander, to whom List sent a telegram, replied:

"I am willing to accept the request for surrender made by the commander of the Greek army in Epirus provided it is understood that the request is made also to the Italian army. It is a matter of prestige on which the Italian army has the right and duty to insist, seeing that it has been fighting the Greek army for six months." The Greeks yielded, and submitted the request to the Italians also, and at midday on April 21 a Greek officer, with a bugler and a white flag, presented himself to the commander of the Milano Regiment of cavalry, which was riding towards the Perati bridge. The Greek officer stated that an armistice was in existence. But "by order of the army commander he was sent back with the message that no armistice negotiations could take place so long as enemy formations were on Albanian territory." Hostilities were therefore resumed. At 5 P.M. another Greek officer presented himself and asked for armistice negotiations, but he too was sent back. In the evening Cavallero announced that "operations will continue without interruption in order to penetrate as deeply as possible in every direction into Greek territory"; and he added that "should further Greek emissaries present themselves, they should be sent to General Headquarters, but without suspending operations."

The strange situation created by the Greco-German armistice immediately began leading to incidents. At Kakavia, advanced units of the Casale Division ran into a German officer who announced that an armistice was in effect. Argument between German and Italian officers ensued, and the latter, being unaware of any cease-fire, decided to continue their advance. It was at Kakavia that Colonel Scognamiglio was killed leading the 4th Bersaglieri, and Starace had his hand slightly grazed by a shell splinter, whereupon he immediately and without authority began wearing a wound stripe, an action that seems to have led to his final disgrace.

A little farther on, the advanced units of the Casale Division ran into another German roadblock on the night of April 21–22. The Italian troops, who were now nearing the Perati bridge, asked permission to pass, but the German Colonel Diethle declined to grant this. The divisional commander, Enea Navarrini, intervened, and it was decided that both Germans and Italians should remain in their positions. The Milan Lancers were also stopped by a Wehrmacht regiment near the Perati bridge. What with Italians, Germans, and Greeks, chaos prevailed. Meanwhile Mussolini had got on the telephone to his good friend Hitler to ask him that no decision about a cease-fire should be made in the absence of the Italians. Hitler telephoned to General Alfred Jodl, his deputy chief of staff, who was at Salonika, telling him to prevaricate before signing any definite agreement, and then to List to assure him that in his position he would have acted in exactly the same way, but that Italian susceptibilities had to be taken into account. General Halder noted in his diary on April 21:

> The Führer has given orders that the armistice must not be applied without his approval. This to give the Italians a way out. But this solution makes the marshal in command of the Twelfth Army look foolish, besides bolstering a systematic distortion of history, creating the myth that the Italians forced the Greeks to surrender. Actually at the time of the armistice there was no contact between Greeks and Italians.

This last statement is incorrect; Cavallero noted almost triumphantly that on the last night of fighting the Bari Division lost thirty officers and 400 other ranks. He derived a great deal of satisfaction from this. Field Marshal List, however, was indignant at the loss of face he had suffered in Greek eyes.

Let us try to reconstruct the background to all this, and look at events which took place not in Tirana, Larissa, or Yanina, but in Rome, Berlin, and Vienna. At 6 A.M. on April 21 General Guzzoni, the undersecretary for war, awoke von Rintelen and, with an anxious air, informed him that a message from Cavallero had arrived overnight saying that he had received a message from List informing him of the armistice negotiations and asking the Italians to interrupt their advance in order not to hamper them. The Duce had replied that the Greeks must also apply to Italy for an armistice. Two hours later von Rintelen, after a conversation with Jodl, tried to reassure Mussolini; no agreement, he said, would be made without Italian participation. But the Duce was beside himself, and considered that the Greeks had committed an "act of perfidy" in approaching the Germans only, which would enable them in the future to claim that they had never surrendered to the Italians. "Italian troops have fought against the Greeks for six months," the Duce protested. "Five hundred thousand men have been engaged, and 63,000 casualties have been suffered."

That morning Mackensen, the German envoy in Rome, was in Vienna, where Ciano was meeting Ribbentrop, and he was called to the telephone by the Italian Foreign Minister, who was in a state of "considerable agitation."[3] The Duce, Ciano said, was "very disturbed" at armistice negotiations taking place without Italian participation. Mackensen first approached the German Foreign Minister, who replied that these were only "vague rumors"—they were nothing of the sort, as we know—and then consulted Hitler. The Führer did not want to upset his Rome comrade, but he was cautious. The sooner there was an armistice or a capitulation the better, he said, because the lives of German soldiers were at stake. However, he was willing to instruct List not to come to any agreement without Italian participation, but pointed out that it was possible that the instructions might not reach him in time. If an armistice had already been signed, a supplementary clause would be added, satisfying the Italian wishes.

In Rome at 10:30 P.M. on April 21 von Rintelen, caught between Italian protests and German pressure, telephoned Guzzoni and sought a way out. He said—not in accordance with the facts—that it was not so much a question of an armistice as of a Greek unconditional surrender. The Germans had reached Yanina after taking 20,000 prisoners. If the Greeks are throwing their arms away, von Rintelen seemed to say, what can we do about it? Can we go on fighting an enemy who has ceased resistance?

Guzzoni telephoned to Tirana and was informed that the Greeks were still fighting and that no plenipotentiary had presented himself. Guzzoni concluded that there was no alternative but to continue hostilities. At a little after midday on April 22 von Rintelen had another conversation with Jodl, after which he asked Guzzoni to send a plenipotentiary to Larissa to negotiate the Greek surrender. Soon afterwards the German military attaché was with Mussolini, in Guzzoni's presence, and read him the draft of the capitulation (this must have been the first one, signed by Dietrich). Mussolini rolled his eyes and protruded his lips in his characteristic dictatorial grimace, struck the table with his fists, and insisted that the Greeks must surrender to him. He said that he would settle the Greeks by himself. Von Rintelen, without smiling, claimed that the situation had merely been that the surrender offer had been made to troops arriving from Yanina, but Mussolini was not to be taken in by that, and he underlined two clauses in the draft that he considered unacceptable: the concession by which the Greek troops were to be allowed to go home and the permission given to officers to retain their arms.

The Greeks did not deserve this honor, he declared; they had treated Italian prisoners, both officers and men, outrageously, and he, Mussolini, had evidence of it. Von Rintelen patiently explained that it was impossible to guard and feed hundreds of thousands of prisoners, and that the honor of retaining their arms was granted to an enemy who had fought well. If the Greeks had not fought bravely, von Rintelen added, not without malice, the Italians would not have had so much trouble in holding them at bay. Mussolini granted the soundness of von Rintelen's arguments on these points, but would not shift his ground.

At 3 P.M. on the same day, April 22, General Biler, the commander of the German 73rd Division, reached Yanina and informed Tsolakoglou that he must send plenipotentiaries to the Italians, and that the German zone was to be separated from the

Italian by the Igoumenitsa-Metsovon line. Tsolakoglou reacted indignantly. He announced that, as a prisoner of war, he had no power to do anything at all, and protested that for the second time the Germans were not keeping to a pact they had signed. Then he ordered the remnants of the troops under his command to retreat hastily southwards in order to leave the Italian zone and avoid becoming prisoners of Cavallero's troops. The units that still preserved some cohesion dispersed after raiding the military stores, and very soon practically nothing of the armies of Epirus and Macedonia remained.

At 6:20 P.M. on April 22 Tsolakoglou, after consulting Bakos and Demestikas, finally agreed to send plenipotentiaries, a colonel, a major, and a warrant officer, who at 9 P.M. presented themselves in the sector of the Casale Division and said they wished to confer with Geloso. The latter informed them that an Italian-German commission had already been formed to accept the surrender. Next morning the three were back with Tsolakoglou, telling him that the cease-fire had been fixed for 11 P.M. that day, the twenty-third. General Ferrero, appointed by Cavallero to head the Italian delegation, went to Yanina and then to Salonika, where Tsolakoglou was also taken by air. At 2:45 P.M., the wooden and overbearing Jodl, and Ferrero and Tsolakoglou, signed the definitive armistice agreement,[4] which repeated the Yanina agreement except that it mentioned the Italians side by side with the Germans and stipulated the immediate release of Italian prisoners in the hands of the Epirus army. Jodl was the only one who could derive any satisfaction from the ceremony; to Tsolakoglou it was an hour of tragedy, and Ferrero was conscious of the ambiguity of his position. With the signing of this agreement the Italian war on Greece came to an end. Tsolakoglou set up a quisling government, was later displaced and, after being sentenced to death in 1945, he died in prison. In Greece he has not many defenders. But objectively it must be acknowledged that he made decisions and assumed responsibilities which, although shared with others, fell on his shoulders.

Italian war communiqué No. 323, dated April 24, stated: "Up to 1800 hours yesterday, when hostilities ceased on the Ninth and Eleventh army fronts, the advance into Greek territory continued without interruption. In the fighting of the last few days we suffered about 6,000 casualties, including about 400 officers." These heavy losses were announced with relish. That was the Mussolini way; in armistice negotiations, whether with France or with Greece, he threw into the scales not the results achieved, but the heavy losses incurred for no useful results. Those killed in the last few days' fighting were truly sacrificed to the pride of a dictator who was already prepared to speak unblushingly of victory, as indeed he did in a telegram to Cavallero:

> In this hour of victory I must acknowledge your indisputable merit in having in the course of four months created the conditions necessary and sufficient for attaining it. These conditions consisted in breaking all further enemy counteroffensive efforts, as you have done, and in imparting to all the moral and material impulse for recovery. I highly appreciate your work and that done by your colleagues and the troops. Remember me to all. Mussolini.

To the troops Mussolini addressed an order of the day recalling that "after six months of bitter fighting the enemy has laid down his arms and our bloody sacrifices have been consecrated by victory" and that "at this moment the Italian people remembers with deep emotion and salutes its heroic sons who fell in the battle of Albania and expresses its undying gratitude to you who have avenged them." The Duce had already forgotten the bitter disappointments of the preceding months. It was not for nothing that Hitler remarked, in one of those dinner-table monologues of his, in which acute observations were interspersed with ranting: "What lucky people! [the Italians] When they are beaten, three days later they have forgotten it. When they win a victory, they remember it for all eternity." There is no doubt that he was referring to the Greek campaign when he said this on August 28,

1942, just as he was a few months earlier when he disparagingly remarked: "When Italy was in difficulties on the Albanian front I wondered what was the thing to do when troops retreated without orders to such an extent that they could not be stopped. I came to the conclusion that the only thing to do was to carry out summary executions. But it is not the little infantryman who ought to be shot . . . but the commander of the retreating unit." But when black hours came for his army that did not help him.

During the period of the Greek collapse, Mussolini, who often had generous and humane impulses in private, demonstrated his inability to be chivalrous in public. The many communiqués issued in the course of those days contain not a single reference to the enemy's valor. The Greek war communiqué of April 23 claimed that the armistice was signed with Greek troops still on Albanian territory. The irritable Italian reply was: "The following are the names of the Italian divisions which were on Greek territory when the act of capitulation was signed: the Venezia, Pusteria, Tridentina, Bari, Casale, Lupi di Toscana. The Greek command has lied yet again. We have reason to assume that this time will be the last." This anonymous prose bears the Mussolini stamp. The Duce, who was well aware of the background to the armistice, might well have refrained from a statement as arrogant as it was disputable.

A campaign bearing all the marks of recklessness and improvisation swiftly turned to tragedy and ended pettily with questions of pride and prestige paid for by hundreds of dead. The advancing Italian troops, without hatred or resentment, became occupying troops, and recognized in the thousands of stragglers at that time their enemies of yesterday, and discerned in their faces a fellowship of suffering and resignation. They were aware that the brightness of their victory was marred by too much bitterness and too many humiliations. They marched along cheerfully—the Italian soldier needs little to forget past hardships—to the roar of German motorcyclists or the rumble of huge German tanks. That April the Italian troops of the Albanian campaign consisted of 31,841 officers, 494,709 other ranks, 65,320 transport animals, 13,169 lorries. The following divisions had taken part in the campaign: the Julia, Pusteria, Tridentina, and Cuneense Alpine; the Ferrara, Siena, Bari, Parma, Cacciatori delle Alpi, Puglie, Modena, Acqui, Cuneo, Lupi di Toscana, Pinerolo, Bergamo, Cagliari, Brennero, Casale, Arezzo, Venezia, Sforzesca, Forlì, Taro, Piemonte, Firenze, and Legnano infantry divisions; the Centauro Armored Division; the Guide, Aosta, and Milano cavalry regiments; and the 3rd Grenadiers. The Marche and Messina divisions reached the theater of operations after the end of the campaign.

After the Greek government gave its consent to the re-embarkation of the British, Australians, and New Zealanders, General Wilson arranged that the evacuation, known as Operation Demon, should begin on April 28, but the surrender of the Epirus army made it necessary to accelerate the operation. The Thermopylae Line was held for three days while the Germans prepared to launch their offensive; then the withdrawal to the small ports of Attica and the northern Peloponnese chosen for the evacuation began. The British were faced with another Narvik, another Dunkirk. The Luftwaffe kept harrying them, and the troops generally embarked by night, whereupon the ship sailed immediately. A number of ships, including the troopship *Slamat* and the torpedo boats *Diamond* and *Wryneck,* were sunk (of 700 men on board the three ships only 50 survived). In the warm springtime nights of Attica the troops left Greece under a hail of fire after a brief and unhappy campaign, using the harbors of Rafina, Rafti, and Megara, and Nauplion, Tholon, Monemvasia, and Kalamai in the Peloponnese.

The Germans were hot on their heels. On April 26 their parachutists seized the Corinth Canal. Apart from a few small contingents that managed to embark in the following two days, the re-embarkation was completed on April 29. Wilson's expeditionary force paid dearly for the Greek campaign. It consisted* altogether of about 58,000 ground troops (plus about 4,200 who went ahead of the main convoys), and it included about 17,-000 Australians and 17,000 New Zealanders. Total casualties were about 12,000, but many of the wounded returned to duty later. In the port of Kalamai alone the Germans surprised and captured 7,000 British troops, commanded by Brigadier Parrington, who were waiting for ships in which to embark after a first contingent had got away. Altogether about 50,700 service personnel re-embarked, including an indefinite number of Greek, Yugoslav, Cypriot, and Palestinian refugees. When account is taken of the fact that it consisted only of two divisions and a brigade, apart from auxiliary units, it is evident that the expeditionary force was exceedingly robust. But it was also terribly inadequate in relation to the strength of the enemy. The Greek population understood the tragedy of these allies who had been unable to provide real aid; and when the defeated British, Australians, and New Zealanders made their way through Athens towards the ports of ro embarkation they were applauded.

At dawn on April 23, King George, the royal family, and the government left for Crete. On the morning of April 27, three weeks to the day after the beginning of the German offensive, one of List's motorized columns entered the outskirts of Athens from the north. Not a shot was fired, and no aircraft flew over the city. The sky was clear, the sun hot, the streets deserted. A Greek military commission met the German motorcyclists, who were advancing almost in parade formation, preceding a lieutenant colonel. The latter accepted the surrender of the city, after which

* These figures are approximate, and the official figures have necessarily been subject to revision. *The Official History of the Second World War, United Kingdom Series* (*The Mediterranean and the Middle East*, Vol. II [London, 1956]) by Major-General I. S. O. Playfair, gives embarkation and casualty figures on pp. 104 and 105. Earlier estimates of these figures are given, for example, in *The Second World War*, Vol. 3, by Winston S. Churchill, London, 1950, pp. 205–6, and *Greece and Crete* by Christopher Buckley, London, 1952, p. 136.

the motorcyclists roared off again to the Acropolis, on which they hoisted a swastika flag. In the Greek campaign the Germans lost 263 officers killed or wounded, 1,160 other ranks killed and 3,411 other ranks wounded. These losses were less than those that the Italians suffered in the prestige advance of the last few days.

On April 28 Italian parachutists and airborne troops called on the Greek garrison in Corfu to surrender. Yet another incident between Italians and Germans occurred; the Greeks were willing to surrender only to the latter, and three German officers hurried to the island to arrange for a cessation of hostilities. Meanwhile troops of the Acqui Division began to land. Before the tension resulted in clashes between Greeks and Italians, the Greeks reluctantly agreed to hand over their arms to Italian troops. The same procedure was resorted to in Cephalonia.

Thus the Greek campaign ended, six months after it began. In Rome the big shots were already putting it away in the files or including it among the successful results of their policies. Ciano was displeased at the setting up in Athens of a government headed by Tsolakoglou, because "it is clear that this general intends to preserve the national and ethnic unity of Greece." Cavallero also resented Tsolakoglou, because he had fought against the Italians[5] (if he had not fought them, he would have fought against the Germans; after all, a general had to be somewhere during that time).

In connection with Tsolakoglou's appointment the Germans had another opportunity of noting how violently the Greek blow to Mussolini's pride still rankled and how he reacted to it with childish sulks. Tsolakoglou declared himself ready to form a government on April 27. At midnight Ribbentrop telephoned Mackensen from Vienna and asked him if he could awaken the Duce to inform him of the possibilities open to the occupying powers; Tsolakoglou, in List's view, was the right man for the job. Mackensen got in touch with Ciano, and was received by the latter at his home at 1:15 A.M. Ciano decided that the matter should not be left over till next morning, but that the Duce had better be awoken straight away. So Mussolini was roused from his bed in the middle of the night—the "unsleeping" dictator in fact used to go to bed rather early—to listen to what the two men had to say. He ended by consenting to the defeated general's appointment, though "without enthusiasm"; he crossly observed that the Axis could have no confidence in Greek sincerity.

Cavallero had his own grave problems, such as what was to be done with the volunteer members of the Fascist hierarchy. He consulted Ciano by telephone on the subject. "Have you anything to tell me about the members of the government and the national councillors? Many desire to leave. Dino [Grandi] is on the Dalmatian coast, Starace left this morning with orders to go to Dalmatia. Arrangements have still to be made for Bottai, Ricci, Cianetti, and Del Giudice."[6] Cavallero was more optimistic than ever, and with good reason. Geloso went to Athens to take part in the victory parade of Italian and German troops, and he remained in Athens for a long time as commander of the Eleventh Army of occupation.

Pricolo noted with alarm in Tirana that in the governor-general's office they were brazenly talking of victory. Victor Emmanuel III visited Albania and the front from May 10 to May 17, and among other places stopped at Hill 731. The dead there had at last been buried, but the height, denuded by shell fire, made such a slight impression that General Puntoni, his aide-de-camp, did not mention it in his diary. On the day of the King-Emperor's departure a hotheaded young Albanian fired four pistol shots at him, but missed. One of the shots holed a tire of the royal car, but the royal nerves stood up very well to the shock.

On May 14 Cavallero wrote Mussolini a long letter proposing the setting up of a shrine on Hill 731.[7] It was a verbose document that used the proposal as a pretext to extol Mussolini's merits as a strategist, and above all his own:

No other position would so effectively demonstrate by its present aspect the stubbornness with which the victorious March offensive was conducted by our soldiers, the offensive proposed and directed

by you which delivered such heavy blows to the structure of the
Greek army as to shatter its power of resistance and make all further initiative quite impossible.

Mussolini, who two months previously had left Albania in a state
of extreme depression after that strange victorious offensive,
brazenly replied as follows:

I received with deep emotion your proposal to erect a shrine to our
dead in the war against Greece on Monastery Hill, 731. This is the
area in which from March 9–14 the battle was engaged that the
enemy himself calls the greatest and most bloody in his modern
history. It was between the Vojussa and the Ossum, on the fronts
held by the IV, VIII, and XXV army corps, that the enemy's back
was broken. It is the area in which our troops demonstrated their
great and unsurpassable heroism. The demonstration must and shall
remain imperishably in these places bathed in the blood of the com-
batants and in the heart of the Italian people.

15. Epilogue

The guns fell silent, and quiet returned to the Albanian mountains. Greece lay supine under the heel of the conqueror, Hitler prepared his fateful Operation Barbarossa, the invasion of Russia, and Visconti Prasca bombarded the General Staff with appeals and complaints that he had been unfairly and arbitrarily shelved. Mussolini tried to "recover face" by engaging in an unequal duel with enemy propaganda that emphasized the humiliating aspects of his Greek adventure. The tone for these Allied attacks was set by Churchill in a broadcast on April 27, in which he talked to the British people about the unhappy outcome of the British intervention:

> I dare say you have read in the newspapers that by a special proclamation the Italian dictator has congratulated the Italian army in Albania on the glorious laurels they have gained by their victories over the Greeks. Here surely is the world record in the domain of the ridiculous and the contemptible. This whipped jackal Mussolini, who to save his skin has made of Italy a vassal state of Hitler's empire, goes frisking up to the side of the German tiger with yelps not only of appetite—that could be understood—but even of triumph. Different things strike different people in different ways, but I am sure a great many millions in the British Empire and the United States will find a new object in life in making sure that when we come to the final reckoning this absurd impostor will be abandoned to public justice and universal scorn.

These Churchillian barbs went home. The inflated language of Mussolini's propaganda comebacks ill concealed his humiliation.

The note that the Greek government had handed to Palairet in Athens consenting to the British re-embarkation provided the Duce with a point of departure for an attempted reassessment of his disastrous campaign. The note said that "after victoriously conducting a vigorous struggle against a numerically superior and better equipped enemy for more than six months, the Greek army is in a state of exhaustion because it is totally lacking in certain resources that are indispensable for the conduct of war." The Fascist propaganda comment on this was:

> Apart from the victory that never was, as it is easy to demonstrate, and the numerical superiority that never was, the admission of the Koryzis government that the struggle with the Italian army had exhausted the Greek army is correct and, we may add, historical. It is not straining logic to conclude that at latest in the seventh month the Italian army would have liquidated a Greek army that was exhausted in the sixth. The Axis operation in the Balkans provoked by the coup d'état in Belgrade and the intervention of the iron German divisions—together with the Yugoslav collapse—accelerated the Greek collapse, which was certain and inevitable. The official admission by the Greek government reported by Eden deflates once and for all the rhetorical and propaganda bubbles that for some time deceived the Greeks about the outcome of the struggle and, with the Greeks, their so-called allies and sponsors in Europe and America.

The language of this announcement is undoubtedly Mussolinian, and it succeeds in condensing many lies into a short space. The Greek army had certainly made a tremendous effort, but there is no doubt that it could have gone on causing the Italians in Albania a great deal of trouble for a long time to come, and the Italian March offensive had brought to light no signs of any Greek collapse; Papagos, as we have seen, was still planning offensive operations. With one of those logical gaps typical of the Mussolinian mentality, the statement almost boasted about the Italian lack of numerical superiority (though it did not deny the superiority of Italian equipment, which it could have done with good reason). It denied the Greek right to talk of victory, which it claimed for Italy, and distorted historical truth by asserting that the German attack on Greece had been a consequence of the Yugoslav coup d'état. As we know, Operation Marita was planned a long time before the events in Belgrade forced Hitler to amplify and modify it. Underneath Mussolini's arrogance his inferiority complex in relation to the Germans and world public opinion was plain to see.

Hitler threw him a crumb of comfort in a speech he made to the Reichstag on May 4. The tribute he paid to the bravery of the Greeks should have been welcome to Mussolini, because it went some way to explaining his failure, though the Duce would have preferred him to have talked of an Italian victory *tout court,* without lingering on the painful ordeal of the previous six months. "Greece," Hitler said in his speech, while the Italian newspapers were printing the first photographs of Mussolini visiting the Albanian front, "which had less need than any other Balkan state to be guaranteed by Britain, lent itself fully to London's criminal plans. I wish to render homage to historical truth by distinguishing between the Greek people and the clique of corrupt leaders headed by the King which subjected itself to British interests. . . ." Then, referring to the Italian attack, Hitler found a rather astute formula that transformed the Italian misadventure into a chance offered the Greeks. "The difficult weather conditions that intervened, the snow, blizzard, and rain, together, I must admit for the sake of historical truth, with the extremely brave resistance put up by the Greek troops, left the Greek government ample time to consider the consequences of its disastrous decision and to seek an opportunity for an honorable way out." They had certainly had time for reflection, but that had not been Mussolini's fault. "The Duce," Hitler went on, "never asked me to put a single division at his disposal. He was convinced that with the beginning of the fine weather season the war against Greece would be

crowned with success. I was of the same opinion. Thus the German forces were not deployed to help Italy against Greece."

Distasteful though it is to admit it, throughout the Greek affair
Hitler's attitude to Mussolini was invariably sensible, reasonable,
and chivalrous. The inhuman exterminator of the Jews, the para-
noiac who in his Berlin bunker still raved about a German recovery and victory, the crazy strategist who abandoned his
Stalingrad army to the slaughter, appears here in an infinitely better light. He could have got back at Mussolini for impudently
confronting him with a *fait accompli* and thus committing a disastrous mistake, but instead he falsified the truth more than was
strictly necessary in order to safeguard the prestige of his Rome
comrade. True, their triumph permitted the Germans such indul-
gences. They had taken prisoner 344,000 Yugoslavs, 218,000
Greeks, and 9,000 British, while suffering minimal losses themselves. Nevertheless Hitler paid another tribute to the Greeks in
his speech. "Towards the unhappy Greek people we feel a sense
of genuine compassion," he said. "Greece fought so bravely that
the esteem of her enemies cannot be denied her."

A month later, when the Greek people, by a significant psychological *volte-face,* had already begun to appreciate the humanity
of the Italian troops and to hate the hardness of the Germans,
Mussolini delivered his summing up of the affair in a speech on
June 10, the first anniversary of Italy's entry into the Second
World War. By this time the Germans and Italians were occupying Crete as well, and he spoke to a cheering and applauding
Chamber of Corporations. The Duce attributed his decision to
make war not to a sudden outburst of anger, but to mature and
deliberate reflection: "As early as August 1940," he said, "I had
evidence that Greece was no longer preserving even the semblance
of neutrality. . . . I convinced myself that Greece in reality constituted a British key position in the east central Mediterranean
and that Yugoslavia's attitude was also exceedingly ambiguous.
. . . The facts have fully confirmed that this view of mine was
right." After this extraordinary statement, which in a democratic

parliament would have been demolished by the opposition in two minutes, Mussolini said that "on October 15 it was unanimously decided to stop dillydallying and enter the field towards the end of the month."

This appeal to unanimity, under a régime that left all decisions and responsibility to its leader, was hypocritical as well as comic. The Duce admitted that beginning a campaign in October "imposed a tremendous logistical effort" (without mentioning that this effort had not been made), though it had the advantage that "the long nights facilitated the navigation of the convoys . . . and was a safeguard against malaria." Visconti Prasca's plan, "approved by the Rome General Staff and by myself, was logical and convincing." In the course of this book I have tried to make clear that it was the opposite. After describing the ordeal of the Julia Division, Mussolini talked of the building of the "wall," and then embarked on an account of the war that amounted to a plea in his own defense, and added that "when I went to Albania at the beginning of March I smelt a foretaste of victory in the air." This claim can be checked against the description of the Duce's tour of inspection. "In the week from March 9 to March 18, which marks the resumption of Italian activity," Mussolini continued, "the Greek army practically ceased to exist as a force still capable of fighting. This was subsequently admitted by the Greek government itself. It is a mathematical certainty that, even if nothing had happened to change the Balkan situation, the Italian army would have overwhelmed and annihilated the Greek army in April. It must, in honesty, be admitted that many Greek units fought bravely."

After this concession, the first he had made since October 28, 1940, Mussolini went on: "The Greek incident demonstrates that the valuation put on armies is not immutable and that surprises, though not frequent, are always possible," an admission inconsistent with the beginning of his speech, in which he claimed that everything had more or less gone according to plan. After presenting his version of the campaign, with many omissions and distortions, Mussolini reached the painful chapter of the Italian losses. These were very high. Cavallero, who attached importance to demonstrating the "nature of the effort made," could be very satisfied on this score. Mussolini announced the casualties as 13,502 killed, 38,768 wounded, 4,391 sufferers from third-degree frostbite, who had been "for the most part saved," 8,592 victims of second-degree frostbite, who had been "completely cured," and 4,564 victims of slight frostbite. Albanian casualties numbered fifty-nine killed and sixty-eight wounded. Thus spoke the Duce, amid acclamation. His figures, however, were largely underestimates. According to official figures by the Defense Ministry, the Greek campaign cost Italy 13,755 killed, 50,874 wounded, 12,368 victims of frostbite, 25,067 missing, 52,108 hospitalized. In the opinion of the Defense Ministry, most of the missing were killed in action. The Greeks suffered heavily too. Their official casualty figures were 13,408 killed and 42,485 wounded. Altogether nearly 50,000 men were killed, 100,000 wounded, and many others condemned to a life of suffering because of mutilations caused by frostbite, because, on a now distant October day, Mussolini's pride was offended by the German take-over of Rumania and he wanted to pay back Adolf Hitler in his own coin. We have not mentioned all the consequences of that moment of pique. Eighteen of the ships that went backwards and forwards in convoy between Italy and Albania were sunk, sixty-five Italian aircraft were brought down, 229 airmen were killed (the number of aircraft lost by the Greeks and British was much greater), and Greek towns were devastated by bombing. All these sacrifices and all this spilling of Italian blood was rewarded by discredit and disrepute in the eyes of world opinion.

The Italians were in serious danger of being thrown out of Albania, as was admitted in an article in the *Rivista Militare* in 1950 by Carlo Geloso, the commander of the Eleventh Army; and the admission was made, paradoxically enough, in order to demonstrate that Papagos (as we may well believe) was not a paragon of generalship, and that it was because of Italian blundering that his abilities seemed to shine. Geloso wrote:

In November 1940, after the fall of Erseke the Ossum Valley was almost completely defenseless. The enemy dallied . . . against two battalions of customs guards. The Pusteria Alpine Division was thus enabled to reach the line and deploy in time. In December . . . the Sciuscizza Valley and the coast road lay practically open to the enemy if he had made use of the opportunity. . . . In January 1941, after the fall of Klisura, the enemy had an open road in front of him towards Berati. He stopped, and the Pinerolo and Cacciatori delle Alpi divisions moved in.

Such were the results of the "logical and convincing" Italian plan.

I shall be happy if in these pages I have succeeded in diverting discredit and disparagement to those responsible for the disastrous enterprise, and in showing that the troops who fought had no weaknesses except the human and, I might add, excusable weaknesses which they shared with the fighting men of all nations. The shrine at Hill 731—who knows what has become of it today with its tall cross and glorious and melancholy relics?—should not so much recall a vain offensive and an insane campaign as a huge sum of endurance and suffering. Mussolini and Cavallero, who exchanged complimentary messages, each trying to use the bones of the sanctuary to add a stone to his own personal monument, are dead; let us leave them aside.

Thinking back about the pages I have written, I feel they have turned out perhaps to be even more bitter and uncomforting than I expected. Truth is a hard taskmaster, but nothing in this book, no truth, can devalue the memory of those killed on Monastery Hill and the thousand other mud- and blood-stained heights in Albania. Let honor be done to those who did their bitter duty in obedience to stupid and iniquitous orders. In April 1941, not a single Greek unit was willing to surrender to the Italians. A few months later, when they had got to know the human warmth of the Italian troops, the Greeks preferred the Italians to the Germans. Let their valor and also their human decency be acknowledged. In the Greek campaign the Italian troops were, without any doubt whatever, the worst-led troops in the world. They deserved better of their country.

Appendix

The Head of the Government, Mussolini

Rome, August 22, 1940.

Directive

In connection with developments of the European and world politico-military situation, operational possibilities in the Yugoslav, Greek, and Egyptian theaters have recently been examined.

In view of the imminence of the attack on the British forces in Egypt —which will coincide with the German land attack on Great Britain— the Libyan sector becomes the main one on which attention and effort should be concentrated; it is the sector in which *mass* must be used on land, at sea, in the air.

The other two theaters—the Greek and the Yugoslav—unless the Yugoslavs or Greeks or British take the initiative—become theaters of observation and vigilance, necessary vigilance in view of the equivocal policy followed by those two states and the state of mind of their peoples.

The previously arranged rate of deployment in these two theaters may therefore be slowed down, the date for the completion of that on the eastern front to be October 20 instead of September 20 and that on the Greek front to be the end of September instead of the end of August.

It is clear, furthermore that, once Great Britain has been defeated, the states that have more or less covertly sympathized with London will not make difficulties about falling into line with Axis decisions, whatever these may be.

The Head of the Government, Mussolini,
to the Chancellor of the Reich, Hitler
(Extract)

Rome, August 24, 1940.

Since our conversation of June 18 we have not had another opportunity for an exchange of ideas.

I think it appropriate to tell you what I think of the present situation.

In the first place, in regard to the Danubian-Balkan basin, there is
no change in the policy mutually agreed on, which consists in keeping
that area out of the conflict. Military measures on the Greek and
Yugoslav frontiers are merely precautionary in nature, in view of the
fact that those two countries are deeply hostile to the Axis and would
be ready to stab it in the back if a favorable opportunity presented itself . . .

[Greece has shown that her understanding with Great Britain continues.] All the Greek ports are bases against us. . . . Unless anything
unforeseen occurs, it is not there that I intend to direct my military
effort, but against Egypt.

Conversation between the Head of the Government, Mussolini,
and the Foreign Minister of the Reich, Ribbentrop

Rome, September 19, 1940.

Minister von Ribbentrop began by describing the present state of
the hostilities between Germany and Great Britain. He said that the
Luftwaffe raids had caused great damage, particularly when it had
been possible for the German bombers to be accompanied by their
fighter escort. During the past few days the British reaction had notably
diminished. The biggest obstacle was still represented by the weather,
which with unforeseeable consistency had remained bad for six weeks.
For the further development of air operations, and to carry the land
war on to British soil, at least eight or ten days of good weather were

necessary; as soon as this came about, an attack—for which preparations, in regard both to the air and the landing forces, were now complete—would be launched on a huge scale.

In these circumstances the question was what excuse there could be for the British attitude, which had recently appeared to be notably defiant. The Führer thought it was an attitude dictated by despair, and also, in some quarters, by incomprehension of reality, as well as the hope of two interventions in favor of Great Britain: by the Russians and by the Americans.

It was to counter this possibility, and above all to paralyze America, that Ribbentrop had prepared, and now submitted for the Duce's approval, a plan for a tripartite alliance with Japan. Negotiations had been conducted secretly through a personal emissary of Minister Ribbentrop's and not through the official embassy channels. In the German view, the conclusion of such an alliance would have the advantage of strengthening the isolationist trend against the interventionism of Roosevelt. Also, in presenting the event to world public opinion it would be necessary to emphasize that a world bloc against extension of the war was being established.

It remained to be seen what the reaction of Russia would be. Some might think that the conclusion of the alliance might throw the Soviets into the arms of the democracies. Ribbentrop did not believe this, for two reasons. In the first place the Soviets were still too weak, and knew that a large part of the German land forces were now concentrated on their frontiers. In the second place, Russia was a land power, and no aid could come to her from a combination of the British and American fleets, while the hostility of Japan would bring down on her the immediate weight of the Japanese army in Manchuria.

There was no doubt that recent events had made relations between Russia and Germany less cordial. The Vienna agreement, the guarantee given to Rumania, the setting up of the Danube Commission, were all events displeasing to the Russians. That did not mean that the Axis intended to, or should, conduct a policy of hostility to Russia. A policy of friendship could continue, though within strictly defined limits. These limits were those outlined in Vienna. The occupation of Bessarabia was foreseen and accepted; but any future move that increased Russian influence in Bulgaria or Yugoslavia or brought the Russians nearer to the Bosphorus would be regarded in a completely negative way by Germany, and Ribbentrop believed that Italy thought likewise.

So far as Greece and Yugoslavia were concerned, Ribbentrop reiterated that these were exclusively Italian interests, and that it was up to Italy to choose her own solution.

In Yugoslavia Germany reserved the right only to the district of Maribor. Ribbentrop reiterated what he had said to Count Ciano in Berlin; that in existing circumstances the principal effort should be directed against Britain. But he confirmed that Yugoslavia and Greece were two spheres of Italian interest in which Italy could adopt the policy she chose with the full support of Germany.

Minister von Ribbentrop then went on to give an account of his conversations with Serrano Suñer. Spain was ready to go to war, and had informed the German government of her requirements. These consisted of oil, wheat, and raw material supplies, the sending of certain special arms, as well as an assurance that at the end of the war the coastal strip of Morocco extending from Oran to Cap Blanc would be transferred to Spanish sovereignty. The Führer was in principle in favor of making such concessions for the sake of procuring us Spanish entry into the war, the immediate purpose of which would be the seizure of Gibraltar. The German General Staff was completing studies with this end in view, and Ribbentrop would communicate these to the Duce during his stay in Rome. If the Duce agreed, Ribbentrop undertook to conclude an agreement with Serrano Suñer on his return to Berlin to settle the conditions of Spain's entry into the war.

Minister von Ribbentrop concluded by saying that, whatever future developments might be, the Führer regarded the war as already won.

The Duce said he completely agreed with the Führer in this last statement. The British situation was bad, and was growing steadily worse as operations against the island were stepped up and the time of the landing approached. The British leaders were still bluffing, but the people were tired. They were not living, they were not working, and the war of nerves could be regarded as won. The southeast of the island was now lost to the British air force. And it should not be forgotten that, once London was lost, the Empire was lost.

As for America, it should be borne in mind that the United States was in practice on the British side already. He did not believe it would send armies to fight in Europe, but the sale of the fifty torpedo boat destroyers, the continuous aid given to Great Britain, showed that America was already against us in practice. That, however, need not cause us special concern. What the United States could do, it had already done.

The Duce declared himself in full agreement with the projected alliance with Japan, which would paralyze American action. It should be borne in mind that the Americans greatly feared Japan, and its fleet in particular, since the American navy, though quantitatively large, must be considered an amateur organization, like the British army.

There remained Russia. It was not important to decide what the Russians would say; it was important to see what they would do. It could be stated here and now that they would do nothing. Italy had recently made some gestures towards the policy of rapprochement with Russia. But the only purpose had been to block the British rapprochement maneuvers towards Moscow. At all events, the Russian reaction to the alliance would in practice be nil, since the Russians' chief worry was about losing what they had gained.

There remained the problem of Yugoslavia and Greece. Italy had half a million men on the Yugoslav frontier and 200,000 on the Greek frontier. To Italy the Greeks represented what the Norwegians had represented to Germany before the April operation. It was therefore necessary for us to set about the liquidation of Greece; particularly as, when our land forces had advanced farther in Egypt, the British fleet would be unable to remain at Alexandria and would try to seek shelter in Greek ports. However, the Duce agreed with Ribbentrop that the primary objective was the defeat of Britain.

He also agreed that the entry of Spain into the war would be a very important event. The loss of Gibraltar would be a severe blow to the British Empire, and would assure us, Italy, of freedom of passage through the straits, through which we could now hardly pass submarines.

Another advantage would be bases in the Balearics. And lastly, the entry of Spain into the war would serve finally to liquidate the de Gaulle danger in North Africa, which in the Duce's opinion had increased recently, particularly as contacts between Pétain and de Gaulle were not to be excluded. The French were still making the great mistake of thinking they had not been beaten.

Ribbentrop said that the Führer's intentions were that France should never again play an important part in the life of Europe.

The Duce said that the most favorable moment for the entry of Spain into the war remained to be settled. There were two alternatives: the war would either end before the winter, or it would continue into next year. The Spanish card should be played according to which alternative seemed the more probable.

Ribbentrop replied that Serrano Suñer had not yet fixed a date for entry into the war. The military thought it might take place in four weeks' time. In any case, the Spanish declaration of war, after the alliance with Japan, would be a tremendous blow to Britain, also from the psychological point of view. The Spanish declaration of war on Britain should be made with the first gunshot.

The Duce asked for information about the attitude of Portugal.

Report of meeting held in the Duce's study
in the Palazzo Venezia, October 15, 1940, 1100 hrs.
(Shorthand Note)

Those present:
The Duce,
Their Excellencies Ciano; Badoglio; Soddu; Jacomoni; Roatta; Visconti Prasca.
Secretary: Lieutenant Colonel Trombetti.

DUCE—The object of this meeting is to lay down—in broad outline—the course of action that I have decided to undertake against Greece.

In the first phase of this operation the objectives are both naval and territorial.

The territorial objectives are to lead to our taking possession of the whole of the southern coast of Albania, that is, they are to result in our occupation of the Ionian Islands of Zante, Cephalonia, and Corfu, and the conquest of Salonika. When we have attained these objectives, we shall have improved our position in the Mediterranean in relation to Britain.

In a second phase, or concomitantly with these operations, [the objective is] the total occupation of Greece, to put it out of action and ensure that in all circumstances it shall remain within our politico-economic sphere.

Having thus defined the issue, I have also decided the date, which in my opinion must not be postponed even by an hour; that is, the twenth-sixth of this month.

This is an operation that has been maturing in my mind for a long time, since many months before our entry into the war and even before the outbreak of the conflict.

These essential points having been settled, we now come to the question of how the operation is to be conducted, and I therefore sent for the governor-general and the military commander in Albania to enable them to put us in the political and military picture, so that we may decide on all the suitable steps for the attainment of our objectives in the best possible manner and within the most appropriate time limits.

Let me add that I foresee no complications in the north. Yugoslavia has every interest in remaining quiet, as is shown incidentally by official public statements that exclude the possibility of complications except in self-defense.

I exclude complications from Turkey, especially since Germany has established herself in Rumania and Bulgaria has strengthened herself. The latter may be a pawn in our game, and I shall take the necessary measures to ensure that this unique opportunity of attaining her aspirations to Macedonia and an outlet to the sea is not wasted.

The objectives and the date having been settled, the other aspects of the situation must now be looked at, so that the measures and means may be decided on.

(The Duce invites the governor-general of Albania to state how he sees the situation.)

JACOMONI—This operation is eagerly awaited in Albania. The country is impatient and full of enthusiasm; it can actually be stated that the enthusiasm is so lively that recently there has been some disappointment that the operation has not yet begun.

We have taken various serious steps to ensure the country's supplies. There is a "port of Durazzo" danger, in the sense that if it were bombed, we should have supply difficulties. In regard to the road prob-

lem, great progress has been made, though it cannot be said to have
been resolved.

What is the situation in Greece as seen from Albania?

DUCE—That is an important point.

JACOMONI—It is very difficult to describe. Public opinion is mani-
festly indifferent.

We announced that the niece of the well-known assassinated Albanian patriot had been murdered, but they responded with a denial.
From information supplied by our informants it appears that, while
two months ago the Greeks did not seem inclined to put up serious resistance, now they seem determined to oppose our action. The clandes-
tine wireless that we have set up at Argyrokastron, with which we
carry out active propaganda, has a wide audience, and seems to be
having an effect. I believe that the nature of Greek resistance will
depend on whether our operation is swift, decisive, and impressive, or
cautious and limited.

There is also the question of what aid the Greeks may receive by sea
from the British.

DUCE—I absolutely exclude the possibility of their sending men; also
their air force has no strength to spare.

JACOMONI—The only worry might result from a partial occupation
of Greece, inasmuch as the British, if they were able to send substantial air strength, might carry out raids on southern Italy and Albania
from the remaining bases. The Greek aircraft are 144s, which are no
serious cause for worry.

DUCE—What is the state of mind of the Greek population?

JACOMONI—It appears to be profoundly depressed.

CIANO—There is a clear distinction between the population and the
ruling political, plutocratic class, which animates the spirit of resistance and keeps alive the country's anglophile spirit. It is a small and
very rich class, while the rest of the population is indifferent to everything, including the prospect of our invasion.

JACOMONI—The news that I caused to be spread about the high
wages in Rumania has made a big impact on the Greek population.

(The Duce invites General Visconti Prasca to describe the military
situation.)

VISCONTI PRASCA—We have prepared an operation against Epirus which will be ready on the twenty-sixth inst., and the prospects are very favorable.

The geographical situation of Epirus does not favor the intervention of other Greek forces, because on the one side there is the sea and on the other an impassable range. This theater of operations will enable us to carry out a series of rounding-up operations against the Greek forces—estimated to number about 30,000 men—which will enable us to occupy the Epirus in a short time, ten or fifteen days.

This operation—which might enable us to liquidate all the Greek troops—has been prepared down to the most minute details and is as perfect as is humanly possible. Its success would bring about an improvement in our position, give us a more secure frontier, and possession of the port of Preveza, resulting in a complete change in our situation.

That is the first phase of the operation, to be carried through with the utmost vigor.

The operation is, however, subject to climatic conditions. In a few weeks' time the rainy season will cause serious difficulties to the conquest of Epirus and the Preveza base.

DUCE—The date of the beginning of the operation can be brought forward, but cannot be put back.

VISCONTI PRASCA—The spirit of the troops is excellent, enthusiasm is as high as it could be. I have never had cause for complaint about the troops in Albania. The only signs of indiscipline among officers and men have been the result of excessive eagerness to go forward and fight.

DUCE—What is your strength?

VISCONTI PRASCA—About 70,000 men, apart from special battalions. In regard to the troops in the front line—about 30,000 men—we have a superiority of two to one.

DUCE—And in regard to *matériel*, the enemy's tanks, field defenses, etc.?

VISCONTI PRASCA—The only worry is the aid that might be given to the enemy by the British air force, since so far as I am concerned the Greek air force does not exist.

As for the Salonika front, there must be some reservations because of the advance of the season.

The operation in Epirus might be developed.

DUCE—The Salonika operation is important, because Salonika must be prevented from becoming a British base.

VISCONTI PRASCA—That operation requires a certain amount of time. The port of disembarkation is Durazzo, which is 300 kilometers distant from Salonika. A couple of months would therefore be required.

DUCE—All the same, the British can be prevented from landing at Salonika. It is important that two divisions should be sent to that front, because it might ensure us of Bulgarian co-operation.

VISCONTI PRASCA—The basis for everything, including the beginning of the march on Athens, is the occupation of Epirus and the port of Preveza.

DUCE—And the occupation of the three islands: Zante, Cephalonia, and Corfu.

VISCONTI PRASCA—Certainly.

DUCE—These operations must be carried out simultaneously. Do you know what the state of the morale of the Greek troops is?

VISCONTI PRASCA—They are not people who like fighting.

DUCE—And now another thing. Having settled the date, we must decide how we shall establish the necessity of this operation of ours. One general justification is that Greece is allied to our enemies, who make use of her bases, etc., but an incident is also required to enable us to say that we are entering Greece to establish order. If such an incident occurs, well and good, but if not, arrange one, it does not matter which.

JACOMONI—I can arrange something on the frontiers: incidents between Tsamouriots and the Greek authorities.

VISCONTI PRASCA—We have procured French arms and bombs to organize a simulated attack.

DUCE—All this is absolutely trivial to me; it is just to put up a bit of smoke. All the same, it will be a good thing if you can arrange for an occasion for lighting the fuse.

CIANO—When do you want the incident to happen?

DUCE—On the twenty-fourth.

CIANO—The incident will occur on the twenty-fourth.

DUCE—No one will believe it, but for metaphysical reasons it will be possible to say that it was necessary to conclude the matter.

What is required in operations of this kind is to act with the greatest energy and the greatest decision, because that is the secret of success, also in relation to possible aid from other countries.

We must give them an alibi, to enable them to say: "There is nothing to be done. Are we to go to the aid of a country that is already beaten?"

That is what the Turks would be able to say, and the British, too, would find it convenient to follow suit.

VISCONTI PRASCA—The operation has been planned in such a way as to create the impression of an overwhelming blow in a few days.

DUCE—In view of my responsibilities in the matter, I tell you not to worry excessively about possible losses, though showing solicitude, from the humane point of view, for the life of the single soldier. I say this because sometimes leaders stop when heavy losses have been suffered.

VISCONTI PRASCA—I have ordered the battalions always to attack, even if faced with a division.

BADOGLIO—There are two aspects to the question: the Greek, and that of British aid. I am with you completely in believing that the possibility of British landings can be almost completely excluded. They are much more worried about Egypt than about Greece, and they are very reluctant to put troops into ships in the Mediterranean. The only possible aid would therefore be in the air.

In view of this, we might take the precaution of making the operation against Greece coincide with that on Mersa Matruh. If that were done, it would be very difficult for them to spare aircraft from Egypt to send them to Greece.

It can be done, because Graziani can also be ready on the twenty-sixth of this month.

DUCE—I should be in favor of Graziani's operation taking place a few days in advance. The capture of Mersa Matruh, especially if we do not stop there, will make it still more difficult for the British to give such aid. After the loss of the Egyptian key point, even if London were still able to carry on, the British Empire would be in a state of defeat. India is in a state of unrest, and the British would no longer be able to receive aid from South Africa and through the Red Sea. Let me add a consideration in the field of morale, that is, that this success in Africa would act as a spur to the troops in Albania. That is why I want synchronization of the two operations, the African operation to have slight precedence.

BADOGLIO—Looking at the Greek problem, I should like to say that stopping short in Epirus is not consistent with the situation. I do not exaggerate in saying that if we wish to occupy Greece we must also occupy Crete and Morea.

The Epirus operation worked out by Visconti Prasca is all right. With our left flank assured, the enemy forces should not present great difficulties. We have the air force. . . .

DUCE—We shall commit at least 400 aircraft to the operations, also because of what the British aid to the Greeks might be.

BADOGLIO—If the operation is to be worthwhile, the whole of Greece must be occupied. For this about twenty divisions are required, while in Albania we now have nine, plus a cavalry division. In these conditions it is obvious that three months will be needed.

ROATTA—Taking everything into account, we can count on the equivalent of eleven divisions. In order not to have to stop in Epirus the sending of troops would have to be stepped up, also to avoid creating the impression that we have run out of breath to go forward. The problem of the total occupation of Greece must therefore be studied at once.

DUCE—The beginning of the operation having been settled for the twenty-sixth, and the liquidation of Epirus being expected by about November 10–15, that gives us another month for sending fresh forces.

VISCONTI PRASCA—The sending of extra troops depends on how the operation develops, and they can be sent only to occupied Epirus. It is not a question of speed, but a security operation. At this season operations are possible only in southern Greece.

Using Durazzo as a base for advancing on Salonika would require a month for the transport of each division.

DUCE—To clarify the ideas we are discussing, let me ask how the march on Athens is envisaged after the occupation of Epirus.

VISCONTI PRASCA—I do not foresee great difficulties. A group of five or six divisions would be sufficient.

BADOGLIO—I should regard it as more important to march on Athens than on Salonika, for one thing because a British landing at Salonika does not seem likely.

CIANO—Particularly in view of possible Bulgarian intervention.

ROATTA—Pressure is desirable in that quarter too.

DUCE—Do you think two divisions are enough?

ROATTA—Yes.

DUCE—Now I think things are getting clearer. The Epirus operation —Salonika. Consideration of possible consequences of Bulgarian intervention, which I consider probable. I fully agree about the occupation of Athens.

VISCONTI PRASCA—Basically we shall cut Greece in two from Athens, and we shall be able to go to Salonika from the Greek capital.

DUCE—What is the distance from the prospective occupied area of Epirus to Athens?

VISCONTI PRASCA—250 kilometers, with a poor road system.

DUCE—And what sort of terrain?

VISCONTI PRASCA—High, steep, difficult, hilly country.

DUCE—And in what direction do the valleys lie?

VISCONTI PRASCA—East–west, and so just in the direction of Athens.

DUCE—That is important.

ROATTA—To a certain extent that is true, because a mountain chain 2,000 meters high has to be crossed. (He shows the Duce a map of the area.)

VISCONTI PRASCA—It is country in which there are a great many mule tracks.

DUCE—Have you traveled along those roads?

VISCONTI PRASCA—Yes, a number of times.

DUCE—Now we come to two other points. Having settled all this, how many extra divisions do you think it necessary to send to Albania to occupy the whole territory leading to Athens?

VISCONTI PRASCA—During the initial period three mountain divisions would be required; of course, circumstances will decide. Now, these troops could be sent to the port of Arta in a single night.

DUCE—Another point: Albanian support, by way of regular troops or bands, to which I attach a certain amount of importance.

VISCONTI PRASCA—We have put forward a plan in that respect. We propose to organize bands of from 2,500 to 3,000 men, under our officers.

JACOMONI—There are a tremendous number of questions. Too many

Muslims should not be sent, or we shall have too many feuds on our hands.

DUCE—Then you can organize a certain number of bands?

VISCONTI PRASCA—It is all arranged. I have already drafted a telegram so that everything can be in readiness and individuals warned.

DUCE—How are you arming them?

VISCONTI PRASCA—With a few light machine guns and grenades.

DUCE—Now another aspect of the matter. What steps have you taken on the Yugoslav frontier?

VISCONTI PRASCA—We have two divisions there and a battalion of carabinieri and customs guards. What it amounts to is that we are reasonably well covered.

DUCE—I do not think there will be attacks from that quarter, and besides, the troops are deployed along prepared strongpoints.

VISCONTI PRASCA—It should be added that the terrain is well adapted to defense. There might be some infiltration through the woods by small formations, but nothing to worry about, because the frontier is completely covered. There is a customs post every 500 or 600 meters.

JACOMONI—In Albania there is a desire that some classes should be recalled to the colors.

DUCE—What does each class yield?

JACOMONI—About 700 men.

DUCE—That is a point to be considered carefully. Such troops are not to be ignored or rejected, but they must not provide an excessive contribution, as we do not want it to be thought that Epirus was won by them. What seems appropriate is a certain participation by Albanian elements that would not disturb the population. I should call up two or three classes.

Anti-aircraft defense must be an object of special attention, because bombing of the oil-producing zone and the Albanian towns, and the comparisons that might be drawn with the better defenses of the towns of Apulia, must as far as possible be avoided. Substantial anti-aircraft defense must therefore be provided.

SODDU—I have already arranged for the 75 Skodas we have had from Germany to be sent.

VISCONTI PRASCA—The defense of Tirana is limited to two groups, while the defense of Albania as a whole consists of barely five groups.

DUCE—At least 100 guns are needed in Albania because we must avoid the demoralization of daytime raids. Send all the Skoda and Oerlikon guns.

soddu—We have not had them all yet. As soon as they arrive I shall send them. I shall send the Oerlikons by air.

duce—The ground defense must be supplemented by fighters. Fortunately we have a substantial number available. On October 1 there were fifty-two aircraft ready for immediate employment and fifteen not ready for immediate employment. Sixty-seven aircraft altogether.

ciano—The 74th wing is leaving now.

duce—I think we have now examined all the aspects of the problem.

badoglio—The details will be arranged by the Army General Staff.

duce—To sum up, then. Offensive in Epirus; observation and pressure on Salonika, and, as a second phase, the march on Athens.

(The meeting ended at 1230 hours.)

Self-typed.

This report was approved by the Duce in the Palazzo Venezia, October 16, 1940—XVIII, at 1400 hours.

(Signed)

G. A. Trombetti.

Secretary,

Lieutenant Colonel attached to the Duce's Supreme Command.

The Head of the Government, Mussolini,
to the King of Bulgaria, Boris III

Rome, October 16, 1940.

I have decided to begin the settlement of accounts with Greece during this month of October.

A historic opportunity is presented to you and to Bulgaria to fulfill the old and just aspiration for an outlet to the Aegean.

In informing you of my decision I have no intention of influencing yours or of soliciting the co-operation of your armed forces.

You will do what your conscience and your royal responsibilities and the interests of your people dictate.

I ask you, your Majesty, to accept this expression of my respect and my cordial greetings.

The King of Bulgaria, Boris III,
to the Head of the Government, Mussolini

Sofia, October 18, 1940.

Deeply appreciative as I am of your consideration in informing me of your decisions in your historic message of October 16, I thank you for it with all my heart. I am particularly sensible of the human attentiveness and courtesy you showed me in pointing out the existence of possibilities that will present themselves to my country of realizing certain of its national aspirations, while giving me liberty of conscience and advice to act in accordance with my royal responsibilities and the interests of my country. In view of the present general conditions and above all the quite special position of Bulgaria, I am able more than ever to appreciate the grandeur and nobility of spirit that dictated this so clear and kind message.

You have indeed divined, your Excellency, the specially delicate situation of Bulgaria. As a result of the unfavorable circumstances which have prevented and delayed a sufficient rearmament of her army, and surrounded as she is by neighbors that you know, she is obliged to act with a great deal of circumspection and prudence without, however, renouncing her sacred rights and historic mission.

For the above-mentioned reasons Bulgaria is forced to refrain from armed action. Nevertheless, and without wishing to attribute exaggerated merits to ourselves, Bulgaria, by reason of her geographical situation, the reputation enjoyed by her army, and above all her attitude, which permits of no equivocation, will hold and will continue to hold a considerable part of her neighbors' forces.

In cordially thanking you for your feelings of friendship for the Bulgarian people and the friendship that you always show me, I ask you, your Excellency, to accept this expression of my feelings of friendly admiration, to which I join the most genuine warm wishes.

May your brilliant initiatives always promote the greatness of your noble country and lead to the establishment of a new order in Europe based on a just and lasting peace.

The Head of the Government, Mussolini,
to the Chancellor of the Reich, Hitler

Rocca delle Caminate, October 19, 1940.

After our meeting of October 4 on the Brenner, I have thought a
great deal about some of the problems that were the subject of our discussion, and I have come to conclusions which I consider it my duty
to communicate to you.

I begin with France.

Our informants and with even better reason yours, too—I think—
are unanimous in stating that the French hate the Axis more than before, that Vichy and de Gaulle have shared out the roles between themselves, and that the French do not consider themselves to have been
beaten, because—they say—they did not want to fight. Vichy is in contact with London through Lisbon. The great majority of them put their
hope in the United States, on the ground that it will assure the victory
of Great Britain. In view of this *Stimmung,* their collaboration is out
of the question. Nor should it be sought. If it came about, the French,
after denying their own defeat, would believe and cause others to believe that victory over Great Britain was due to them and them alone,
and would be capable of presenting us with the bill. Hence, dismissing
the idea of the French joining an anti-British continental bloc, I believe the time has come to decide the face of the metropolitan and
colonial France of tomorrow, reduced, as you rightly desire, to proportions that will prevent her from ever again dreaming about expan-
sions and hegemonies. Let us begin with the population. The 1936
census attributed to France 41,950,000 inhabitants, of whom 2,700,-
000 were foreigners and 2,300,000 naturalized of either recent or distant date. That makes five million non-Frenchmen. Of the 850,000
Italians, who formed the biggest category of foreigners, I am having
500 repatriated daily, and I hope to reach a total of at least 500,000 in
a year. I calculate that your and my territorial acquisitions will de-
prive France of another four million inhabitants. Thus the peace treaty
should and will reduce the population of France to 34–35 million,
with a tendency to further diminution, since I consider a demographic

revival in France to be highly improbable. As for the metropolitan and colonial acquisitions proposed by Italy, these are, as I have told you, very modest: they are limited to Nice, Corsica, and Tunis. I do not count Somalia, because it is a classical desert. They are, that is to say, demands that could have been discussed before the war but for Daladier's unconscionable reply of *jamais* and were put forward—as a basis of discussion—for the maintenance of non-belligerence on Italy's part. After the settlement of the financial and economic questions arising from the war, Italy does not and will not put forward further demands in relation to France.

The question—now—is whether the time can be considered ripe for this clarification of relations between the Axis and France. And I shall be very happy to learn your views on this essential point.

British positions on the continent.

I believe that, assuming a prolongation of the war, you agree with me in thinking it essential to eliminate the remaining British positions on the European continent. Such elimination is another condition for victory. These positions are the following: Portugal, Yugoslavia, Greece, Turkey, Egypt, Switzerland. As for Portugal, her attitude is neutralized by Spain. We must nurse no illusions about the true Yugoslav *Stimmung* towards the Axis. It is irremediably hostile. I enclose a report by my police which shows the nature of Yugoslav neutrality and criminal activity in relation to Italy. She is a bad neighbor and has a bad conscience. Yugoslavia cannot survive as she is today. Serbs and Croats are more distant from each other than ever. The Macek experiment has been a complete failure. For the time being I do not intend to change the attitude of Italy in relation to Yugoslavia, which is one of lively vigilance.

As for Greece, I am determined to stop dilly-dallying, and to act very soon. Greece is one of the strongholds of British naval strategy in the Mediterranean. A British King, a British political class, a people that is immature, but brought up to hate Italy. Greece has set about mobilizing her forces, and has put air and naval bases at the disposal of Great Britain since May, as is shown by the documents that von Ribbentrop courteously sent me after the finds at Vitry la Charité; during the past few days British officers have practically taken possession of all the airfields in Greece. In short, Greece is in the Mediterranean what Norway was in the North Sea, and must not escape a similar fate. I believe that Turkey, another pawn in the British game, will not move, particularly if you increase your occupation forces in Rumania, as you certainly will. As for Egypt, the resumption of operations is subject to a huge task of logistic preparation, similar to that which you have had to undertake in preparation for the landing in Great Britain. At all events, I hope to carry out operations simultaneously on the Greek and Egyptian fronts. At the conclusion of the second phase of the offensive, which is to lead to the capture of the strongpoint of Mersa Matruh (230 km. from Alexandria) the decisive battle of the Delta will remain to be fought. It is for that phase that the aid of your armor must be considered. General Toma, who has gone to Cyrenaica, will report to you.

I am sure it will not surprise you to see Switzerland included among the remaining continental positions of Great Britain. By the incomprehensible hostility of her attitude Switzerland herself raises the question of her future existence.

I also wish to mention something in regard to Spain. Suñer's assumption of the Foreign Affairs portfolio gives the assurance that trends hostile to the Axis have been eliminated, or at least contained. But I do not think that the internal economic situation has improved. I still take the view that Spanish non-belligerence suits us better than would her intervention. We must hold her intervention in reserve; it is a card we must play at the most favorable moment, in definite circumstances, such as the prolongation of the war throughout the whole of 1941 or an open intervention by the United States. Meanwhile Spain will have the time necessary to prepare.

Contrary to my custom, I am writing you a long letter, but I could not refrain from giving you my ideas on the many questions we discussed at our meeting on the Brenner.

I ask you, Führer, to accept this assurance of my comradely friendship, which events and our own trials will only intensify, and to accept my most cordial greetings.

Proclamation by Metaxas to the Greek People

October 28, 1940.

The hour has come to fight for the liberty of Greece, her integrity and honor. Though we have maintained the strictest neutrality, the same to all, Italy, who does not recognize our right to live as free Greeks, asked me at three o'clock this morning to hand over areas of the national territory, selected at the choice of Italy herself, and informed me that her troops would begin moving to occupy those territories at six o'clock. I replied to the Italian ambassador that I considered this request, and the manner in which it was delivered, in itself a declaration of war on Greece.

Now we shall show whether we are really worthy of our ancestors and of the liberty our forefathers secured for us. The country rises unanimously. Fight for our country, for your women and children, for our sacred institutions.

Now, above all, fight.

Message from Churchill to Metaxas

October 28, 1940.

Italy has found threats and intimidation of no avail against your calm courage. She has therefore resorted to unprovoked aggression against your country, seeking justification for a wanton attack in baseless accusations. The way in which the Greek people, under your trusted leadership, have faced the dangers and provocations of recent months has gained for Greece the admiration of the British people; the same qualities will uphold them in their present hour of trial. We will give you all the help in our power. We fight a common foe and we will share a united victory.

Conversation between the Head of the Government, Mussolini,
and the Chancellor of the Reich, Hitler

(Extract)

Florence, October 28, 1940.

The Führer began by saying that he wished to make this journey to
Florence to present a report to the Duce on his recent conversations
with the Spanish and French governments and to offer full German
solidarity in the operation begun by Italy against Greece. The Führer
put at the Duce's disposal for whenever they might be needed the parachute divisions that could be used for the occupation of Crete.

Letter from Hitler to Mussolini

Vienna, November 20, 1940.

Duce,

Permit me to begin this letter with the assurance that during these
past few days my heart and thoughts have been with you more than
ever. Take note, Duce, that I am willing to do everything that may be
of assistance to you in the present situation.

When I asked you to receive me in Florence, I set out on the trip
in the hope of stating my thoughts to you before the dangerous conflict
with Greece, of which I had heard only in the most general terms,
began.

I wished above all to ask you to delay the operation a little, if possible to a more favorable season, but in any case until after the election
of the American President. In any case, Duce, I wanted to ask you not
to undertake the operation without a previous *Blitz* seizure of Crete.
For this reason I wished to bring you practical proposals for the employment of a parachute division and another division of airborne infantry.

The state of affairs thus brought about has had very grave psychologi-

cal and military consequences, on which it is important to throw full
light.

I refer to the individual circumstances because the countermeasures that are absolutely essential can in my opinion be deduced from
them.

(a) *Psychological consequences.*—The psychological consequences of
the situation are displeasing, inasmuch as they unfavorably affect diplomatic preparations which are in full swing. In general, we feel the
consequences in the form of a strengthening of the tendency not to
engage prematurely in the conflict on our side, but instead to await further developments. Bulgaria, which previously showed very little desire indeed to join the Tripartite Pact, is now completely averse even
to considering such a step.

Also, in regard to Russia it is more difficult to bring our interests
into line and to divert Russian ambitions towards the east. On the contrary, Mr. Molotov has let it be seen that he is increasingly interested
in the Balkans.

For the time being it is impossible to ascertain from here the impression created in Yugoslavia. But even in France the position of those
who urge caution, and say that perhaps the last word in this war has
not yet been spoken, has undoubtedly been strengthened.

Whatever the psychological consequences may be, what counts is
that there should be no resulting obstacles to our further operations,
and in particular that unfriendly positions should not be adopted by
those powers which, like Yugoslavia, might be able to provoke, if not
actually a disaster, at any rate an unpleasing extension of the war.

The attitude of Turkey is of special importance, because it will have
a decisive influence on that of Bulgaria.

(b) *Military consequences.*—The military consequences of this situation, Duce, are very grave.

Britain will obtain a certain number of air bases that will bring her
not only into the immediate neighborhood of the Ploesti oilfields, but
also into the immediate neighborhood of the whole of southern Italy,
and in particular the ports of embarkation and disembarkation both in
metropolitan Italy and in Albania.

While hitherto the Rumanian oilfields have not been within range
of British bombers, these have now been brought within a distance of
less than 500 kilometers. I do not dare even think of the consequences

that might ensue. Now, Duce, it is necessary to be clear on one point. That is that there is no such thing as true and real protection for an oil-field. Even our own anti-aircraft artillery is capable of endangering such an area as much as enemy attacks. If such oil refineries were destroyed, the damage would be irreparable.

Southern Italy, its ports, and the whole of Albania, are now within easy range of British bombers. It is obvious that Britain will be completely indifferent if Italy destroys Greek towns in reprisal. It is attacks on Italian towns that will be decisive. In this connection I consider a land offensive from Albanian territory against the new British bases before the beginning of March to be completely vain.

The destruction of British air bases by means of air attack is, on the basis of previous experience of air warfare, similarly excluded. Almost anything is easier to destroy than an airfield. Thus the fact is, as I feared, that Britain has now occupied Crete, and is in the process of setting foot on a large number of other islands and also of establishing air bases in a whole series of places in Greece, including two near Salonika and two others presumably in Thrace. Rhodes also is now within range of the British heavy fighters, and if, as seems likely, the British also establish air bases in western Greece, all the coastal areas of southern Italy will be gravely threatened.

From the military viewpoint this situation is a threat. In the economic respect, so far as the Rumanian oilfields are concerned, it is actually alarming.

To remedy matters I propose the following measures:

(a) Political:

(1) Spain must now be persuaded immediately to enter the war. It can be assumed that this should happen at latest within six weeks. Spanish intervention will help to rid us of Gibraltar and free the straits, and to send to Spanish Morocco at least one or two German divisions, and thus secure ourselves against a possible defection from France of part of French Morocco and North Africa. Such a defection, Duce, would assure the Anglo-French air force of bases that would become disastrous for the whole of Italy, a matter that must be avoided and cannot in any circumstances be left to hope or even to chance. With the fall of Gibraltar, the door to the Mediterranean would be bolted from the west. Britain would be obliged to send all her shipping round

South Africa. Thus the eastern Mediterranean would be relieved, and North Africa would be preserved for Pétain's government.

(2) Every effort must now be made to divert Russia from the Balkan area and direct her towards the east.

(3) Attempts must now be made to reach some sort of agreement with Turkey in order to relieve Bulgaria from Turkish pressure.

(4) Yugoslavia must be persuaded to disinterest herself in, or, to the extent that this may be possible, to take an interest in positive cooperation to settle the Greek question in the way we wish. Unless Yugoslavia is secure, no operation can be risked in the Balkans with any promise of success.

(5) Hungary must permit the immediate transport of big German formations to Rumania.

(6) Rumania must accept this increase in the German armed forces in the interests of her own security.

I am determined, Duce, to oppose with decisive strength any possible attempt by the British to establish a true and real position in Thrace, and that at any risk.

I am, however, unfortunately obliged to note that warlike operations in the Balkans before March are impossible. Hence any pressure or threat to Yugoslavia would be vain, as the Serbian General Staff knows very well that the carrying out of such a threat in practice is impossible before March. Hence we must secure Yugoslavia for ourselves if possible by other means and methods.

(b) Measures of a military nature:

The most important military measure seems to me to be above all the unblocking of the Mediterranean. To this end I shall try, as I have already mentioned, to persuade Spain to intervene speedily in the war in order to shut the western passage.

Now, Duce, I consider it necessary that you should try to reach Mersa Matruh as soon as preparations can be completed, with a view to establishing an air base there which will make it possible in the first place to drive the British fleet from Alexandria once and for all by means of Stukas, and then to lay mines in the Suez Canal by long-range bombers so as to make it practically impossible to maintain effective traffic through it.

I also think it necessary to proceed to a strong and systematic concentration of our joint air forces in regard to bombing objectives. The present war has incontrovertibly demonstrated that raids on civilian areas have no importance whatever. Only attacks on important military and economic positions promise success. The most important aim in the Mediterranean is therefore always and above all that of dislodging the British fleet from its lair.

In my view, the vigor of our collective attack must be concentrated on it, while firm direct support for the troops operating in Albania is maintained. Uninterrupted watch and continuous attack must be begun on all shipping crossing the Mediterranean under the enemy flag. That this is possible, Duce, is shown by our struggle in the North Sea, which British shipping dares cross only under the protection of fighters tied to the coast.

For this purpose, Duce, I suggest that you recall the Italian armed forces stationed by us in the west, except for the submarines, the effectiveness of which is continually increasing, and that they be employed in a now more important sector. These forces are now stationed in the Channel sector at the most unfavorable season, and are suffering under climatic conditions that are just as troublesome to them as southern climes would be to us in summer.

At all events, I am of the opinion that the Mediterranean question must now be liquidated in the course of this winter, because it is in this season that the employment of the German armed forces is most appropriate, while the employment of Italian forces in western and northern Europe at this season of the year seems unpractical for climatic reasons.

I should therefore like to have my German armed forces back in spring, and at latest at the beginning of May; the right moment for our operation will follow from that too.

For the co-operation of our air arm in the Mediterranean, I should like in the first place to send you a squadron of Ju 88s, with the necessary reconnaissance aircraft, fighters, etc.

I have not yet discussed the details of this question with Marshal Göring, and therefore I shall leave to him the task of finally deciding what contingents are necessary in his opinion. Thus in the Mediterranean there would be two great zones of air operations: the Italian, which in short dominates the Albanian and Italian sky, as well as the Egyptian, and the German, which, because of our long-range bombers, would in the first place include the whole of the eastern Mediterranean. With wise use of our air forces, in three or four months the Mediterranean will become the tomb of the British fleet, and that is the vital premise for the military operations which in my opinion it will not be possible to begin before the beginning of March, so far as Greece itself is concerned. I consider this period of time necessary for the simple reason that before then it would not be possible for me to concentrate in Rumania forces such as will in all circumstances ensure an unequivocal success. Only then can success within the briefest possible period be expected.

For the time being the question of Egypt can remain completely open, because after mature reflection I have become convinced that an attack on the Nile delta will not be possible before the autumn of next year. To me, the most important thing seems to me to secure a position near Mersa Matruh from which the British fleet at Alexandria can be attacked by Stukas protected by fighters.

These steps are also well adapted from the psychological point of view for bringing about an alleviation of the situation and again creating a positive atmosphere in regard to the Axis.

I communicate these thoughts to you, Duce, with the warmest cordiality of a friend who is ready to help you with the greatest fanaticism to overcome the crisis in the shortest possible time, so that an apparent unsuccess shall be transformed into a situation that will impose final defeat on the enemy.

With the most cordial greetings and feelings of loyal comradeship,

Adolf Hitler

Letter from Mussolini to Hitler

Rome, November 22, 1940.

Führer,

I regret that my letter of October 19 failed to reach you in time to give you an opportunity of expressing your opinion of the projected operation in Greece; I should have taken careful note of it, as on other occasions.

The advance of the Italian forces in Greece stopped after a promising and swift beginning, enabling the Greek forces to take the initiative in their turn. This was due to three causes in particular:

(a) The bad weather, which deteriorated with violent rains and stopped the advance of the mechanized forces. An armored division, for instance, literally sank in the mud.

(b) The almost complete defection of the Albanian forces, who turned against our troops. A single division of ours, for instance, had to disarm 6,000 Albanians and send them to the back areas.

(c) The attitude of Bulgaria, which enabled the Greeks to withdraw eight divisions they had in Thrace and send them to reinforce those already facing us.

All this belongs to the past and we must not allow ourselves to be shocked by it, though I realize that these events have had unfavorable repercussions. Italy is now preparing thirty divisions, with which she will be able to annihilate Greece. There is no reason for concern about the bombing of southern towns, which causes little damage.

I wish to call your attention to two things:

Spain: The Spanish card can be played. I am willing to meet Franco to put pressure on him to enter the field.

Yugoslavia: This card at present may be even more important. I am ready to guarantee the present frontiers and grant Salonika to Yugoslavia on the following conditions: (a) That Yugoslavia joins the Tripartite Pact; (b) that it demilitarizes the Adriatic; (c) that its intervention is carried out in such a way that Yugoslav forces enter the lists only after Greece has received a first blow at Italian hands.

On this basis I already agree to whatever you decide to do to attain this purpose.

I think it essential in present circumstances to intensify co-operation between our air forces.

I too have had my black week, but now the worst is over.

Internal conditions in Britain seem to be really serious from news reaching us, and the possibility of a collapse is not to be excluded.

Accept, Führer, my comradely greeting.

Mussolini

Broadcast Address to the Greek Nation by Metaxas

November 22, 1940.

Twenty-six days ago an underhand and cowardly enemy attacked us without any provocation whatever, and for the sole purpose of taking away from us what gives value to our life; that is to say, our liberty, our national independence and our honor. All Greece has united into a monolithic block; and at the King's orders we hurried to arms. Hard fighting began from the outset, and the brunt was borne by the Epirus army, whose tenacious resistance protected the mobilization and assembly of our forces. When the army was assembled, victories followed one after the other. Army, air force and navy competed in valorous deeds that will always honor the name of Greece. I therefore on behalf of the whole nation express gratitude to the heroic men of the army, the air force and the navy, just as I express gratitude to the inhabitants of the towns and villages who have undergone enemy air attack. Further, I am convinced that I am interpreting the general will in expressing the gratitude of the Greek people to our valorous allies the British for the wholehearted aid they are giving us and for the successes they are gaining with their incomparable fleet and magnificent air force.

For the past ten days the fighting has assumed its greatest intensity in the western Macedonian sector, where the battle has been hard and continuous for the whole of that time, and it ended, after the fall of the mountain massif of Morava, with the capture of Koritsa and the flight of the enemy along the whole of the western Macedonian and Epirus front. When the Italian dictator made his last speech, so full of hatred of and anger at Greece, I did not imagine the Greek army would give him such a swift reply. After this reply, which he will not forget, not many words are needed from me. There are only a few things I must add. Greece does not forget Santarosa, or Fratti, or Garibaldi, or the many other Italians who shed their blood for her, for liberty, and for Italian independence in the last century.

The Italians who fought by our side in our national struggle will always be close to us, and if they were alive today they would be perse-

cuted victims of the Fascism that could never accept into its embrace
men prompted by the high ideals for which those Italians fought and
for which we are fighting today. I should also like to add this. Signor
Mussolini, astonished that his proposals to enslave Greece should
have roused the hatred of the Greek people, has made the destruction
of Greece a war aim of Fascist Italy. We assure him that we have
decided not to allow ourselves to be destroyed, but to live as a free
and independent nation; and we shall live and, together with our British allies, we shall win. The consequences of this to Italy will be decided by the Italian people when the day comes to settle accounts with
its dictator.

And now, Greek men, women, and children, whether mobilized or
not, let us grit our teeth and clench our fists, let us steel our spirit to
fight with all the fury that is called for by this base and dishonorable
attack on us. All must know that the struggle will be hard and long,
and that our road will not be strewn with flowers, but we shall overcome all difficulties, face all perils, and defeat the enemy. We are
fighting, not only for our own life, but also for that of other Balkan
peoples, and for the liberation of Albania. We are fighting for values
the significance of which goes beyond our own frontiers and those
of the Balkans and extends to all humanity.

Let us thank God that His will has again destined Greece to fight
for such a lofty cause.

Letter from Hitler to Mussolini
(Extract)

Obersalzberg, December 31, 1940.

Duce,

At the end of this year I feel the need to express to you from the
bottom of my heart my wishes for your happiness during the New
Year. I do this with a feeling of friendship that is the warmer in that
I am able to believe that recent events will have detached you from
many persons who are in themselves devoid of importance but in com-
pensation will have made you more sensible of the sincere comrade-

ship of a man who feels tied to you in good times and bad, in prosperity and adversity.

At the beginning of this letter let me state one thing, that is, that the events that move us all today have innumerable precedents in the history of wars and nations. In most cases great powers have started attacks on small states nearly always with inadequate means, and then, in the first stage of the struggle, have very often suffered reverses. German history contains a whole series of instances of this. It is precisely for that reason that I think it necessary in such cases to attack, when possible, with superior forces, even at the risk of losing the sympathy of those who like to regard parity of strength as a necessary premise for giving the winner his due.

Following the events in Greece, as in Albania and North Africa, I am continually considering the really effective countermeasures that can be adopted, especially on my part. By the word "effective," I mean avoiding all that kind of aid that is aid and no more, and instead conducting really decisive operations which will therefore in themselves be an alleviation.

As for direct aid to Italy, your desires, Duce, are known to me. To the extent that they are within our powers, they will be satisfied. In some fields this will not be possible. But it will be possible to provide other aid that will lead to the desired result.

Letter from Hitler to Mussolini

Obersalzberg, February 28, 1941.

Duce,

In the first place, accept my thanks for your letter, and for sending the report on the conversation with Franco. Since I too am expecting a communication from Franco, I should like to postpone stating my position until I have received it, but in any case the meaning of the long Spanish speeches and their written explanations is that Spain does not want to and will not enter the war. This is very displeasing, because thus the simplest way of striking Britain in her Mediterranean position is now eliminated for the time being. But the Spanish decision is also to be deplored because it removes the best possibility of putting an end to the oscillations of French policy. I can only describe Franco's statement that the attack on Gibraltar would be carried out by Spanish troops as a naïve overvaluation of the strength and offensive capacity of the Spanish army.

Apart from this, I regard the situation in general as having noticeably improved.

(1) I too think that the situation in Albania can now be regarded as stabilized.

(2) In North Africa, if another fifty-one days' time still remain to us, I am sure that a new British attempt to advance towards Tripoli will fail. I am very grateful to you, Duce, for having put your motorized troops in Tripoli at the disposal of General Rommel. He will certainly not disappoint your confidence. I am certain that he will quickly gain the confidence and, I hope, also the affection of your troops. The opinion expressed to me by Colonel Schmidt, who has been to Tripoli, on the Italian troops has been very reassuring. He has returned convinced that with such men the situation will undoubtedly be restored. That we should be permitted to help you, and that we shall be able to do so, is a matter of genuine pleasure to me. I believe that the mere arrival of the first armored regiment will constitute an extraordinary reinforcement of the situation in your favor.

The arrival of the armored division will provide the basis for further reflections which I hope, Duce, to be able to discuss with you personally.

(3) Greece. The liberation of the Danube from the ice danger, now probably definite, enabled me to order the construction of the bridge to be begun on February 28, and thus a number of armored units are to set out tomorrow to reinforce the anti-aircraft defense of Bulgaria. With the completion of their deployment all the way to the Greek frontier, a notable alleviation on the Albanian frontier will be achieved immediately. One other thing concerns me, Duce, and that is your islands in the Dodecanese. It would undoubtedly be extraordinarily helpful for the conduct of the air war in the eastern Mediterranean if these islands could be held. A great strengthening of Rhodes would probably finally close the Suez Canal to Britain. At all events, the loss of Rhodes would greatly lengthen the flight to Suez. But the important thing, Duce, is that now at last winter is passing, and with it the paralysis of our operations imposed by nature.

Concluding my today's letter, I also wish to inform you that I am writing to the President of Turkey, Ismet Inönü, informing him that the entry of German troops into Bulgaria is not directed against Turkey but that, on the contrary, I am convinced that it would be in the interests of Turkey to stabilize good relations with us; and that Germany has no territorial interests either in Bulgaria or in Rumania, and that it will evacuate these territories as soon as possible, and the sooner the better, immediately after eliminating the British threat. Unless Mr. Eden has succeeded in depriving the Turkish statesmen and soldiers of their capacity to judge their own interests dispassionately, I see no danger here. In any case, we are of course prepared for anything.

Accept my most cordial and most comradely greetings.

A. Hitler

Message from Hitler to Mussolini

March 27, 1941.

Duce,

Events oblige me to communicate to you by this most rapid fashion my view of the situation and the decisions that follow from it.

(1) From the outset I have considered Yugoslavia the most dangerous factor in the conflict with Greece. From the purely military viewpoint, the success of a German attack on Thrace could not in fact be assured so long as the attitude of Yugoslavia remained doubtful and hence might threaten the left flank of the advancing columns on our enormous front.

(2) For this reason I have done everything possible and have made tremendous efforts to make Yugoslavia join our common cause. These efforts have been in vain, however, for one thing because they were begun too late to ensure success in good time. Today's news leaves no doubt whatever about an imminent change in Yugoslav foreign policy.

(3) Now, I regard the situation not as disastrous, but nevertheless as so serious as to make necessary the avoidance of all mistakes on

our part if we are not to see our overall position definitely endangered.

(4) I have therefore made all arrangements to be able to meet a development of the crisis with the necessary military means. A change in our marching orders in Bulgaria also has already been ordered.

I therefore now warmly request you, Duce, not to begin further operations in Albania in the next few days. I consider it necessary that you should try to man and guard the most important passes between Yugoslavia and Albania with all the forces that may be available to you. This is not a measure for the long term, but to prevent the development of a crisis during the next fortnight or three weeks.

I also think it necessary, Duce, that you should reinforce your forces on the Italo-Yugoslav frontier with all the means at your disposal and with maximum speed.

(5) Furthermore, Duce, I think it essential above all that we should ensure that absolute silence be observed on this matter, and that some knowledge of it should be imparted only to those personalities whom it is absolutely essential to inform. Any dissemination of information about our preventive measures would lead to their complete devalorization.

(6) I today sent for the Bulgarian and Hungarian ministers and informed them of the broad outlines of my view of the situation and tried to rouse their interest in the eventuality of military developments by explaining both the negative and positive consequences that would ensue for them. Because without the co-operation of Hungary and Bulgaria, Duce, it will certainly not be possible to operate with the speed that may be made necessary by events.

If possible, Duce, during the course of tomorrow I shall inform you of what is going to happen.

(7) General von Rintelen will present himself to you tomorrow, Duce, if he is able to fly, and will inform you of the next preparatory military steps to be taken on our part tonight.

If silence is maintained about these measures of ours, Duce, I do not doubt that, in the event of our having to act, we shall both see a success no less than that in Norway. That is my rocklike conviction.

Accept my most cordial and comradely greetings.

Your
Adolf Hitler

Letter from the Duce to the Führer

March 28, 1941.   0300 hours.

Ambassador von Mackensen has communicated to me your letter concerning the situation that has arisen in Yugoslavia since the coup d'état. I wish to inform you that I took what has happened calmly, as I was not in the least surprised, particularly when I noted that on the eve of the Vienna signature Stojadinović was sent to Britain. It is my belief that before the signature the coup d'état had already been decided on in full agreement with the Regent. As for the steps required by the situation, I inform you that: (1) General Cavallero has already been personally ordered by me to postpone the offensive which was imminent; (2) infantry units are on the way to the northern frontier of Albania and are taking up positions on the three lines of a possible Yugoslav attack; (3) orders have already been given to send to our eastern alpine frontier seven divisions to join the six already there, in addition to 15,000 frontier guards who have already been put on the alert; (4) all these preparations will be completed as rapidly as possible and are surrounded by absolute secrecy; (5) the second air squadron is ready to operate in the same area; (6) apart from Bulgarian and above all Hungarian co-operation, there should also be borne in mind the Croat separatist movement represented by Dr. Pavelić, who is at a short distance from Rome. I also wish to inform you, Führer, that, if war became inevitable, it would be very popular in Italy. That is another reason why I fully share your belief that the present crisis will lead to full and decisive Axis success.

I ask you, Führer, to accept this expression of my cordial comradeship and my friendly greetings.

Mussolini

Notes

Preface

1 A. Papagos, *The Battle of Greece 1940–1941*, p. 80.
2 G. Ciano, *Diario*.
3 Visconti Prasca, *Io ho aggredito la Grecia*, p. 46.
4 *The Testament of Adolf Hitler*, under date February 17, 1945.

Chapter 1

1 I. Metaxas, *Diary*.
2 E. Grazzi, *Il principio della fine*, p. 27.
3 Ibid., p. 18
4 Metaxas, op. cit., Appendix.
5 L. Mondini, *Prologo del conflitto italo-greco*, p. 149.
6 C. Baudino, *Una Guerra assurda*, p. 111.
7 Visconti Prasca, op. cit., p. 8.
8 M. G. Gamelin, *Servir*.
9 Dispatch from Grazzi to Ciano, June 29, 1940. IDD.*
10 Dispatch from Jacomoni to Ciano, August 9, 1940. IDD.
11 F. Jacomoni, *La politica dell'Italia in Albania*, p. 22.
12 Dispatch from Grazzi to Ciano, August 13, 1940. IDD.
13 Note from Ciano to Politis, August 1940. IDD.
14 Dispatch from Alfieri to Ciano, August 17, 1940. IDD.
15 Dispatch from Ciano to Alfieri, August 17, 1940. IDD.
16 Telegram from Alfieri to Ciano, August 20, 1940. IDD.
17 Directive by Mussolini, August 22, 1940. IDD. See Appendix.
18 Dispatch from Jacomoni to Ciano, August 17, 1940. IDD.
19 Dispatch from Jacomoni to Ciano, August 17, 1940. IDD.
20 Letter from Ciano to Jacomoni, August 22, 1940. IDD.
21 Dispatch from Jacomoni to Ciano, August 24, 1940. IDD.
  * Italian Diplomatic Documents.

Chapter 2

1 Ciano, op. cit., under date August 15, 1940.
2 Ciano, op. cit., under date August 18, 1940.
3 Visconti Prasca, op. cit., p. 2.
4 M. Roatta, *Otto milioni di baionette,* p. 119.
5 Visconti Prasca, op. cit., p. 32.
6 Jacomoni, op. cit., p. 230.
7 F. Pricolo, *Ignavia contra eroismo,* p. 6.
8 Visconti Prasca, op. cit., p. 37.
9 Ibid., p. 37.
10 Ibid., p. 38.
11 Dispatch from Ciano to Jacomoni, August 18, 1940. IDD.
12 Visconti Prasca, op. cit.
13 G. Santoro, *L'aeronautica italiana nella seconda guerra mondiale,* Vol. I, p. 125.
14 Ibid., p. 128.
15 Message from Mussolini to Hitler, August 24, 1940. IDD.
16 Visconti Prasca, op. cit., directive dated October 22, confirming pre-ceding directives dated September 16.

Chapter 3

1 Dispatch from Grazzi to Ciano, July 23, 1940. IDD.
2 Dispatch from Grazzi to Ciano, September 23, 1940. IDD.
3 Dispatch from Grazzi to Ciano, October 3, 1940. IDD.
4 Dispatch from Jacomoni to Ciano, August 24, 1940. IDD.
5 Dispatch from Jacomoni to Benini, August 28, 1940. IDD.
6 Jacomoni, op. çit., p. 253.
7 German foreign policy documents.
8 Metaxas, op. cit., under date August 26, 1940.
9 Report of conversation between Mussolini and Ribbentrop, September 19, 1940. IDD. See Appendix.
10 German foreign policy documents.
11 Roatta, op. cit., p. 117.
12 Visconti Prasca, op. cit., p. 211.
13 Q. Armellini, *Diario di guerra,* p. 111.
14 Pricolo, op. cit., p. 6.
15 E. Faldella, *L'Italia nella seconda guerra mondiale,* p. 265.
16 German foreign policy documents.
17 Visconti Prasca, op. cit., p. 46.
18 Santoro, op. cit., p. 129.

19 P. Puntoni, *Parla Vittorio Emanuele III,* under date October 16, 1940.
20 Jacomoni, op. cit., p. 249.
21 Ibid., p. 252.
22 Roatta, op. cit., p. 123.
23 Report of meeting in Palazzo Venezia, October 15, 1940. IDD. See Appendix.

Chapter 4

1 Report of meeting in Palazzo Venezia, October 15, 1940. IDD. See Appendix.
2 Visconti Prasca, op. cit., p. 48.
3 Ibid., p. 178.
4 Dispatch from Jacomoni to Benini, October 23, 1940. IDD.
5 Letter from Benini to Thaon di Revel, October 24, 1940. IDD.
6 Grazzi, op. cit., p. 220.
7 V. Vailati, *Badoglio risponde,* p. 290 ff.
8 P. Badoglio, *L'Italia nella seconda guerra mondiale,* p. 53.
9 Jacomoni, op. cit., p. 260.
10 Puntoni, op. cit., under date October 20, 1940.
11 Roatta, op. cit., p. 127.
12 Pricolo, op. cit., p. 10.
13 Letter from Mussolini to Boris III of Bulgaria, October 16, 1940. IDD. See Appendix.
14 Letter from Boris III of Bulgaria to Mussolini, October 18, 1940. IDD. See Appendix.
15 Badoglio, op. cit., p. 54.
16 German foreign policy documents.
17 Letter from Mussolini to Hitler, October 19, 1940. IDD. See Appendix.
18 Letter from Badoglio to De Vecchi, October 22, 1940. IDD.

Chapter 5

1 Dispatch from Jacomoni to Benini, October 1940. IDD.
2 Telegram from Ciano to Jacomoni, October 22, 1940. IDD.
3 Dispatch from Jacomoni to Benini, October 23, 1940. IDD.
4 Dispatch from Jacomoni to Benini, October 21, 1940. IDD.
5 Stefani agency press communiqué, October 26, 1940. IDD.
6 Metaxas, op. cit., under date October 26, 1940.
7 Ciano, op. cit., under date October 27, 1940.
8 Visconti Prasca, op. cit.
9 Ibid.
10 Ibid.
11 Ibid.

Chapter 6

1 Grazzi, op. cit., p. 225.
2 Mondini, op. cit., p. 226.
3 Dispatch from Ciano to Grazzi, October 26, 1940. IDD.
4 Metaxas, op. cit., under date October 28, 1940.
5 A. Tsifou, *Memoirs.*

Chapter 7

1 Memorandum from De Ferraris to Anfuso, October 29, 1940. IDD.
2 Visconti Prasca, op. cit., p. 107.
3 Pricolo, op. cit., p. 13.
4 Roatta, op. cit., p. 132.
5 Ciano, op. cit., under date October 31, 1940.
6 Visconti Prasca, op. cit., p. 118.
7 Ibid., p. 147.
8 Santoro, op. cit., p. 167.
9 Pricolo, op. cit., p. 15.
10 Visconti Prasca, op. cit.
11 Ibid.
12 Ibid., p. 125.
13 Ibid., p. 247.
14 Ibid., p. 243.
15 Ibid.
16 Ibid., p. 171.

Chapter 8

1 Visconti Prasca, op. cit., p. 143.
2 Greek General Staff, *The Greek Army in the Second World War.*
3 Speech by Mussolini, November 18, 1940.
4 Santoro, op. cit., p. 182.
5 Visconti Prasca, op. cit.
6 A. Rasero, *Quinto Alpini,* p. 353.
7 Pricolo, op. cit., p. 45.
8 Letter from Hitler to Mussolini, November 20, 1940. IDD. See Appendix.
9 Letter from Mussolini to Hitler, November 22, 1940. IDD. See Appendix.
10 Broadcast by Metaxas, November 22, 1940. IDD. See Appendix.
11 G. C. Fusco, *Guerra d'Albania,* p. 47.

Chapter 9

1 Roatta, op. cit., p. 132.
2 Ibid., p. 133.
3 C. Cavallero, *Il dramma del maresciallo Cavallero*, p. 93.
4 U. Cavallero, *Comando supremo*, under date December 4, 1940.
5 German foreign policy documents.
6 Santoro, op. cit., p. 174.
7 U. Cavallero, op. cit., pp. 34–35.
8 Ciano, op. cit., under date December 14, 1940.
9 Ibid., under date December 24, 1940.
10 Pricolo, op. cit., p. 81.
11 Ibid., p. 125.

Chapter 10

1 German foreign policy documents.
2 U. Cavallero, op. cit., under date January 14, 1941.
3 Ibid., under date January 18, 1941.
4 Ciano, op. cit., under date January 8, 1941.
5 U. Cavallero, op. cit., under date January 22, 1941.
6 Ibid., Directive No. 13.
7 Ibid., under date February 8, 1941.
8 German foreign policy documents.
9 W. Churchill, *The Second World War*, Vol. II, p. 472.
10 Ibid., Vol. III, p. 17.
11 A. Heckstall-Smith and H. T. Baillie-Grohman. *Greek Tragedy*, p. 17.
12 Metaxas, op. cit., Appendix.

Chapter 11

1 *See also* p. 83.
2 German foreign policy documents.
3 A. Terzakes, *Hellenic Epoch* (in Greek), p. 166.
4 Pricolo, op. cit., p. 115.
5 Ibid., p. 118.
6 Ibid., p. 122.
7 Ibid., p. 124.
8 Puntoni, op. cit., under date February 7, 1941.
9 Pricolo, op. cit., p. 131; and U. Cavallero, op. cit., under date March 9, 1941.

10 Pricolo, op. cit., p. 136, and U. Cavallero, op. cit., under date March 13, 1941.
11 U. Cavallero, op. cit., pp. 74–75.
12 U. Cavallero, op. cit., pp. 75–76.
13 Puntoni, op. cit., under date March 10, 1941.

Chapter 12

1 Giuseppe Bona, *Martirio ed eroismo di Genserico Fontana,* quoted by B. Ceva, *Cinque anni di storia italiana,* p. 33.
2 F. Campione, *Guerra in Epiro.*
3 *Giornale l'Alpino,* February 15, 1942, quoted by Ceva, op. cit., p. 31.
4 Silvano Buffa, *Lettere alla famiglia e diario,* quoted by Ceva, op. cit., p. 43.
5 Egisto Corradi, *La ritirata di Russia.*
6 Vincenzo Ambrosio, *Epistolario,* Rome, 1941, quoted by Ceva, op. cit., p. 38.
7 Nicola Forenza, *Epistolario di guerra del Caduto caporal Peppino Caramuta 139 Reggimento, divisione Bari* (Putignano, 1941), quoted by Ceva, op. cit., p. 36.

Chapter 13

1 Churchill, op. cit., Vol. III, p. 63.
2 Heckstall-Smith and Baillie-Grohman, op. cit., p. 23.
3 Papagos, op. cit., p. 323.
4 Ibid., p. 324.
5 Churchill, op. cit., p. 90.
6 German foreign policy documents.
7 Ibid.
8 Puntoni, op. cit., under date March 22, 1941.
9 Ibid., under date March 24, 1941.
10 Message from Hitler to Mussolini, March 27, 1941. IDD. See Appendix.
11 Letter from Mussolini to Hitler, March 28, 1941. IDD. See Appendix.
12 U. Cavallero, op. cit., under dates March 28, March 31, April 6, April 7, 1941.
13 Ibid., under date April 4, 1941.
14 R. Crisp, *The Gods Were Neutral,* p. 54.
15 Papagos, op. cit., p. 338.

Chapter 14

1 Churchill, op. cit., Vol. III, p. 200.
2 Papagos, op. cit., p. 380.
3 German foreign policy documents.
4 Draft convention for capitulation of Greek army, April 23, 1941. IDD.
5 U. Cavallero, op. cit., under date April 28, 1941.
6 Ibid., under date April 30, 1941.
7 Letter from Cavallero to Mussolini, May 14, 1941. IDD.

Bibliography

AMÉ, CESARE. *Guerra segreta in Italia.* Rome, 1954.
ANFUSO, FILIPPO. *Da Palazzo Venezia al lago di Garda.* Florence, 1957.
ARMELLINI, QUIRINO. *Diario di guerra.* Milan, 1945.
BADOGLIO, PIETRO. *L'Italia nella seconda guerra mondiale.* Milan, 1946.
BAUDINO, CARLO. *Una guerra assurda.* Milan-Varese, 1965.
BIANCHI, GIANFRANCO. *25 luglio crollo di un regime.* Milan, 1963.
BONA, GIUSEPPE. *Martirio ed eroismo di Genserico Fontana.* Rome, 1954.
BUCKLEY, CHRISTOPHER. *Greece and Crete, 1941.* London, 1952.
CAMPIONE, FERNANDO. *Guerra in Epiro.* Naples, 1950.
CANEVARI, EMILIO. *La guerra italiana—Retroscena della disfatta.* Rome, 1948.
CAVALLERO, CARLO. *Il dramma del maresciallo Cavallero.* Milan, 1952.
CAVALLERO, UGO. *Comando Supremo, Diario 1940–1943.* Bologna, 1948.
CEVA, BIANCA. *Cinque anni di storia italiana 1940–45 da lettere e diari di caduti.* Milan, 1964.
CHURCHILL, WINSTON S. *The Second World War.* 6 vols. London, 1949. New York, 1960.
CIANO, GALEAZZO. *Diario.* Rome, 1946.
CORRADI, EGISTO. *La ritirata dl Russia.* Milan, 1964.
CRESPI, RICCARDO. *Squadristi in Albania.* Milan, 1941.
CRISP, ROBERT. *The Gods Were Neutral.* London, 1960.
FALDELLA, EMILIO. *L'Italia nella seconda guerra mondiale.* Bologna, 1959.
FANIZZA, RUGGERO. *Da Vecchi, Bastico, Campioni ultimi governatori dell' Egeo.* Forlì, 1947.
FUSCO, GIAN CARLO. *Guerra d'Albania.* Milan, 1961.
GAMELIN, MAURICE G. *Servir—les Armées français de 1940.* 3 vols. Paris, 1946.
GRAZZI, EMANUELE. *Il principio della fine.* Rome, 1945.
GUINGAND, SIR FRANCIS DE. *Operation Victory.* London, 1947.
HALDER, FRANZ. *Hitler as War Lord.* (English Translation.) London, 1950.
HECKSTALL-SMITH, A., and BAILLIE-GROHMAN, H. T. *Greek Tragedy.* London, 1961.
HITLER, ADOLF. *Table Talk, 1941–1944.* (English Translation.) London, 1953. U.S. Ed.: *Secret Conversations, 1941–1944.* New York, 1953.
———. *The Testament of Adolf Hitler.* (English Translation.) Ed. H. R. Trevor-Roper. London, 1961.

354 *The Hollow Legions*

HITLER and MUSSOLINI. *Lettere e documenti.* Milan, 1946.
JACOMONI DI SAN SAVINO, FRANCESCO. *La politica dell'Italia in Albania nella testimonianza del luogotenente del re.* Bologna, 1965.
LONG, GAVIN. *Greece, Crete and Syria, Australia in the War of 1939–45,* Series I, Vol. II. Canberra, 1953.
LUALDI, ALDO. *Nudi alla meta.* Milan, 1965.
METAXAS, IOANNIS. *Diary.* 4 vols. Athens, 1960.
MONDINI, LUIGI. *Prologo del conflitto italo-greco.* Milan, 1945.
MUSSOLINI, BENITO. *Storia di un anno.* Milan, 1945.
PAGLIANO, FRANCO. *Storia di diecimila aeroplani.* Milan, 1947.
PAPAGOS, ALEXANDER. *The Battle of Greece, 1940–1941.* (English Translation.) Athens, 1949.
PRICOLO, FRANCESCO. *Ignavia contra eroismo.* Rome, 1946.
PUNTONI, PAOLO. *Parla Vittorio Emanuele III.* Milan, 1958.
RASERO, ALDO. *Quinto Alpini.* Rovereto, 1964.
REISOLI, GUSTAVO. *Fuoco su Adolfo. Fuoco su Benito.* Naples, 1948.
RINTELEN, ENNO VON. *Mussolini als Bundesgenosse.* Tübingen and Stuttgart, 1951.
ROATTA, MARIO. *Otto milioni di baionette.* Milan, 1946.
ROSSI, FRANCESCO. *Mussolini e lo Stato Maggiore.* Rome, 1951.
———. *Come arrivammo all'armistizio.* Rome, 1946.
SANTORO, GIUSEPPE. *L'aeronautica italiana nella seconda guerra mondiale.* Vol. 1, Rome, 1957.
SCHMIDT, PAUL. *Da Versaglia a Norimberga.* Rome, 1951.
SIMONI, LEONARDO. *Berlino, Ambasciata d'Italia 1939–1943.* Rome, 1946.
TERZAKES, ANGELOS. *Hellenic Epoch.* (In Greek.) Athens, 1964.
TOSTI, AMEDEO. *La guerra che non si doveva fare.* Rome, 1945.
TSIFOU, A. *Memoirs.* Athens, 1945.
VAILATI, VANNA. *Badoglio racconta.* Milan, 1955.
———. *Badoglio risponde.* Milan, 1958.
VISCONTI PRASCA, SEBASTIANO. *Io ho aggredito la Grecia.* Milan, 1946.
WILSON, HENRY MAITLAND. *Eight Years Overseas.* London, 1952.
WISKEMANN, ELIZABETH. *The Rome-Berlin Axis.* London and New York, 1966.
ZANUSSI, GIACOMO. *Guerra e catastrofe d'Italia.* Rome, 1945.

Documents on German Foreign Policy. Series D, Vols. X, XI, XII. H.M.S.O., London.
Documenti Diplomatici Italiani. Series IX. Rome, 1965.
GREEK GENERAL STAFF. *The Greek Army in the Second World War.* (In Greek.) Athens, 1956.
———. *Military History of Greece.* Athens, 1958.

Index

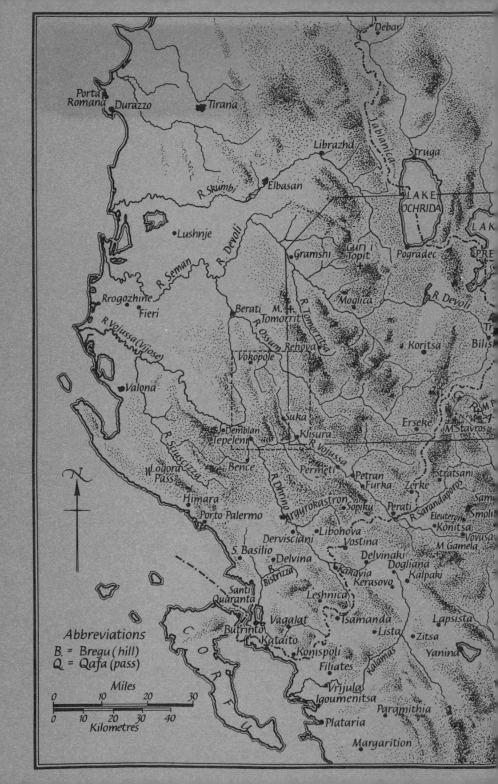